H22 805 086 2

BURTON, R. A.

The heritage of Exmoor   14-95.

942.3'85 .

THE HERITAGE OF EXMOOR

Cow Castle

THE HERITAGE OF EXMOOR

by

ROGER A. BURTON

R.A.B., 1989

COPYRIGHT NOTICE

Researched, written and published by

R.A. Burton

all enquiries to

12 Style Close,
Rumsam,
Barnstaple,
N. Devon
EX32 9EL

Printed by Maslands Ltd., 16a Fore Street, Tiverton, Devon

TO THE MEMORY OF JACK BUCKINGHAM

of Rose Cottage, Simonsbath

CONTENTS

LIST OF ILLUSTRATIONS

List of Illustrations — *continued*

MAPS OF EXMOOR

PLANS OF MINES

ACKNOWLEDGEMENTS

IN my efforts to put together this new study of the history of Exmoor I have become indebted to many people, not least the authors of earlier books and articles relating to the Moor. I trust that in the pages that follow, all sources of information have been properly acknowledged and that I have offended no-one.

I would now like to thank all who have helped or contributed in any way towards the successful completion of this book. Firstly, I would like to pay tribute to the Archivists and Staff of the following Record Offices and Libraries; the Devon Record Office and the West Country Studies Library at Exeter; the Somerset Record Office and the Local History Library at Taunton; the Reference Section of Kidderminster Library, Worcs.; the Public Record Office in London, and last, but by no means least, the Athenaeum and Reference Library in my home town of Barnstaple. Without exception all have been most courteous and helpful during the seven long years of my research.

My grateful thanks too are due to Lady Margaret Fortescue of Castle Hill, Filleigh, and her Agent Mr. Hugh Thomas for generously allowing me access to all the Fortescue Estate papers and other documents held in the D.R.O. Exeter, many of which are not normally available to the general public. My thanks again to Mr. Thomas for reading the whole of my typescript, providing additional information, permission to publish plans of mines etc., and for his enthusiastic reception of my humble efforts.

Here too, I would like to thank Sir Richard and Lady Acland of College, Broadclyst, near Exeter, for their kind permission to publish the two chapters of Exmoor's history that were mainly gleaned from the Acland Archive (also in the D.R.O. Exeter) particularly the extracts taken from the Forest Books of Exmoor 1718-1764.

Others who have given freely of their time and knowledge to help me on my way, include the late Bert Carter and his brother Leslie (formerly of Litton Farm, Exmoor); the late Jack Buckingham of Rose Cottage, Simonsbath, to whose memory this book is dedicated; Harry and 'Madam' Prout (also of Rose Cottage); Tom Little of Barnstaple (formerly of Exmoor); Reg and Rita Westcott of West Ley Farm, Exford; the late William Grant of Pilton, Barnstaple; Mr. and Mrs. Bob Richards of Skilgate (formerly of Horsen Farm, Exmoor); John Bragg of North Molton; Anne Buckingham of North Molton, (formerly of Kinsford and Horsen Farms, Exmoor); the Rev. Atkins, Vicar of Exmoor and Exford, (for making available the Exmoor Parish Registers): Peter Claughton, a close friend on the mining scene for many years, and my sister, Eileen Dolling, for her work on the maps in this book. My heartfelt gratitude to you all for your help and the pleasure of your company.

I would also like to thank Ian Hudson for coming to my rescue in producing the fine dust jacket, and all my friends who have contributed photographs, illustrations, etc., (see under list of illustrations), and anyone else who has helped in any way, but have in-advertently been left out.

Lastly, I would like to pay tribute to my typist Kathleen Margaret Lewis, who has struggled valiantly with my manuscript and the many, many corrections and additions to my account.

Roger Alan Burton
Barnstaple
1989

FOREWORD

WITHIN the boundary of the Exmoor National Park, lies a smaller but well defined area of high moorlands that was for hundreds of years the Royal Forest of Exmoor. Its evolvement as a Royal Forest began in the days of the Saxons, who, although they had established many settlements around the fringe of Exmoor, had for the most part left the inhospitable regions of the central uplands untouched. This land subsequently became the property of the Saxon kings and was kept by them as hunting and game preserves: Exmoor being the largest, wildest, and most remote of five such ancient forests in Somerset.

After the Conquest the early Norman kings greatly enlarged the Forest of Exmoor by adding to it lands, manors and townships that they had misappropriated for this purpose over a large area of the surrounding countryside, both in West Somerset and North Devon, and it was not until long after King John signed the Magna Carta that the last of the misappropriated lands were returned to their rightful owners and the Forest restored to something like its former and proper size. Thus it remained until 1818, when Parliament, acting on behalf of the Crown, divided the Forest into allotments, and sold 10,262 of its 20,344 acres to John Knight, an Ironmaster of Worcestershire, for £50,000.

As it is the history of the area within the boundary of the Royal Forest that we are principally concerned with, it is appropriate here to give a brief description of its main features and certain other aspects of its character, both before and after its enclosure.

First and foremost, despite its name, it was not a forest in the conventional sense, nor has it been in historic times; the term Royal Forest being used in the context of a royal hunting and game preserve, and apart from a little scrub willow here and there, and a few Rowan and Hawthorn trees, there were only two trees of note on Exmoor, about which more will be said shortly.

The Forest itself—roughly heartshaped in appearance—was surrounded on its three sides by the commons of no less than thirteen parishes, seven in Devon and six in Somerset. Of the former; Molland, Twitchen, North Molton, High Bray and Challacombe adjoin its western boundary, with the northern boundary shared by Lynton and Brendon in Devon and Oare in Somerset, leaving the commons of Porlock, Stoke Pero, Exford, Withypool and Hawkridge along its eastern flank. Where the commons of the parishes meet each other and the Forest boundary the spot was usually marked by a large stone which was given a name; smaller stones—known as lesser mere stones—being used in between to mark the continuation of the boundary line.

The most obvious difference between the interior of the Forest and the

10

commons surrounding it, is in its vegetation, the natural herbage of the Forest consisting of coarse grasses, while the commons are, or were, predominantly heather, some having since been reclaimed. In only a very few instances has this heather succeeded in gaining a foothold inside the Forest bounds. The reason for this difference is generally believed to be due to the intensive grazing, mainly by sheep, that the Forest was subjected to during the summer months over a period of something like a thousand years, which, in the course of time, destroyed the heather and encouraged the natural grasses, for it was from taking in sheep for the summer grazing that the Warden of the Forest derived the major part of his income. We will go into this more thoroughly later; for the present we will confine our attentions to the Exmoor landscape.

The Royal Forest can be said to be divided into North and South Forest by the Challacombe-Exford road; the former Forest contains the wilder moorlands, which rise up to nudge 1600 ft. above sea level in that large and desolate area known as the Chains. This windswept plateau, with its deep peatlands, acts as a giant sponge to absorb and release its annual rainfall of some 80 ins. into numerous small rivulets, which quickly give birth to not only the major rivers of Exmoor, the Exe and the Barle, but the West Lyn also.

Here too rises Hoaroak Water, which runs parallel with Farley Water from Exe Plain towards Hillsford Bridge, where they join, and together tumble swiftly on over rocky boulders to cascade their contents into the East Lyn River at Watersmeet. Of the countless numbers who have visited this lovely spot, very few have traced the passage of these two fine Waters back along their moorland paths to the lonely places where they were given birth.

In sharp contrast to the Waters that fall dramatically from the 1500 ft. northern heights of the Chains in their haste to cover the short journey northwards to the Bristol Channel, the Barle and the Exe flow more sedately in a south-easterly direction across Exmoor Forest and the National Park, to join forces below Dulverton, and continue as the Exe via Tiverton and Exeter, discharging its moorland waters at Exmouth on the South Devon coast. What a difference one narrow ridge on the moorlands can make to the journey of a river, for the Exe rises within a quarter of a mile of a north flowing tributory of Hoaroak Water. Its counterpart, the Barle, rises within a similar distance of the headwaters of the West Lyn river.

A trek across the Chains can be wearying even to the most experienced walker as he picks his path from tussock to tussock in an attempt to avoid the water sodden Sphagnum moss, where, with effortless ease, an unwary footstep forward finds a spot a little softer than the last and is instantly rewarded with a bootfull of water; and yet, in the long dry summers of 1976 and 1983, it was possible to walk its length and breadth dry foot, wearing only a pair of 'daps' for comfort.

Wearying as it is walking across the Chains, it is little better on that other part of the North Forest, which lies east of the Simonsbath to Lynton and Brendon road: Lanacombe with its tussock grass, where it is easy to wrench an ankle, and the boggy areas around the Pinfords, are very heavy going.

Within this area lies a massive network of rivulets and small streams that form the headwaters of the lovely Badgworthy Water, which in turn empties its contents into the East Lyn river. Eastwards again, Chalk Water does likewise.

It was within this north-eastern part of the old Forest that Frederic Knight created three of his lonely moorland farms, Toms Hill, Larkbarrow and Warren. The first two were always difficult to let and were later occupied by his moorland shepherds. Of the three farms, Warren has the finest setting, lying on the northern slopes above the River Exe, close to Exe Cleave, where the river has cut its deepest channel, and in the process left behind a scene of grandeur unsurpassed within the Forest.

In the South Forest it is the Barle that reigns supreme, for it was alongside this river at Simonsbath that the first house (since recorded history began) was built by James Boevey in 1654, and it was here along the Barle some 165 years later that John Knight and his son Frederic built the village of Simonsbath and began the long and arduous task of turning the moorlands into productive farms.

Further south, the northern slopes above Kinsford Water, and the area north and south of Sherdon Water (which it becomes before it joins the Barle), have also been extensively reclaimed, but as the creation of these farms is given full coverage later in the book, it would be as well to end our foreword here and set forth in earnest on the Heritage Trail.

INTRODUCTION

ALTHOUGH by 1947 I was familiar with the roads around and across Exmoor, it was not until the early 1950's that my proper introduction to the Moor took place. My initiation came with a walking, camping, nature watching holiday, after my brother—a keen Ornithologist—had decided that 'We' would spend a few days on the Moor. Needless to say, I was more than willing to join him, and eager to be off.

A bakers van brought us as far as Challacombe, where we disembarked, and with packs on our backs set off up the valley of the River Bray to Swincombe Reservoir and Rocks. On and up we went, passing the old ruined farm of Radworthy on route for the Challacombe Longstone. Pinkworthy Pond was our next objective, a very lonely spot in those days and we did not tarry long before setting forth over the Chains and down Long Chains Combe to the long deserted sheepfold near the junction with Chains Valley Water (the upper reaches of Hoar Oak Water). Turning down the Water we soon arrived at the Hoar Oak Tree and the Forest boundary wall. Here we turned eastwards and followed the wall up over the southern edge of Cheriton Ridge, down to Farley Water, and climbing once more came to Brendon Two Gates on the Simonsbath-Lynton and Brendon road. Once across the road we continued alongside the boundary wall down Hoccombe Water, and near its junction with Long Combe Water we camped for the night.

It was the middle of May, but in the ignorance and poverty of our youth we were poorly equipped for camping on the open moorlands. Our outfit (very basic) consisted of a borrowed tent, a groundsheet, and one blanket (the luxury of a sleeping bag was to us still an unknown experience). To complete our outfit we had a hatchet and matches, and the main necessity of life—food—and that at least we had in plenty.

I can still vividly recall that first night, when, after placing our ground sheet on a pile of heather, we slept fully dressed—apart from our boots—under our solitary blanket. Very early the next morning a sharp frost awakened us from our slumbers, and nearly paralysed with the cold we crawled from our tent. It was still dark, but we soon had a fire going, and after lashings of hot coffee had restored our equilibrium, we were ready for the day. It was at this spot that I first saw the delightful Ring Ousel, and later in the day came my first sighting of the beautiful wild Red Deer —three hinds—which, after pausing for a few brief moments, quickly disappeared over the brow of a hill and were seen no more.

For well over 35 years the wonderful enchantment of that encounter has remained fresh in my memory, recalled and renewed on the numerous occasions since, that these magnificent creatures have come into view. Far off, or close at hand, they have never yet failed to set my pulses racing.

A leisurely walk brought us to the ruins of Toms Hill and Larkbarrow farms: Created from the wilderness by the Knight family, they were blasted out of existence during the last war when used for target practise by the big field guns stationed around the Moor, and though I knew nothing of this at the time, I believe it was here that the seeds were sown and the deep longing to know more about Exmoor's past began.

Leaving the farms behind we crossed over heather moorland to Aldermans Barrow, and then worked our way down the lovely combe of Chetsford Water, the home of the elusive Stonechat, whose powers as a ventriloquist had us looking everywhere that he was not. We set up camp beside the Water, a short distance up from Nutscale Reservoir, close to the filter tanks, which in those days were full of Stickleback fish. For some time we stood beside the tanks and watched the fish in silence, fascinated by their antics as they were swirled this way and that by the turbulent water rushing through on its way to the quieter waters of the man made lake, where it was gently stilled.

On the following morning we took a short walk down the valley as far as the ruins of Stoke Mill. After retracing our steps, we struggled up the mountainous combe to the west of the reservoir, and by the time we reached the top—burdened as we were with our heavy packs—we were perspiring freely. A cool breeze greeted us as we passed over Lucott Moor, and thus refreshed we marched down to Weir Water. We spent several hours in this delightful valley before making our way up over Mill Hill and down to Chalk Water, where we raised our tent once more. The next morning was spent in searching for a Merlin we had spotted and our patience was rewarded when we eventually found its nest. We camped early that day, high up Landcombe, overlooking Badgworthy Water. This part of Exmoor is unbelievably beautiful, especially so when the Rhododendrons are in full bloom. From our camp site we explored the valley below as far as the ruins of the 'Doone Cotts', where enough of these ancient buildings remain to stimulate the imagination as to the happenings in this remote fastness so many years ago.

On our last day we descended from the heights of Landcome, crossed Badgworthy Water and made our way up lonely Lankcombe and out over Brendon Common, recrossing the Simonsbath road about a mile north of Brendon Two Gates and the Forest Wall. Continuing westwards we recrossed Farley Water, Cheriton Ridge and Hoar Oak Water, and came to Hoar Oak Cottage (at that time still the home of one of the Exmoor Estate shepherds).

From Hoar Oak to the Chains was only a short step, but is was hard going thereafter, and we were not sorry when at last we reached Chapman Barrows. After a short rest to recharge our flagging energies and to take in the breath-taking scenery that unfolds below and around this place, we made our way down to the main road near Parracombe, where a passing motorist took pity on what can only be described as a couple of tramps and gave us a lift back to Barnstaple.

This, then, was my introduction to Exmoor over 35 years ago. Since that time I have spent countless happy hours, summer and winter, in all kinds of weather, walking its lonely hills and exploring its hidden combes. Gradually I became familiar with its physical features and its many and varied aspects, and with this growing awareness came the realisation of how little I really knew of its people and its history down through the ages.

I became an avid reader of books about Exmoor, and as my familiarity with the Moor continued to expand, certain aspects of its history began to raise questions in my mind, questions that remained unanswered until I came at last to Edward T. MacDermot's *History of the Forest of Exmoor*, and a little later—C.S. Orwin's *The Reclamation of Exmoor Forest,** and it was only after a careful study of these two fine books that some—but by no means all—of the missing pieces of what can only be described as a gigantic jig-saw puzzle, began to fall into place. These two books, which I call the Old and New Testaments of Exmoor's history, are essential reading for all who would seek to increase their knowledge of the Moor, and they have been drawn upon by the authors of practically every book written about Exmoor since their publication. I am no exception, for without their guiding influence I could never have written *The Heritage of Exmoor*. I humbly and gratefully acknowledge my debt.

When I began to write these pages, my intention was to use what was for hundreds of years the Royal Forest of Exmoor as my foundation stone, and to build upon it by including some of the history of the Moorland Parishes adjoining and surrounding it. As my research continued I came to realise the enormity of my task, and with a growing pile of documents and relevant material concerning the Royal Forest, or Exmoor Proper as it is now usually known, the decision was made to concentrate my efforts on the area within the bounds of the Forest. This book is the end product of that decision.

---

*Both of these books were updated by R.J. Sellick and republished in 1970.

CHAPTER 1

EXMOOR'S EARLY DAYS

AT the very heart of what was once the Royal Forest of Exmoor the village of Simonsbath now stands, but if we turn the clock back in 1818, when the Forest, after being held by the Crown for nigh on a thousand years, was put up for sale to the highest tender, all that would be found there was a solitary house and a few fields that went with it to make up a small farm.

Many years earlier, and long before the creation of this farm, when John Leland passed this way in 1540 on a journey from Dunster to Barnstaple, only a bridge of wood spanning the river there marked this lonely spot. Leland, who had been appointed by Henry VIII to travel the length and breadth of the kingdom, to search after and record England's antiquities, found little of interest to detain him on Exmoor, for within the Forest of his day there was neither house or habitation of any kind, or for that matter, any trees, apart from the Hoar Oak, which from ancient times had been a boundary marker; and the Kite Oak, about which we know only that it was in existence in 1622 when it is mentioned in a Forest dispute (MacDermot). Although this tree has been long gone its name has survived in the corrupted form of Kittuck, a hilly area of moorlands north of Larkbarrow Farm.

In order to find trees on Exmoor it is necessary to travel back much further in time, and we only know they were there because from time to time in the old peat diggings tree stumps have been uncovered and brought to the surface. Not that this necessarily means that all of Exmoor was covered by forest, but some parts of it certainly were.

A large proportion of the Exmoor region lies 1200 ft. and more above sea level, and it is on and around these high uplands that many of the historic monuments of bygone ages are to be found, and we are indeed fortunate that the present climate—in more ways than one—and the unsuitability of much of this land for reclamation, has left them undisturbed for many centuries.

It is now known that for several thousand years down to about 700 BC Exmoor enjoyed a far better climate than we now have to contend with. At first it was warm and moist, which encouraged the growth of trees and other vegetation. This cycle was followed by a long period of warmer and dryer weather, which enabled man to live in comparative comfort on the high moorlands, and so, it is back to those early days that we must turn to take our first glimpse at the history of Exmoor.

On the heights of Exmoor there is little to show that the people of the Stone Ages ever passed this way, but on the lower slopes at least two or three semi-permanent settlements are known to have existed. At

Hawkcombe Head, not far from the top of Porlock Hill; and at Ranscombe Head, close to the road leading from the Parracombe-Lynton highway into Woolhanger, many flint artifacts have been discovered. From these two places, and a third on Kentisbury Down, the Stone Age hunters were supplied with arrow and spearheads for their hunting forays into the Forest, in search of animals such as the Mammoth, Bison, Bear, Woolly Rhinoceros, the Wild Ox, and, of course, the Red Deer, the only one of these large mammals to have survived on Exmoor to the present day.

Other settlements await discovery, but one such site, although it is probably not as large or important as those already referred to, lay to the west of Twineford and Tinnerly Combe, on the high ground above Parracombe. In the early 1970's when this field was ploughed, I picked up in the course of half an hour some 15 flint artifacts, mainly scrapers, and no doubt a more experienced eye than mine would have found many more. A constant spring of water rises near this spot; an important factor to be considered when searching for a settled site, and the steep sided valley below is, and probably has been for hundreds—perhaps thousands of years—one of Exmoor's nurseries for young deer; a useful source of food.

A later arrival of Stone Age people are believed to have introduced sheep into this country. These sheep are thought to have been akin to our Exmoor 'Hornies' but much smaller. Goats, pigs, oxen and horses were also kept, to provide skins and food; meat being the staple diet of the age, and leading a nomadic life, the Stone-Agers moved their beasts from place to place as the rough pasture was consumed, but with the onset of winter many of these animals had to be slaughtered, there being insufficient feed available to carry them through to the next years growth of new pasture.

Somewhere about 2000 BC a new race of people arrived in Britain. These people are generally known as the Beaker Folk, because decorative pots have often been found in the burial mounds of their dead. Their arrival did little to alter the way of life of Stone Age 'man', who, as time went by, were gradually absorbed into the new culture. Like the people of the latter Stone Age, the Beaker Folk brought their flocks and herds with them, but unlike the men of the Stone Age, who, we believe, only ventured into the high forest to hunt, the Beaker people made their way up on to the heights of Exmoor, and there they chose to settle, cutting down trees as needed for firing and to use in the construction of their round houses and stockades, in which their flocks and herds were kept at night, safe from the prowling wolves.

The Beaker Folk were certainly not a primitive race, as has so often been suggested, for they lived a communal life, and were among the first to spin and weave the wool from their sheep into cloth, and to supplement the usual diet of meat, a little corn was grown. They also knew how to make beautiful pottery, and from using copper, developed the high technology and skills required to blend metals and smelt them into bronze, after which they became known as the Bronze Age people. The bronzework produced by these people was of a highly decorative but practical nature, even the axe heads were just as suitable for religious or ceremonial occasions as they were for daily use.

The transition from the use of flint to bronze did not happen overnight, and probably for the whole of the Bronze Age, which lasted—if we include the Beaker period—from about 2000-550 BC, flint tools and weapons would still have been very much in daily use, but in the absence of any recorded discoveries of bronze artifacts on Exmoor Proper, either in a hoard or in the burial mounds of this period that have been opened, the use of bronze on Exmoor appears to have been restricted to a few of the Chieftains, and was apparently far too valuable a commodity to be buried with them when they died.

Despite the fact that the heights of Exmoor have not, either before or since, been so densely populated, we know very little about where these people lived. So few positively identified hut circles have been found that it seems likely—especially on the high moor where stone is not so readily available—that turf and wood were used in the construction of their homes, which, with the passing of so many centuries, have returned to the earth from which they sprung.

It was during the Bronze Age that the Round Barrows were raised. They are believed to be memorials to dead chieftains, and were at first, during the Beaker period, quite small, but later in the Bronze Age came the huge mounds that for 2500 years and more have dominated and formed a fascinating part of the Exmoor landscape. Time meant little when these Barrows were raised, and a considerable labour force must have been involved in their construction, for quite often, the earth, turf and stone used to raise them up came from some distance away. One of the best known of the larger groups of these burial mounds are the eleven Chapman Barrows, which are spread along the Challacombe-Parracombe boundary at a height above sea level of over 1500 ft. Another interesting group, called Five Barrows, a misnomer, for here there are nine, can be found at an even higher level on North Molton's Western Common. On the eastern side of Exmoor the best examples are the three Wambarrows, which stand proud and prominent on Winsford Hill. From all these places there are spectacular views, but for me the panorama that unfolds from the Chapman Barrows cannot be surpassed. Many more of these mounds, large and small, singly and in small groups, are dotted about Exmoor. Often they are to be found close to the ancient ridgeways that have been used by the peoples of all the ages past to travel across the Moor, and in many cases still do; the modern Tarmac roads now either covering or running beside these ancient tracks. Two such routes that closely approximate with present roads crossing our region from east to west are, from Porlock to Lynton in the north; and from Dulverton in the south, across East and West Anstey Commons, Molland Common, Twitchen Ridge, Sandyway Cross and on to North Molton and the west. Two other ancient trackways crossing the centre of our region are not so easy to define after they leave the Brendon Hills ridgeway at Wheddon Cross. One route appears to have passed over Dunkery Hill and Almsworthy Common in the direction of Warren Farm, and then on to Exe Head, Chains Barrow and Woodbarrow, going on to Chapman Barrows, and following along the same ridge shortly leaves the Moor. The other route passed somewhere in the region of Exford, and afterwards followed closely the present road from Exford to Simonsbath, where it forked, with trackways going on to Span Head and Moles Chamber.

At least two important north-south routes linked with the major east-west ridgeways. One that later became a well used pack horse trail, crossed from Lynton to Moles Chamber by way of Shallowford, Saddlegate and Woodbarrow, continued on via Setta Barrow, Span Head, Kinsford Gate and Two Barrows to Sandyway Cross; much of the latter part of this route now being covered by a Tarmac road. Another such route can be picked up at White Cross, about 1 mile west of Exford. North of this point its passage is a little obscure, but it probably joined the next east-west ridgeway, either at Larkbarrow, or Aldermans Barrow. Southwards, it continued roughly on the line of the modern road to Dulverton, following the ridge which passes close by the Wambarrows. Numerous other trackways linked the Bronze Age settlements, but whether the ancient clapper bridge, Tarr Steps, can be fitted into this network is open to debate.

This clapper bridge, probably the finest in the Country, has been variously dated from the Bronze Age to Medieval and some of the arguments put forward in defence of the former are most convincing. A good example of this line of thought is given in a report by Professor Sir William Boyd Deakins, FRS in the Somerset Archaeological and Natural History Society publication of 1924, in which he stated that Tarr Steps marked a well defined stage in the history of roads that goes back to the prehistoric period, the bridge across the River Barle uniting the ridgeway descending from Winsford Hill past Liscombe, to the road leading up to the ridgeway passing from Hawkridge in the direction of Worth Hill. He was later supported in this belief by H. St. George Grey, an eminent archaeologist in his day. Nevertheless, the consensus of opinion today is that it is medieval, and cannot be dated any earlier than 1400 AD.

Relics of the Bronze Age on Exmoor also include a wide assortment of stone monuments, such as stone circles, stone rows, odd groups and single stones, and though they lack the proportions of the stones of Dartmoor—with few of them standing more than two feet high—they are, nonetheless, fairly plentiful, and more are still being discovered. The purpose of these stones has never been satisfactorily explained, but recent research has shown that at least some of the stone groups were placed to mark areas where the earth's natural force field is at its strongest, and it was within these well defined areas that the Bronze Age religious ceremonies are believed to have taken place.

The finest example of a stone circle on Exmoor can be found on

Withypool Hill, with another—considerably smaller—at the head of Colley Water (a tributary of Weir Water) which rises close to the Exford-Porlock road.

There is a third reputed circle, on Almsworthy Common, but this peculiar group, with a number of stones missing, thought by H. St. George Grey to be three stone rings one inside the other, is more likely—according to L.V. Grinsell (author of *Archaeology of Exmoor)*—to be the remaining stones of parallel rows.

There are several stone rows on Exmoor, typical examples being the one on East Pinford, and a second on the opposite side of Long Combe Water, on Little Toms Hill, both having parallel rows, three stones in a row. Another stone row (near Five Barrows) called the White Ladder, often referred to in records of the past, was rediscovered in 1975 by Miss Eardley-Wilmot, a keen amateur archaeologist and author of the Micro Study-*Ancient Exmoor*. These stones were better seen in 1976, after the long dry summer had caused considerable shrinkage in the peat surrounding them. Numerous single stones exist, but none are more impressive than the Longstone on Challacombe Common, which, standing as it does nearly 10 ft. high and with a certain weird shape, once gave me a very strange feeling—almost of terror—when it suddenly loomed out of the mist and appeared to be coming towards me.

Towards the end of the Bronze Age the climate began to deteriorate, making it increasingly difficult to live on the high uplands, and a gradual descent to the more sheltered valleys took place. Coinciding with this change in the weather the Iron Age Celts began to arrive on the scene. The earliest of these settlers appear to have blended peaceably with the people of the Bronze Age, but later arrivals were much more warlike, and the competition for the available land inevitably led to some bloodshed. It is highly probable that some of the notable landmarks of the Iron Age—the huge earthworks of their hill forts and camps—are the results of a combined attempt by the Bronze Age people and the early Celts to halt the advancing Celtic warriors, but stem the tide they could not, and it is perhaps significant that few—if any—stones or burial mounds were raised thereafter.

In time, as the region was split between the Celtic families, other hill forts were built, and the Celts, when not fighting a common enemy, were not above fighting amongst themselves. It was then that the massive earthwork enclosures would have been of great value, not to withstand a prolonged siege, but as protection against raiding parties and cattle thieves.

Several of these castles and camps lie close to known iron ore deposits. Shoulsbury Castle is near ancient workings at Moles Chamber and other surface workings on Whitefield Down and Buscombe Down. Cow Castle* is very close to the Picked Stones iron mine. Road Castle is near very old—and more recent workings—on Court Down, Exford; and the Camp

---

*Also known as Ring Castle.

on Staddon Hill is also in the immediate vicinity of early iron mining, and less than half a mile from the site of ancient iron works believed to be in the area of Pinns Quarry, which lies just to the east of the Stone Cross to Winsford road, about 1½ miles from Exford. According to Collinson—writing in 1791*—it was in these iron works—tradition has it—that much of the wood that once grew on Exmoor was consumed. In his time, many of the old pits where the ore was dug still remained and great quantities of scoria (smelting slag) could be found about them. As trees have been non existent on Exmoor at least as far back as the beginning of recorded history, it is just possible that this iron smelter could have been at work in the days of the Iron Age, but is more likely to be of 16th century origin.

None of these Iron Age castles or camps have been excavated, nor have others dating from this period, such as Mounsey and Brewers Castles, which held dominating positions on opposite banks of the River Barle, about halfway between Withypool and Dulverton. Nor, do I believe, has any serious attempt been made to find the site of the iron smelter, which, if it could be accurately located and dated, would add greatly to our very limited knowledge of early mining on Exmoor.

Not all of the considerable energies of the Celtic people—who in the south western region were known as the Dumnonii—was spent in fighting, they were also competent farmers, skilled in the use of iron, and highly capable craftsmen in other fields as well, including spinning and weaving, the manufacture of pottery, and in woodwork. How many of these crafts were followed on Exmoor is uncertain, but with a plentiful supply of iron readily available they may well have traded iron currency bars, or tools and weapons, for some of the other necessities of life.

The Roman invasion of Britain, nearly 500 years after the arrival of the first Celts, does not appear to have been opposed on Exmoor, and it is possible the Dumnonii were able to come to some agreement with the Romans, whereby, as long as they caused no trouble, they would be left free to carry on the Celtic way of life, although no doubt they would have been expected to contribute some form of tribute to their Roman overlords.

Only two Roman fortlets are known to have existed in the Exmoor region; both were on the coastal fringe, where a close watch could be kept on raiders from the sea, principally the Silures of South Wales who had not then been subdued by the Roman Legions. The fortlet at Old Burrow (1090 ft. above sea level) on the Glenthorne Estate near County Gate, was partially excavated in 1911 by H. St. George Grey, and more fully in 1963 by Lady Aileen Fox and Dr. W.L.D. Ravenhill, who discovered it had been constructed about 48 AD and abandoned some four years later when the garrison moved to a new site about 10 miles to the west at Martinhoe, which, although nearly 300 ft. lower, had a far wider field of view, both seawards and inland. This site had been excavated by Lady Fox and Dr.

*History of Somerset, Vol. II.

Tarr Steps

Virgin moorland, The Pinfords

The Harepath near Moles Chamber

Edgerley Stone

T.D. Stone

Ravenhill a little earlier, and they found it had been occupied for about 20 years before it was abandoned for good about 75 AD. It was around this time that the Romans overcame the strongest of the opposition in South Wales, and with the completion of the legionary fortress of Caerleon in South Gwent, the need for a watchful garrison on our coast ceased.

Of the two fortlets, the remains of the one at Old Burrow is in much the better condition today, with the pattern of its earthworks well defined. Its main advantages were in the superb position it held overlooking the always vulnerable area of Porlock Bay, and the excellent view of the South Wales coastline, but this was offset by the very limited field of view inland, and the many days of the year when fog blankets the site. There is a timeless quality about this place that one does not feel at Martinhoe, where the site of the fortlet is very overgrown with gorse and the banks of the encampment considerably run down, but standing as it does on the very edge of a steep run down to the cliffs and sea below, and with a far wider all round view, it is not surprising that the Romans found this site more in line with their requirements. Judging from the deterioration of the earthworks, however, it appears to have been equally—if not more—exposed to the elements than Old Burrow. Only a small garrison of about 80 men were stationed there, and in the absence of any sign of a Roman road in the vicinity of either of the fortlets, they were apparently supplied by sea.

A number of historians have, over the years, suggested there was a third Roman camp on Exmoor, namely the hill fort Shoulsbury Castle, which lies at the western end of the Exmoor escarpment on a ridge between High Bray and Challacombe, but the evidence is less than convincing, and appears to be based on the shape of the earthworks, which, although considerably larger, does resemble that of the fortlets on the coast; and on two swords discovered there, said to have been Roman; also unconvincing, as other and more reliable accounts state they were 17th century rapiers, probably relics of the Civil War. Although Shoulsbury Castle is over 1500 ft. above sea level it cannot be seen from either Old Burrow or the Martinhoe fortlets, a mistake the Romans are unlikely to have made, especially so when a clear and efficient signalling system would have been vital in bringing a strong back up force quickly to the coast to repel any landings there, but, according to Lady Fox and Dr. Ravenhill, the main purpose of the fortlet garrison was to warn the Roman patrol boats of the approach of any raiders crossing the Bristol Channel, who could then be quickly dealt with, thus doing away with the need to keep a large land based force tied up for this purpose[1]. Similarly, there is no evidence to suggest that the native Dumnonii were troublesome, for had they been, it is hardly likely that the small garrison of 80 men in the fortlet would have survived for long. Shoulsbury Castle's position would, however, have been of great strategic value to the earlier Iron Age Celts, protecting as it does the western flank of Exmoor. Moreover, it could have been easily reinforced when the need arose from within the region—resources the Romans could not call upon.

A persistent story that a Roman town called Termolus stood at—or near—Molland should be discounted, there being no historical evidence to support this. The rumour appears to have been started by the Bishop of Cloyne in the 18th century, on the very flimsy evidence of what had appeared to be a Roman camp, but was apparently the remains of an early home of the Bottreaux family.

Of the period following the withdrawal of the Roman Legions from Britain—which was completed in the first half of the 5th century AD—we know very little. After a period of considerable national unrest, with a great movement of people, out of, and into this country, the predominant Celtic culture slowly re-asserted itself, and for nearly 300 years their way of life continued. Only a few settlements and two or three inscribed stones (attributed to this period) are known. Of the latter, the Caratacus Stone standing on Winsford Hill is the most interesting, and from its inscription is believed to be a memorial to a kinsman of the great Caratacus, whose heroic resistance against the might of the Roman Legions kept them at bay for 8 years before he was captured at Caer Caradoc near Church Stretton in Shropshire (tradition), from whence he was taken to Rome and paraded before his captors.

The Cavudus Stone can now be found in the garden of Six Acre Farm, Lynton; not far from where the Rev. J.F. Chanter discovered it in 1913* being used as a gate post in the outer boundary hedge of what was formerly Lynton Common, which was enclosed about 1861. Translated, the inscription reads, 'The memorial of Cavudus son of Civilus', but who they were and where they lived has not yet been discovered. A third stone of this type once stood near Holywell, Parracombe; but when the Rev. Samuel Badcock searched for it in 1786 it could not be found. Later, he was informed that it had been incorporated in the foundations of a little bridge close by, some 10-12 years previously. The builder stated that it was inscribed with about 20 letters, which many who had seen it declared to be Greek. The bridge has since been widened, and at the time of the Lynmouth Flood Disaster, partly destroyed, but the stone is believed to be safe, if safe is the right word, still buried in the main structure.

In Culbone Woods stands a stone of a completely different type. This stone is inscribed with a Wheel Cross, and there is little reason to doubt that it belongs to the late Celtic era, making it one of the earliest—if not the earliest—Christian Cross in the Exmoor region.

Settlements at Charles and Walland, and others at Walscott and Wallover are all believed to date from late Celtic times. Walland and Charles have strong links with St. Petroc, a missionary saint who came over from South Wales in the 6th century, probably landing at Combe Martin, where he is believed to have founded a church, with another at nearby Berrynarbor. After leaving Combe Martin he skirted around the edge of Exmoor, founding churches at Trentishoe, Parracombe, Charles,

---

*Near Caffins Cross.

West Anstey and Bampton. A little later he continued his missionary work in Cornwall, where a number of churches are also dedicated to him, and it was at Bodmin in Cornwall that he died, and where his relics are preserved in a silver or ivory casket.

The present church at Charles is dedicated to St. John and has no connection with St. Petroc, whose church or chantry was built a half mile to the west beside the old road from Barnstaple to North Molton. Once the chantry had been established it was served by a 'hedge priest' and the chaplain of the nearby manor of Walland. It was rebuilt and rededicated in 1426, but after the Reformation fell into ruin. In more recent times it was rebuilt as a cottage, and more recently still, altered and added to.*

One or two fortified farmsteads were believed by the late Charles Whybrow** to date from the last unsettled years of Celtic rule, but without a proper excavation and accurate dating, the confirmation of these sites is impossible, and so at this point we will take our leave of the mysterious Dark Ages.

---

*The Moorland Parish of Charles by W.W. Joyce.
**Author of Antiquary's Exmoor and other local works.

CHAPTER 2

THE ROYAL FOREST OF EXMOOR EMERGES

AFTER the defeat of the Celts at Penselwood on the Wiltshire-Somerset border in 658 AD, the Saxons gradually pushed westwards, but it was close to the turn of the century before their influence was felt in the Exmoor region. We do not know if they met with any opposition from the local Celts, but the mass disruption following the departure of the Romans may have left them too weak and divided to offer more than token resistance, and in a short while the Saxons had established settlements on the potentially good agricultural land around the fringe of the Moor, with a few of the more venturesome finding their way up on to the high uplands of Exmoor, as can be seen from the surviving Saxon names.

Of Elsworthy—which lies between Larkbarrow Corner and the Warren —there is now no trace, although there is one site within this area that awaits an explanation. This is near the head of Ramscombe, where the hillside has been cut into and levelled out to make a platform some 25 yards long by 15 yards wide. With ample water close at hand it would have made an ideal spot to build on, but does not appear to be of such ancient date, and is more likely to belong to the 1850's when exploratory work was being carried out on the iron ore deposits about half a mile to the east: Whether any buildings were ever erected on this site has not been ascertained.

Other place names suggestive of Saxon settlements on Exmoor Proper are Cornham, which is derived from Quarnham; and Pinkworthy, although there is a division of opinion regarding the latter because it is shown in earlier records as Pinkery or Pinkry, but as these records do not go back very far it is impossible to confirm that this was its original name and Pinkworthy could well be correct. None of these farms—or suspected farms—and settlements survived long enough to gain an entry in the Domesday Book, but on the high ground north of Challacombe, on a south facing hillside in a comparatively sheltered position from the worst weather was the Saxon Manor of Radworthy. This area was in favour at least as far back as the Bronze Age, as the nearby Chapman Barrows and the Challacombe Longstone would attest. In 1983, a few acres of rough moorland on the south side of Radworthy Combe were ploughed up and worked down for tillage, and following my usual custom I walked over this ground from north to south, and from east to west, taking a strip at a time. All that I found there were two unknapped flints and a hooked scraper; all were close together, and I believe they may have been grave goods, possibly dating from the Beaker Period. Close to where the flints were found—near the head of the side combe off the Radworthy valley— the ground level is raised slightly in two places, suggesting the possible remains of two burial mounds, and two or three large stones a short distance away may have been dragged with the flints from these sites.

In late Saxon times Radworthy was held by Alric, but after the Conquest it was given to William de Poillei, who then let it to Rainauld. From the Domesday Book we find this manor was of about 743 acres, mostly rough pasture, with a little meadow for hay, and a virgate (about 30 acres) of arable, and it was this land only that was subject to the Geld or Land Tax. Ten shillings per annum being paid, as against 6/- in Alric's time. Half the arable land was in Demesne, the remainder shared between Rainauld's three Villeins, who, in return for the right to have land and a house of their own, were bound to the manor under the feudal system. The only animals belonging to the Villeins appear to have been two plough oxen, whereas Rainauld's stock consisted of 6 beasts (cattle), 7 swine, 17 sheep and 11 goats.

Like many other manors, Radworthy's history is somewhat obscure for several centuries, but it reappears in 1687, when in a dispute concerning the commons surrounding Exmoor, Jeffrey Lock stated that he had—in right of his wife—a quarter share of Radworthy, by grant of Thomas Hacche of South Molton. As Jeffrey was tenant of only 35 acres, Radworthy would appear to have been reduced to 140 acres, but this, of course, would not have included the commons, which at that time formed the largest part of the manor. The ruins of Jeffrey Lock's farmhouse, sheltered by a few beech trees, and a number of small fields close by, are a testament to his hard labour, and though the fields have reverted to heather, the banks surrounding them are in remarkably fine condition and look set to stand for many centuries yet.

A little more of Radworthy's history crops up from time to time after the Lock's had left it for the softer climes of Parracombe. In the early 18th century it was rented by a William Dovell, and a survey of Challacombe taken in 1732, shortly after the death of John Hacche—the owner of much of Challacombe—reveals that William Gubb was holding a lease for it on the life of his daughter Agnes. The lease of the next tenant was also held on the life of Agnes Gubb, but at some time before 1816, John Slader took the tenancy of Radworthy Tenement and 32 acres at a rental of £14 a year. Some 25 years later, when the Census of 1841 for Challacombe was taken, Radworthy was uninhabited, but by 1851 it was again occupied when John Harris, a farmworker, and his wife—who was a flax spinner*—were living there with their three sons and two daughters. They were still there in 1861, but neither Radworthy nor the Harrises are recorded in the Census of 1871 and 1881, and it would appear that they were probably the last family to live there. If this was so, then this family is remembered in the following story still told in Parracombe about the old days:

'When the men of the village were in need of a haircut they used to walk up over Parracombe and Challacombe Commons to the old homestead of Radworthy for a trim:' A more lonely and less likely place for a Barber's

---

*At this time flax was grown in some quantity around Parracombe.

shop is hard to imagine, and it is to be hoped they chose the right weather, or it could have been very chilly around the ears on the way home.

These, then, were the few settlements—or suspected Saxon settlements—on high Exmoor, but on the lower land around the Moor farm after farm were carved from the wilderness. As the settlements grew, more land was cleared and enclosed with the high and wide banks of earth and turf for which the Saxons were noted, and in their little fields, corn and other crops were grown. In the summer the cattle and sheep were driven up on to the old rough pastures, but towards the end of the year were brought down again to winter on the farms, and thus began a custom that has been carried on for over 1,000 years, although many hardy animals do now remain on the high uplands of Exmoor all the year round, except perhaps in the severest weather.

As time passed it became the custom of the Saxon kings to appropriate all land not in the continual use of the farming communities. Much of this land was either too steep or wet to plough, or the soil too thin, so these wastelands became the King's deer and game reserves, afterwards Royal Forests. Such was the case with Exmoor.

For a short while the Saxons enjoyed an untroubled life in our region, but early in 877 AD a nameless Viking—believed to be the brother of Ivar and Haelfden—crossed from South Wales (where he had wintered) with 23 ships and landed on the North Devon coast. Although various sources contradict one another as to the precise point where the battle that followed took place, many leading historians now believe that it was in trying to overcome a company of the King's Thegns who were entrenched within the huge earthworks of Wind Hill at Countisbury, high above Lynmouth, that the unknown Viking and 840 of his men were killed, giving a great victory to the Saxons.

In 914 AD a band of Lidwiccas crossed the sea from what is now Brittany and made a savage attack on Porlock, where they met with courageous resistance and after losing many men were driven back to sea. Other raiders followed, but none appear to have secured a beach-head along our coast. Outside the region King Alfred saved Wessex from the Danes, but a later wave of Danish invaders after Alfred's death met with weaker resistance, and by 1016 AD the country was under the rule of King Canute. He died in 1035 and was followed a few years later by Edward the Confessor. Towards the end of his long reign, a free for all struggle for power took place amongst the Saxon nobility. In this struggle, Harold and his father Earl Godwin were thwarted by Leofic, Earl of Mercia, and dispossessed of their lands. Harold was forced to flee to Ireland, where he promptly set about raising an army, and in due course, intent on revenge, he landed at Porlock, which belonged to Leofric's son Algar. After a bloody battle, in which many Porlock men were slain, Harold looted everything of value and set fire to the town, destroying with it (according to tradition) the Palace of a Saxon king, which, in all probability, was Algar's home.

On Godwin's death Harold became an Earl, and later King; a title held for less than a year when he marched triumphant from a victory in the North to meet William near Hastings, where, in 1066 AD, he was slain. The traditional manner of his death (that it followed shortly after being struck by an arrow) is now disputed by a recent re-interpretation of the Bayeaux Tapestry, which gives a completely different version of events, and it is now believed that he fell beneath the hooves of a Norman horse as he tried to defend himself with an axe. Yet another story is that four Norman Knights broke through to where he stood, and unable to parry four thrusts simultaneously he was struck to the ground by one knight with a lance, two others hacked at his body, and the fourth cut off his head.

With Harold's death the Saxon resistance crumbled, and a few years later, when all England was under the Norman thumb, we find the Barons —who had fought beside William—in possession of the manors, villages and farms created by the Saxons, and few indeed were the Saxons left with any estate, as can be seen from that monumental work, the Domesday Book. The object of the survey that resulted in this book was to obtain an accurate account of the value of all estates, livestock and other property in the country, for the purpose of raising taxes for the King's coffers. To historical researchers it gives an unparalleled insight into the wealth and state of the country at that time.

All the lands and property that had belonged to the Saxon kings, automatically passed to William the Conqueror. In this way he acquired not only the Royal hunting and game preserve of Exmoor, but also the nearby manors of North Molton, Molland, Winsford and Dulverton.

Although the Normans were noted castle builders, few of their works are to be found in our region. Our finest example (although no buildings remain) are the impressive earthworks of the Motte and Bailey of Holwell Castle, Parracombe. It would be interesting to know more of the history of this castle, but to date we are not even sure who built it.

At West Park, Molland, a different type of castle was built on a raised platform surrounded by earth ramparts and a moat, or ditch, which was approached by a causeway that crossed the low lying land near the River Yeo. The adjoining land was enclosed as a deer park, and a little to the west fish ponds were constructed to supplement the food supply of the inhabitants. In Saxon days Molland was a valuable estate worth £24 by weight, and prior to the Norman Conquest it belonged to Harold. William the Conqueror gave it to the ancestor of William de Beumeis, but at some time before 1160 AD it was purchased by William de Bottreaux, who is said to have built the castle there. For nearly 600 years its history is shrouded in mystery, but it re-emerges in 1717, when a lease granted by John Courtenay to Thomas Williams included the 'Eastern House' (East Park) and the ancient mansion. It appears from this description that at some time between the two dates the castle had been transformed or rebuilt as a mansion. It is possible that by this time it was uninhabited, because less than 30 years later in 1755 it is described in the Milles Parochial

Returns as a ruin, and no trace of either the ancient house or the fishponds can be found on the tithe map of Molland of 1842. Another castle of Norman origin stands at Dunster, but being outside the region we are dealing with does not concern us here.

The Normans were passionately fond of hunting, especially the chase, but the Royal Forest of Exmoor held few deer in comparison with the woods and coverts outside its bounds, where they also chose to breed. Because this was so, the early Norman kings appropriated or afforested this land also. Once afforested it came under extremely harsh laws, which were specifically designed to protect the Royal deer and game therein, to the benefit of the King and a chosen few. Anyone else caught illegally killing the deer of the Forest, were liable to the death penalty, or the lesser (if it could be called lesser) sentence of mutilation or blinding. In later years, when the severity of these laws were eased, heavy fines were the order of the day, with a few years rotting in gaol for those unable to pay. To further protect the deer, all dogs capable of hunting them (living within the area of the Forest) were required by law to be put through a very cruel practise in which the animals were deliberately lamed by cutting off three toes of a fore foot.

Such was the harshness of the Forest Laws that now affected large numbers of the rural population, that it led to the men of Devon raising 100 marks (about £666) in 1204 to be disafforested. This money, paid to King John, released not only the afforested lands on the Devon side of Exmoor, but also similar lands around the Forest of Dartmoor. A little later, in 1215, on the terms of the Magna Carta, King John was forced to return his illegally held lands on the Somerset side of Exmoor, but it was not until after his death that any attempt was made to put things right, when his successor, Henry III, decided to re-establish the proper Forest boundaries and a perambulation of the bounds took place. There appears to have been little haste on his part, however, to fulfill his obligations because nearly 60 years elapsed and still nothing had been done to restore the misappropriated lands to the rightful owners.

In 1279, seven years after Henry's death, a new perambulation took place, but from the storm of protest that came from the inhabitants of Withypool, Hawkridge, and parts of Porlock, Exford and Winsford, it was obviously far from correct, and later in the same year a second perambulation took place which left only Oare and a part of Withypool at Lanacre still included in the Forest. Twenty years later Lanacre was placed outside the Forest bounds, but when Oare was excluded is not recorded. All that is known is that is was no longer a part of the Forest when the survey of 1651 took place.

Up until this time we have dealt with Exmoor in its widest sense, but now seems the appropriate moment to define the proper boundaries of the Forest, and hereafter, this book will be mainly concerned with events that took place within its well defined area of 20,344 acres, which remained a Royal Forest until it was disposed of by Parliament—acting on behalf of the Crown—in 1818. It should be noted that this large block of land, now usually referred to as Exmoor Proper, should not in any way be confused with the much larger area known as the Exmoor National Park, even though it is part and parcel of it.

Only a brief description of the general route of the Forest boundary will be given here, for there is no point whatever in including boundary stones and other markers that have long since disappeared. By taking the last survey of the Forest in 1815 as a guide, and by using modern as well as ancient landmarks, the boundary should not prove too difficult to follow, and with the aid of a 1 in. OS map of Exmoor, or better still, the 2½ in. series, the task will be made easier still.

Our starting point (for my own convenience) is Higher Willingford Bridge, the southernmost point of the Forest. Taking a clockwise direction the boundary follows Litton Water, first westward and then northwestward up towards its source near Sandyway Cross. From this point it continues in a northwesterly direction side by side with the road to Kinsford Gate and Moles Chamber, leaving the road for a mile or so to cut across rough moorlands to Setta Barrow, rejoining the road again just short of Moles Chamber. It leaves the highway there, and veering northward runs alongside the ancient Lynton track for a short distance before striking out alone over boggy ground to the Challacombe-Simonsbath road, where its position is marked by the Edgerley Stone. The boundary now veers northwestward for a short distance, but on converging with the Lynton track once more, turns northwards with it, and side by side, track and boundary continue on to Woodbarrow and Saddle Gate. A few yards more and the northernmost extremity of the western boundary of the Forest is reached at Saddle Stone (no longer there). Here the boundary turns sharply eastward, and within a mile drops steeply into Ruckham Combe, to climb just as steeply out the other side. Once across Thorn Hill the route becomes a litte easier as it crosses the head of Warcombe and the Hoar Oak enclosures, continuing on down to Gammon Corner and the Hoar Oak Water.

On the far side of the Water stands the historic Hoar Oak, which marks the spot where the Forest boundary meets the boundary dividing the commons of Lynton and Brendon. The first recorded Hoar Oak had grown into a large tree and was past its prime when it succumbed to its very age and rotten-ness about the year 1658. Its replacement, planted some four years later, is said to have survived until 1916, but this I find questionable, because there is certainly no sign in the photograph of the Hoar Oak in S.H. Burton's *Exmoor,* that the tree shown is anything like 255 years old, and a scale relationship between the Forest wall and tree makes it very little—if any—larger than the present tree, which is a mere 70 years old (1986). The latest tree, when measured on 23.1.83 had reached height of 24 ft. 2 ins. with a girth at base of 3 ft. 6 ins.

Leaving the Hoar Oak Tree behind and continuing eastwards, the boundary passes over the southern end of Cheriton Ridge before dropping down to Farley Water, and climbing again meets the Brendon and Lynton-Simonsbath highway at Brendon Two Gates. Once across the road it follows Hoccombe Water down to its junction with Badgworthy Water.

Thus far, the Forest boundary and that of Devon and Somerset are one and the same, but from here on it is entirely in Somerset. The boundary now turns southwards up Long Combe Water (the name given to the higher reaches of Badgworthy Water) but shortly after turns eastwards again, and leaving the Water behind crosses Little Toms Hill—just to the south of the stone row noted in Chapter 1. Within a mile the boundary turns abruptly northwards to the head of Stowford Bottom, where it veers northeast-wards following the combe down to Chalk Water, crossing it, and bearing eastwards continues on to Black Barrow. Here it begins its journey back to Willingford by turning south to Aldermans Barrow, and then southwest-wards alongside the road to Larkbarrow Corner. It leaves the road at this point and shortly after drops down beside Sparcombe Water to its confluence with the Exe. Once across the river it heads southeastwards up over Red Stone Hill, to meet the Exford-Simonsbath road at a point about threequarters of a mile east of Red Deer Farm. The boundary continues alongside the road past the farm and then turns southwards beside Gypsy Lane, and on beyond the end of the lane to meet the River Barle at a point opposite Sherdon Water. After crossing the Barle the boundary runs alongside the Water for about half a mile, and then turns up over Dillacombe, crossing in turn the Lanacre road and the Sandyway-Withypool highway, continuing on southwards to Willingford, where the perambulation of the Forest boundary is completed.

In order to administer the Forest and its laws, a number of officials were appointed. The most important of these on Exmoor was the Warden, who held his position by courtesy of the King, and in return for a small annual rent he was entitled to the income from the Forest, which was mainly derived from the summer grazing of sheep, cattle and ponies; sheep providing the largest source of revenue. The main duties of the Warden were to protect and preserve the deer and game for the King, and to keep the Forest in good condition. The most notable of the early Wardens was William de Wrotham, who in his day held many important posts. He was one of the Kings Justices, Warden of the Stannaries of Devon and Cornwall, and was also for a time the Sheriff of Devon. In 1204, he was granted a Charter by King John, giving him and his heirs forever the Wardenship of the Forest of Exmoor, which the family held until about 1341, when a descendant exchanged the Wardenship and his income from the Forest for the Manor of Ubley (on the north side of the Mendip Hills). Other officials, included the Forester, who was responsible for the day to day running of the Forest; and the Verderers, who were directly responsible to the King for maintaining Law and Order and presiding over the Courts which dealt with the minor claims and disputes of the Forest. There were also the Regarders, whose chief duty was to inspect and report on the state of the Forest once in every three years; and the Agisters, who were responsible for counting the stock pastured there in the summer.

The supreme court of the Royal Forest of Exmoor was the Eyre, and it was in these courts that the harshest punishments were handed out. The last Eyre which concerned Exmoor appears to have been held in 1270, and by the end of the 13th century this type of court had been abandoned in favour of an inquisition—or trial by jury—for the more serious offences; the lesser complaints and minor crimes being dealt with by the Swainmote Court.

How this court came into being is interesting, and is, I believe, best described in a booklet, *The Swainmote Courts of Exmoor* by J.F. Chanter, as follows:

'The Manors of the Saxons were given by William the Conqueror to a few Lords, mostly his relatives, and in time parishes were formed from these manors and the Forest was defined and perambulated. Between the Forest bounds and the old manors were large tracts of unenclosed lands called the commons on which the manors had certain rights, derived from the old Saxon landowners having exercised a free right from time immemorial of sending their flocks and herds to graze on Exmoor. These commons were once part of the Forest, before disafforestation, but were not included in later perambulations. The parishes surrounding Exmoor included the commons rightly or wrongly within their bounds, each parish to the Forest boundary. By the time the Kings Forest Laws were evolved the old freeholders were able to maintain some of their rights against the Crown, and on agreeing to keep the Forest safe from marauders were given pasturage and other rights at an annual rent, and so gradually became the Free Tenants, Suitors at Large and Free Suitors of the Swainmote Court.' Two of these Forest Courts were held every year, the first at Lanacre, the second a fortnight later at Hawkridge in the churchyard; this court always adjourned to Withypool in the afternoon.

The Free Suitors appear to have had their origin in Saxon days when three of the Kings Foresters held Withypool and Hawkridge in return for duties in the Forest, and for 200 years after the Conquest the Normans continued this custom. Similarly, the tenants of the 52 tenements that went to make up these two parishes, held their farms on condition that they provided suit and service as required within the Forest. These duties included attending the Swainmote Courts, and to drive the Forest nine times a year on horseback; five times for horses, twice, sometimes three times for cattle, and once for sheep. The drive for sheep took place nine days before midsummer, by which time all sheep pasturing on the Forest should have returned to their home farms for shearing; any left behind were driven to the Forest Pound at Withypool and shorn, the fleece going to the Warden, and the sheep also if not claimed by Midsummer Day. Any other animals found trespassing on the Moor were also impounded, until an appropriate fine was paid. The Free Suitors were also expected to perambulate the Forest bounds once in seven years, and serve on a Coroners inquest should any corpse be found within the Forest. In return for these services each of the Free Suitors were entitled to day pasture 140 sheep in the Forest (later amended to include night pasturage as well). They were also allowed free pasture for 5 mares and their foals, and as many cattle as could be wintered on their tenements, plus other privileges, which included all the peat, heath and fern they could use on their farms in winter, and certain rights of fishing on the rivers of the Forest.

The Suitors at Large represented the other townships and manors (which later became parishes) around Exmoor. They were obliged to attend the Swainmote Courts each year in order to maintain the right of common in the Forest they had held since time immemorial. Each of these parishes had their own iron mark—or branding iron—which had to be produced when the Forest Courts met, and as we shall see in Chapter 3, great importance was placed on the production of this iron and the use to which it was put. The chief landowners among the Suitors at Large, although obliged to attend the Swainmote Courts, were usually represented by their bailiffs. This was allowed, providing a fine was paid. In time, these fines became known as Quit Rents and later still they are entered in the Forest Books as Court Rents, this money being also a part of the Warden's income.

Apart from attending the Forest Courts the duties of the Suitors at Large appear to have been mainly confined to maintaining the boundary stones which separated the Forest from their own commons, and for these minor services they became entitled, at some time during the evolvement of the Forest, to pasture their sheep, cattle and horses on Exmoor at half the going rate paid by outsiders. These rates were proclaimed early in the spring of every year in the market towns around the Moor, and as time went by this custom came to be known as 'Crying the Moor'.

It was sheep that provided the largest source of income to the Warden of the Forest, for wool had been the greatest source of wealth of the Country since early medieval times, and in Telling Houses placed at strategic points covering the main routes from the towns and villages, principally from North Devon, the sheep were counted on to the Moor and the tally for each farmer noted.[1] The sheep were taken off the Moor at shearing time, and on returning a new count was taken; repeated once more when the seasons grazing was over in October and the sheep returned to their home farms for the winter. All money due for the grazing was paid on the 25th July (St. James Day) at Withypool.

How many Telling Houses were placed on or around Exmoor is not recorded.

MacDermot refers to one that was said to have stood on North Molton Common at Span Head, but this does not tie up with the location given on the 1809 1″ OS map, which places it south-east of Yarde Down Cross, (Poltimore Arms), now a T-junction. This, however, proves nothing, as this map is frequently in error where Exmoor is concerned, and as Miss Eardley-Wilmot points out in the 1981 Exmoor Review, this position, although eminently suitable for counting the large numbers of sheep

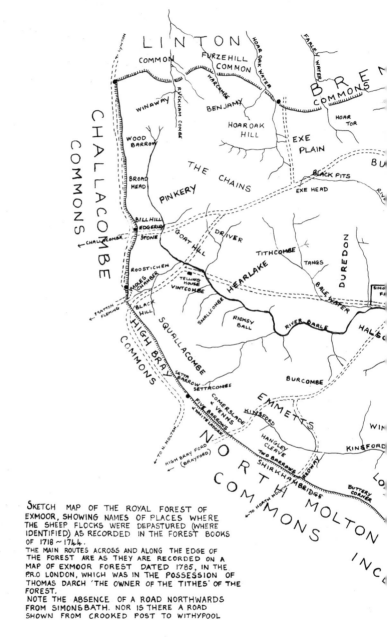

SKETCH MAP OF THE ROYAL FOREST OF
EXMOOR, SHOWING NAMES OF PLACES WHERE
THE SHEEP FLOCKS WERE DEPASTURED (WHERE
IDENTIFIED) AS RECORDED IN THE FOREST BOOKS
OF 1718 ~ 1744.
THE MAIN ROUTES ACROSS AND ALONG THE EDGE OF
THE FOREST ARE AS THEY ARE RECORDED ON A
MAP OF EXMOOR FOREST DATED 1785, IN THE
P.R.O LONDON, WHICH WAS IN THE POSSESSION OF
THOMAS DARCH 'THE OWNER OF THE TITHES' OF THE
FOREST.
NOTE THE ABSENCE OF A ROAD NORTHWARDS
FROM SIMONSBATH. NOR IS THERE A ROAD
SHOWN FROM CROOKED POST TO WITHYPOOL

• MERE STONES MARKING EXTENT OF THE
COMMONS OF THE BORDERING PARISHES.

coming from the North Molton area (and South Molton), was hardly in the right place to count those coming from Brayford and beyond. She confirms the late Charles Whybrow's opinion that this Telling House stood in a field north-east of the Yarde Down fork, where a steep sided mound of earth and stones is believed to be the remains of this building, which abutted on to what was apparently a sunken drovers trail (now under grass) that headed straight for the lowest part of Fyldon Ridge and the entrance of the Forest at Kinsford Gate.

Miss Hope Bourne, in her *Little History of Exmoor,* suggests there was a Telling House in the Hoar Oak Valley, but although I am familiar with the area I am still uncertain of its location.

By tradition, another Telling House was situated somewhere near Moles Chamber, a tradition that is in fact confirmed by Day and Masters Map of Exmoor of 1782. Unfortunately, as is true of some of the later maps of Exmoor, it does not quite relate to the lie of the land. It shows the trackway known as the Harepath running down from Moles Chamber, parallel to the tributory of the River Barle that was at one time believed to be its source, but does not show the combe and water coming down from Black Hill to join it, and to confuse us still further shows a non-existent valley coming out of the hillside on the opposite side of the main stream. Two hundred yards or so beyond the point, where the Black Hill Water joins the main stream, the Harepath forks into two tracks; the southern-most leading on to Simonsbath, the other to Exe Head, and though this part of the latter route is no longer in use, it is still plainly visible on the ground. The position of this fork is important, as it holds the key to the whereabouts of the Telling House, always assuming that Day and Masters have placed it correctly on their map. This shows it situated on the south side of the Harepath, approximately opposite the mouth of the non-existent valley, and by retracing our steps a little, places it in the close proximity of the junction of the Black Hill Water and the Harepath which crosses it.

Despite the care taken to establish its position, nothing appears to be left of a Telling House in this area, but about 250 yards beyond the fork in the trackways, and some 75 yards short of where the Simonsbath track goes through a gateway in a wire fence, there is, on the south side of the old Harepath, a small circular earth and turf bank which all but covers a base wall built of stone, and this, I believe, could well be the building we are looking for.

Although this Telling House (as it surely was) stood three quarters of a mile inside the Forest, its position would have been ideal for its intended purpose because of the commanding view it held over a wide area of the Forest, including two of the major routes by which the sheep from the North Devon area entered the Moor. One, through and from Challacombe, the other from High Bray; and Bratton Fleming and beyond, via Moles Chamber.

Throughout the 12th, 13th, and early 14th centuries the farms around

Exmoor had prospered and grown in numbers, until that fateful year 1348, when the Black Death, in a series of terrifying visitations, caused such a decimation of the population throughout the country, that whole villages and townships were wiped out, and many of the farms left uninhabited by this foul disease fell quickly into ruin. The better land was taken over by the farmers and peasants who survived, but corn, which had been extensively grown in earlier years, now played only a small part in the agricultural economy, for labour to do the tillage was scarce and at a premium, and stock farming, mainly sheep, flourished in consequence.

The breakdown of the farming community following the Black Death was the beginning of the end of the old manorial system, but many years were yet to pass before the feudal structure and its customs finally came to an end.

CHAPTER 3

FOREST DAYS AND FOREST WAYS 1350-1750

FOR a century and a half following the Black Death, little of consequence happened within the Forest, but in 1504 there came an event which completely changed the course of the history of Exmoor. Prior to this date, the deer of the Forest belonged to the King, and to the King alone, but to Henry VII this meant little, for he was far more interested in increasing the revenues from his estates, and so, in the last year of his reign, the royal entitlement to the deer was given up when the Forest of Exmoor was leased to Sir Edmund Carew, a lease which included the right of hunting and killing the deer, the only stipulation being that at the termination of the lease 100 deer were to be left in the Forest, which may have proved difficult to comply with, unless the deer were more obliging than in earlier years. The annual rent payable to the Crown was fixed at £46. 13. 4.; a figure that remained unchanged right down to the termination of the last lease in 1814.

The lease granted to Sir Edmund Carew had set a precedent, and thereafter, all leases granted for the Forest included the deer and hunting rights. Little else changed, except that the Lessee was now also the Warden of the Forest, and as such received all the income from the grazing, etc. therein. The profit to be made from this was considerable, and led in later years to large sums of money changing hands in order to obtain a lease. The running of the Forest was usually left to a Deputy Warden—or Forester. The laws of the Forest were still maintained. The Swainmote Courts continued to meet, and so life went on as lessee followed lessee down through the 16th and into the 17th century, when the Forest came into the possession of a most interesting character by the name of James Boevey.

Before continuing with Boevey's story, however, we must take a look at another matter that was causing great concern around Exmoor, where the stock pastured on the Moor had grown in numbers over the years, and towards the end of the 16th century it was said 40,000 sheep, 1,000 cattle, and 400 horses were placed annually upon the Forest to enjoy the summer pasture.*

On the evidence of Forest Books of later date I would query only the numbers of cattle, and believe the other figures given are probably not far from the truth.

About the year 1600, the parsons of some of the parishes bordering Exmoor began claiming the full wool tithes for the sheep belonging to their parishioners, which, in fact, they were not entitled to, as for six months of

---

*MacDermot.

the year many of the sheep were grazing on the Forest. These claims went to Court, where judgement was given in favour of the farmers. Their jubilation did not last long, however, because the Crown had been made aware that as Exmoor was not a parish, but extra-parochial, it was they who were entitled to the tithes of the Forest. They promptly responded by granting the tithe rights to George Cottington in 1623 for a lump sum of £133. 6. 8, plus a yearly rent of £13. 6. 8. Cottington wasted no time in claiming his tithes, but only a few farmers willingly paid up, others completely ignored his demands, although some were later persuaded to settle their accounts. The remainder were taken to court by Cottington, who, being legally in the right, won his claims, with the result that far fewer sheep were sent to Exmoor in the years that followed, which could not have pleased the Warden of the Forest who sustained a considerable reduction in his income.

During the Civil War—which began in 1642—Exmoor saw little of the fighting and bloodshed that was happening elsewhere in the country. The farming communities around the Forest were generally more sympathetic to the cause of the Parliamentary Forces, which is hardly surprising when taking into consideration the way the Crown had treated them in respect of the tithes. There was the odd skirmish here and there, and though little is recorded of events on or close to Exmoor, a cannon ball, believed to date from this period, was unearthed at Home Farm, Challacombe, about the end of the last century. This ball was believed by J.L.W. Page to have been but one of several found in the locality.

In 1642, the Luttrells of Dunster Castle were attacked by Royalist Forces who were quickly sent packing; most of the escaping Cavaliers either crossed Exmoor via Exford, or skirted the Moor by way of Dulverton, on route for what they hoped would be a better reception in Cornwall. Two years later, after a change of fortunes, they were back, and about 600 of the Kings men were crossing Exmoor when they were sighted by a smaller number of Luttrell's men, who were with Bennetts troops from Bristol, who, being outnumbered, and believing discretion to be the better part of valour, quickly scattered in all directions, thus avoiding a fight. Shortly afterwards about 200 of these men arrived at Barnstaple, where, less than a week later, after being betrayed, the whole garrison and town fell into the hands of the Royalists, and remained so until April 1646, when it was relieved by Parliament Forces.

There is in existence a document which relates to the village of Charles —on the fringe of Exmoor—at this time.[*] It is a set of accounts for keeping troops and horses there, these being part of the Royalist Garrison at Barnstaple. These accounts, all for 1646, are itemised but in poor condition. Usually each item covers just one or two troopers and their horses, and on one occasion a Col. James Ansley paid a short visit. Only once was a troop of any size garrisoned there. This was when 34 men and horses of a French regiment spent 16 days at Charles, at a cost of £19. 18. 0.

---

[*]Acland Archive D.R.O. Exeter.

Because only one such document has been found it does not necessarily mean that Charles was the only village around Exmoor that was expected to provide food and shelter for whichever faction was in control at the time, and it would be interesting to discover more documentary evidence to this effect, and even more interesting to know that if such services were rendered, were they ever paid for?

After the execution of Charles Stuart in 1649, the Civil War was—or should have been—at an end, but there was still the odd occasion—even in our area—when small groups of fervent Cavaliers rose up and caused some disturbances, but as they do not directly concern Exmoor we will pass on to more important issues.

In the same year of the King's execution, an Act of Parliament was passed to dispose of all the royal properties and estates, and shortly afterwards, a survey of the Royal Forest of Exmoor took place, followed in 1652 by its sale to Joseph Strange, who shortly proved to be only the front man for the real purchasers, James Boevey and John Smith. The price agreed for the freehold of the Forest was £12,329. 5. 5, which was based on 25 years of its annual gross income, which at this time was nearly £500 per annum. To allow for Lady Thurles life lease on the Forest this sum was reduced to £7,417. 14. 6, and reduced still further because Exmoor had been sold tithe free, which, of course, it was not. This must have been a worrying time for John Mills, who now owned the tithes—these having been purchased by his father (also John) from Cottington, for the exorbitant sum of £2,000—because to all intents and purposes his rights had been completely ignored. On appealing to the Commissioners he was allowed £560, bringing the final figure paid for the Forest down to £6,851. 14. 6, but, by the time this settlement had been agreed, Boevey had acquired the tithes from John Mills.

The Forest was now divided between the two partners, with Smith taking the greater share, which was also the better land south of the Exford to Challacombe road. It is apparent that he was only concerned with obtaining a good return on his investment, whereas, Boevey—although like minded—is thought to have had a real hankering for the country life after years of indifferent health while making his fortune in the City of London, where he had set himself up as a merchant, and to this end he built a fine house in the centre of the Forest at Simonsbath and around it enclosed 108 acres for a farm. He also built a new Pound there, to replace the centuries old Pound at Withypool, although, in fact, the latter did remain in use. This was as far as he got with the development of Exmoor, where it is thought he intended to establish several farms and to colonise the Moor in much the same way as John Knight and his son succeeded in doing some 200 years later. On the completion of his new house in 1654, Boevey and his second wife, Isabel, moved in. In the same year he leased all of John Smith's portion of Exmoor, for a term of 2,000 years, at a fixed annual rent of £130, and thus gained control of all the Forest.

All went well until 1660, when the Monarchy was restored, and with it all the Crown property that Parliament had disposed of. This meant that Boevey and Smith no longer owned the Forest, which to them was a major blow, because not only did they lose the Forest, but they also forfeited the money they had paid for it. Boevey, however, schemer that he was, had forseen this possibility and had purchased Lady Thurles life lease of the Forest, and so, he now became the sole lessee and tithe owner of Exmoor. We do not know what John Smith's remarks were on the subject, but he could not have been a very 'happy chappy'. Boevey's next step was to extend the life of his lease, and this he succeeded in doing by the purchase of leases on three more lives plus 31 years.

One of the first changes Boevey had made on gaining possession of the Forest was to more than double the rates for the stock pastured there. In the following year he was forced to reduce them somewhat, because as usual the farmers retaliated by sending fewer sheep to graze on Exmoor, and by moving them on and off the Forest at night, and by various other schemes, they avoided paying their dues. When Boevey got wind of what was going on he took the offending farmers to court in an attempt to recover the money owed him, and so began a succession of law suits that was to keep him busy for the next 40 years. The rates charged for the summer grazing at this time were 4d. a head for sheep, 2/- for cattle and 4/- for horses, the latter being for all the year grazing; rates that remained unchanged until John Knight bought the major portion of the Forest in 1818. To allow for the tithes, 1d. was added to the normal rates of each and every sheep pastured on the Forest, and thus the tithes came to be worth about one fifth of the income of Exmoor. The Free Suitors, of course, still paid nothing, and the Suitors at Large, half rates.

James Boevey's first wife had died in 1649, but as her next of kin he inherited a large legacy left her by a relative in Holland, where, after some time had passed with no inheritance forthcoming, he set forth to claim it.

On arrival in Holland, he was strongly opposed by one Peter Bowden, who had him arrested and thrown into prison, where he remained for three years. On his release he immediately resumed his claims, and was promptly returned to gaol for a further two years, after which he appears to have got the message and returned to England, where, in the meantime, his ex-partner had had the audacity to sue him for arrears of rent, on the terms of his lease, which, of course, was no longer valid, his interest having been forfeited at the time of the Restoration of the Monarchy. The outcome of the case is not recorded, but it is most unlikely that Smith was successful in his claim.

The respite gained by the farmers while Boevey languished in prison was now over, and with great determination he resumed his claims against the many farmers who owed him money, but these legal proceedings paled into insignificance, when, in 1675, Boevey laid claim to the commons of all the parishes bordering the Forest, on the grounds that they were once a part of the Royal Forest. His objective was clear, for if he succeeded in securing the commons, he would be entitled to the tithes of all the sheep pastured thereon, thus greatly increasing his income. Naturally enough he met with strong opposition, not only from the parsons of the parishes concerned, who were accustomed to receiving the tithes, but also from the commoners, who confirmed this, and stated that the parish boundaries—including the commons—were regularly perambulated, and though Boevey fought hard to make his case convincing, judgement was given against him, for which the parsons and the farmers must have been exceedingly thankful.

In or about the year 1680, James Boevey married for the third time (his second wife having died in 1669) and shortly afterwards he and his wife, Margaret, née Cresset, left Exmoor to retire to Cheam in Surrey, leaving the day to day running of the Forest and the collection of the Forest dues to his Deputy Forester, Henry Smith, who had held this office since 1674. MacDermot loses track of Smith in 1691, when a gap of some 13 years appears in his list of Deputy Foresters, but there is reason to believe that he continued to hold the office until 1704, when William Smith (probably a relative) took over the duties. Henry Smith was certainly still around in 1694, when his signature occurs on a document concerning Simonsbath Farm that has recently come to light in the Somerset Archives at Taunton, which is, without doubt, one of the most important discoveries in recent years concerning Exmoor. MacDermot was apparently completely unaware of the existence of this document, which is in the form of an inventory of the farm taken after the death of the tenant, Richard Hill, in 1694, just two years before Boevey's own death in 1696, and only 40 years after the house was built and the farm enclosed.

The inventory—which from two or three words that have completely disappeared from the parchment—is in remarkably fine condition considering it is nearly 300 years old, and because of its importance I have recorded it in full.

Simons = Burrow Invoice

Richard Hill

An inventory of the goods of Richard Hill of Simons = Bath lately deceased, taken and priced the 18th day of April, 1694, by Henry Smith and Richard Crang as followeth

		£.	s.	6.
Item	his wearing apparell	2.	0.	0.
,,	two cows and calves	9.	0.	0.
,,	four yearlings	5.	0.	0.
,,	three pigs	2.	0.	0.
,,	one old . o . . (boar? pony?) (could be anything)	0.	5.	0.
,,	three score ewes . . . r (poor?) leen sheep	20.	10.	0.
,,	Poultry	0.	5.	0.
,,	two table boards and three formes	0.	15.	0.
,,	three . . . stools	0.	2.	0.
,,	one cubbord	0.	10.	0.

Item	four pewter dishes, two plates, a candlestick and a salt	0.	10.	0.
,,	two brass pans and a kettle	1.	6.	0.
,,	three brass pots and a skillet	1.	1.	6.
,,	two brewing vates, three tubs, four screens? and three little vessells	0.	16.	0.
,,	an old cheese press and four cheese vates (vats)	0.	4.	0.
,,	six flagons	0.	6.	0.
,,	two feather beds, bolsters, coverletts and blankets belonging to them	7.	10.	0.
,,	two other beds with coverletts and blankets to them	1.	13.	4.
,,	three pairs of old sheets, two table cloths and six table napkins	1.	0.	4.
,,	three bedsteads . . . . . . chest and two coffers	1.	7.	4.
,,	Andirons, pot hooks and pot hangings	0.	2.	0.
,,	two pack saddles, a hackney saddle, girls and a rooks	0.	4.	6.
,,	two brandices, a fender and two spits	0.	5.	0.
,,	an old gun, a yoke, bows and a seale	0.	6.	6.
,,	a trundle salter and vates (vats)	0.	18.	6.
,,	other small tools and things out of mind and unseen	0.	3.	4.
		£56.	1.	10.

N.B. Although the valuation was probably an accurate assessment of the value of the estate, the arithmetic leaves a little to be desired and the total should, I think, be   £58. 1. 4.

There is nothing in the inventory to suggest that Richard Hill was also the Deputy Forester, which was the usual custom thereafter, but as we can see, Henry Smith was one of the two men taking the inventory and was almost certainly still in office.

Certain items in the inventory, such as the table cloths, table napkins and sheets, indicate that Richard Hill was not of ordinary farming stock, but what we would now call a gentleman farmer, and from the number of brewing items listed it would appear that he supplemented his income by the sale of ale, or beer. There was certainly some demand for this commodity, because we know from later accounts that the yearly cutting (castrating) of colts at Simonsbath, was always followed by an allowance of beer for the men assisting with this hard and thirsty work. Beer was also provided when a survey (sale) of colts took place, and the Deputy Forester usually managed to justify its consumption on other occasions as well. There would also have been a limited passing trade, comprised of packhorse train drivers, drovers and stockmen going about their duties, and so, although Simonsbath House was not licenced as an inn until 1789, we can be fairly sure that the brewing of ale took place there at least one hundred years earlier, and continued to be brewed there up to and after a licence was granted.

Very little new material has been found concerning James Boevey, but among the Acland papers are a number of receipts for the Crown and Tithe rents for the Royal Forest of Exmoor, paid by him to Queen Catherine.* Although of little interest in themselves, they do cover many of the years that he was Lessee of the Forest. In the year 1660, the receipt was made out to Jacobus Boevey. From 1661-1663 to Jacob Boevey, but was in the name of James Boevey thereafter.

Boevey's death in 1696, ended 43 years of unbroken rule of the Forest; the longest period that any one man held it during its lengthy history as a Royal Forest, and for nearly 40 of these years he was involved in litigation of one kind or another: After Boevey's death his widow retained the Forest for a further eight years, before selling the remaining 15 years of her last lease to Robert Siderfin, who lived at Croydon House, Timberscombe. He took over the Forest in 1704, and was fortunate enough to be able to acquire a further lease, giving him possession to 1750. Margaret Boevey did not, however, sell the tithes, and on her death in 1714 they passed to one of her relatives, James Cresset, for the benefit of his children.

One of the most satisfying experiences when researching for material for a book of this nature, is to find documents that were either not available, or have been missed by the experts, and in the Acland deposit in the D.R.O. Archives at Exeter, can be found Forest Books for entering sheep, cattle and horses, pasturing on Exmoor, which cover a period of some 47 years from 1718-1764. A few of these books are missing, but from other brief accounts very few years are left unaccounted for.

It was previously believed that only two such books existed, so this find is of major importance, and, because the Forest Books are almost continuous, it has been possible to build up a picture of a way of life that probably began with the evolvement of the Forest as summer grazing pasture, with a capacity for heavy stocking, and thus capable of producing a considerable annual income, and for year after year, century after century, continued to do so, until a change of policy by the Crown in the early part of the 19th century brought the traditional way of life on Exmoor to an abrupt end.

The Forest Books can be divided into two parts, 1718-1749, and 1750-1764; the former being of the greatest interest because they are given in greater detail. The earliest book, that of 1718, when Robert Siderfin was Warden of Exmoor, shows that he ran the Forest with the aid of two bailiffs; John Hill and John Clatworthy, but this was not the normal custom of the Forest, where these duties were usually carried out by a Deputy Forester, and on the 29th June 1718, James Hill was appointed to collect the Forest dues and to carry out the customary duties. Although he too is recorded as a bailiff, we can be sure that he was in fact the Deputy Forester, because after collecting £510. 16. 0 out of the total income for 1719 of £581 he received the customary payment of 18 pence in the pound as salary; in this case, £41. 13. 3. This method of payment to the Deputy Forester continued—with only a

---

*MacDermot: Queen Katherine of Braganza. After her death the tithe rent ceased and the tithes became absolute freehold.

couple of exceptions—until the Forest was sold in 1818, but when it originated and who first paid it we do not know.

The disbursements, or expenses of the Forest in 1719 amounted to £201 leaving a profit—after tithes of £110 were paid—of £270 to Robert Siderfin, but by the time the accounts were settled he was dead, and the profit was shared between Madam Siderfin and Robert Darch—his nephew.

Among the disbursements one item is of particular interest, and is, I believe, the only record of not only how many Tellers were employed on Exmoor to check the numbers of sheep booked in, tallied with the numbers on the Moor, but also gives the Tellers names. At this time there were four Tellers; three of them; William Passmore, John Ridd and Henry Moorman, were paid £1. 6. 0 apiece; the fourth Teller, Robert Williams, received 12/-. In the following year the Tellers were paid £5. 8. 0 between them, and this figure remained about the same until 1745, when it was increased to £6. 9. 0.

Although four Tellers are recorded (and this appears to have been the usual number) only two Telling Houses have been identified, one near the Poltimore Arms at Yarde Down, the other near Moles Chamber. Both are placed in the best possible positions to overlook the primary routes to Exmoor from the North Devon area, where the bulk of the sheep flocks came from, and thus to count them as they passed, and contrary to Miss Hope Bourne's belief that there was a third Telling House in the Hoar Oak valley, all the evidence points against it, as the Forest Books for 1722 (the peak year) show that only 440 sheep from Lynton, and 40 from Brendon, are likely to have passed this way, and none of these were placed on the Forest until after shearing. Similarly, it is unlikely there were any Telling Houses on the Somerset side of Exmoor, because here too, the sheep from Oare (500), Porlock (1,336), and Exford (2,590), did not arrive on the Forest until after sheartime. By examining the Forest records a little closer, we find that out of a total of 36,605 sheep pastured on the Forest in 1722, only 6,607 did not pass by the two known Telling Houses, and of these, 4,921 belonged to borderers who did not place them on the Moor until after shearing. This being so, there was little need for any additional Telling Houses, as the few sheep flocks outstanding could have been easily checked and counted *in situ* as required.

When Robert Siderfin died in 1719 or 20 (MacDermot gives 1720) he was deeply in debt and the moiety or profit of the Forest was afterwards shared between his two chief creditors; his nephew Robert Darch was one, James Hill the other, and though MacDermot states that Robert Darch did not purchase the tithes from the Cresset family until 1723 (for £800), the Forest Book of 1720 shows that they were already in his possession.

The income of the Forest—which had for some years been rising—reached a peak in 1722 of £644, and though this figure was exceeded on two or three occasions after, this was due to exceptional circumstances which did not reflect the true annual income. Out of the total income for

1722, £592 came from sheep pasturing dues. A breakdown of the sheep flocks show that 15,429 sheep came from the bordering parishes, and 21,178 more—all from the North Devon area. If the 52 Free Suitors of Hawkridge and Withypool took up their full rights of 140 sheep for each tenement, then a possible 43,887 sheep could have pastured on Exmoor that year, far exceeding the 40,000 figure given by a witness in the late 16th century. Additional stock on Exmoor in 1722 included 166 colts (horses of all description), 150 of them from the borderers of the following parishes: Brendon 10, Challacombe 12, Exford 39, High Bray 24, Lynton 19, Molland 8, North Molton 16, Oare 2, Twitchen 2, Withypool 18, but there were none from Porlock, Hawkridge, or Stoke Pero.

Of the 128 Bullocks grazing on the Forest, 14 came from Brendon, Exford 12, Porlock 56, Molland 9, Oare 3, Stoke Pero 18, Luccombe 10, Culbone 4, and Selworthy 2. As can be seen, the majority of these came from West Somerset. It should be noted here that the Free Suitors were also entitled to free pasture for 5 mares and their foals and as many cattle as could be wintered on their tenements. If these rights were fully taken up, there would have been a considerable number of additional stock on Exmoor which were not recorded in the Forest Books. We still have the Warden's own stock to consider, and though we have no figures for sheep or bullocks, we do know that at times the numbers of horses or ponies kept there were as high as 300-400.

Because 1722 was the peak year, I have prepared a list giving the numbers of sheep from each of the parishes sending them to the Moor, and for the sake of convenience and comparison, I have also included the figures for 1743, when, in the midst of England's war against Spain and France, the income of the Forest dropped to £274, the lowest level recorded in the Forest Books.

We will begin with the numbers of sheep entered by the bordering parishes, the first figures are for 1722; those in parentheses 1743.

Brendon 40 (50)	Challacombe 399 (160)	High Bray 930 (428)
Exford 2590 (980)	Lynton 440 (46)	Molland 810 (577)
North Molton 7492 (4909)	Oare 500 (nil)	Porlock 1366 (896)
Twitchen 797 (567)	Withypool 65 (nil)	

giving a total for *1722* of 15,427, the corresponding figure for *1743* was 8,613.

The other parishes sending sheep to Exmoor were:

Arlington 1013 (266)	Atherington 152 (nil)	Ashford 87 (41)
Bishops Nympton 246 (43)	West Buckland 783 (459)	East Buckland 911 (329)
Bishops Tawton 1755 (134)	Bickington 104 (107)	Brau ton 305 (40)
Chittlehampton 1406 (295)	Charles 823 (58)	East Down 305 (40)
Fremington 44 (56)	Goodleigh 463 (168)	Heanton 237 (93)
Loxhore 872 (535)	Landkey 1599 (762)	South Molton 1056 (160)
Marwood 354 (98)	Pilton 67 (15)	Filleigh 237 (91)
Stoke Rivers 560 (471)	Shirwell 1083 (413)	Tawstock 1896 (846)
Swimbridge 3773 (982)	Warkleigh 727 (164)	Westleigh 259 (125)
		Yarnscombe 325 (63)

making a total for *1722* of 21,178 and for *1743,* 7,070.

From these figures it can be deduced that while the numbers of sheep placed on Exmoor by the borderers dropped by less than half, those of the other parishes declined by two thirds, but, of course, the borderers did have the advantage that in most cases they paid only half the outsiders dues. As can be seen from the list of borderers, the largest number of sheep came from North Molton, and though most of the sheep from this parish were placed on Exmoor before shearing, this was not necessarily the case with some of the other bordering parishes, and it is rare to find any sheep from Brendon, Exford, Lynton, Oare and Porlock on the Moor before sheartime, even though there was no reduction in the dues paid.

Of the other parishes, Swimbridge was by far the largest contributor to the income of the Forest, but Arlington, Bishops Tawton, Chittlehampton, Landkey, South Molton, Shirwell and Tawstock also sent large numbers of sheep year after year to Exmoor.

Having to some extent dealt with the animals grazing on Exmoor, it is time to take a look at the expenses of the Forest, many of which varied but little year in, year out, but occasionally items of special interest do crop up and these will be included as we come to them. As the year 1722 is typical of the earlier Forest Books, we will take the disbursements of that year and include them in full.

		£.	s.	d.
Pd	for crying the Moor at Barnstaple		3.	6.
,,	for crying the Moor at Molton		2.	6.
,,	for crying the Moor at Dunster		2.	6.
,,	for crying the Moor at Porlock		1.	0.
,,	for mending Pound Gates and timber		1.	6.
,,	ye Bailiffs and charges about ye Ejectment at Simonsbath	8.	2.	6.
,,	for crying a Survey at Simonsbath		1.	6.
,,	for beer at the Survey		3.	6.
,,	the cryer		1.	0.
,,	for a lock for the Pound		1.	6.
,,	expenses both Courts		10.	6.
,,	keeping the two Courts	1.	5.	0.
,,	mending the Pound at Withypool		3.	4.
,,	for carrying sand into Pound		1.	6.
,,	for keeping 6 colts 172½	4.	1.	0.
,,	for mending Poundwall at Simonsbath		2.	4.
,,	for cutting Nine colts		9.	0.
,,	for beer in cutting and Ironing Colts		1.	6.
,,	for two Posts and placing		2.	6.
,,	the Talers (Tellers)	5.	8.	0.
,,	my son to Braunton to See Colts		2.	6.
,,	for taking up and keeping two Mares at Brushford		3.	6.
,,	for two men to own and fetch them		4.	0.
,,	for Beer in taking up Suckers			6.
,,	for driving Suckers to Croydon		2.	6.

Pd	for cutting and keeping one Colt		2.	0.
,,	The Kings rent due at Michaelmass*	40.	18.	10.
,,	my Son to pay it to Mr. Darch		2.	6.
,,	ye Poundherd attending 9 drifts and warning the suit	1.	2.	6.
,,	him attending two Courts		2.	0.
,,	Warning the Sute at Hawkridge		5.	0.
,,	for Driving the Comons		4.	6.
,,	Expenses at Molton about my Duties		2.	6.
,,	a messenger to Dunster re letter		1.	6.
,,	the pound tax (land tax)	39.	3.	0.
,,	postage of letters		5.	6.
,,	Survey charges, Halters, etc.		16.	0.
,,	Salary for £523. 10. 8½ at 18d. (part)	39.	5.	3.

£144.	9.	4.

tithe land tax deducted £7. .8. 0.

disbursements £137. 1. 9.
tithes deducted £120. 12. 5.

leaving £386. 8. 11½ to be divided between the two moieties of Robert Darch and James Hill.

The sum of £8. 2. 6 paid to the bailiffs for the ejectment at Simonsbath is of some interest, and must refer to the Dinnacombe family who had been living and farming there since 1702. The rent paid by John Dinnacombe for the house and farm was minimal at £9 per annum, but he had taken the property for 5 years on a full repairing agreement, and to prove his honourable intentions he deposited a bond for £500 with Robert Siderfin as security. Towards the end of the 5 years, with nothing having been done to carry out his obligations, the premises were in a ruinous state and Dinnacombe was given notice to do the necessary repairs. He pleaded with Siderfin that he could not afford the repairs, but if his landlord would do them he would repay him. The repairs were done and Dinnacombe was allowed to stay on as a yearly tenant after his 5 years were up, but in 1717 he was given notice to quit. In 1718, Dinnacombe's wife pleaded with Siderfin for permission to remain in part of the house until midsummer. This was agreed, but when the time came, Dinnacombe refused to go and was arrested and taken to Ilchester Gaol; the usual treatment for debtors. In the Forest Book of 1718, the disbursements include expenses of assizes £14. 3. 7½ and for myself (Deputy Forester), what you please, which in this case was £1. 3. 6. These items were presumably in connection with the same case. A year later, the rest of the Dinnacombe family were thrown out on to the Moor. A Chancery suit followed soon after, in which Dinnacombe claimed Siderfin had no right to throw him out as he had laid out large sums of money in the last year on improvements and manure for the farm. This was disputed by his landlord, who replied that he doubted if

---

*£46. 13. 4, less land tax.

5/- had ever been spent on the farm by Dinnacombe. Furthermore, the tenant had burnt just about all the timber, doors, etc. in the house and buildings. The outcome of the case has not been found but one cannot see Dinnacombe getting any benefit from the Court's decision.

Prior to 1725, the four towns of Barnstaple, Molton, Dunster and Porlock were listed separately in the expenses for 'Crying the Moor', but after this date they are lumped together under the title of 'Crying the Moor in several places'; the total sum paid being exactly the same at 9s. 6d. In the 1719 returns, 1s. 6. was also paid for 'Crying the Moor at Dulverton', but as no stock was forthcoming from this area it was not repeated.

Not a year went by without a small sum being included in the disbursements for repairs to the Pound at Simonsbath, and usually the Withypool Pound as well. Exceptional expenses in regard to the latter were paid in 1733, when timber costing £9. 10. 0 was bought to remake the Pound rails, plus 10s. 6d. for the carriage of same, together with £2. 13. 0 for a carpenter and 2d. 6d. for spikes and nails. As was usual on Exmoor, the job could not be done satisfactorily without an allowance of ale, and 3s. 0d. was paid out for this essential activator of the proceedings. The account ended with a payment of 5s. 0d. to the Deputy Forester for his labour in buying the timber and looking after the carpenter, plus a further 1s. 6d. for beer for selling the offcuts of the trees and old timber from the Pound. After a great flood in 1736, 8s. 2d. was paid out for the repair of the Pound wall at Simonsbath. Three years later, following a great rain, 8s. 0d. was paid for the repair of the Exford road, and a similar amount for repairing the other highways of Exmoor. In most of the other years covered by the Forest Books, one or two shillings only were spent on the roads, which was probably just sufficient to keep them in a passable condition. Another customary payment was for cutting out bogs; the sum allowed was usually about 4s. 6d.

Robert Darch, the owner of a half share in the profits of the Forest—and the tithes, died in 1737, leaving both to his wife Hannah for life. On her death in 1740, the tithes passed on the terms of Robert's will to their son Thomas, who also received a half share in his father's half moiety; the other half going to his sister Mary, the wife of the Rev. Jonathan Hall. At this time, James Hill still held the other half moiety, but in 1746 we find his interest in the Forest in the hands of a William Draycott. How this came about is not clear, but with the disastrous year of 1743, when the income of the Forest was only £274, which, after expenses, left only a meagre profit of £76. 16. 10½ to be shared; and with 1744 showing little signs of improvement, James Hill may have decided that with only 6 years of the lease left to run, it was time to cash in on his remaining assets.

The Forest Book for 1745 is missing, and those of 1746 and after are in a very slimline version only 4½ in. wide which leave out such details as brand marks and where the flocks of sheep were placed on Exmoor; details that were always included in the earlier books.

Before 1745, the books were always signed by John Hill, who appears to have taken over from his father as Deputy Forester about 1720, but though Thomas Darch and his brother-in-law Jonathan Hall, were still in possession of a shared half moiety after the new books appear, they are no longer signed by John Hill, or, for that matter, anyone else after William Draycott took over the other half moiety; although other records show he was still the Deputy Forester in 1762.

By comparing entries in the Forest Books prior to 1745, it has been possible to arrive at some conclusions. Firstly, where flocks of sheep were sent to the Forest regularly year after year by the same owners, they were always placed on the same part of Exmoor, and it has in some cases been possible to trace these flocks passing from father to son still using the same grazing grounds. I strongly suspect that if complete records were available for the Forest in earlier years, it would be possible in this way to trace the ancestry of some of these flock owners back to very early times. Similarly, by cross checking flocks of sheep placed on particular parts of Exmoor, we find flock owners of the same name, with sheep in the same place, even though they come from different parishes, often many miles apart. This occurs too frequently for it to be coincidence, and I believe if this could be followed up it would not take long to find a common family connection.

If we look back into the history of the Forest of Exmoor, we find that the Suitors at Large and their tenants were the only people—apart from the Free Suitors—with a right of common on the Forest. They were obliged to attend the Swainmote Courts accompanied by a number of hands—usually five for the larger parishes, less for the smaller ones, and to bring with them their iron mark—or stood iron as it came to be called; failure to attend the Courts, or failure to bring with them their iron mark resulting in a fine. As none of these stood irons appear to have survived, we cannot be sure of the form they took in the Exmoor region, but it is not unlikely that they were in the shape of a crown with a different letter affixed for each place represented by the Suitors at Large; the form it took in at least two of the other Royal Forests where similar rights existed (Essex and Waltham). Special importance came to be placed upon the stood iron, because it implied—legally or otherwise—a right of pasture in the Forest for its owner and the occupiers of land in the manor or parish it represented; animals branded with this iron mark being charged at half the rates paid by outsiders for pasturage. In time, as the Forest Laws became less vigorously enforced, the use of the stood iron gradually died out, and as Warden followed Warden on the Forest, the customary rights of the Suitors at Large began to be questioned.

This was the case shortly after Robert Siderfin took over the Forest from Margaret Boevey in 1706, when we find twelve of these borderers being summoned for failing to pay the full dues. Nine of these men presumably paid up, but the other three, all named Shapland, who were tenants of Sir Charles Copplestone Bampfylde of North Molton, contested the case, and though the outcome is not recorded we do know that thereafter, with very few exceptions, the borderers paid the customary half rate. The interesting thing about this is that in the Forest Book of 1718, and for many years after, we find the stood iron still in use by two of the Shaplands in the case, George and William, and it may well be true that the production of the stood iron in court provided the evidence needed to persuade the jury to give judgement in their favour. We lose track of George Shapland in the 1730's, but William was still branding his sheep with the stood iron in 1739, after which he disappears from the Forest Books, but in 1741, when for one year Philip Shapland placed his sheep on Exmoor, they too were branded in this way.

In two of the other bordering parishes the iron mark was also still in use during this period: Joseph Quick of High Bray and his stood iron made a yearly appearance until 1729, but neither appear after. The other stood iron was in the possession of John Moore of Molland, who is regularly listed in the Forest Books from 1718-1742. Sheep branded with this iron appear once more in the following year, entered with the name of James Quartly (who had married John Moore's daughter), but he is not listed in 1744, the last year to include the brand marks of the sheep flocks pastured on Exmoor, and this makes it impossible to check if this stood iron or any of the others were used at a later date.

The stood iron appears in the Forest Books of Exmoor either written as such, or as a sign ⚤ , but on two occasions, in 1718 and 1719, the iron mark belonging to John Moore of Molland is shown in a different form, ⊕ and ⊕ respectively. The former is of greatest interest, because it is the only time when a distinct letter, in this case L, is revealed, which tends to confirm that a lettering system similar to that used in the Forests of Essex and Waltham was also used on Exmoor.

It was customary for the Lessee or Warden of Exmoor to keep some stock of his own on the Forest, and though we know nothing of the numbers of sheep or cattle kept, we do know something of his ponies, which in some years contributed a fair addition to his income.

Sufficient Forest Books remain for a fairly accurate assessment to be made of not only the numbers of ponies on Exmoor, but also what happened on at least one occasion when the Warden's term of office ended and a new Lessee took over.

Although we do not know if James Boevey kept any ponies on Exmoor, we can be fairly sure that when his widow handed over the Forest to Robert Siderfin in 1704, few—if any—ponies passed to him with the transfer. Fourteen years later there was still only a small herd, with just two colts sold and six cut, and it is strange to find that the £4. 6. 0 realised by the sale was not included in the income of the Forest as was the usual custom. This happened again in 1719, when 13 ponies were sold for £23. 2. 6. This was in the year of Robert Siderfin's death, when the profit from the Forest was shared equally between Madam Siderfin and Robert Darch, but the records do not show who took the proceeds from the sale, and though this money may have been paid to Madam Siderfin, it is more likely to have gone to Robert Darch, as part payment of the debt owed him by his lately deceased uncle.

From this time on we can follow with some accuracy most of the major events, and many of the minor ones, in the story of the Forest ponies. In 1720, when Robert Darch and James Hill took equal shares of the profits, we find the proceeds of the pony sale included in the Forest income, indicating that at this time the small herd of ponies on Exmoor were a joint venture, and though only seven were sold, they made £17. 0. 6, an exceptional price at the time. In the following year, the same number made £9. 10. 0, which was about the usual price. The numbers of ponies sold annually in the next ten years rose only slightly; the emphasis being placed on building up the herd, and though 38 colts were cut in 1731, only 10 were sold—for £16. 4. 6. This policy continued; the numbers sold each year falling far short of the numbers born, and by 1736, when 34 ponies were sold for £39. 0. 0, the herd had grown considerably.

The death of Robert Darch in 1737, followed by his wife in 1740, changed nothing, even though this half moiety was now split between their two children, but in 1741, we find the price paid for ponies had dropped, and only £23. 8. 6 was realised from the sale of 31 ponies. Three years later, in 1744, prices were at the other end of the scale, when most of the 19 ponies sold made £2-£3 apiece, with a top price of £3 15. 0.

In 1745—or thereabouts—James Hill's interest in the Forest passed to William Draycott, and with it his half share of the pony herd which was still increasing. A little later, with only a short time left before the expiration of the Forest lease, it was time for the Darch family and William Draycott to turn their pony assets into cash. In previous years, it was rare to find more than 30 ponies sold at the annual sales, but in 1747, 61 were sold for £98. 19. 6. In the following year, 105 made £117. In the final clearance sale in the last year of the Forest lease, 284 ponies came under the hammer, realising £294. 17. 0; making a total for the three years of 450 ponies sold for £510. 16. 6; an average of £1. 2. 8 apiece.

We know that this sale completely cleared the Forest of all but the commoners or agisted ponies, because from 1750 until after 1767, when Sir Thomas Dyke Acland re-established a small herd, not one pony was sold or one colt cut on the Forest of Exmoor.

This has raised a point that has apparently escaped the notice of historians in the past, and it is highly probable that this was not the only occasion in the history of the Forest that on the termination of a lease—or when the Forest changed hands—the entire horse or pony herd belonging to the outgoing Warden was sold, leaving the incoming Warden to build up a new herd. It is, of course, possible that in many cases the new Warden took over the whole or part of the herd at valuation, but as we have just seen this was not necessarily so.

Serious crimes on Exmoor during the period covered by the Forest Books appear to have been comparatively rare, but in the books for 1742 and 1743, the disbursements include the costs of bringing prosecutions in the case of two felonies.

In 1742, Mr. Halls bills for prosecuting persons for felony was £9, and witness expenses £3. 3. 0. The Deputy Forester, John Hill, put in his quaintly worded 'expenses if you please' for apprehending two people; carrying them before a Justice of the Peace, and his journey to attend the Bridgwater and Taunton Assizes, but his expenses were not included in the 1742 accounts for the Forest.

In 1743, a Mrs. Crowys was paid £5. 13. 6 for bringing a prosecution against several persons, and John Hill was paid £2. 2. 0 for his trouble and expenses, but it is not clear which of the two cases this covered, possibly both.

Unfortunately, although the Forest Books list the costs of bringing the criminals to justice, they neither give the nature of the crimes committed, or the names of the people involved, and the relevant Assizes Crown Minute Books and the Indictment Files for 1742 and 1743 are missing. They are not to be found in either the Public Record Office in London, or the Somerset Records Office at Taunton, and it is feared they have not survived. All we have left for this period are the Gaol Books of Somerset, which do not tell us a great deal, and the only name that rings a bell is that of William Draycott, who was one of the joint lessees of the Forest from about 1745 to 1750. The trial with which he was concerned took place at the Somerset Assizes during the Winter Circuit of 1743, when a William Pearce (the older) was imprisoned for wrongfully taking a share of the goods belonging to William Draycott and others, but as no further particulars are furnished, it is impossible to say if his crime was in any way connected with the Forest of Exmoor.

CHAPTER 4

THE SUN SETS ON THE ROYAL FOREST

IN the second period covered by the Forest Books (1750-1764), we find Robert Walpole's son and grandson—the second and third Earls of Orford—in possession of the Forest. The second Lord Orford had married Margaret, the daughter and heiress of Samuel Rolle of Heanton Satchville in 1724. She brought him the great Rolle Estates, and as he already possessed a fine pack of staghounds he was looking forward to extending his hunting territory when he applied for a reversionary lease for the Forest of Exmoor in 1737.

How he acquired this lease is interesting, and at the same time illuminating, for it proves the truth of that old adage 'It is not what you know that counts, but who': Being the Prime Minister's son gave him certain advantages and connections not freely available to lesser mortals, and he pressed home his advantage by getting the Surveyor General to play down the value of the Forest, emphasising that the office of Warden or Forester was one of pleasure rather than of profit. The Surveyor General must have done his work well, because Lord Orford obtained a lease of the Forest for 18 years, which cost him nothing. Furthermore, unless the usual custom of including the King's rent in the disbursements of the Forest had been waived in favour of a different method of payment, then not one penny of this rent was paid either for the whole of the term that he and his son held the Forest.

With Lord Orford in control of the Forest, the interest in the deer, which for many years had played only a very minor role in the affairs of the Warden of Exmoor, took on a new lease of life, and with his staghounds ready and eager, Lord Orford was all set to enjoy his new hunting grounds, but it was not to be, for in less than 12 months after taking office he was dead.

Some time before his death, however, he had acquired a second lease for Exmoor, but this was after his father's death, and with less influence in the right places this lease cost him £500. With 26 years of the two leases left to run, the third Earl of Orford became the Warden of the Forest. Whether he was interested in hunting we do not know, but throughout his term of office the hunting of the deer was left to Sir Thomas Acland of Holnicote, and two years after the third Earl obtained a third reversionary lease of the Forest, he sold the remaining 28 years of his three leases to Sir Thomas for £4,200. Not a bad profit on an investment of £1,800, plus the profits from the income of the Forest that he had enjoyed for the last 16 years, which was somewhere in the region of another £4,000. Not bad at all considering his father's plea that the Wardens Office was one of pleasure rather than of profit. One wonders what Lord Orfords expectations would have been of a profitable undertaking.

Very little of moment is recorded in the Forest Books of this period, we find the customary expenses and the occasional flood. Repairs to the Pound walls at Withypool after a great flood in 1756 cost 6s. 6d., plus £3. 7. 10 for repairs to the Pound rails. This included the carpenters wages, timber, spikes and nails, and a further £1. 6. 0 was paid for scraping out and cleaning the Little Pound. Hitherto, it was thought that after James Boevey built the new Pound at Simonsbath, only the Little Pound at Withypool remained in use, but from these disbursements, and the way they are worded, it would appear that both of the old Pounds at Withypool were still regularly maintained and used.

A source of income from the Forest that has not so far been discussed, is that of Turf and Quarry. In the early part of the 17th century, anyone wishing to cut peat on Exmoor was able to do so, and could dig whatever quantities required at a set price of 4d. per day. This was later increased, and after Boevey settled on the Moor, increased further to 1s. 6d. per day. In the Forest Books of 1718-1750, the income from this source rose from £10 to £12, and later to £14, nice round figures, which strongly suggest the system of letting had changed and that the concessions of Turf and Quarry were now let *en bloc* to the highest tender. The later Forest Books confirm this suspicion, showing the income from 1751-1758 inclusive, at £35 per annum, a considerable increase. This was reduced to £30 in 1759, after which it ceased completely. Why it should end so abruptly we do not know, and though it is hard to believe there was no longer a demand for peat or stone, they do not appear thereafter, either in the remainder of the Forest Books, or in Sir Thomas Acland's accounts for the Forest for 1767-1790.

For many years, successive Lessees of Exmoors' only interest in the Forest, lay in its ability to yield them a considerable yearly profit. This attitude had done little or nothing towards upholding the former high standards of the Warden's office. In latter years, when the moiety had been shared, these standards declined still further, until the laws of the Forest, which had been primarily designed to protect the deer therein, had become very lax, and as we have already seen, some of the customs had likewise become little more than token gestures.

The decline had to some extent been halted after Lord Orford gained control of the Forest, when, for the first time in over 100 years, hunting was resumed on a regular basis, but it is to Sir Thomas Acland, his son, and grandson, that the credit should go for restoring the Forest and the office of Warden to something approaching its former high standard. It is fitting that this fine family should be destined to be the last to hold the Forest under lease, for in so doing they have preserved for posterity not only accounts of their own time on Exmoor, but also the irreplaceable Forest Books of earlier years, which have given us such a detailed picture of the way the Forest was run in the 18th century. Being local men, with a country seat at Holnicote in the beautiful Porlock Vale, and with considerable other property in the Exmoor region, they were already familiar with the customs of the Forest and in a better position to deal with problems arising therein than their predecessors, who, for the most part, lived at a distance. Moreover, because the Aclands were a family of great wealth and property, the income of the Forest was not of primary importance, although of course, not to be sneezed at.

The position of their country home at Holnicote meant that the Acland's were able to freely indulge their keen love of hunting on Exmoor. It also meant that they were able to afford some protection to the deer, which had for many years—before the restoration of hunting—been declining rapidly at the hands of poachers. Although this may appear to be contradictory, it is a proven fact that the Red Deer have thrived in times of hunting, not the other way around as one would suppose.

As we have already seen, the third Earl of Orford had left the hunting of the deer on Exmoor to Sir Thomas Acland, who continued as Master of the staghounds until 1770, some three years after he became the Warden and Lessee of the Forest. His son (also Sir Thomas) who became known as 'His Honour' then took over the reins. He was only 18 years old at the time, but he hunted the hounds until 1775, before handing over the Mastership to Colonel Basset of Watermouth, who continued as Master until 1786, when Sir Thomas again took over. In the nine years that followed he accounted for 150 deer; 73 of them stags and 77 hinds. In 1794, in the year of his death at the early age of 42, the old manor house at Holnicote was completely destroyed by fire, and with it many of the antlers in the fine collection he had built up during the period he was Master. Sir Thomas's comments on receiving the condolences of a friend on the loss of his house and contents were, 'that he cared little for the house or the 40,000 ounces of the family silver plate it is said to have contained, the one he could rebuild, the other repurchase, but the loss of his collection of antlers grieved him greatly, for he had preserved them from the stags killed by his own hounds'.

The hospitality of the Acland family during what is known as the Golden Age of hunting was boundless and extended to all comers, rich and poor alike, not only at Holnicote, but also at Pixton Park and their hunting and shooting box at Highercombe; both in the parish of Dulverton.

It is apparent from the Forest Books of Lord Orford's time that very little of his income from the Forest had been spent on its maintenance, and one of the first entries in the Acland account book shows that in consequence, the one house at Simonsbath, built by Boevey, was showing signs of this neglect and was in need of major renovation: £203. 3. 2½, including £60 worth of timber cut at Hacche Farm, South Molton, was spent on its repair, but even this was not enough to complete the work needed there, and two year later, in 1769, a further £52. 16. 9½ was paid out, £25. 12. 5 of which went to pay a mason and £16. 1. 10½ to a carpenter; the remainder for materials used.

The Acland account book is not in the form of any of the earlier Forest Books, and gives only the income received from each of the usual sources, all other details being omitted. The disbursements, however, are fully covered, and it is possible between the two to plot the progress of Sir Thomas Acland's new pony herd, which was placed on the Forest soon after he became Warden. In 1768, the poundherd cut 16 colts, for which he was paid 16/-, and with the cutting and branding of these colts the old custom of providing ale for those assisting was restored; on this occasion at a cost of £1. 1. 6, and though only 6 colts were cut in the following year, there was a steady rise in numbers thereafter. It was not, however, until 1772, that the herd of ponies had grown sufficiently to warrant a sale, and with this sale another old custom, that of 'crying a survey of the colts' was also restored. The numbers of colts and mares sold is not recorded, but the sum realised was £32. 5. 0. The next sale was in 1773, when 36 colts and nags were sold for £73. 9. 6, just over £2 a head. Further sales took place in 1777 and 1779, when two lots of Exmoor nags sold for £78. 8. 10 and £56. 1. 0 respectively. The pony sales now became a more or less annual event, with just the occasional year missed out.

In later accounts for 1805, 1807 and 1808, a total of 83 colts and nags made £466. 7. 0, an average of £5. 12. 4, with a top price of £12; a considerable rise in value on earlier years. Out of the 83 ponies sold, only a possible 17 bays and 9 duns would have been eligible for entry into the Exmoor Pony Stud Book under its present rules, and this was on colour alone. This number would probably have been reduced still further when height, etc. were taken into consideration. It is possible that at this time, Sir Thomas was culling his herd, because the other ponies sold were a motley selection of 34 Blacks, 20 Greys, 2 Chestnuts and a Piebald, and it is certainly true that only a few years later when the Forest was sold in 1818, he was able to take with him a herd of pure bred Exmoor ponies, which he re-established on Winsford Hill, on his own land adjoining Ashway Farm. He also left a small number of ponies of similar quality behind on Exmoor for the benefit of John Knight, the incoming new owner of the largest part of the old Royal Forest.

Sheep pasturage dues were still the main source of income of the Forest, and in a separate account for 1770, we find that 27,506 sheep were pastured there; 12,621 from the bordering parishes, and 14,885 from further afield; a total of 51 parishes being represented, 12 more than in 1722. Roughly the same number of bullocks and colts were agisted on Exmoor as in previous years. An additional source of income came from the house and farm at Simonsbath, which had for some years been let at £35 per annum; apart from three years when Robert Court had paid £40, but he must have been hard pushed to meet this extra rental, because in 1780—the year before he died—it was reduced again to £35, and remained at this figure until it was purchased by John Knight in 1818.

The Acland accounts show the usual Forest expenses of 'Crying the Moor', keeping the Courts, cutting out Bogs, repairs to the Pounds and roads, etc., and the Tellers, who for many years had received £6. 9. 0, were now usually paid £10. 10. 0—shared between them, but the greatest expense and drain on the resources of the Forest, were the customary King's Rent of £46. 13. 6, and the Land Tax, which was first applied to Exmoor in Boevey's time, and much to his annoyance, to help relieve the burden of taxation on the rest of the district, and though Boevey at first refused to pay it and began another of his interminable law suits, the verdict went against him and the Land Tax became a permanent part of the annual outgoings of the Forest.

One of Boevey's adversaries in the case for the introduction of the Land Tax was Robert Siderfin, who, as one of the West Somerset Commissioners, helped to get it passed, but it is doubtful if he would have been so insistent if he could have foreseen that very shortly he would be the one to pay it. In its early years, when the rate of Land Tax was low, £58. 14. 6 was the annual sum paid, but when the rate became 4/- in the pound, with the value of the Forest for taxation purposes assessed at £416 per annum, the amount payable each year was £83. 6. 0.

Although the Forest had been in the possession of the Aclands since 1767, the tithes had remained the property of the Darch family, and it was not until about 1789 that Sir Thomas Acland was able to acquire them for an unknown sum, and thus, for the first time since Boevey, the tithes and the income from the Forest became the property of one man.

For the two years that John Zeale was the Deputy Forester (1768 and 1769) he was paid a fixed salary of £30 a year, but afterwards the usual custom of paying the Deputy Forester 1s. 6d. in the pound of the Forest income was again employed. Another small item, which had become a regular feature in the disbursements, was the payment of £5. 5. 0 per annum to Sir Thomas Acland's steward, John Shapland, for keeping the Swainmote Courts and settling the accounts.

Like the Forest accounts of earlier years, there were considerable fluctuations in the annual income. An exceptional £699. 15. 3½ is recorded in 1779, which, after expenses and tithes had been deducted, left a profit margin of £416. 1. 11½, a figure that exceeds the total receipts on a number of occasions in the earlier Forest Books, but a closer look at this particular year, reveals that this exceptional amount was not in fact a true statement of affairs, because it included arrears of £151. 0. 2½ from the previous year.

The average income of the Forest for the years 1767-1790 was £503, which compares favourably with that of the period from 1718-1767, which was £491, with the average profit being a little more than half the annual income, increased after Sir Thomas Acland purchased the tithes, by approximately one fifth.

At the time of 'His Honour's' death in 1794, there was less than a year to run on the leases purchased from Lord Orford, but Sir Thomas had been successful in acquiring two more leases for Exmoor, at a total cost of £980, extending his term of office to 1814, but by the time his son and heir (also Sir Thomas) came of age in 1808, only six years remained. He immediately applied for a new lease, but on failing to obtain one offered to buy the Freehold of the Forest if this was preferred. In the meantime, however, Parliament, on behalf of the Crown, had been looking into ways of making better use of Exmoor, and surveyors were sent to see if the land was suitable for growing oak woods to supply timber to the navy, but before we continue with the change of policy (which was to lead shortly to the division of Exmoor into allotments and the sale of the freehold of the Crown's portion), we will take a little diversion, and have a look at a small matter that indirectly concerns Exmoor, which occurred in 1807 in the parish of High Bray.

For hundreds of years the annual pilgrimage of sheep to Exmoor had taken place following the well defined roads or tracks leading to the Forest, and though it was perhaps customary for the men of the bordering parishes to take short cuts across their own commons, it was certainly not the done thing for outsiders to use such routes, but in the Presentments of the Manor of High Bray for 1808, at the Court Baron of William Long Oxenham esq.—who was the Lord of the Manor—four men were brought before Ralph Barnes, gentleman steward, for just such offences. It may be of some interest to note here that the Court was comprised of four Free Suitors; Philip Harding, Richard Thorne, John Mules and William Westcott, and ten others listed under Names of Homage; William Marker, William Westcott, John Dendle, George Hole, Nicholas Clegg, James Thorne, George Shapland, Richard Dyer, John Hole, and John Holloway. Evidence was given by James Hewett, a 'sheepherd', who said that Stephen Crocker of Fremington did, about the latter end of August last, drive his sheep from Exmoor over Muxworthy Common and through Muxworthy Green, and said he should continue to drive his sheep that way until prevented by law, notwithstanding the notice he had received to discontinue to do so.

Another culprit was John Bowden of Swimbridge, who did on the 16th day of September last, drive his sheep over the same route, and said that he had a right to do so, but if he was prevented from driving that way he would sell his sheep.

The other two men, James and John Gratton of High Bickington, were seen by another witness, Reginald Shapland, doing the same, even though it was stated at the Court that no persons had a right of way there except the tenants of the Manor. We do not know the outcome of these Presentments, which could have proved interesting as to just how much power the Manor Courts held at this time.

To continue with the story of Exmoor we find that after due consideration, Parliament had come up with three proposals for its future.

1. To renew the lease to Sir Thomas Acland.
2. To sell the Freehold of the Forest.
3. To enclose the Forest, reserving a large allotment for the Crown on which to grow timber.

After some deliberation, the third proposal was decided upon, but before any of the Forest could be enclosed there were many people to be compensated for their loss of grazing and other rights.

By an act of Parliament passed on the 4th July 1815, the Forest was divided up in the following way. The Crown took the largest portion of 10,262 acres around Simonsbath. Sir Thomas Acland received 3,201 acres as compensation for the loss of his tithes, and thereafter Exmoor became tithe free. The land assigned to him was situated in the north-eastern part of Exmoor, that being nearest to his estate at Holnicote.

Two Commissioners were appointed to deal with any problems; Richard Hawkins on behalf of the Crown, and Thomas Abraham for all the other persons claiming rights on the Forest. At the same time, a Mr. M. Wasborough, one of the surveyors on the Forest, appears to have had much to say in regard to the allotment awards, and in a letter to A. Milne (14.5.1814) ('who was representing the interests of both the Free Suitors and the Suitors at Large'), he does his best to clarify the situation. He quotes John Locke—the Coroner of the Forest—who was the son of William Locke, (for many years the Deputy Forester of Exmoor) as saying 'that he—John—believed the enclosure of the Forest will generally be approved': This may well have been true in the case of some of the larger landowners of the parishes bordering Exmoor, who had everything to gain and nothing to lose, but what of their tenants who had for countless years been accustomed to either free pasturage or at half rates. What could they expect to gain in return for their loss of privileges? As will be seen shortly; very little.

Mr. Wasbrough goes on to reveal how the acreage of the allotments awarded to the Free Suitors and Suitors at Large was to be arrived at. In the case of the 52 Free Suitors of Hawkridge and Withypool, who had been accustomed to free pasturage for 140 sheep, 5 mares and foals, and as many cattle as could be wintered on their tenements, the following table was worked out:

  for 140 sheep at 4 to the acre   = 35 acres
  for 5 mares and foals   3 acres

As no cattle had been placed on the Forest in recent years this particular right was disregarded, and so the amount for each Free Suitor was to be 38 acres. Total for 52 Free Suitors.

                                          × 38 acres = 1976 acres
  less tithes computed at one eighth   247

                                          1729 acres.

We do not know how they arrived at the figure for tithes, because the Free Suitors paid neither grazing rights, or, as far as is known, any tithes for sheep pastured on the Forest, and when the final awards were made, the actual acreage awarded was 1633 acres, an average of 31 acres for each tenement.

The Suitors at Large, were by far the largest body with an interest in the

Forest, representing a total of 57 manors or reputed manors, but at the time of the allotment award 15 were apparently in default with the Forest Court rents. The average yearly sum received from these manors for stocking the Forest at half rate was £130 from 12,480 sheep, which, by working on the same basis as before of 4 sheep to the acre, would have worked out at 3,120 acres to be shared among the remaining Suitors at Large, on behalf of their tenants. Mr. Wasborough goes on to say that if the land be valued at 5/- per acre annually, to produce the £130 paid yearly by the borderers with half rights would require 5,207 acres, and by this mode of calculation the claimants would have the full value of the difference between the nominal price of stocking and its real worth. The total land eventually allowed to the Suitors at Large was 4,700 acres.

In order to obtain an allotment on Exmoor, each and every person who had previously enjoyed a right of common in the Forest had to fill in a claim form in respect of the tenement for which he claimed this right; only one tenement and claimant to be entered on each form. Three of these claim forms have been found among the Acland papers, all—for one reason of another—invalidated. One, from the Rev. Hugh Bent, was in respect of North Glebe and the tithes of High Bray, which were together valued at £253. 4. 0 per annum. This claim was for half rights in the Forest, and we do know that he was later awarded 46 acres. The other claims relate to a tenement with an illegible name, and to Whitley Gate (Withygate) in the parish of North Molton. This form was obviously rejected because it also included North and South Bray Mills, North and South Dean, and High Wood; all in the parish of High Bray.

The final survey and perambulation of the Royal Forest of Exmoor took place in 1815. It differed in only one respect from the survey of 1651, and this was where the parish of Oare adjoined the Forest, and there can be no doubt whatever, that the boundary stones had been deliberately moved back into the Forest, which in effect added about 400 acres to Oare Common. This land, the habitat of the Red Deer and the Black Grouse, thus came into the possession of Nicholas Snow of Oare Manor, a notable sportsman in his day, as was his son (of the same name) who followed him.

It is in fact possible to prove that the Forest boundary had been moved back, because Clannacombe, which had formerly been within the Forest, and was frequently recorded in the early Forest Books of Exmoor (1718-1745), was now outside the Forest bounds. It is equally certain that this cheeky act of land grabbing did not escape the notice of the Crown Commissioners, because although the first allotment award of Exmoor in 1817 shows neither Oare, Porlock or Stoke Pero with an allotment in the Forest, the later award of 1819 leaves only Oare without.

As late as the early part of 1818, the Crown were still determined to plant oak trees on their portion of Exmoor, but it is thought that Sir Thomas Acland persuaded them of the futility of this idea, and with a complete about-face, the Crown Allotment of 10,262 acres was put up for sale to the highest tender, and so, after being part of a Royal Forest since the days of the Saxons, it was sold to John Knight esq., for £50,000. His address was given as Portland Place, London, but he also owned considerable property in his native Worcestershire, including Wolverley House and Lea Castle. The latter, a large brick castellated mansion, which he is said to have built about 1809,* was put up for sale in 1818, around the time that John Knight purchased the largest part of the old Forest. The next highest tender came from Lord Fortescue, who offered £30,000, with Sir Thomas Acland a poor third at £5,000. At the time, however, his tender was probably the most realistic, being based on 20 years net income from the Forest.

Included in John Knight's purchase were the mineral rights, which were considered to be of little value and were thrown in for nothing. The small farm at Simonsbath, which included the only house on Exmoor, was sold as a separate lot, and this too he purchased, at a cost of £1,200. The remainder of the Forest now passed into the hands of the Free Suitors, Suitors at Large, and others who had formerly held pasturage rights in the Forest.

Having secured the heart of Exmoor, John Knight now set about buying up as many as possible of the other allotments. Among those willing to sell was Sir Thomas Acland, who had, in right of his tithes and one or two tenements, been awarded a total of 3,298 acres, and he must have been well satisfied with the £16,415 he received for his allotment; especially so when his valuation of the Crown's portion of 10,262 acres was only £5,000.

Another large slice of Exmoor had been awarded to Sir Charles Warwick Bampfylde of North Molton, and this was purchased for £7,985. Most of this allotment of 1880 acres was subject to the life tenancies of his tenant farmers, and in order to gain possession a further £550 was split between them, and for this pittance, the pasturage rights which the North Molton farmers had enjoyed on the Forest since time immemorial, were gone for ever.

The mineral rights to Sir T. Acland and Sir C.W. Bampfylde's allotments had been retained by the Crown, but leaving nothing to chance, John Knight purchased them a few years later for £762. A few smaller allotments were also acquired at a later date, giving him possession of 16,137 acres (about four fifths of the Forest), at a cost of just under £80,000.

Even this did not satisfy his hunger for land, and from Sir Arthur Chichester of Youlston, Shirwell, he bought the manor of Brendon, which included several useful farms, Brendon Common and Badgworthy, 5,331 acres in all, for which he paid £23,225. One or two other farms in this locality were also purchased about this time, adding 174 acres to his estate, and £4,000 to his capital outlay. Most of the Brendon Farms were in the hands of tenant farmers, and John Knight was content for the time being to let them continue in this way.

---

*Vic. History of Worcestershire Volume III, Page 570. The Reclamation of Exmoor Forest gives John Knight's father, also John, of Lea Castle 1740-1795.
N.B. It was in fact built by Edward Knight (John Knight of Exmoor's Grandfather) in 1762.

CHAPTER 5

THE LIFE AND TIMES OF JOHN KNIGHT OF EXMOOR

JOHN KNIGHT was now fully committed to the major challenge of his life, and his aim, right from the start, was to turn what was considered by many to be nothing more than a barren wilderness, into a productive and prosperous farming community. In order to carry out his plans, not only was a large amount of capital required, but also enormous drive and determination; attributes that he was well endowed with.

His fortune had been built up over several generations in the family forges and iron foundries in Shropshire and Worcestershire, where the Knights also owned considerable other property, but, despite this background, he still found the Moor extremely hard and expensive to tame. Nevertheless, by the time old age finally forced him to give up the struggle and hand over the estate to his eldest son Frederic, he had made some progress in achieving his dream.

When John Knight took over the greater part of the old Royal Forest, only a few stones, mounds, and streams separated it from the commons of the surrounding parishes, and one of the first formidable tasks confronting him, was to build a high wall to enclose his estate. This wall, nearly 29 miles in length, was completed in 1824, just three years after he took possession. Other work in hand at this time included the remaking of the old roads, or building new ones, to replace the rough muddy tracks that had formerly existed, and in a few years fine roads led from Simonsbath towards Exford; North and South Molton; and Brendon and Lynton.

Although stock was still taken in for the summer grazing (albeit at twice the old rates),[1] John Knight had not purchased Exmoor for this purpose, and he now turned his endeavours to the monumental task of reclaiming the rough moorlands; a task he was already familiar with, having earlier in his life reclaimed a large heathland area in his home county.

The first areas selected for improvement, were along the south facing slopes above the River Barle at Cornham and Honeymead, and both of these places were provided with three workmens cottages and the appropriate farm buildings. John Knight's method of reclamation was to first enclose the moorland into fields of 50 acres or so. This was followed by paring off and burning the old rough herbage, after which the land was ploughed up and worked down by teams of oxen, but the soil of Exmoor was very acid, and before any crops could be grown large quantities of lime were needed to sweeten and fertilize the ground. Having done this, root crops—usually turnips—were grown, followed by successive corn crops, but owing to the unfavourable weather at this height above sea level there were few successful harvests, and this land was later put down to permanent pasture.

The greatest enigma to come down to us from John Knight's early days, is, without doubt, Pinkworthy—or Pinkery—Pond and its so called canal,* and for what purpose did he intend to use it? Able minds have puzzled over this problem for many years, but it was not until Dr. Youell of Leeds University, discovered two letters in the Somerset Record Office at Taunton,** that any indication of John Knight's intentions became known.

From the contents of the first letter, dated 28th March 1826, it is now known that he proposed to construct a railway from Simonsbath to Porlock Weir. At both ends of this railway power would have been needed to raise the trucks up steep inclines, and it was the water from Pinkery Pond which would have supplied the necessary power at the Simonsbath end.

In the 1974 *Exmoor Review,* Dr. Youell wrote an article based on the two letters, but did not go into great depth on the significance of his discovery, and recently (1985) I wrote a further article on the subject for the *Review,* and from that report the following is derived.

In order to reclaim the moorlands, vast quantities of lime were needed, the largest local supply was at Combe Martin, but at £1 per ton it proved an enormous expense when considering the tonnage required, plus the problems of transporting it home. For some inexplicable reason—but one that may well have had some bearing on the need for a railway—the road to Challacombe, and thus to Combe Martin, was not made up at this time, and it was not until nearly 20 years later that a new road was built to make the lime hauling easier. John Knight made great efforts to find a cheaper source of supply and some lime was bought from John Williams of Newlands Quarry, Exford, but this also proved costly, and he was well aware that without cheaper lime and economic transport, the rapid expansion of his farming enterprise was out of the question.

It was about this time that Pinkery Pond and canal were constructed. It was obviously a scheme of great importance, and there must have been some urgency, because 200 Irish labourers were brought over especially to work on the project, and since we now have a link connecting the pond and canal to the proposed railway, the purpose of the whole scheme becomes a little clearer: For many years, cargoes of limestone had been shipped regularly from South Wales to the limekilns dotted along the North Devon and Exmoor coast, and there can be little doubt that it was this source of supply that John Knight wished to tap. Obviously, other goods would also have been brought in, and later, as his farms became more productive the railway would have provided a useful outlet for the

---

*Although usually referred to as a canal there is nothing to show that it was to be used to convey either canal barges or boat traffic. All the evidence points to it being constructed solely to carry vast quantities of water to work the inclines of a proposed railway.
**The Blathwayt Archive.

Pinkery Pond in sombre mood

The canal on Duredon

Ruined tower near Simonsbath

Canal from the River Exe adjoining the Hayes Allotment — Pinford Fence

surplus produce. He was also aware of the minerals under his land, the rights to which he had acquired, and it is possible he could foresee a mining era, and the even greater benefits a railway to the coast would bring.

A closer look at the first letter sent by John Knight to Charles Bailey of Nynehead near Wellington—who was the Agent to the Blathwayt Estate at Porlock—provides supporting evidence for some of the above conclusions. In this letter, a 99 years lease was sought and John Knight's requirements set out. These included enough land at Porlock Weir to build wharfs, warehouses, agents and labourers cottages, and limekilns, with the privileges of taking stones and other materials from the Blathwayt Estate for their construction. He also requested permission to divert several streams, for the purpose of scouring the harbour, supplying engines, and filling the wet dock to raise vessels for easier unloading, together with enough land to build inclined planes and railroads across Porlock Common to where the common joined his own estate at Larkbarrow. From this point he would be able to bring the railway over his own land to Simonsbath. He also asked for space to build reservoirs and leats to supply water to the inclines, which would probably have been worked by water wheels to raise the loaded trucks. In return, John Knight promised to keep it all in good repair, allow it to be used as a free port, and to pay an acknowledgement annually.

An undated map,* depicting a railway, was found with the letters. This map was probably drawn up in the mid 1850's in Frederic Knight's time, in that it shows the mineral veins of Exmoor and tramways connecting the principal mines—which were then at work—to a station at Simonsbath, but there is reason to believe it was based on his father's earlier scheme. There are two other stations marked on the map; one near Larkbarrow would have served that part of the Moor; the other station is shown just to the east of the head of Limecombe—on Dure Down. From this point the railway would have run steeply down to Simonsbath, following the east bank of Limecombe. The section between these two stations would have required an incline, and as the canal from Pinkery Pond can be traced to within a few yards of the proposed top station, there can be no doubt whatever that its purpose was to supply the water power needed there.

Frederic Knight's railway proposals some 30 years later in the 1850's, differed in two respects from the map and his father's earlier scheme. Firstly, at the Porlock end he intended to work the inclines by self action; the weight of the ore laden trucks from the mines pulling up the mainly empty ones. Secondly, he proposed to bring the railway down from Dure Down to Simonsbath in a series of curves, thus doing away with the need for an incline there.

In his second letter to Charles Bailey, written 23rd June 1827, John Knight requested an urgent reply to his letter of the previous year. It is not

*Another copy in the Fortescue Archive D.R.O., Exeter.

known if a reply was received, but if it was, it would appear to have been a refusal to his requests, and so, bitterly disappointed, he was forced to abandon the scheme and the project was never completed.

In hindsight, it seems likely that John Knight was over hasty in constructing Pinkery Pond and canal, when he does not appear to have reached an agreement with the Blathwayt Estate to construct a railway and buildings on their land. It was not until some 30 years later, in 1860, that Frederic Knight succeeded in obtaining a lease from Colonel Blathwayt, and by then it was too late to save the iron mines on which he had pinned his hopes and had such high expectations; so this railway also remained unbuilt, although a start was made on cutting the bed for the rails.

Since the publication of my article in the *Exmoor Review* (1985), in regard to Pinkery Pond and John Knight's proposed railway, new evidence has come to light* concerning the Pinkery canal, and another of the same type that was taken off the River Exe. Such is the importance of this discovery that I believe most—if not all—of the outstanding queries relating to John Knight's proposed Simonsbath-Porlock railway can now be answered.

Firstly, let us consider the Pinkery canal, which did not, as I first believed, end above the proposed station near Limecombe Cottages, but in fact continued eastwards alongside the hedge above the Limecombe sheep pens, crossing the road at Prayway Head, to continue along the north side of the bank hedge parting Great Ashcombe from Prayway. Just beyond the Ashcombe sheep pens it passed through the hedge at a point where there is a distinct kink in the hedge line, and following the 1425 ft. contour level cuts across Great and Little Ashcombe and the Honeymead Allotments. The passage of the canal across these fields is not so easy to follow, as the banks have been bulldozed and the ground levelled in more recent times, but just before it enters a small fir plantation above Three Combes Hill (about half a mile south of Warren Farm) it is still intact, and can be followed through the plantation and out-the other side, but a few yards beyond peters out. It has now reached the point where it can no longer continue on at the same level without falling rapidly away. The last visible section of the canal is heading straight for a kink in the stone wall that runs along the top of Three Combes Hill, where the water from Pinkery Pond would have tumbled swiftly down the steep hillside to join the River Exe below. There can only be one reason for this otherwise pointless exercise, and that is that John Knight intended to construct an incline there to bring his railway across the river, thus avoiding the difficult wet and boggy ground at Blackpits and Exe Head, where we believe Frederic Knight intended to take his later railway.

If, as now seems certain, John Knight intended to construct an incline on the hillside south of the Exe, then he would also have needed an incline on the hillside north of the river, and this would probably have been placed

---

*From conversations and walks with Jack Buckingham of Rose Cottage, Simonsbath.

close to where Warren Farm stands. Here again we have evidence of John Knight's intentions, because on the northside of the bank hedge dividing the farm from the rough moorlands above, a similar canal is to be found. This canal runs beside the bank all the way back around the hillside, following the 1400 ft. contour level, to a point just above Blackpits Bungalow, where it crosses the Simonsbath-Lynton road and continues on to join the River Exe, about half a mile west of the road. This would then have solved the problem of supplying water to work the northern incline. If we follow the bank wall beyond the headwaters of the River Exe we will find that this has been placed in such a way as to collect surplus water from the Chains in order to increase the flow of the Exe, and thus that of the canal. So far, so good, but it does not explain why the canal was continued on for a mile beyond the point where the incline would have been built before it discharged its surplus water in Rams Combe; nor does it explain why a similar waterway was taken off the main canal about one mile north-west of Warren Farm. This waterway; equally as wide and deep as its brother, ran eastwards across open moorlands between Warren and West Pinford, and then continued its journey alongside the northern boundary bank fence of Sparcombe (Hayes) Allotment until it ends abruptly at a point about three-quarters of a mile west-north-west of Larkbarrow Corner. The bank fence continues on to the Corner, but no longer follows its former level and is on rising ground.

Where the canal ends is no more than half a mile distant from the bed of Frederic Knight's unfinished railway, cut in the early 1860's.. Both were on the same level and converging rapidly, one passing around the northern edge of the allotment, the other around the southern fringe. As the route of Frederic Knight's proposed railway can be followed easily from this point, along the bed that was cut for it, across the head of Madacombe, around the headwaters of Weir Water and on to Hawkcombe Head, it becomes clear that he was doing no more than using the route worked out by his father many years earlier. The reason for a canal heading in the same direction on a parallel course is explained in John Knight's letter to the Agent of the Blathwayt Estate; in which he sought permission to build reservoirs and leats on Porlock Common, and as the railway and the head of the incline were above the level where he could obtain sufficient water to power the incline, then he was left with no alternative but to bring water from high up the River Exe in order to gain the necessary height to carry out the project. As to the section of the canal between Warren Farm and Rams Combe, I believe that John Knight's original intention was to carry it on over Porlock Common to Hawkcombe Head, but there may have been some difficulty in crossing the head of Rams Combe, so an alternative route was begun. This section is of further interest, because on the lower side of the canal the bank has been made exceptionally wide, and it now appears likely that John Knight proposed to run his railway along the top of it, and not along the higher side of the waterway as his son decided to do later. The size of the project, and the lengths that John

Knight went to in his efforts to bring his railway plans to fruition, is mind boggling, and but for circumstances beyond his control, would, I believe, have been brought to a successful conclusion.

We will now turn to Frederic Knight's projected railway, which despite claims that he did little more than was absolutely necessary to get Dowlais* to carry out the terms of their agreement, assuredly went much further than that. Besides cutting and levelling the bed of his railroad for a distance of 6½ miles,* he obtained an agreement in 1860 to construct a level crossing over the Yarnor (Yearnor) road; and also began work on a section of the railroad near Exe Head. The footpath from Blackpits Bridge to Exe Head intersects this piece of levelled trackway about half a mile from the road. Eastwards this trackway runs back towards the road, but ends before reaching the turning point around Dure Down, where it was obviously intended to take it and at this level it would have come around the hill to meet the position of the intended Limecombe station. West of the junction with the footpath the trackway continues to the Exe, passing over at least three well built stone culverts in the process, and crosses the river by a well hidden stone built bridge. Beyond the bridge we lose sight of the trackway, but it would undoubtedly have curved around to travel eastwards, following approximately the route of the canal to Warren, where it would have joined the track already cut.

After the failure of John Knight's railway project, the search for limerock on his own land was renewed, but with little success. In 1836 a miner named Thomas Morcombe was employed to sink two shafts at Balewater, one 23 ft. deep, the other 21 ft., for which he was paid £44, reduced by £2. 10. 0 because some of the digging was soft work.** The outcome of this work is not recorded, but according to the *Reclamation of Exmoor Forest* a limekiln was built in this area about 12 years later and a little lime was produced. There is no explanation for the time lapse, but the indications are that both the exploratory work, and the later excavation of limestone, took place on the piece of waste land south of the Challacombe-Simonsbath road and Bale Water; the limerock coming from a small quarry type working close to the south bank of Bale Water, about a quarter of a mile down stream from the road bridge. This working, began virtually at stream level, and a closer inspection of the area revealed that a leat had been cut around the hillside from further up the water and ceased on reaching the now flooded quarry, which suggests that a small water wheel was installed there for pumping purposes to keep the workings dry. Between the stream and the road, on the bank opposite the quarry, can be found the scant remains of a stone building, which may or may not have been the limekiln, but as the size of the quarry is very small, and the present depth of water in it only about 10 ft., it follows that unless limerock was brought in from elsewhere to burn there, then the working life of this limekiln was very short indeed.

*From the Porlock-Lynton road to Warren Farm. (See Chapter 8).
**John Knight's labour accounts 1835/36. Kidderminster Library.

A further discovery of limerock on Exmoor was made at the Warren in 1841, but here too, although some of the limestone was of top quality, expectations were not realised and very little lime was produced.

What is harder to understand, is why no mention has been made to the fact that the Knights did have a limestone quarry of their own, although it was not on Exmoor Proper, but in the adjoining parish of Exford at Newlands. John Knight's involvement here began in 1824, when he purchased about 73 acres of the waste land (commons) of Monkham Manor from James Bunce Curling for £155. According to the *Reclamation of Exmoor Forest* this purchase included three cottages, but this is not borne out by the Exford Tithe Map and Apportionment of 1839; which lists only one cottage, a barn and a garden, 16 perches in all, in his possession, plus an undisclosed share of the Exford Commons. The one cottage, let to a carpenter by the name of James Pippin, was situated near the old footpath from Chibbet Ford to Blacklands, at a point about 200 yards south from its junction with the Chibbet Ford-Sellbed Cross road. After James Pippin's death the cottage was let down, but his name lived on for many years in a building close by known as Pippins Barn. This too is now in ruins. The garden that formerly went with the cottage, afterwards known as Monkham Gardens, was later let by Frederic Knight to Thomas Baker for many years at a rent of 5/- a year. This, of course, is incidental to our story, but it does pinpoint the site of the only cottage in the parish of Exford known to be in the possession of John Knight at the time of the tithe apportionment.

Only one small quarry was at work in the Newlands area in 1839, and this did not belong to the Knights, but was on land owned by John Comer, being part of South Newlands and Delbridge Farms. This quarry was situated in the field north of the road, opposite the most westerly building of South Newlands Farm, and it may have been here that John Williams extracted his limestone in the 1820's. There was, however, another place nearby that may also have once been a quarry. It is shown on the Tithe Map as a small pond, but being within the confines of what was later the scene of a much larger quarrying operation for limestone, the possibility of this pond being natural has to be suspect. Unfortunately, the Tithe Map and Apportionment fail to give details as to who owned this area, presumably because at this time it was still part of the unenclosed common.

The 1851 Enclosure Map of the Exford commons is much more helpful in this respect, for by this time sufficient development had taken place to enable John Knight's land purchases to be accurately identified. This shows him with four separate enclosures, plus Pippins Cottage, barn and garden, the nearest to the cottage being the triangular piece of rough hillside held in the fork of the roads from Sellbed Cross towards Lanacre, and the same Cross towards Newlands, some 4½ acres in all.

The largest area enclosed by John Knight, was 60 acres of the extreme west of the commons (inside the parish boundary at Gypsy Lane, and from the lane end back along the main Exford road as far as Red Deer) where opposite the old Gallon House Inn two cottages had been built (not on the Tithe Map). The third enclosure, was of 7½ acres of land adjoining the west side of the road from Newlands to Sellbed Cross, and here too a cottage—known as West or Lower Newlands—had been erected. Across the road from this cottage was a further 1½ acres, and it was this piece of land that was to prove the greatest asset to the Knight family, for it was here, and here alone that they found limestone in quantity, and for 10-12 years prior to 1851 this quarry had been developed to the extent where practically the whole of the 1½ acre plot had been opened up, and large quantities of limerock taken out. Such had been the extent of the operations here that the workings were already below water level, and a water wheel for pumping purposes had been installed directly on Pennycombe Water. This had been diverted from its natural course—east of the small pond already referred to—to pass around its western edge, the pond now becoming part of the much larger quarry workings. Just to the west of the wheel, a double limekiln had been constructed to process the limestone from the quarry, and though no record of output from these kilns has been found, there is little reason to doubt that for some years they contributed greatly to the large supply of lime needed by the Knights for their reclamation work on Exmoor.

Although the Tithe Map does not show John Knight's quarry at Newlands, we do know that some exploratory work was carried out there prior to this date, because in 1836, the same year that Thomas Morcombe sunk the two shafts at Balewater, he also sunk a 19 ft. deep shaft at Newlands, and with the help of a man and a boy, open cut the limerock there at a total cost of £21. 10. 0. About the same time, a mason named Robert Adams was paid 5s. 8d. for work done at Newlands, presumably connected with the quarry, but no details are given in John Knights labour accounts.

Nothing more has come to light relating to the early history of this quarry, but in 1851 we find a Francis Comer firmly established at West Newlands, where, according to the Census, he was employed as a Limeburner; in all probability working for Frederic Knight, but by 1861 he had prospered greatly and was now listed as a Lime Merchant, renting not only the cottage and limekiln, but also farming a total of 517 acres, mainly around Picked Stones Farm, where he moved in 1864. Newland Cottage and the limekiln were given up in 1868, when Francis Comer was 67 years old. At the same time he reduced his farming interests at Picked Stones to 385 acres; further reduced in 1871 to 180 acres, which he continued to farm until his retirement in 1875.

Although West—or Lower Newlands—Cottage and the land around it was relet, there is no mention of the limekiln after 1868, and this would appear to be the closing date of both the quarry and the limekiln.

Note: The other quarry at Newlands (adjoining but not belonging to the Knights) was also in production in 1851, but there was little sign of development on the Enclosure Map of this date, although a double limekiln had been built. This quarry continued in production until November 1916, when an underground spring broke and the workings flooded overnight, causing the abandonment of the quarry and the loss of all the trucks and tools there.*

In following the story of John Knight's search for limerock on his own land, we have once again gone ahead of other events happening on the Forest, and it is time to return to 1826, where we find that the reclamation of the moorlands had reached the stage where considerable extra stock was required to make use of the improved land, and to fold (feed) on his root crops. A number of large allotments of rough pasture that had been enclosed were also now ready for stocking.

In order to obtain the cattle and sheep required, John Knight travelled all over the country, buying only animals of the finest quality. Little was known at this time as to what breeds were best suited to the high upland conditions on Exmoor. Summer grazing was one thing; wintering stock, a completely different proposition, and apart from the pony herd running on the Moor, had never before been attempted.

At first, John Knight purchased large numbers of cattle of the West Highland breed, together with about 200 Herefords, but the latter appear to have been given up at early date. The 'Highlanders' were inclined to be on the wild side, and later many of the cows and heifers of this breed were put to Shorthorn bulls; a useful cross, but whether it improved their temperament is not recorded, and later sales indicate that the herd reverted to purebreds. Selecting the right breed of sheep for all the year round living on Exmoor also caused problems. Cheviots were introduced for the first time to compete with the native Exmoor Horn's, but because of the shortcomings of the local shepherds, thieving on a large scale, and other difficulties, they were not the success that he had hoped for. A small flock of Merinos, and another of Welsh sheep were also experimented with, but within two or three years both flocks had been sold off.

As well as improving his land, John Knight was constantly trying to improve the quality of his livestock, and the small herd of Exmoor ponies left behind by Sir Thomas Acland were no exception. A fine Dongolla Barb stallion was purchased to run with some of the Exmoor mares. The resulting crossbreds were in great demand by the local hunting fraternity, being ideal for this rough work, but they were not as hardy as the pure bred 'Exmoors', and could not be wintered on the open Moor, and though some of the Dongolla blood was still around within two or three years of Frederic Knight's death in 1897, the experiment had long since ceased and the Exmoor ponies had once again come into their own and multiplied greatly.

Immediately after he had acquired the Exmoor and Brendon Estates, John Knight had gone to live at Lynton, residing in what later became the

---

*From a conversation with Mr. Reg Westcott of West Ley Farm, Exford.

Castle Hotel, but about 1830 the family moved into Boevey's old house at Simonsbath, which, since 1789, had also been an inn, and shortly afterwards work was begun on building a large mansion to the rear of the old house.

This work was never completed; probably because an inheritance which John Knight had been expecting, failed to materialise and passed instead to a female branch of the family. According to *The Reclamation of Exmoor Forest,* the mansion was pulled down in 1899, but as we shall see later, this was not entirely true.

No large landed country estate in those days was considered complete without a deerpark, which was desirable not only for the sport and venison it provided, but also for its aesthetic appeal. John Knight's Exmoor Estate was no exception, and a large area of rough moorlands adjacent to the road leading from Simonsbath towards South Molton was enclosed and set aside for this purpose. It was then well stocked with Fallow Deer, which along with his sheep were considered 'fair game' by many of his labourers and shepherds; who, by all accounts were a pretty wild bunch and much given to thieving. Nor were they the only ones interested in a share of the profits. According to F.J. Snell *(The Blackmore Country,* 1906), two particularly notorious villains, Jan and Betty Glass, who lived at Larcombe Farm—halfway between Exford and Luckwell Bridge—regularly stole 50-60 sheep a year from the Exmoor Estate. Not content with this, they also stole sheep from their neighbours. Jan was eventually caught and transported to the Colonies. After serving his sentence he returned to his wife, who had kept the farm going by stealing just about anything she could lay her hands on.

In a later description of the Exmoor deerpark in *The Reclamation of Exmoor Forest,* it is stated that it stretched as far as Prayway Head, which does not seem to be the obvious choice of direction in which to expand it, as this would have meant a detour around the old farm at Simonsbath. Be that as it may, there is certainly some evidence to suggest this might have been the case.

To the west of the Brendon and Lynton road, about halfway between Simonsbath and Prayway Head, stands a round stone built tower that is now partially collapsed on its western side. The tower is entered from the east through a nicely arched doorway. The inside of the building has a diameter of about 12 ft. and in its ruined state the walls reach a height of 11-12 ft. It is thought by some that the tower was used as an observation post from which to watch or study the habits of the deer, but there are others who believe that it was once part of a deer trap into which the deer were driven and then killed: This is quite logical, because a deep gully formerly ran from a little to the west of the tower, passing beside it, and before John Knight built his new road to Brendon, probably continued to where a depression can be seen on the other side. Shown on the earlier OS Maps as Gravel Pits, they are now no more than shallow depressions in the fields, but before they were filled in, were much deeper, and would therefore have been ideal for the purpose intended, whereby once the deer had been driven into the trap there would have been no escaping the hail of bullets or arrows fired from the tower above to kill them.

There are no records to show when this tower was built, which raises the distinct possibility that it predates the Knight era, in which case it is most likely to date from the time of James Boevey, but like so many of Exmoor's unexplained mysteries, this is purely a matter of conjecture.

Throughout the 1830's the reclamation continued at a steady pace. Some idea of the cost of the work being done on Exmoor during this period is given in a breakdown of accounts covering labour and small items for the years 1835 and 1836. These accounts, the only ones to survive from the John Knight era, represent only a very small part of the large collection of papers and documents concerning the Knight family held in the Kidderminster Library, but they are of immense value when trying to estimate the total amount expended by John Knight on his reclamation.

The labour bill for 1836 amounted to £4,087. 11. 6, of which £1,650 went to the three Exmoor farms, Honeymead, Cornham and Simonsbath, and an insignificant amount to men working on the Brendon Estate.

If we assume that this was an average year—and the figures for earlier years are unlikely to have been less—this would represent an expenditure of some £80,000 for the 20 years period (1821-1841) when John Knight was actively involved in the running of the Exmoor Estate. This does not take into consideration the great expense of lime used on the 2,500 acres he is said to have reclaimed; which at 2-3 tons an acre would not have been less than £5,000, or at the higher tonnage, £7,500. Nor does it take into account the cost of some of his larger schemes, such as the enclosure of his estate, the making of roads, Pinkery Pond and canal system, the building of his mansion, cottages, farm buildings, etc., and when these are taken into consideration it is highly unlikely that John Knight's involvement with Exmoor cost him less than £100,000* and this of course is excluding the initial purchase price of the Exmoor Estate and the cost of stocking it.

The accounts also provide a useful picture of what was happening on Exmoor at this time. In 1835, Honeymead, Cornham and Simonsbath farms each had their own bailiff; James Aynsley, Edward Henderson and Charles Pearson respectively, but by the end of the year Pearson had left and Osmund Lock—who as John Knight's steward was responsible for the day to day running of both the Exmoor and Brendon Estates—took charge of the Simonsbath farm as well. In or about June 1836, a John Bridger was put in charge of the other two Exmoor farms; Cornham and Honeymead, although we know from the Exford Church Registers that James Aynsley was still the bailiff at Honeymead in 1840. In the following year he appears on the Brendon Census at Cranscombe, where he was employed in the same capacity on one of John Knight's Brendon farms, but he had moved away from the district before the Census of 1851 was taken.[2]

---

*Not less than £30,000,000 at today's value. Based on labourers wages, then and now.

Although in the *Reclamation of Exmoor Forest* it is stated that the Brendon Estate continued to be farmed by tenant farmers after it was purchased by John Knight this was not entirely true, for in August 1835 the accounts show that 42 of the Brendon inhabitants, at least three of them women, were employed by him on a temporary basis to assist with the hay harvest on three of the Brendon farms; Cranscombe, Farley and Brendon Barton, all or part of which were in hand. Two hundred and twenty four acres of grass in all were mowed and successfully harvested, at a cost of £103. 10 1½.

The Exmoor Estate workforce fluctuated according to seasonal demand and the size of the projects in hand, but some of the employment was on a more permanent basis, and the account for December 1835, which is fairly typical, provides the following breakdown of labour. There were 6 grooms, whose wages varied from 2s. 0d. down to 1s. 8d. a day; 2 carpenters at 3s. 4d. a day; 3 blacksmiths at 3s. 4d., 2s. 6d. and 1s. 8d.; 1 mason at 2s. 3d.; 4 shepherds at 2s.; 2 ploughmen, an oxman and a driver, all at 1s. 9d; 3 gardeners, 1 at 2s., 2 at 1s. 8d., and a boy at 6d.; and 8 labourers at 1s. 8d.; all paid by the day. A gamekeeper, George Shore, was also employed at a quarterly salary of £12. 10. 0, which was £2. 10. 0 a quarter less than his counterpart Archibald Olgilvy received for the same duties at Brendon. In December 1835, and January 1836, George Leworthy received a total of £3. 6. 0 for the 33 dozen moles he had trapped (they could have done with him at Whitehall), and a litle later, James Cann was paid 19s. 4d. for the 116 rats he had killed (no comment).

A closer examination of the accounts reveal that by this time a considerable proportion of the moorland had been sectioned off into large enclosures. At least two men were kept busy on repair work, not only to the enclosure banks, but the Estate boundary wall as well. Other work carried out in 1836, included two major drainage schemes and a few minor ones. On Ashcombe, 628½ chains (a little over 7¾ miles) of Floting? gutters were cut by George Crocombe, at a cost of £7. 17. 1½, and were, I believe, a complete success, but others cut at Blackpits and on the Chains were of very doubtful value. On the latter, Richard Bale cut 2,741 perches (8½ miles) of surface drains, for which he received £8. 11. 5, but from the appearance of the Chains today they were of no benefit whatever, and have on more than one occasion since caused the downfall of unwary horsemen and walkers.

With the increase in population around Simonsbath a great expansion in the production of peat for fuel took place, and by September, 129,500 turves had been cut and dried at Blackpits, 117,500 of them by Richard Wilkey, who at 4s. a thousand was paid £23. 10. 0 for his labours. Fifty two thousand five hundred more were cut on Ashcombe, but how many were sold and how many were burnt in the Exmoor hearths is not recorded.

On some of the better land on Ashcombe, a total of 33 man days were spent in June hoeing a field of potatoes, but whether the resulting harvest justified the expense of tilling them, we do not know.* What is certain, is that Exmoor was still incapable of producing anything like the quantity of feed needed to sustain John Knight's stock on the Moor all the year round, and despite the efforts of William Ash, who was chaffing home grown oats at the rate of over 3,000 bushels a month—at 6d. a score bushels—throughout the long winter, hay, corn and meal were still being bought in regularly month after month.

Before we close the Exmoor accounts, one further item, the only one of its kind recorded may be of interest, when in September, 39 gallons of beer were purchased from John Haynes for £2. 12. 0, the equivalent of 2d. a pint.[3] The cause of the celebration is not given, but the date suggests it may have been for the harvest helpers, either in the field or for the Harvest Supper, or both.

To house his labourers and stockmen, who at that time were mostly—but by no means all—single men, John Knight built at least 17 cottages in addition to the 3 built to serve Cornham Farm, and a similar number at Honeymead. A few of these early cottages have survived, but usually where there were two or more together they have been converted or reduced to one. Such is the case at Limecombe where once there were four, now only one remains.

The position of the Limecombe cottages is interesting, because they would have been very close to where John Knight proposed to build his railway station on Dure Down, and the exceptional number of cottages in this lonely combe suggests that the Simonsbath to Porlock railway scheme was already in mind, and the construction of Pinkery Pond and the canal to supply water power to this station under way; thus implying that these cottages were built at least in part to serve this station. I can think of no other reason for so many cottages there, as not even the three Exmoor Estate farms of this period had more. Other cottages built by John Knight that still remain in use, are at Cloven Rocks (originally two), with two more at Bale Water, although the cottage now standing on this site is of more recent date and was built soon after a disastrous fire destroyed the original in 1898. White Rock Cottage, and Pound Cottages in Simonsbath are also of early date, but others built close by at the same time have been demolished.

Most of the single labourers on Exmoor were housed on the Scotch 'Bothy' system, sleeping in hammocks slung from the beams of cottages, which were known as barracks. In the 1820's and 1830's, when large numbers of labourers were brought in to carry out John Knight's larger projects, some of these cottages must have been bulging at the seams. Farm buildings were also utilized at this time to provide accommodation. One, a two storey building at Cornham, had its own fireplace and chimney. It also had fitted glass windows in the upper storey and was whitewashed throughout internally. It would have provided quarters for many

---

*Pits in Birch Wood Simonsbath, known locally as Potatoe Clamps, may have been dug and used at this time to store potatoes.

labourers, but with the completion of the first stage in the development of Exmoor in or about 1841, the need for this type of accommodation declined and very few labourers were housed in this way thereafter. There were, however, still a few small groups living in these conditions when the Census of 1841 was taken. One of the Simonsbath cottages had 5 agricultural labourers in residence, another at Cornham 7. Two cottages at Honeymead held 4 and 7 respectively, and those at Bale Water 9 and 3, plus a mason. A number of Irish labourers were also living on Exmoor at this time. There were 6 at Cloven Rocks, 11 in one of the Limecombe cottages, and 4 more at Hoar Oak, but this cottage was not the Oar Oak in Lynton parish where James Bale was living in 1841, and the former cottage, which does not appear on later Exmoor Census Returns, is believed to have been situated further up the same valley (see pages 77 and 115).

The married men on Exmoor, who were for the most part employed as stockmen and shepherds, were more fortunate in this respect and did not suffer the same over-crowded conditions. Their problem was quite the reverse, for living as they did in outlying cottages hidden away in lonely combes far out on the Moor, it was the solitude and the lack of convivial company that often proved too much to bear. One of the first of these shepherds was Robert Cann, who came from Coldridge. He was already living on Exmoor when he married Catherine Lock of North Molton in 1821. They had at least 4 children* while living on the Moor, but by 1830 they had moved on to the neighbouring parish of Exford.

It is now very difficult to trace all the cottages built by John Knight, but the scant remains of a pair of lonely moorland cottages can be found on the west bank of White Water, close to the ford and trackway from Winstitchen to Picked Stones. In 1841 they were known as Slate Rock; with James Nisbeck a shepherd from Wiltshire and his wife and son living in one, Charity Pearce in the other. In 1851 these cottages were called Cow Castle, after the nearby Iron Age fortress. The Nisbeck family had been twice added to, but Charity Pearce was gone and a miller from Holcombe Rogus, James Needs, was living in this cottage, but where he carried on his trade has yet to come to light.

In the Census 10 years later, there is no trace of either of these two families or the Cow Castle cottages, but we must be extremely wary of jumping to the conclusion that they were already in ruins, and two cottages, each with a single labourer, listed together as Winstitchen and Picked Stones, do not fit into the known picture of either of these farms at this time, and as they do not appear in the 1871 and 1881 Census, it is fairly safe to assume that these cottages were the ones formerly known as Cow Castle, and that at some time before 1871 the last occupants had departed and the decline into ruin had begun.

The remnants of two more cottages stand on a mound surrounded by

---

*John born 1822, Mary born 1824, Richard born 1826, George 1829.

beech trees about halfway between Warren Farm and the road bridge across the River Exe. Very little is known about the inhabitants of these, or any other cottages on Exmoor before the Census of 1841, but Samuel Horwood and his family—who were then in occupation—were probably living in one of the Warren Cottages for a number of years prior to this, as we do know they were on the Moor at least as early as 1835, when Sam was listed in the labour accounts as a leveller, and one of his boys was a gardener at John Knight's residence in Simonsbath. At some time before 1851 they left the Warren to live in one of the Red Deer cottages, where Sam remained until 1864. The next occupants of the two cottages in the Warren were John Farley—who lived there with a female lodger, and Anne Blackmore, a farmworker's wife, who also had a lodger of the opposite sex. There is no further mention of either the occupants or the cottages, and it would appear that at some time between 1851 and 1861 they were abandoned and the ravages of storm and time have since taken their toll.

There is a tradition that a house stood in the Warren long before the days of John Knight: R.D. Blackmore made full use of it in *Lorna Doone,* and the Rev. W.H. Thornton* believed it to be the hiding place of a nobleman who had fled from one of the 'Henrys', who, strange to say, was credited with being an excellent florist, and was said to have maintained a good garden there. The Reverend goes on to say that unless the climate was better then than now he must have been a clever man, and one well accustomed to managing hot houses.

Where there is a tradition there is usually a grain of truth and the Warren is no exception, for in an area south of Warren Farm; below the road leading to it, there is strong evidence to show that man was at work here long before the Knights built the cottages and the farm. In the area referred to, three pillow shaped mounds have been thrown up. These mounds are all about 30 paces long from north-south, and from 5-6 paces wide and about 3½ ft. in height. The lower end of the mound nearest the farm has in more recent years been cut across to allow water from the farm to drain away. The position of a second mound is about 180 yards to the west, with a third mound lying between the two, but much lower down the hillside, nearer the river. Here too the mound has been disturbed, probably at some time during John or Frederic Knight's ownership, when a leat cut around the hillside to supply water to the meadows of the farm was taken right across its centre. To add to the mystery there is a fourth mound above the farm road, lying west of the shelter belt of trees protecting the farm, but this mound, although of similar dimensions, runs from east-west. In the same field there is a small banked enclosure, which may or may not be related, but is just as likely to have once been the gardens of the Warren Cottages which stood close by.

From the above and other observations it is clear that there was once

---

*First Vicar of the Parish of Exmoor.

something of great importance in this area. First and foremost is the name of the area itself, which was called The Warren long before the Knights came to Exmoor, and this, I believe, provides the key to its real identity. Warrens, or Conygars as they were once called, formed an important part of many of the larger manors and estates, and some can be dated from early in the 12th century, when the humble rabbit was introduced into this country by the Normans to provide a valuable and highly protected source of food.

The notable features of a Warren are:[*] They were usually on a warm south facing hillside, often near a manor house. Conygars or Warrens were frequently in the form of long pillow-shaped mounds, several of them close together: Apart from the lack of a convenient manor house close at hand the description is tailor made for the area in question, and there can be no doubt whatever that the mounds were created long ago as artificial burrows to house a Warreners breeding stock of rabbits, but only a pollen dating analysis will provide the answer as to which period in time they date from.

As the Warren was well within the bounds of the old Royal Forest, which until Boevey built his house at Simonsbath in 1654 was reputedly uninhabited; who was to be supplied with the rabbits, and where did they live? The answer to these questions could well alter the history of Exmoor as we know it, which in turn raises other queries.

Having come this far, I would like to venture one stage further, because documents do exist which could possibly relate to the above. These documents concern the Manor of Exmoor, but because of the apparent lack of visual or substantiated proof of its existence they were believed by MacDermot to have come about by mistake when a clerk who was drawing up a list of manors and properties possessed by Henry VII at the time of his death in 1509, failed to notice that four of these properties were Bailiwicks of Forests in Somerset—Exmoor included—and recorded them as manors. Errors that were repeated later. All the late King's real estate was conveyed to his son Henry VIII in 1511, and it was not until 1603 that further reference is found concerning the Manor of Exmoor. This was when James I—following Henry VIII's example—settled it, with the Forest of Exmoor and other estates, on his Queen.

In 1618, Queen Anne granted a reversionary lease of the Forest and Chase of Exmoor and the manor to the Earl of Pembroke; to follow the lease he already held, which was due to expire in 1625. The content of the reversionary lease is of great interest, because for the first time the Manor of Exmoor is shown as a separate entity, for which a rent of 40s. a year was to be paid.

After Queen Anne's death in 1619 there appears to have been some doubt as to the validity of the lease she had granted to the Earl of Pembroke, as the Queen did not in fact have the power to grant such a

---

[*]From Geoffrey Gregson's *Countryside,* 1982.

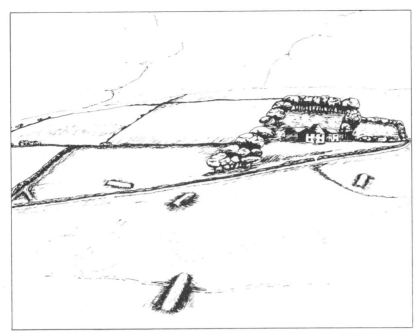

Warren Farm and the Warrens

Enclosure on Lanacombe

Simonsbath prior to 1900

Simonsbath today

lease, but before Lord Pembroke's first lease expired he obtained another from the King. This lease included the usual conditions, plus permission at the Earl of Pembroke or his assignees expense to erect a dwelling house or lodge with stables and other buildings within the Forest, and to enclose not more than 100 acres therein. At this time, Lewis Pollard of Kings Nympton was in sole possession of the Forest, having sub-leased it from another member of the Pollard family who was Lord Pembroke's assignee, but with only 22 years of lease secured on the Forest it is most unlikely that Lewis Pollard would have gone to the expense of building there, and as no mention of any dwelling was made in the survey of 1651, or when James Boevey built his house at Simonsbath in 1654, it is fairly safe to assume that nothing was built on Exmoor by the Pollards.

On looking through his deeds, James Boevey must have become aware of the existence of documents concerning the so called Manor of Exmoor, and leaving nothing to chance purchased the title in 1655 for the sum of £32, which was 16 years of its annual value of 40/-, as set down in the Forest Lease of 1625.

There is nothing in the documents so far found that actually confirms that the Manor of Exmoor was a reality, neither do they disprove its existence, but on the evidence revealed, both on the ground and in tradition handed down, it is not impossible that the Manor did exist, and if so, its location was undoubtedly somewhere in the Warren area.

John Knight is believed to have built other cottages on Exmoor during the early years of his reclamation, but the Hoar Oak recorded in the Census of Exmoor for 1841, and for that Census only, is not the Oar Oak listed in the Census for Lynton of the same date, and the former cottage is probably the one referred to by MacDermot as being situated in Long Chains Combe.*[4]

Although I have searched this area well, I am still uncertain of its location. Attached to the lonely sheepfold which stands on a mound near the junction of Long Chains Combe and the Chains Valley Water is a ruined building which was large enough to house a single shepherd, but I do not believe that this is the remains of the lost cottage, and it is to J.L.W. Page's book *The Exploration of Exmoor and the Hill Country of West Somerset* that we must turn for a possible clue to its location. Page refers to a shepherds cottage standing on an eminence below which is a forsaken sheepfold and a quantity of scattered stones. This description fits the above scene far better than where he places it in the higher regions of Farley Water, for no trace whatever can be found of a sheepfold or cottage there.

If, as I believe, Page was in error regarding the position of this cottage, and if, as he said, it was on high ground overlooking the sheepfold, then its most likely site would be high up on the eastern hillside of Hoar Oak Water, and about 60 yards below the ditch bank which runs northwards

---

*Higher reaches of Hoar Oak Water.

along the Western edge of Exe Plain, at a point opposite Long Chains Combe, a pile of scattered stones might just be all that remains of the cottage we are looking for. This is not an unlikely site, there is water at hand, and although the present path from Exe Head to Hoar Oak and Lynton runs down to the sheepfold and then follows the valley bottom for some distance, the older trackway kept to the high ground east of the Hoar Oak Valley and would have passed very close to the suspected site of the shepherds cottage.

One more cottage generally attributed to John Knight concerns us, although it was not on the Forest proper, but just outside the boundary wall. The ruins of this cottage stand on a rise about 100 yards north of Hoccombe Water, adjoining the wall that separates Brendon Common from the Badgworthy enclosure. All of this land was purchased by John Knight from Sir Arthur Chichester with the Brendon Estate, and a cottage here would have provided a base, not only for a stockman, but also to enable a close watch to be kept on the men of Brendon, who are said to have been fearful that John Knight intended to enclose the commons, and by so doing deprive them of their common rights, and so, as fast as walls and banks were built during the day, the Brendon men pulled them down at night.

In his book, *Exmoor,* S.H. Burton relates that a Pound built on Brendon Common also suffered considerable damage. He does not say where this Pound was, but the enclosure at the head of Lankcombe, close to where the water rises, may have been used for this purpose, for with two or three acres of fair pasture and the stream running through the middle of it, the main essentials for impounding stock were taken care of.

Although neither of these stories have been substantiated by factual evidence there is certainly some truth in the tradition about the Brendon men, or should I say, one man; for in all likelihood it was just one man who gave rise to the tradition, but as is usual with stories of this nature, each retelling of the tale is embellished further, until it has grown out of all proportion to the actual crime committed, with even the scene of the crime changed where necessary to suit the story.

In a case of trespass brought by John Knight against John Crick, one of his Brendon tenants, it was claimed by the plaintiff that on the 4th day of July 1832, and on divers other days, John Crick did wrongfully without leave or licence, and against the consent of the plaintiff, break into and enter Southern Ball Close, and there dug down, demolished and destroyed the wall fence and gate and posts parting the said close from Brendon Common, so that cattle feeding on the common might go and depasture there. Crick replied that he had a one fifth interest in Southern Ball Close, and he also held rights on Brendon Common, and it would appear— although it does not say so in John Knight's deposition—that he had some cause for complaint, and that he genuinely believed that John Knight had no right to construct a wall partioning the two

The plaintiff had on a number of occasions asked John Crick to restore the bricks, stones, gates, etc., but he had not done so, and from the gist of the document, had converted 20 cart loads of bricks, the same amount of stones, 10 gates and 10 wooden posts to his own use, to the plaintiff's damage of £500. The deposition does not record the outcome of the case, but it is apparent from the numbers of gates that disappeared, that John Knight's complaint was one of long standing. We do know, however, that John Crick did not remain the tenant of Malmsmead for much longer, because in 1834 Robert Crick was in possession of John Knight's farm there at a yearly rent of £30. The Census for Brendon of 1841 lists a John Crick at Fullingscott (Fellingscott), a farm adjoining Southern Ball, but this farm was not a part of the Knight Estate. John Crick's age is given as 88, and under the heading of occupation he is listed as 'Independent'. In taking on a man of John Knight's calibre and substance he most certainly was.

After John Knight moved into Boevey's old house at Simonsbath about the year 1830, its use as an inn ceased, the licence lapsed, and there were no licenced premises in Simonsbath until the mid 1850's, when an existing cottage was converted to an inn, mainly to cater for the thirst of the miners who were then at work on Exmoor. There were, however, at least two other inns on Exmoor Proper prior to 1841. At Moles Chamber, in a corner of the allotment awarded to Thomas Palmer Acland of Little Bray, the Acland Arms was built, and according to MacDermot these premises were first licenced in 1825. Standing as it did at the crossroads of the important routes from Barnstaple to Simonsbath and from North and South Molton and Molland to Lynton, it relied heavily on the pack horse train drivers and the seasonal sheep and bullock drovers for much of its trade, and being as it was far from the arm of the law it gained the reputation of being a disorderly house in its early days, where much of the Brandy and other illicit goods smuggled in along the North Devon and Exmoor coasts, passed through on its way to satisfy a wide local demand.

The earliest record of a house or a proposed house in this area is given in a lease granted by T.P. Acland esq., on 25.3.1820, to Daniel Bright, a labourer of West Buckland for a term of 60 years, or alternatively on the lives of three young children, one of them also a Bright. The lease was granted for a consideration of 5/-, plus 1/- per annum rent, and a Heriot of 10/-,* the land leased being 6 acres of Little Black Hill, which was to be enclosed, with the usual stipulations regarding tillage, application of lime, etc. A condition of the lease was that before the 24th day of June 1821, Daniel Bright would, at his own cost, build and complete in a workmanlike manner a good substantial slated dwelling house containing 2 good sized rooms on the ground floor and 3 chambers over. A good stable and yard and necessary outhouses were also to be erected on some part of the land, and the whole of the property was thereafter to be kept in good order.**

---

*Payment on the death of a tenant to his landlord.
**Acland Archive.

Whether Daniel Bright did in fact build his house is not known, but on 24th March 1824, a Henry Hole, Gent, of Newport in the parish of Bishops Tawton, was granted a lease by T.P. Acland esq., for 1¾ acres of land at Moles Chamber, which may or may not have been part of Daniel Bright's land, as this lease too was held on the lives of the same three children, and for 56 years (the same term as that remaining on Daniel Bright's lease). Henry Hole, moreover, was paying a grossly exorbitant rent for this small plot of unenclosed moorland at £1 per annum for the first 7 years, £1. 10. 0 for the next 7, and £2 thereafter.

There is no indication given in Henry Hole's agreement that there was already a house on his land and there was certainly no provision included to build one, and though we know that neither of the two men became the first landlord of the Acland Arms, Henry Hole did stand surety for the customary £10 when the first licence was granted to a James Hewett, which came into force on Michaelmas Day 1824. James remained there for about 2 years, when the licence was transferred to a John Chick. He remained the landlord of the Inn until his death in May 1834 at the age of 46, just a year after his wife Charlotte had given birth to a daughter, Mary Ann. In what may appear to have been indecent haste Charlotte remarried (25.1.1835) and continued in business at the Inn with her new husband George Chapple. Before the year was out their only daughter Susannah was born. George, who was born at High Bickington, supplemented his income in the usual manner by taking in lodgers, but with the decline in passing trade, following the opening up of the new roads out of Simonsbath he combined the inn with a small holding of 20 acres to make a living. The mining era of the 1850's gave the Inn a temporary boost, but thereafter trade again declined. The Chapples remained at the Acland Arms for a few more years until 1863, when the Inn and small holding were handed over to Jeremiah Smith, or Smyth as he perferred to be called. George Chapple's daughter, Sussanah, was the same age as Jeremiah Smyth's wife, also Sussanah, and they were surely one and the same person. (This proved to be the case, they were married at Simonsbath June 1858).

By 1871 Sussanah and her husband were raising 4 sons and 4 daughters; a family that was increased during the next 10 years to 7 sons and 6 daughters, although one of the sons, Richard, died at the tender age of 1 year and 8 months and was buried at Simonsbath. In the Census of 1871 Jeremiah Smyth is listed as a licenced victualler and farmer of 160 acres. Most of the improved land around Moles Chamber is the result of his endeavours, although a fair proportion of his farm was rough grazing on the Acland Allotment, which was either rented, or set against his account for looking after the stock taken in to keep on the allotment.

In *Exmoor, Sporting and Otherwise* H.J. Marshall tells of the Acland Arms, when, soon after Sir Thomas Acland inherited the Little Bray Estate following the death of his cousin Sir Peregrine Acland (in 1871), he expressed a desire to see the Acland Allotment, and accompanied by his steward, Mr. Battishall, duly arrived at the Inn, where they found Mrs. Smyth up to her arms in soapsuds, it being washday. (One suspects that with her large family every day was a washday). The kettle was boiled and bread and butter and tea were served to her guests. A very merry hour was enjoyed by all before Sir Thomas and his steward departed through hail and snow to return to Little Bray.

Although the licence of the Inn was not given up until about 1883, it is doubtful if there had been much call for liquid refreshment stronger than tea for some time, as the Census of 1881 refers to Jeremiah Smyth only as a farmer of what was now a much reduced holding of 96 acres. In 1889 or 90, the Smyths vacated the old Inn and moved to Natsley Farm about a mile away, though they continued to farm the land at Moles Chamber for some years after. Susannah Smyth died at the age of 66 in September 1901, and was laid to rest in High Bray Churchyard; Jeremiah rejoined her on his death at the age of 82 in November 1912.

With their passing another link in the long chain of Exmoor's history was broken, although one of their sons continued to farm at Natsley until his death in 1927.

In F.J. Snell's publication, *Book of Exmoor* (1903) the Acland Arms was described as a desolate building with its 'Upping' stone and porch still in a fair state of preservation, but the garden was a ruin. Today only a small section of one wall remains, and soon all trace of this infamous Inn will be gone forever.

Far more noticeable today is the inscribed stone placed beside the bank of the lane leading to the site of the Inn. This stone; which marks the boundaries of High Bray and Gratton Commons—where they meet the Forest boundary—was erected in 1742. The inscription on its face reads: William Longe Oxenham esquire, Lord of the Manor of High Bray, 1742; and on the reverse; Christian Slowley Lady of the Manor of Gratton.

In 1841, John Knight purchased another of the Exmoor allotments, which included a dwelling house and 42 acres of land from Philip Hancock junior, for £450. This house, standing in a prime position just off the road from Simonsbath to Exford, was already an Inn at the time of his purchase, and was certainly built prior to 1822 by Philip Hancock senior; for in that year, under the name of New Inn it was granted its first licence. The landlord, James Lake, remained there until 1824-5 when Richard Bromham took over the tenancy. The man standing surety for Richard was Thomas Tipper, who had been landlord of the Simonsbath Inn (Boevey's old house) since 1821, but his licence lapsed when John Knight took up residence there about 1830. For the last five years that Thomas Tipper held the licence at Simonsbath he continued to stand surety for Richard Bromham, who in a convenient arrangement reciprocated by doing the same for him.

Richard Bromham was still at the New Inn in 1841, and was said to have been John Knight's only tenant on the Exmoor Estate. At this time the Inn was known as Gallon House, the reason being, or so the story goes, was that nothing less than a gallon of ale was served at a time to its customers. In those days, heavy drinking sessions, often followed by a brawl, were practically the only recreations available to relieve the monotony of the moorman's lonely existence.

A change of tenant at some time before 1843 brought a change of name to the Inn, and until recently Census and other records list it as Red Deer, but locally it has never lost its former title of Gallon House, and the house has now officially reverted to this name; Red Deer being used as the address of the cottages opposite: Like the Acland Arms trade declined after the miners departed, and its licence too was relinquished about 1883.

In 1841, at the age of 75, John Knight handed over the management of the Exmoor and Brendon Estates to Frederic, his eldest son, and a year later left our shores forever to retire to Rome, where even in retirement he retained a keen interest in all that was happening on Exmoor until his death in 1850.

There can be no doubt whatever that John Knight was a remarkable man, for he had taken up the challenge of reclaiming one of the wildest parts of the country at an age (52) when most men would have been content to live off their established wealth, and despite many setbacks and mistakes he succeeded in reclaiming about 2,500 acres of the moorland. His attempts to grow corn where there was little guarantee it would ever be harvested may now seem to us to have been tempting providence, but at the time much that we now take for granted was still in the experimental stage. Many acres of his poorer land also benefitted to some degree from the miles of drainage gutters that were cut, his meadows too, where water was brought by leats to encourage the growth of early and abundant grass.

Only one reference to the numbers of stock kept on the Exmoor Estate during the John Knight era has been found. This gives the figures for 1841 as 300 breeding cows, 1,000 ewes and some pony mares and their offspring. From these returns it is obvious that he was still very dependent on letting the summer grazing pasture to stock farmers around the Moor, not only to keep the moorland in good condition, but also to help finance further reclamation.

The cost of the improvements had been enormous, the return on his investment trifling; more than enough to make a lesser man cut his losses and move on, but through all his trials and tribulations John Knight had remained resolute in his aims, and on his death the Exmoor and Brendon Estates passed intact to his son Frederic.

So far we have dealt mainly with John Knight's portion of Exmoor, but it is now time to take a look at what had been happening elsewhere on the old Forest, where, somewhat surprisingly, very few new farms or cottages had been built during the same period, and apart from the Inn and farm at Red Deer, and the Acland Arms at Moles Chamber, only 4 other houses are listed on the Census of 1841; all of them in the south-eastern corner of Exmoor; all occupied by married men and their families.

The first of these farms is not named, but must surely be Ferny Ball, the only farm in the area that ties in with the hunting records of the North Devon Staghounds, when in 1818 the hunt passed close by Sangers new house; John Sanger of Whitechapel, Bishops Nympton, having purchased this land from Edward Hill of South Batsham, and Samuel Moore of South Hill, two of the Withypool Free Suitors.

Ferny Ball must therefore have the foremost claim to being the first house and farm built on Exmoor after Boevey completed his residence at Simonsbath in 1654. That this was the only house in the area at the appropriate time is confirmed by the Electoral Roll of 1841, but by this time, following the death of John Sanger on August 4th 1834, it had changed hands, and Alexander Fisher of Bishops Nympton now owned the freehold of the house and land, but according to the Census Returns he did not live there; the occupants being William Blake and John Barrow, with their wives and families; both men being listed as agricultural labourers. By 1851 William Poole had moved into Ferny Ball, where he was farming 130 acres. He remained there until 1863, when he took over the Red Deer Inn and 200 acres of land on the Exmoor Estate, leaving his son-in-law, William Thorne (who had been living at Ferny Ball since about 1861) in the farm, and for the next 50 years William continued to farm there, until shortly before his death in 1917 at the grand age of 85.

The next farm or house listed on the Census of 1841 for the south-eastern corner of Exmoor, was Holes Allotment; a name that meant nothing to me, but a perusal of the Inclosure Award Map of 1819 shows an allotment of that name, 35 acres in extent, positioned between the Hon George Courtenay's allotment in respect of Molland, and the Earl of Carnarvon's allotment of 246 acres, which he subsequently sold to John Knight, and where Litton Farm was later built. A comparison of the Award Map with the present 2½ OS Map, reveals that John Holes Allotment (awarded in respect of Slade in Hawkridge) included the area where Willingford Farm now stands, and without a shadow of a doubt they are one and the same, but it was not until 1861 that it appears as Willingford, being listed in the Census of 1851 as Lower Liddens. In 1888, Willingford was put up for auction at the Barnstaple Inn, South Molton, but failed to reach the reserve price and was withdrawn. It was subsequently sold to Sir William Throckmorton, the owner of the Molland Estate, and has remained in the possession of that family to this day.

The tenant of Holes Allotment in 1841 was William Carter, who later farmed at Litton. This is of some interest, because it not only predates by some 20 years the time he is believed to have started farming on his own account, but also confirms a family tradition that when he began farming, it was Willingford where he lived. With the help of two of his descendants, Bert and Leslie Carter, it has been possible to put together some of this family's history, which we will come to in a later chapter.

Burcombe, the third of the farms created on this part of Exmoor before 1841, has a comparatively straightforward history. The farmhouse was erected on part of the allotments awarded to the Earl of Carnarvon that had been retained. These allotments, along with Litton land, had been awarded in respect of the Earl's tenements in Hawkridge, but whether any allowance was made to the Free Suitors of Hawkridge—who as lessees of his Lordship were also supposed to benefit from the enclosure—is not recorded.

According to Hamilton *(Red Deer of Exmoor,* p. 252) there is a tradition handed down in Hawkridge and Withypool that the Free Suitors—who were not in the fortunate position of owning their tenements—had been unfairly treated in this matter, and the sale of the Litton land to John Knight, and the creation of Burcombe, which took up most of Lord Carnarvon's remaining allotments, may have contributed more than a little to this tradition. In 1841 Burcombe was occupied by a farm labourer, William Sexton, but less than 10 years later a John Selby was farming 80 acres there. He was succeeded in 1860 by Samuel Shapland, who was in turn followed by his son (also Samuel) and during this period the farm was expanded to 120 acres.

By 1861 Burcombe had become Barkham, the name it holds today. Samuel Shapland junior died before the Census of 1881 was taken, and late in the same year his widow Jane remarried. For a few years more she and her second husband continued to live there, but they had moved on by 1888, when Barkham was in the occupation of a Philip Haskins. He was gone before 1897 when the farm came into the hands of John Milton, who with his son William farmed there until about 1925.

Greenbarrow;[5] the only other small farm on Exmoor prior to 1841, was built on the Rev. Emra's allotment of 27 acres, awarded him in respect of Hallsgrove, but all that now remains of the farm house and buildings, is the lower part of one wall, which is incorporated into the field boundary hedge on the south side of the road from Sandyway to Withypool, at a point some 550 yards west of the Greenbarrow Cattle grid. The occupants in 1841 were John Carter and his family. He was still there in 1851, but was sharing his home with a man named Sylvester Williams, who according to the Census was farming 80 acres. At this time the house was listed under the name of Crooked Post, but had reverted to Greenbarrow before 1861. Sylvester Williams was gone by this time, and the John Carter farming 70 acres there was not the earlier occupant but his son.

On 21st July 1870, Hallsgrove Farm, Withypool, and Greenbarrow, which at that time still went with it, were put up for auction at the Royal Oak, Winsford, in 2 lots. Hallsgrove was purchased by the Williams family of Blacklands for £2,430, but Greenbarrow was apparently unsold. John Carter continued to farm there for a while longer, but by 1881 it had reverted to a labourers cottage, and continued as such until it was let down in the 1920's. It its latter days Greenbarrow's history is tied up with the Carter family of Litton, and so it will be more appropriate to continue with it when we come to them later in the book.

CHAPTER 6

FREDERIC KNIGHT AND THE MAKING OF EXMOOR

NO attempt had been made by John Knight to colonise Exmoor in the traditional landlord and tenant farmer relationship, and when he relinquished control of his estates in 1841, the total rents received on Exmoor were only £70. *The Reclamation of Exmoor Forest* gives only one tenant at this time. He was Richard Bromham, the innkeeper of Gallon House (Red Deer), who was also farming at least 42 acres and probably more. *Murrays Handbook for Devon* 1887, gives 2 tenants for the pre 1842 period; paying rents of £40 and £30 respectively. Unfortunately, neither the location of the properties or the tenants names are given, which leaves us to guess the identity of the other. My own preference is for the offlying land at Crooked Post (Litton) but as yet nothing has been found to confirm this.

It was in trying to farm the whole of his 16,000 acre estate on Exmoor, with only his three sons and hired hands to help him, that John Knight had made his greatest mistake. This policy had placed too great a burden on one man's purse. Moreover, it had denied him the all important family unit so essential to the establishment of a settled farming community. Frederic, on assuming the management, quickly realised this, and in order to bring the necessary changes about new farms were proposed, with the sole purpose in mind of letting them to tenant farmers, who with their growing families would not only increase the population of Exmoor in the way desired, but would also provide him with badly needed cash to finance the continuing reclamation of the remaining moorland.

The enormous outlay of capital by his father, and the loss of the expected inheritance, had imposed a considerable strain on the Knight resources, and though the incoming tenants would be made responsible for the improvement of their farms, Frederic was still left with the great expense of erecting farmhouses, buildings and cottages to serve them.

In the year that he took over the management of the Exmoor and Brendon Estates, Frederic Knight was elected a Member of Parliament for West Worcestershire, the family homeland; and this, with other commitments in the City, took all the boundless energy, drive and determination that were so much a part of the family make-up. At this time it is apparent that his brothers, Charles and Lewis, played an important role in the affairs of Exmoor; the day to day running of the Estates being left to John Mogridge, who had come from Molland to take over from John Litson* as Agent and Steward.

---

*He succeeded Osmund Lock.

Frederic Knight pressed on with the creation of his new farms. Honeymead and Simonsbath Barton—two of the three of John Knight's earliest farms—were quickly let, and by the time William Hannam took the tenancy of Cornham on Ladyday 1845, most—if not all—of the reclaimed and improved land had been—or was on the point of being—let and it was no longer possible for Frederic Knight to carry on farming in the way his father had done.

That this was so is borne out by an advertisement in the *North Devon Journal* of 27th February 1845, which stated that the whole of John Knight's livestock and implements of husbandry were to be sold without reserve on 12th and 13th March next. Cattle breeders, farmers and the general public were informed that this was the last opportunity they would have of purchasing pure bred Scotch cattle from the Forest of Exmoor; it being Mr. Knight's last sale. On the first day some 434 Scotch cattle of all ages, including 6 bulls, were on offer. On the second day it was the turn of 606 Cheviot sheep, also the farm machinery and husbandry implements, but comparing the machinery and implements with those advertised in 1851 following John Knight's death, it would appear that many of the lots on offer were not sold at this time.[1]

Although the sale of livestock advertised for March 1845 was intended to be John Knight's final cattle sale, this was not the case, and there was a further sale of livestock in September of the same year, when 405 Highland Cattle of all types and ages were on offer; also 700 Cheviot sheep of varying ages, plus a few well bred horses. This completed the sale of John Knight's breeding stock of cattle and sheep, and for many years after only Exmoor ponies and a few good class horses were advertised for sale.

The die was cast; the change of policy complete, and the letting of the new farms with as many acres as possible took priority over all else. After a promising start, difficulties arose in negotiating the letting arrangements, and some of the would-be tenants—suddenly realising what was expected of them—took fright and departed before their agreements were signed. John Mogridge, Agent and Steward of the Exmoor and Brendon Estates, did not handle these sensitive negotiations at all well, and by 1848 he had been relieved of all his duties and replaced by Robert Smith, a well known progressive agriculturalist, who had recently been farming in Leicestershire. On his arrival, Smith moved into—and took the tenancy of—Emmetts Grange, one of the new farms, together with 674 acres; combining his duties as Agent with the equally demanding challenge to become a successful hill farmer. He took particular pride in his water meadows, the creation of which entailed cutting many miles of leats around the south facing slopes of the Grange, where they can still be traced to this day although no longer in use. For a few years around 1851 the improvement of this farm required a large labour force and some 15 men and 4 boys were employed, but by 1861 most of the essential work had been done and only 6 men were now employed on a regular basis.

Under Robert Smith's agency little difficulty was experienced in finding tenants for the new farms, and it was not unusual for the farms to be let before the farmhouse and buildings were completed. Robert Smith had devised a system to help the new farmers to get established, whereby at first rents were very low, but as the farms started to become productive the rents were increased, and a few years later increased again: This system, sound as it was in theory, unfortunately attracted the wrong type of farmers, generally those of very limited means from areas where they could not afford to farm, and so, very few of the early tenants remained on Exmoor long enough to pay the increased rentals.

Although Frederic Knight had been managing the Exmoor and Brendon Estates since 1841, his father still held the purse strings, and a mortgage which had been taken out in 1826 for £16,000, was increased in 1848 to £36,000. The timing of the second mortgage suggests that most of the £20,000 raised in this manner was needed to finance the creation of the new farms.

A list of farms built on Exmoor prior to 1841 has already been given, but it was in the following decade that most of the farms and cottages now standing on Exmoor were erected. In fact, only three farms and a few cottages have been built on Exmoor Proper since; these farms being Pinkery, Woolcombe and Aclands.

The earliest mention of a house or cottage at Pinkery is that given by F.J. Snell in *The Blackmore Country,* in which he refers to a tough old creature, one Ursula Fry living there. This was soon after the Rev. Matthew Mundy came to live at Lynton in 1833. Mundy became intrigued by the tales of the Doones and other traditional stories that were in vogue in the area long before R.D. Blackmore got hold of them and used them as the basis for *Lorna Doone.*

Common as these stories had once been, they were in danger of being forgotten, and the Rev. Mundy set about collecting them and writing them down. The woman who could have helped him most was Ursula Johnson (née Babb), an old inhabitant of Lynton, who was famed for her remarkable memory, but she had died some 7 years earlier in 1826. A few of her friends or associates were still living however, and the Rev. Mundy turned to them for help. One of these was Ursula Fry, and she was visited at Pinkery by two of Mundy's friends, Dr. and Miss Cowell, who pumped her for information. Ursula Fry died in 1856 at the age of 90, but she is not recorded as being on Exmoor in either the Census of 1841 or 51.* There is no record of a cottage at Pinkery for these years either, nor indeed for 1861, and it was not until about 1864 that the farmhouse at Pinkery was completed. Be that as it may, Ursula Fry assuredly lived at Pinkery, but the location of her cottage—like one or two others of John Knights early days—has not yet been discovered.

Part of Pinkery was let as a farm on Ladyday 1849 to George Groves,

---

*Ursula Fry was in fact living in Lynmouth in 1841. Her occupation given—in the Census of Lynton—as a Laundress, age 75.

who came to Exmoor from Lincolnshire, and subsequent events pinpoint exactly where he was living. According to William Hannam* of Cornham Farm, 'Groves was hardly the most suitable type of man to take such a farm as he was quite an invalid with about one foot in the grave, and after occupying the farm for about 12 months and getting deeper in debt, he took his gun and blew his brains out'.

The *North Devon Journal* (28.3.1850) duly recorded his death, when it stated that George Groves of Goat Hill Farm, Exmoor; a bachelor of 46, committed suicide by blowing his brains out in the road near the lone cottage where he lived and was attended to by the wife of a labourer who lived in a part of the house. The cottage was described as being 2 miles from Moles Chamber and 4 from Challacombe, and it was from the Acland Arms at Moles Chamber that Mrs. Chapple—the wife of the innkeeper—had come on Thursday morning last, arriving at the cottage at about 10 o'clock, where she remained in conversation with the labourer and his wife for about half an hour. On coming out of the house to return home she saw a horse and cart standing in the road outside, and found a Mrs. Irwin of Combe Martin—who was on her way to Simonsbath—in a very distressed condition, having just found the body of a man beside the road bank just around the corner from the cottage, at a spot that Mrs. Chapple has passed only half an hour before. Mrs. Chapple called to Agnes Huxtable—the labourers wife—and together they went to where the body was lying, which was identified as being that of George Groves.

At the inquest that followed, Mrs. Huxtable stated that the deceased had been dejected of late, eating nothing but a little dry toast and drinking only water. A verdict of suicide while the balance of his mind was disturbed was recorded.

It is not so much the story of George Groves death—tragic though it was—as the identity of Agnes Huxtable, that provides us with the vital clue as to where George Groves had been living and using as a base for his farming activities on Pinkery. Agnes was the wife of Anthony Huxtable (one of at least 4 of that name who were born or lived on Exmoor in the 19th century) and their home in 1851 was Driver Cott, at the entrance of the lane into Driver Farm; the cottages now known as Moorland Way.

In addition to the old farms at Simonsbath, Cornham, Honeymead and Red Deer, there were now the new farms of Simonsbath Barton, Toms Hill and Larkbarrow, Warren, Horsen, Wintershead, Emmetts Grange, Duredon and Driver, with another on the offlying land at Litton: Picked Stones and Winstitchen were also built prior to 1851, but were at that time part of Honeymead, and it was not until 1861, when Henry Matthews—the only one of Frederic Knight's early tenants to make good—gave up his long tenancy (19 years) that they became farms in their own right. Other farms, all—apart from Kinsford—in the south-east corner of Exmoor were also built at this time and later we will take a look at them.

Reclamation of Exmoor Forest.

The story of the farms created by John and Frederic Knight has already been given in some detail in the *Reclamation of Exmoor Forest,* and it is not my intention to reiterate or attempt to compete with it here, but rather to take a wider view and include items of interest gleaned from original documents and other less well known sources, that are relevant to the continuing history of Exmoor as a whole.

The work that had been done before the new farms could become profitable presented a daunting task to the incoming tenant farmers. There were fields to be enclosed, the land ploughed up, worked down and tilled; lime to be paid for and hauled from Combe Martin and other limekilns in the area, and so, it is hardly surprising that there was a steady procession of tenants as one after another ran out of money and moved on. This was of little help to Frederic Knight, as he all too often lost out when the farmers became bankrupt, even to the extent of compensating them for the residual benefits accruing from the work they had done.

The new farms were mainly geared to stock farming, with some being further equipped with dairies: John Hebditch of Driver, James Meadows of Larkbarrow and William Hannam of Cornham—who later fell on very hard times—all produced excellent cheeses and some butter. Hannam alone, in the early part of 1852, had one ton of cheese on offer at the Golden Fleece, Barnstaple *(North Devon Journal* advert 24.2.1852). There were also dairies at Honeymead,[2] Emmetts Grange and Warren. Winstitchen appears to have been similarly equipped, because in 1851 Uriah Dyke and his daughter—who were living there—are listed in the Census as a dairyman and dairymaid.

Because many of Frederic Knight's early tenants lacked the necessary capital to farm properly, they had supplemented their income by taking in stock from outside the Moor for the summer grazing. Sheep, which in the past had always provided the largest source of income to the Warden of the Forest, had now been overtaken by cattle, and Frederic's income from this source alone had reached a useful £1,000 a year. Nevertheless, he frowned on his tenants for doing likewise, because he believed—and probably with some justification—that if they could obtain a regular living in this way, little progress would be made in the improvement of their farms.

On John Knight's death in 1850, the Exmoor and Brendon Estates became the sole property of Frederic, his eldest son. In that same year, he married, and like his father before him at first used Lynton as his base, which enabled him to let Simonsbath House with nearly 600 acres as a farm. Before this farm could be let, however, two important sales took place. The first, in the autumn of 1850, was a disposal sale of the late John Knight's prime breeding stock of some 80 horses and ponies; a sale that came close to breaking Frederic's heart, but one forced on him by his need to quickly raise some ready cash.

The stud consisted of 40 Thoroughbred horses of various ages, plus 7 Exmoor horse ponies, 7 Exmoor mares, 9 working carthorses, 5 mares,

2 foals and 5 yearlings, realised £945. 15. 10. The need to reduce the number of Thoroughbred's, which required enormous quantities of forage and oats during the course of a year can well be appreciated, but the sale of so many of his working horses can only mean that with so much of his land now let as farms, a large proportion of the reclamation work had been taken out of Frederic Knight's hands.

This sale was followed in 1851 by the auction of the whole of the late John Knight's valuable household goods, furniture and stock of wines; this being the contents of Simonsbath House; also a number of surplus agricultural machinery and husbanding implements. The sale, which began on the 8th July, took three days to complete. Among the household contents were many valuable items, including a set of Spanish mahogany telescopic tables with 8 chairs, 2 dozen antique mahogany chairs in Claret leather and Moreen, 2 dozen Rosewood chairs with stuffed seats, a Rosewood Cabriole sofa, a Horseshoe table with revolving centre and brass fittings, a Rosewood Davenport, a handsome mahogany bookcase with glass doors and drawers, an Oval pillar and claw mahogany table, a Zebra wood Loo table, 2 Rosewood Whatnots, a very good Piano Forte and music stool, a mahogany Celeret (Cellarett) brassbound, an iron safety chest; a copying machine and apparatus, various Brussels and Kidderminster carpets, a mahogany sideboard and many minor items. Bedroom furniture included a 4 poster bed, a Trafalgar and Tent bedsteads, bed furniture, etc. Although it is not known how much money this sale brought in many of these items today would be worth a small fortune.

On the last day of the sale the agricultural machinery and husbandry implements came under the hammer. Among the items sold was a four horse threshing machine, a full size corn drill with every requisite for sowing corn, turnips and seeds, manufactured by Garret; a manure drill for turnips on the ridge or flat, iron double ploughs, iron and wooden harrows of every kind, 2 good chaffcutters and another suitable for horse or mill power, a bean mill, a malt mill, a water engine, iron rollers, long and short butts, hay machines, a circular saw with iron frame, and many other items, including an immense quantity of old cast and wrought iron.

Having been interested in old barn machinery for many years; particularly that driven by horses in the traditional round house or by waterpower, I have tried to ascertain just how many farms on Exmoor Proper were equipped in this manner. It has not been easy to establish an exact number, because after John Knight's earlier failure to achieve a regular satisfactory corn harvest, the tendency was to grow mainly oats, which were either fed direct from the stack in the sheaf, or put through a chaff cutter, thus doing away with the need for a barn thresher, and the sale of the threshing machine in 1851 would tend to confirm that this mode of operation was already the norm.

Another thresher driven by horsepower, was installed at Litton Farm, where is remained in use until early this century; and it is now known that

Simonsbath House

Simonsbath House (rear of) showing Lord Fortescues conversion of John Knights mansion

Exmoor Forest Hotel, Simonsbath.

Simonsbath Village in the 1920's

Lower Sherdon was equipped with a horse powered chaff cutter;[1] one horse being sufficient for this task.

It had been previously thought that very little use had been made of the abundant water power that the streams and rivers of Exmoor were capable of supplying, but recent research has shown that this was not the case. A water wheel was installed near Simonsbath Bridge, to provide power for a saw mill, chaff cutting and other purposes as well. Henry Matthews' retirement sale at Honeymead in 1860 included a water wheel and barn thresher. This machinery appears to have been purchased by the incoming tenant, as there was still a water wheel and barn thresher in use at Honeymead in the mid to late 1920's, when Harry Prout of Rose Cottage was working there for Tom Elworthy. The water to drive this machinery came via a leat from high up White Water, near Cloven Rocks. Warren Farm was similarly equipped, but the water wheel and barn machinery have been gone for over 70 years.[*] According to William Hannam's account in the *Reclamation of Exmoor Forest,* there was also a water powered chaff cutter at Cornham, but nothing is recorded of other barn machinery there.[3] One would also expect that Emmetts Grange—where Robert Smith in his earlier years attempted to grow a large acreage of corn —would have been provided with the necessary machinery to deal with it, but as yet I have found nothing to confirm this, although a leat did carry water to the farm.

The sale of John Knight's prime breeding stock of Thoroughbred horses and the auction of the contents of Simonsbath House had been largely brought about by Frederic Knight's acute financial problems following his father's death, when he found himself with considerable real estate but very little money.

On the terms of John Knight's will, Frederic had inherited not only the Exmoor and Brendon Estates, but also a substantial amount of property in Worcestershire. John Knight's interest in the Wolverley and Cookley Ironworks were shared equally between Frederic and his brother Charles. The latter, and the youngest brother Lewis, were bequeathed £16,000 apiece, a huge fortune in the 1850's, and a similar sum was to be paid to their three sisters, Margaret, Isabella and Helen; making a total cash requirement from the estate of £80,000, with the residue of John Knight's personal estate to go to Frederic.

The problem was, that at the time of his death, John Knight did not have this kind of money, and to make it easier for Frederic and Charles— the executors—to administer the estate he had stipulated that the legacies were to be paid in full, plus 3% accrued interest, on the expiration of 5 years after his death; thus allowing time in which to improve the finances of his properties, and so accumulate the money needed to meet the payments of the legacies without having to sell off too large a part of the real estate.

---

[*]From conversations with Jack Buckingham and Harry Prout both of Rose Cottage, Simonsbath.

From a Bill filed in the High Court of Chancery on 15th March 1852 it is obvious that Frederic's three sisters were not too happy with the current state of affairs, and looked at from their point of view they had every reason to be concerned, as there appeared to be little prospect that the Exmoor and Brendon Estates would become a viable proposition within the foreseeable future, with hardly enough money being generated to meet existing mortgage repayments, let alone enough to put aside to pay in full their legacies on the date they were due, which was now less than three years away.

The course of action decided upon by the Knight sisters, was to enlist the aid of the Chancery Court to have an account taken of all the real and personal estate of their late deceased father, now in the possession of Frederic, Charles and Lewis Knight, with the debts, funeral expenses and other charges incurred in the administration of the estate, and that any personal estate remaining should be applied in due course to the payment of their legacies. Should these funds be insufficient for the said purpose; to take account of the rents and profits of the real estate since John Knight's death and this money retained for the same purpose, and if this too was inadequate, then, as a last resort, to sell such real estate as was deemed necessary under the direction of the Court to meet the legacy payments plus the interest.

Frederic did not have long to wait for the Chancery Courts decision, which in general terms complied with the demands made by his three sisters. The Court was, however, sympathetic to his problems in regards to raising the huge sum of money needed to meet the legacy payments, and the original time limit of 5 years in which to do it, was extended again and again, but it was not until some 14 years after the death of John Knight that the last instalments on the legacies were paid up and Frederic was finally free of all restraints and orders placed upon him. While his estates were tied up in Chancery, a Receiver, William Fowler, was appointed to help sort out Frederic's financial affairs. Every penny had to be accounted for, and apart from fulfilling his obligations to his tenants, very little—if any—new reclamation work was carried out. All rents and profits were paid into a separate bank fund under the jurisdiction of the Accountant General of the Chancery Court, and after a decree was passed on 13.12.1852, a considerable proportion of Frederic Knight's properties in Worcestershire were sold off, bit by bit, to augment this fund. Much of the Exmoor and Brendon Estates would assuredly have been disposed of in the same way, had it not been for the discovery of a number of promising iron veins traversing these estates. Frederic was able to convince the Court that it would be prejudicial to his interests to sell any part of this property prior to the commencement of mining, and it was due to this alone that the whole of his estates in Devon and Somerset remained intact.

The sale of the Worcestershire properties had not been solely for the benefit of Frederic's brothers and sisters, but had to some extent been forced upon him by further complications in his financial affairs, when, following the death of Sir Samuel Clarke Jervoise, of Hanover Square, Middlesex, and Idsworth Park, Hants, on 1st October 1852, his son and heir Sir Jervoise Clarke Jervoise sought the repayment of £10,000 loaned by the former to John Knight in 1826, and secured by a mortgage on the Manor of Brendon and the Advowson.

With the consent of all the Knight brothers and sisters, £755 of this money was quickly repaid, this being the proceeds from the sale of the Advowson (next presentation) of the Rectory of Brendon to the Rev. Charles Tripp. Two years later, following a court order of 10.6.1854, the balance of £9,245 was also repaid. A repayment that required a considerable sacrifice by the members of the Knight family, who as yet had received little or nothing of their inheritance.

It was during the period under consideration that the next major development in Exmoor's history took place, although strictly speaking it had begun a little earlier in 1846, with an attempt to exploit the mineral wealth of the Exmoor Estate by a local syndicate, an attempt that ended in failure 9 years later, but undeterred by this Frederic now turned to the mineral resources of his land as a way out of his financial difficulties. On the Brendon Hills to the east of Exmoor, iron was being mined in large quantities, and there was little doubt in his mind that similar quantities lay under his own property. The story of the efforts made to find and mine this ore has been well told in *The Reclamation of Exmoor Forest* but there are many gaps, which a fresh look at the available information—and considerable legwork—have helped to fill. In a later chapter we will attempt a re-appraisal of the mining scene, but for the present our attentions will be confined to the financial contributions made by the three mining companies induced to take setts upon the Moor. The dead rents alone paid by the three companies amounted to £3,500 per annum, and though they were not long on the Moor, the total contribution to Frederic Knight's Chancery Fund could not have been less than £5,500, a figure that was greatly added to by settlements totalling £17,000 awarded to Frederic in Court Actions brought against the two larger companies; Schneider and Hannay of Ulverstone and Dowlais of Merthyr Tydfil, South Wales, after they had given notice to quit without fulfilling the terms of their mining agreements as set down in their leases (according to Frederic Knight).

Despite the large amounts of money that from one source and another had been paid into Chancery, it was still insufficient to meet the legacy payments and other claims upon it, and just two months before William Fowler passed his final account as Receiver, the mortgages on the Exmoor and Brendon Estates were raised from £36,000 to £91,000, but even with this additional money, by the time all the claims against Frederic Knight and his late father's estate were met, only £1,126. 2.3½ was left to his credit.

This, however, was more than enough to satisfy the Receiver, and on the 25th April 1864, after 12 long years of hardship and personal sacrifice, all restraints and conditions imposed by the Chancery Court were lifted by order of the Master of the Rolls, John Romilly, and Frederic Knight became a free agent once more.

Frederic's problems over the past 12 years had not been confined to finance alone. Another source of worry—albeit minor by comparison—was the herd of Fallow Deer introduced on Exmoor many years earlier by his father; which despite the harassment of poachers had increased in numbers to the stage where they could no longer be contained within the Deer Park, and had consequently become a pest, not only to Frederic's own tenants but also to farmers further afield. The damage done by the deer had to be paid for, and with repeated demands for compensation there was no way that this state of affairs could be allowed to continue unchecked and the decision was taken to rid the Moor of these pests, and in a very short time they were completely wiped out.*

I believe it was in the late 1950's or early 1960's, that I came across some of these 'Ghosts from the past', when, early one morning a small herd, 8-10 strong, trooped in single file over a corner of Lanacombe not far from Brendon Two Gates. They were travelling east, but where they came from and whither they were going I do not know, but Fallow Deer they certainly were.

The Red Deer came close to suffering a similar fate when hunting virtually ceased for a period of some 30 years after 1825. Poachers quickly moved in, and within a few years the numbers of deer remaining on Exmoor and the surrounding countryside reached an all time low. It was due in no small part to the efforts of John and Frederic Knight—who set aside a quiet area of the Brendon Estate on Scob Hill and the adjoining woods—where the deer remained unmolested—that they survived.

Another staunch preserver of the deer was Sir Thomas Acland, and later, when hunting was resumed and Scob Hill was divided between four adjoining farms, Nicholas Snow of Oare Manor took over the role of chief preserver and proctector of the deer, and by enclosing over 300 acres of the hillside of Oare Common, on the east side of Badgworthy Water, and planting small plantations of Larch and Fir, provided them with shelter. In this enclosed area the Red Deer were jealously guarded against all intruders, thus encouraging them to breed there. This continued until his death in 1914, by which time the deer had recovered sufficiently in numbers to survive unaided. As time passed the deer park has been gradually run down, although the deer have remained loyal to the place where they were 'leared' and their descendants can still be often found there.

Gradually, very gradually, the pattern of life on Exmoor had been changing, and with an ever increasing rural population, boosted still further by the arrival of three mining companies, the time had come to fulfil the last requirement of the Disafforestation of Exmoor Act of 1815,

---

*In the early 1850's.

which had made provision for the erection of a church and parsonage when the population was deemed sufficiently large to warrant them. By the autumn of 1856 the desired buildings had been erected on the 12 acres of land reserved by the Crown for this purpose: For a thousand years Exmoor had been a Royal Forest; for a few years more it was an extra-parochial district, but with the completion of the church and parsonage, and the appointment of its first minister, the Ecclesiastical and Civil Parish of Exmoor was born and another landmark in the history of Exmoor was reached.

The first incumbent at Simonsbath was the Reverend W.H. Thornton, a close friend and confidant of the Knight family, who had previously held the curacy of Lynton and Lynmouth, with sole responsibility for the Parish of Countisbury. He had little good to say about the contractors who built his new church and home, and by all accounts the contractors were not too happy with the contract either, because it all but bankrupted them, despite the Rev. Thornton's opinion* that they were on the fiddle and used inferior materials. All the lead work had to be replaced, and the church was faced with Bath stone which had spent some time in the sea at Combe Martin, after being brought there by boat and dumped. In the winter of 1856-7, heavy rains, followed by severe frosts, took their toll and the stone peeled off in flakes, a cart load under every window. Soon after, in a gale, slates by the hundred whirled away into the distance, and it was discovered that iron nails—not copper as specified—had been used and these had quickly rusted away. Inside the house things were little better; locks and fittings gave much trouble and had to be replaced. The Rev. Thornton, whose stipend was—at £150 per annum—not great when considering the demands made upon it, and the lifestyle he was expected to maintain, was put to great expense in setting things right. He was also left to build the garden walls, clear the site of large rocks, make the paths, and then buy shrubs and trees with which to stock his garden.

In less than twelve months after the completion of the church a new school was built in Simonsbath. A document dated 22nd October 1857 certifies the completion of the school in a satisfactory manner, and that no debt or charge remains on it. It goes on to say that the promoters were Frederic Knight and the Rev. Thornton, who were both great believers in the education of the poorer working classes, and though the latter was to leave Exmoor in 1861, Frederic Knight remained a school manager until his death some 40 years later in 1897. The completion of the school and the setting up of a Trust to run it is of some importance, because it has a bearing on a later matter concerning it. This school was not, however, the first on Exmoor, because when the Rev. Thornton arrived at Simonsbath there was already a Dames School, which was held in what was later the kitchen of one house, and the sitting room of another (at that time part of three cottages by a different arrangement). The occupants recorded there

---

*Reminiscences of an Old West Country Clergyman, Vol. 1.

in 1926 by the Rev. Surtees in the Exmoor Parish magazine—Mr. George Webber and Mrs. White respectivly—reveals that he was in fact referring to White Rocks Cottages; beside which the new school was built in 1857.

Although the Reverend Thornton's reminiscences leave out much that would have enlightened us concerning Exmoor; especially that relating to the Knight family; they do nonetheless give us an insight into the happenings on the Moor during what in many ways was still a far from civilised time. Some of his personal exploits are almost unbelievable: He thought nothing of walking from Simonsbath to Barnstaple and back—a distance of 32 miles—just for the exercise, or to run over to Glenthorne on the coast near County Gate to visit his friends the Hallidays for the evening, and afterwards run home again. On another occasion—with two others—he rowed from Minehead over to Wales, and after dinner on roast Curlews (which he did not recommend) rowed back again. Another time on returning from a trip to London, he left the train at Tiverton Junction and ran in hand ran the 27 miles home.

In the year following his induction at Simonsbath he was married, and a year later their first child was born. She lived only a few short moments and lies at rest in the little churchyard there. Deeply shocked by this tragic loss, for which his wife blamed the isolation and the distance from the nearest doctor, who was 11 miles away at South Molton, she became very depressed, urging him to leave Exmoor for a more civilised and populated area. It became increasingly difficult for him to remain on the Moor he loved, but even so, two more daughters were born there, the second involving a mad dash across the Moor at night to fetch the doctor from South Molton. This was the last straw, and early in 1861, after a great fall of snow had brought the people of Simonsbath close to starvation, the Thorntons moved to the softer climate of Dunsford, a village between Exeter and Moretonhampstead, and later, to North Bovey on the fringe of Dartmoor, where he remained and served faithfully for 50 years.

The reminiscences also give us a brief glimpse into the characters of the Knight brothers, who were all intrepid horsemen and for wild and reckless - daring in their younger days had no equal. All were crack shots who could put a bullet into a penny piece at 12 paces. Frederic was also a keen falconer, taking Peregrines from their nests in the Exmoor region, and training them himself. He also strictly reserved the fishing on his rivers and streams, so it would appear that he was also a keen fisherman. Charles was later crippled in the Roman Campagna, and Lewis was tossed nine times by a buffalo cow in the depths of darkest Abyssinia, near the third Nile Cataract, which effectively cured him of the uncontrollable shakes that he had contracted the previous year (1854) when the SS Ercolano went down off Civita Vecchia, after being rammed by another vessel. In a few terrifying seconds, his wife* and two young sons were drowned, and it was only with the greatest difficulty, after losing a thumb and two fingers in

---

*Formerly Elizabeth Harris of Canada.

the collision, that Lewis saved himself by clinging to the bowsprit rigging of the vessel that ran them down. Two years later, after returning from his travels abroad, Lewis married Henrietta Mary Sanford, the daughter of E.A. Sanford, Esq., of Nynehead Court near Wellington, Somerset, and it was their children who became Frederic Knight's heirs, as his only son was to die at the early age of 27.

During his sojourn on Exmoor the Rev. Thornton became greatly involved in the troubles of his parishioners, and it is obvious that he was sometimes taken for a ride by some of the more lawless elements among his scattered flock. One such occurance happened shortly after Burgess—the notorious Exmoor murderer—(whose story will be told in a later chapter) had been found guilty of murdering his youngest daughter and was hanged.

This story relates to a John Smith—a well known scoundrel from Lynmouth—who at the time in question was lodging with Joseph Steer in Simonsbath with his 6 year old daughter Elizabeth. Smith was frequently drunk, and when in drink was very rough and cruel to his child. Mrs. Thornton, worried by the Burgess affair, could foresee that Lizzy Smith stood every chance of following Anna Maria Burgess to an untimely grave.

Smith, a mason by trade, settled up his account with Joseph Steer and prepared to leave the Moor to take a job with a builder at Williton. Mrs. Thornton, on hearing the news, was furious, saying murder would surely be committed. She persuaded her husband to go at once to see Smith to find out if he was prepared to let them take care of his daughter.

It was late on a wild night when the Rev. Thornton arrived at Smith's lodgings. He aroused him from his bed, and proceeded to strike a bargain with him in regards to his daughter. Smith agreed to pay 2s. 6d. a week towards her keep, and the Rev. Thornton promised to clothe, board, educate and generally provide for her until she was old enough to be respectably put out into the world. Joe Steer witnessed the agreement, and to safeguard his interest, the builder's address where Smith would in future be working was taken, and a letter was sent at once with his consent to have 2s. 6d. a week deducted from his wages to be forwarded quarterly to the Rev. Thornton.

At the end of the month 10/- arrived from the builder, with a letter saying that Smith had sold his tools and departed, leaving no forwarding address. The Rev. Thornton was now saddled with a 6 year old child, full of bad blood and of worse education; timid until re-assured, when she then told lies for a pastime. He kept her at his own expense until she grew into a big girl of 14. He had done his best for her but she turned out badly, untruthful, thievish, dirty and at 14 showed promise of being unsatisfactory in other ways. She was now old enough to earn her own living and he wrote to her relatives at Lynmouth enquiring as to her father's whereabouts. A reply came saying that Smith was now working at Weston-super-Mare at this trade.

Next morning the Rev. Thornton and Lizzy left for 'Weston'. On arrival they went to the Police Station for information. Lizzy was left there in the Police Sergeant's custody while Rev. Thornton set forth to search for Smith, finding him at work on some half finished houses. Confronting Smith he told him he had kept his daughter at his own expense long enough, and he could now have her back. Smith declared he was remarried with a second family to support and could not afford the expense. He did, however, accompany the Rev. Thornton to the Police Station, where he promised that he and his wife would do what they could for the girl and see that she was not maltreated. Shortly afterwards, news was received at the parsonage that Lizzy had been put into service and had robbed her mistress, for which deed she had been sent to a reformatory, whence she proceeded to Australia and was heard of no more.

In 1858, a major diphtheria epidemic hit Simonsbath. It was brought there by a girl from Barnstaple who had been hired as a servant and the poor girl nearly died. The Thorntons immediately sent their baby daughter and her nurse out of the village to a remote farmhouse, where they remained for the duration of the epidemic. The remainder of the household; the Thorntons, the housemaid and cook, promptly went down with the diphtheria; all at the same time. This was, of course, long before the days of modern medicine and antibiotics, and at a time when bleeding by the application of leeches was still the cure for many ailments. The treatment for diphtheria was no less drastic. The equipment comprised of a rammer, which was soaked in Sulphuric acid and then thrust down the throat; this operation being repeated as necessary, several times a day; the burning effect being soothed by copious libations of old Port wine. They eventually recovered, but not before a great hole had been made in the Thornton's cellar. Only one life was lost in the village; that of a small baby who could not take the Port and succumbed in consequence.

In the 1850's and 60's, the area of moorland reclaimed grew rapidly. Local men with a knowledge of the Moor and its ways were now taking over the farms, and men who had spent some years working for Frederic Knight—and often for his father before him—who had managed to save a little money, were helped and encouraged to get a start farming on their own account by the creation of a number of small holdings of about 50 acres each. There were at least nine of these holdings, four of them between Winstitchen Lane and Simonsbath, but a list has not, as far as I know, been published. If they were the same as those later held under Viscount Ebrington, they are as follows: Balewater, West Gate (Viscount Ebrington only), West Cottages (2), Post Office, Lower House, South View, Cloven Rocks, and one more—not named. This list, although correct for the early part of this century, leaves out the White Rocks Cottage holding, and three other small blocks of land let in this way

An interesting story regarding these holdings was told me by Tom Little (a descendant of one of the Scottish shepherds brought down by Frederic Knight in the early 1870's), a story that can be traced back to 1855, when after many years without an inn, a cottage in Simonsbath was converted and granted a full licence, mainly to cater for the thirst of the miners then at work on the Moor. As time passed, Frederic Knight became aware that the Inn was having a detrimental effect on his men's work, ambitions and pocket and he stopped the sale of beer and spirits; only wine and light refreshments could be obtained there. This was in 1862, and from that time on his workers prospered and many who had taken the smallholdings were able to add to them, or took larger farms on the estate. Later still, some of these men were able to purchase farms of their own around the Moor. Viscount Ebrington—who later became the 4th Earl Fortescue—continued the practise of letting these holdings when he became the owner of the Exmoor Estate, and none of these smallholdings as they became vacant ever lacked a new tenant, until 1933, when a full licence was restored to the Inn. From that day on, not one of these holdings was ever again re-let when the existing tenant gave them up or retired, and all of this land, which, incidentally, was often some distance away from the cottage it went with, was eventually taken into the estate farm.

In 1860, Frederic Knight returned to Simonsbath, to live once again in the old house, which, with the land he had let with it, had become vacant, and though he was often away for long periods the house was not let again in his lifetime. His homecoming was celebrated by a voluntary gift of 10% off the half yearly rent paid by the tenants of his Exmoor and Brendon Estates at the rents audit held at the Red Deer Inn in September. This act of kindness, altogether unsolicited, was received with grateful emotion and pleasure by his tenants, who looked forward to his return at some time during the Parliamentary recess.*

In March of the following year, Robert Smith left—or was dismissed from his position as Agent to the Estates—although he continued to farm Emmetts Grange for a further 7 years. He had done his work well, not only as the Agent responsible for the letting of the new farms and the competent way in which he ran the Estates, but also in the considerable time he had devoted to the search of the elusive iron ore, prior to—and during—the mining era. Nevertheless, for reasons best known to themselves, Robert Smith's employment was terminated, and for the next 5 years the estates were run by a bailiff, William Scott.

Robert Smith was without any doubt an enlightened and resourceful man, and an extremely competent and practical farmer. Articles written by him on a variety of subjects concerning agriculture, show an acute awareness of the problems relating to farming in general, particularly those that arose from bringing the moorlands into cultivation, and the loss of his services to the Exmoor farming fraternity as a whole was keenly felt for many a long year.

Emmetts Grange, which Robert Smith rented from Frederic Knight, was a model farm, and a fine example of just what could be achieved at this height above sea level, providing the right methods were adopted and adhered to. By this time, the futility of growing corn—other than oats—had been realised, and the accepted mode of farming was now mainly

---

North Devon Journal 6.9.1860.

geared to animal husbandry, with a large proportion of the newly reclaimed land tilled to rape and turnips for the sustenance of this stock.

According to a report in the *North Devon Journal,* following Robert Smith's dismissal in 1861—which in glowing terms extolled his virtues and achievements—the small herd of Exmoor ponies left behind by Sir Thomas Acland had grown from 30 to 300 strong; figures that do not tally with those given by F.J. Snell *(The Blackmore Country,* 1906) who states that in 1860 the pony stock consisted of 100 Brood mares, mainly Bays and Buffy Bays, with ages ranging from 1-13 years, plus 10 stallions: Up to the age of three the ponies shared 800 acres of Badgworthy with the Red Deer and Blackcock, but on reaching maturity they were removed to one of the Exmoor allotments to run with a stallion.

Prior to 1850 the surplus ponies and suckers had been sold by private contract, but for a few years after that date they were sold at Simonsbath —following ancient custom. In 1853, 200 people gathered at Stony Plot (in the area where the church now stands) for the pony sale, but in 1856 and thereafter, due largely to the need to attract a wider range of buyers, many of the ponies were driven to Bampton and sold at the annual fair. Although it may have been a better market, it could not have been the easiest to tasks to drive 50-60 wild and unbroken Exmoor ponies and suckers from Simonsbath to get there. There was certainly a keen demand at this time, with an average of about £10 a head. An exceptional 60 guineas were paid on one occasion by the Rev. Thornton for a pair of Frederic Knight's unbroken ponies, which were purchased on behalf of a friend.

Contrary to popular belief, Bampton was not always the venue for Frederic Knight's Exmoor ponies, and from 1861 to about 1883, a large number of ponies were sent annually to Reading in Berkshire to be sold. Some years later, one of the Exmoor pony stallions was purchased by a buyer from the New Forest, where it was taken and released. It proved to be a most successful sire, and one largely responsible for a great improvement in the quality of the New Forest pony herd.

Frederic Knight was not alone in keeping a herd of ponies or horses on Exmoor, because in 1851, only 3 years after Robert Smith arrived at Emmetts Grange, an inventory of his stock included 120 head of cattle, 50 pigs, and 120 horses. A few of the latter were Exmoor ponies, but he specialised in breeding Cobs and Galloways, for which there was always a great demand. The true Galloway pony originated from the region of the same name in South West Scotland, where they are believed to have roamed since time immemorial. They were an extremely useful breed, being very hardy and active, with the added advantage of having a docile nature. Standing some 14-15 hands high, they resembled a typical Clydesdale in miniature and were equally at home with saddle, cart or plough; a useful breed indeed, but one seldom if ever heard of today. Whether the Galloway pony on Exmoor was the true one is not certainly known, because the name has also been used to describe a cross between a pony and a thoroughbred, and it is not unlikely that this was the case here.

For some years the number of ponies sold by Frederic Knight was matched by those of Robert Smith, but as the latter increased his sheep flock, so he decreased the numbers of his cattle and pony stock, and in his concluding sales in 1867 and 1868—prior to his leaving Exmoor—when over 1,000 sheep of the Exmoor Horn breed were sold, only 40 cobs, Exmoor ponies and Galloways were up for auction: Henry Matthews, the first tenant of Honeymead, also kept a useful mixed herd of horses and ponies. His retirement sale in October 1860 included pure bred Exmoor ponies, Galloways, Cobs, Coach and Bus horses, 60 in all: Also included in his sale was his stallion Quicksilver, which for strength, symmetry and beauty could not be equalled; his grandsire, the property of Frederic Knight, had been purchased in Rome for 600 guineas.

Life on Exmoor was always hard, with little time for relaxation or recreation; the highlights of the year coming mainly in the hunting season, when for a few short moments men downed tools when the occasion brought the stag or foxhounds within viewing distance. Many of the fine runs by the Devon and Somerset staghounds have been recorded in some detail, but less attention has been given to the foxhounds, which were equally successful. Nicholas Snow; the last of his line at Oare Manor, maintained a fine pack of hounds which were known as the Stars of the West; a name that was later changed to the Exmoor Foxhounds on Frederic Knight's insistence, as a condition of his allowing the hunt free access over the Exmoor and Brendon Estates.[*] It was not until much later that a resident pack of foxhounds were established on Exmoor Proper, when kennels were built at Bale Water in 1939, where the hounds have since lived, and continued to thrive to this day.

Another sport, which began in the mid 1850's, and afterwards became an annual event, was the Horse and Pony races. The first such event took place at Honeymead Farm on 15th August 1855 *(North Devon Journal 23.8.1855)*, by kind permission of the tenant, Henry Matthews, on the instigation of a William Smith, who had suggested it a little earlier. A purse of silver was quickly collected, and the date fixed for holding the 'Maiden Exmoor Races'. By 4 p.m. on the day, several hundred spectators from the surrounding district had gathered on the romantic heights of Big Hill, where a course had been selected and marked out with posts.

The race was for ponies under 12½ hands high and there were 5 contenders for the prize of a fine new saddle. The contenders were Mr. Matthews Bay pony Busy Bee; Mr. Knight's grey, Tipton Slasher; Mr. Fry's Brown pony, Wide Awake; Mr. Smith's Chestnut, Eva; and Master G. Smith's Bay, Bessie. The race was divided into heats, with the same 5 ponies competing in them all. The reported account as to who was the ultimate winner is a little confused, but I think it was young Master Smith on Bessie, with William Smith's pony Eva second, but they were hard pressed by the other ponies, especially Busy Bee.

[*]According to a small booklet written by Bertha M. Harford in 1925.

The highlight of the day came with a Donkey race, when five ragged gentlemen were brought to the starting post to contend for a new and excellent bridle. This was the 'most laughter moving offering imaginable from beginning to end', the donkeys were lined up for the start and they were off, but although they started together each had his own ideas as to where the course ought to be, and the 5 donkeys proceeded accordingly on 5 different lines of country, none of which was the race course! After numerous falls—the jockeys being remounted again and again by their friends—they were marshalled into some sort of order to gallop over the course. At length, after 4 heats were completed to the tune of incessant laughter from the spectators, and really hard bare back riding by the jockeys, the bridle was won by William Howe's brown mare donkey, Gallopard, who narrowly gained victory from the other contenders, Kickemoff, Jibemoff, Snatchemoff and Boltemoff. Thus ended the first races ever held on Exmoor Forest, and such was the success of the event that an open handicap race was proposed for the following year, and also one for Galloways.

The horse races continued for many years on Exmoor, and later in the 19th century, when Mr. Sanders was the Master of the Devon and Somerset Staghounds, some highly successful Point to Point races were held over a particularly difficult course which began and ended at Larkbarrow.

After leaving the farm, horses and riders crossed the boggy area around Pinford, up over Trout Hill and then circled around to the Warren where they turned and raced up over Dry Hill, and, skirting the fringe of Swap Hill, raced on to the finishing post at the rear of the farm. Casualties, however, were somewhat plentiful, owing to the rough and holding nature of the ground, and later the course was changed for a safer one near Hawkcombe Head.

In the small book *Jottings from the Diary of Joseph Webber* another sport that was in vogue on Exmoor for many years until the 1860's is described. This unique race, which was on foot and open to all comers, was in pursuit of a wild Exmoor sheep over the wildest part of Exmoor, where there were no hedges. The one who caught the sheep kept it as a prize. It was a kind of Marathon, and the sheep, which had been especially selected, was subject to special feeding for some time before the event, and being bred on the Moor was as fleet as a deer for the first few miles. The race developed into a feat of endurance between the sheep and pursuers and could not be captured until it was thoroughly tired, because the rules stipulated that it had to be caught and held by its short tail, which, to make things more difficult, had been well greased, and until the sheep was completely exhausted it would slip from ones grasp and the race was on again, until eventually after many miles had been covered the prize was taken.

Joseph Webber—although born at Molland—was descended from an old Challacombe family, and on two occasions his father, Edward Webber, was the successful contestant, and thus the winner of the sheep.

In 1862, a year after Robert Smith's dismissal, an advertisement in the *North Devon Journal* reveals that over 10,000 acres of the Exmoor Estate were in hand and that William Scott, the estate bailiff, was to attend fairs and markets at Barnstaple, Torrington, Bampton, South Molton, Tiverton, Witheridge, Crediton, Bideford and Chulmleigh, to take bookings from farmers interested in placing stock on Exmoor for the summer grazing from May 1st to October 7th; the rates for the various types of stock being; Bullocks three year old £1, 2 year old 15/-, 1 year old 12/-. Ponies under 13 hands 15/-, Horses £1. 5. 0. Sheep without lambs 2s. 6d., with lambs 2s. 9d. As an incentive, Frederic Knight supplied Devon bulls to run with the heifers free of charge, and experienced herdsmen were kept to look after the stock. In addition to taking in stock, 400 acres of improved land at Winstitchen was to be let in lots of 50-100 acres, plus several other allotments of 400-1,000 acres, which were to be let by private contract.

A worthy replacement to Robert Smith was found in 1866, when Frederick Loveband Smyth, who was farming over 1,000 acres at Wistlandpound Farm, Kentisbury, and at Challacombe, as a tenant of Lord Fortescue, was appointed to the onerous duties of Agent of the Exmoor and Brendon Estates, although William Scott continued as bailiff for several more years. F.L. Smyth was an ideal choice for the work in hand, having already reclaimed much of the deep peatlands of Challacombe Common for Lord Fortescue. His system of tilling successive crops of rape after heavy liming, and folding them with sheep over a period of three to four years, was far more efficient in breaking down the peat than the single cropping previously practised. This proved to be of immense value on Frederic Knight's so far untouched heavier peatlands, and later, when steam ploughing was introduced on Exmoor, a large area around Titchcombe was reclaimed in this manner. Incidentally, the entrance that leads to Titchcombe, where the sheep pens now stand, is still known locally as Engine Gates, although very few people today recognise the significance of the name. Titchcombe, which had been designated as a farm, was never to reach that status and only a shepherds cottage and one or two outbuildings were ever built there.

It was in the mid 1860's that the letting of Frederic Knight's farms and other lands reached its peak, when we find the situation of 1862 reversed, with 10,000 acres of the 16,000 acre Exmoor Estate now let, which in 1866 brought him rents to the value of £3,674, and never again while the Estate remained intact, was this level of letting exceeded, although later, as the farm rents were increased, the income from this source did go a little higher.

Just how successful Frederic Knight had been in letting his farms and allotments, can be gathered from a closer look at the 5,909 acres he was left with, on which to keep his own stock and that taken in for the summer grazing. Most of the land in hand was unimproved moorlands, and only 128 acres of Simonsbath Farm, and 407 acres of Winstitchen had been reclaimed, and on this he was dependent for his own winter keep. The remaining land consisted of 2,158 acres of Warren, but did not include the farm or better ground; 400 acres of Prayway; 1,306 acres of Exe Plain; 150 acres at Exe Head; 500 acres of the Deer Park; 442 acres of the rougher moorlands at Wintershead, and 150 acres of the poorer ground at Toms Hill. A further 268 acres, listed under the name of Kittuck Farm, raises a point of interest, for although no farmhouse or buildings were erected on this land, which adjoined Larkbarrow Farm, the name suggests that a farm may have been intended there.

Towards the end of the 1860's some of the Exmoor farms became vacant and proved impossible to re-let; a problem that was not confined to our region, and was due to the perilous state that the farming industry had been brought to by Robert Peel's Free Trade measures, which opened the way for the importation of cheap food from abroad, mainly from America, Australia, New Zealand and Argentina; further aided by the advent of steam ships and an expanding railway network, both at home and abroad. The rapid strides made by America in farming mechanisation had opened up the vast Prairies for growing wheat on an unprecedented scale, which inevitably led to over-production and the flooding of the world markets with surplus grain. The effect in Britain was that the price of a loaf of bread fell by half, and at this price our corn growers just could not compete.

This put immense additional pressure on an already fragile farming economy, which was not improved when the corn growers turned to dairy and stock farming as a way out of their troubles. This in turn added further impetus to the decline in farming fortunes and by the end of the 19th century, three quarters of a million farmers and farmworkers had been forced to emigrate; for the most part to the self same countries from which their problems had emanated.

The impact on the farmers of Exmoor was less severe than in the corn growing districts, where rents were substantially higher, and as far as is known not one of Frederic Knight's tenants left the country for the Colonies during this period. Nevertheless, it was a time of great hardship, but by keeping expenditure down to the absolute minimum they survived.

The agricultural depression had a double barrelled effect on Frederic Knight's plans, because not only was he now left with a much larger proportion of unstocked land, but, because of the pressures that all farming was under, there was virtually no demand for the traditional summer grazing. In the circumstances the only possible way he could maintain or increase his revenue was to increase the numbers of his own stock, and because it was impractical to keep large numbers of bullocks all the year round, he was left with no alternative but to increase his sheep flocks. He was still far from satisfied with the native Exmoor Hornies, which he considered needed far too much additional feed during the long winter months, so he decided to try once more the Cheviot sheep that his father had experimented with some 40 years earlier, but this time when he travelled north to make his purchases he persuaded some of the northern shepherds—who were accompanying their sheep down to Exmoor—to bring their families with them to settle on the Moor.

By the end of 1871 the mass exodus of some 5,000 sheep and their shepherds from Scotland and Northumbria was completed,[1] and from this time on the economy of the Moor became largely dependent on their experience and skills, and so, after 50 years of trial and error, the type of farming best suited to the high moorland conditions had finally come about.

Very little of the story of these shepherds and their descendants—and the sheep herdings they were responsible for—has ever been told, but enough is now known about them to provide a separate chapter, so for the present we will leave them, to continue with other matters concerning Exmoor.

The introduction of steam operated ploughing on Frederic Knight's Estate took place in 1873, some three years earlier than the date recorded in the *Reclamation of Exmoor Forest,* and was initially carried out with the ploughing tackle belonging to Mr. Lake of Cruwys Morchard. His journey to Simonsbath was not without incident, and caused the following comment in the *North Devon Journal* (27.11.1873), under the title of 'The Iron Horse'. 'A minor sensation was created in East Street, South Molton, on Wednesday afternoon of last week by the passing of a traction engine and 5 trucks containing the apparatus constituting a steam plough. The carriages were driven on the North Molton road towards Simonsbath, where the plough is to be employed on the extensive property of F.W. Knight esq., M.P.'. How much ploughing was carried out at this time is not recorded, and it was probably not until after a particularly long spell of severe weather in the early months of 1875 had brought Frederic Knight's sheep flocks close to starvation, that steam ploughing began in earnest, in a bid to increase the acreage under cultivation, to ensure that in future, adequate feed was available in times when hard frosts or snow made it impossible for the sheep to survive unaided.

By this time much of the easier working and more suitable land had been reclaimed, but the heavier peat lands had proved impossible to tackle with teams of oxen or horses. With a single 10 horsepower steam engine it was possible to work either a huge single furrow reversible plough or—where the ground was more suitable—a 4 furrow plough, which was pulled back and forth on a wire rope fed through anchored pulleys at each end of the field. When the return journey was completed the anchors were raised, moved forwards a little, and the process repeated; the huge plough cutting through the deep peat as though it was butter. In a short while many acres were reclaimed, and after heavy liming quickly brought into production. On some of the more difficult ground where water lay on or close to the surface, a large iron hook was trailed in the furrow behind the plough to

---

*See notes in Appendix III.

penetrate the iron pan, which lay at varying depths below the peat. Once this crust had been broken through the water quickly drained away.

In 1879, Frederic Knight's only son, Frederic Sebright Winn Knight, died at the untimely age of 27, after a short illness at Simonsbath. He had become a respected member of the community, the Deputy Lieutenant and a Justice of the Peace for the Counties of Devon and Somerset and occasionally took his place on the bench at the Petty Sessions of Combe Martin and Dulverton. Frederic never fully recovered from his tragic loss, and with no other immediate relatives to succeed him, or to carry on his work of reclamation, it was time to pause and reflect upon his own position. He was fast approaching 70 years of age, and with his estates now mortgaged to the tune of £123,060 it would appear that he could see little hope in spending his remaining years burdened with crippling mortgage repayments and a capital debt he could not hope to repay without selling off a considerable proportion of his remaining property. After giving the matter a great deal of thought he reluctantly came to the conclusion that if he was to enjoy his remaining years free from worry, then the whole of the Exmoor and Brendon Estates would have to go, but with the forlorn hope that they could still be kept in the family they were first offered to his nearest relatives, who politely but firmly declined his offer. The properties were then put into agents hands and on the 12th April 1881 Messrs. Skewis and Son of Southsea Chambers, Bishops Gate Street, London, received an offer of £285,000 from an un-named syndicate for the whole of the two estates, including all the live and dead stock.

With the price agreed to the satisfaction of both parties, all looked set for a speedy completion of the sale, but it was not to be. It is difficult to pinpoint the cause of the breakdown in negotiations, but the content of one or two of the letters passing between the two factions show that Frederic Knight was concerned that the Exmoor and Brendon Estates should not fall into the hands of unscrupulous speculators. In the first place, the principal party of the syndicate wished to remain anonymous until such time as the business transactions were completed, but Frederic would not hear of this. In a letter to Messrs. Skewis and Son, he insisted that the name of the principal purchaser (a responsible man) and the address of his residence be given; that an agreement be drawn up in the usual manner and signed, and a deposit of £28,500 paid not later than the 24th June 1881, with vacant possession of the whole on the 1st January 1882. Unless the above terms were complied with within 7 days of the date of the letter the contract was to be absolutely withdrawn. At this stage he was fairly confident that the sale would go through. In a letter to Mr. Finch (his solicitor) he assumed that he was entitled to the rents and profits up to 1st January 1882, as there was the matter of £5,700 (mainly rents) outstanding.

In a further letter to Skewis and Son, Frederic rebuked them for demanding their full commission for the sale to be forwarded from out of the £28,500 deposit as soon as it was paid, which was not only contrary to their agreement, but unethical. He stated that their commission on the deposit would be paid as soon as this was banked in such a way that it could not be claimed again from them (the agents), and that the remainder of their commission would be paid in the usual manner when the sale was completed. There were no further letters on the subject, but for some reason—in all probability one of those given above—the transactions were not completed, and four more years elapsed before a contract was signed for the sale of the Exmoor and Brendon Estates. This sale—which we will come to shortly—was conducted on completely different terms.

Frederic Knight retired from Public Life in 1885. A year later he was rewarded with a Knighthood. Not, as one would suppose, for services to agriculture, either in or out of Parliament, but for his lesser known involvement over a period of many years with the Yeomanry and Volunteer Movement, in which he held the rank of Colonel. He was now 74, but still an active man, both mentally and physically, and though he was still prepared to sell his two major properties in order to capitalise on his assets, he was no longer prepared to relinquish all control of them, and when they were sold to Lord Fortescue (3rd Earl) of Castle Hill, Filleigh, in that same year for £193,060, the Exmoor and Brendon Estates were sold subject to Sir Frederic retaining a life interest in them, which he continued to enjoy for a further 11 years. The contract was signed on the 10th April 1886 and an initial deposit of £12,000 was paid, followed 6 months later by a further payment of £33,000. At the time of the agreement Lord Cornwallis of Linton Park, Maidstone in Kent held the deeds of many of the Exmoor and Brendon properties as security for the £123,060 loaned on mortgage, and 5 days before the contract was signed—in a letter to Sir Frederic Knight—he requested the repayment of the principal capital, plus whatever interest was owing.

According to the *Reclamation of Exmoor Forest,* 'Lord Fortescue accepted responsibility for the repayment of this money', but as time went by, and Sir Frederic lived on, he must have had serious misgivings as to whether he had done the right thing in buying on these terms, even though his purchase price had allowed for this possibility. There is a locally held belief among some of the older men that if Sir Frederic had lived much longer, Lord Fortescue's own position would have been very serious indeed:[4] There was still a further £25,000 owing to Sir Frederic, but on the terms of the agreement this was not due to be paid until 1 year after the death of the widow of the 2nd Lord Fortescue, although Sir Frederic was entitled to interest on this money from the date of signing of the contract in 1886. He did not, however, live long enough to receive the benefit of this capital, as he and Lady Fortescue died within a short time of each other.

In 1887 Frederick Loveband Smyth died, and his son, George Cobley Smyth—who shortly added Richards to his name—took over as Agent responsible for the Exmoor and Brendon Estates, a position he held for over 50 years, first for Sir Frederic and later for Lord Fortescue and his son Viscount Ebrington. Many of his letters—often daily—to the latter are deposited with the Fortescue papers in the D.R.O. Exeter. They are of particular importance because they cover the period immediately after Sir Frederic's death, when Lord Fortescue and Viscount Ebrington finally gained possession of their long awaited estates; and thus provide us with a very clear picture of the problems Viscount Ebrington faced, and the steps taken to ensure that his inheritance was run in a manner calculated to produce the maximum possible revenue during very difficult times. It is too early, however, to go into the details of Viscount Ebrington and George Cobley Smyth Richards contribution to the history of Exmoor, as we have not yet concluded the story of the Knights.

On the 3rd May 1897, in his 85th year, Sir Frederic Knight died at Bath. Four days later his body was interred in the grave of his only son in the little churchyard at Simonsbath at the very heart of his beloved Kingdom of Exmoor. In the *North Devon Journal* of the following week an obituary notice appeared, which reads as follows:

'Colonel Sir Frederic Winn Knight of Exmoor and of Wolverley, Worcestershire, who represented West Worcs. for 44 years as a Conservative M.P., died last week at the age of 84. He was the eldest son of John Knight of Wolverley by his second wife, the elder daughter of the 1st Lord Headley, and a descendant of Richard Knight of Madely, Shropshire, a considerable iron master in the time of the Commonwealth. He was born in 1812 and educated at Charterhouse. He was a Deputy Lieutenant and magistrate of Worcs. and a magistrate for Devon and Somerset. A family trustee of the British Museum as representative of the late R. Payne Knight of Downton. He served for many years in the local Yeomanry and Volunteers. He was married in 1850 to a daughter of the late Mr. E. Gibbs and was created a K.C.B. in 1886. In 1841 the deceased was elected for West Worcs. and continued to represent the constituency until the passing of the Redistribution Act of 1885 when he retired from Public Life. In 1852 and again in 1858-9 he was Parliamentary Secretary to the Poor Law Board under Lord Derby's government having in his early parliamentary days been a supporter of Agricultural protection. The interment took place on Friday last. In addition to the members of his own family and the tenants of the deceased, the funeral was attended by Lord Ebrington, Mr. Snow (Oare Manor), Mr. R.S. Crosse of South Molton, Mr. Smyth Richards of Barnstaple and others. The day being rough and the place inaccessible naturally reduced the numbers of those who would otherwise have attended'.

Looking back over the past three quarters of a century, it is almost impossible to comprehend the magnitude of the changes wrought on Exmoor by John and Frederic Knight, for not only had the physical landscape been changed beyond all recognition, but also the way of life. When John Knight took possession of four fifths of the old Royal Forest in 1821, there was but one small farm and just 5 people living on the Moor. From this small nucleus the village of Simonsbath had grown, and much of the old rough moorlands had been enclosed and reclaimed. As a result of their endeavours nearly 200 people had become dependent on the farms and sheep herdings they had created, and men who had worked for the Knights had, with their encouragement, risen from humble beginnings and climbed up the social ladder to become successful farmers in their own right.

From the time he had taken over the running of the Exmoor and Brendon Estates in 1841, Frederic Knight had been beset with financial difficulties, and though his income rose steadily year after year, it is obvious the increase in revenue did not keep pace with the demands made upon it. In 1848 his total income from all sources was just £2,746, but after the new farms were completed and let it rose rapidly to reach £4,017 in 1852, and £5,498 8 years later. In 1861 it passed through the £6,000 barrier, increasing steadily to £6,784 in 1863, £6,934 in 1869, and subsequently to £8,492 in 1878. No comparable figures have been found for the years 1879 to 1897, but one would expect to find a continuous steady improvement. In the latter half of the 1850's he had—as we have already seen—benefited considerably from the contributions of dead rents and related settlements made by 3 mining companies, but even this was not enough to stop him from progressing from a £16,000 mortgage in 1826, to £36,000 in 1848, and by a huge jump to £91,000 in 1864, and ultimately to £123,060 in 1877.

Three of these increases have already been accounted for: The cost of creating his new farms: The large family settlements: The claim of Sir Jervoise Clarke Jervoise; and this, one would have thought, would have been quite sufficient borrowing, but other demands on his finances had yet to be made.

Sir Frederic Knight had—or so we have been told—*(Reclamation of Exmoor Forest)* inherited the whole of the Exmoor and Brendon Estates, but in fact he did not come into possession of all the former property until 1869, when he paid his brother Charles, £7,317. 17. 8 for his interest on it.

The full extent of Charles Knight's holding on Exmoor is not known, but at least 3 of John Knight's earlier purchases were assigned to him. These were; Red Deer (Gallon House) and 42 acres; Chichesters allotment of 36 acres—which adjoined the offlying farm of Litton, and a 15 acres allotment that had been first awarded in respect of South Furzehill, Lynton. Sir Frederic was also unable to resist the temptation to buy more land as it became available locally. Between 1869 and 1871 he purchased a further 138 acres in the parish of Brendon for £4,100, even though his existing Brendon properties were already mortgaged to the hilt. He was, moreover, a man who never shirked his public responsibilities, with the welfare of his tenants and their families especially close to his heart, and as well as the school built at Simonsbath in 1857 he also erected a school for 60 children at Brendon, plus a house for a teacher, both of which were completed in 1875.

Whatever the benefits of the reclamation work done on Exmoor they were not in the form of financial gain to John and Frederic Knight, but rather to the farming community of Exmoor as a whole. Of profit there was precious little, and that mainly in the last 11 years of Sir Frederic's life when, after the burden of the mortgage repayments had been lifted from his shoulders, he was able to reap the full benefit of the income from his tenanted farms, and also that from his own farming and sheepherding enterprises. Even though this was a considerable sum,it was but a drop in the ocean when compared with the total outlay on the reclamation. If this could have been achieved by ploughing back the profits of a successful business—thus allowing a steady expansion of the same—then all would have been well, but in borrowing such large sums of money to achieve the same ends he had gone to the limit of his means, and once in the rut he had been unable to get out.

After deducting the £123,060 capital charge of his mortgage, Sir Frederic was left with £70,000, which was some £41,000 less than his father's original outlay in buying the Exmoor and Brendon Estates, and no amount of juggling with figures can alter this fact. The rents and profits he received in the last 11 years of his life—although allowed for in the purchase price paid by Lord Fortescue—are incidental to the issue, as Sir Frederic could have died the day after the contract was signed.

At the time of his death Sir Frederic was farming about 10,000 acres. Most of this land was divided between 8 sheepherdings, with an additional herding just outside the boundary wall at Badgworthy. The combined number of sheep of all ages recorded just 2 days before his death was 10,043, plus 167 rams. About half of the flock were ewes and ewe hogg replacements, the remainder, lambs. In addition, there were 184 head of cattle, mostly heifers—which were sold in calf in the autumn; 20 carthorses and 60 Exmoor ponies. The latter being all that remained of a herd that had at one time been nearly 400 strong, but as the sheep became more profitable than the ponies, the latter were gradually reduced, and the herd may have been further depleted in the winter of 1896-7 when many of the Brendon ponies died as a direct result of the severe drought in the previous summer.

There was no large sale of live and dead stock following Sir Frederic's death, as this was taken over by Viscount Ebrington at a valuation of £14,400, but there was a smaller sale of some of the contents of Simonsbath House, which took place on 23rd July 1897;* the only livestock on offer being 6 choice pigs and a quantity of poultry. On the day prior to the sale, Lady Knight removed an old lock from one of the doors of the old house—this lock having originally been brought either from Wolverley or Sir Frederic's house in London, was of great sentimental value to Lady Knight—but before she left a new lock was paid for and fitted, and after this final symbolic gesture she was gone from Exmoor.

Just three years after Sir Frederic's death, Lady Knight was laid to rest beside him, and with her passing another chapter in Exmoor's history

---

*North Devon Journal.

closed, as Charles Allanson and Edward Lewis Knight had predeceased them both; May they rest in peace.

Footnote: Exmoor today is still very much as Sir Frederic Knight left it, and it is, I believe, a blessing that he did not have the means to do all he intended, for in failing to complete his mighty task he has left Exmoor with a delicate balance of farms and wild moorlands that in many ways complement and supplement each other. Long may it continue so.

CHAPTER 7

THE SCOTTISH SHEPHERDS AND THEIR SHEEP

DURING the 20 years or so of John Knight's active involvement with the reclamation of his Exmoor Estate, much experimentation with different breeds of sheep had taken place in his efforts to find the breed most suited to the high moorland conditions, and to meet his own high standards for quality of wool and mutton, but the results were both disappointing and inconclusive, and it would appear from later records that by the time Frederic succeeded his father, only a few Exmoor Horn sheep were left to make use of such land as could not be let or used by his ponies and the bullocks taken in for summer grazing.[1] Later still, when local men took over the Exmoor farms, the traditional custom of the moorland region was followed, and they too kept only the local breed, which in their own district were reputed to be better suited to the local conditions than the imported Cheviot and Blackface sheep from Scotland, providing a little extra feed and better pasture were available immediately after lambing. They were very prolific and made good mothers, and once such a start had been given the Exmoor sheep were quite capable of fending for themselves and doing well off the rough herbage of the unreclaimed commons and moorland. Their worth was proved later, when at the Royal Show in 1913 they held off all challengers amongst the mountain breeds to win the coveted award for the finest wool. One of the objections to the horned sheep in the mid 19th century was that when they were on the open moorland they were very susceptible to 'Scab', but with good shepherding and the advent of compulsory dipping this has been all but eliminated.

Despite the local preference for the breed—which remains to this day—Frederic Knight was for some reason prejudiced against them. The story that they could not be wintered without additional feed was to prove no less true of the Cheviots that he re-introduced in the late 1860's and early 1870's, and probably only the Blackface sheep—brought down from Scotland at the same time—were capable of surviving unaided all the year round on the rougher moorland enclosures.

The re-introduction of the Cheviot and Blackface sheep took place some 20 years after Gerard Spooner had come down from Scotland in 1852 to take Wintershead Farm, bringing with him his own shepherd, William Scott,· and a mixed flock of Cheviots and Blackfaces.[2] Although the time was not right for his style of sheep ranching—or the acceptance of these breeds locally—Spooner proved during the six years he remained on Exmoor that given the right conditions his way of farming could be made

---

*He later worked for Frederic Knight as bailiff.

to pay, and when, in the late 1860's Frederic Knight's farms began to come in hand, it was this method of sheep ranching that was decided upon to make the best use of this land.

The Blackface sheep, although the hardiest of all the breeds tried on Exmoor, lacked the finer qualities of their competitors and it would appear that as time went by they were gradually replaced by Cheviots. There were still Blackface sheep on the Hoar Oak or Chains herding in the late 1950's (when this part of the Exmoor Estate was sold off) but they were not descendants of the original stock, having been introduced in the 1940's to replace a flock of Cheviots that were not hardy enough to withstand the harsh winter conditions there.

Of all the sheep that had been tried on Exmoor the Cheviot has the most interesting history.* Once known as the Long or White sheep they had roamed the Cheviot Hills for close on 600 years, improved a little from time to time by the import of Merino sheep from Europe. Six centuries on the exposed hills in all weathers had made them naturally hardy, but they carried little meat, and even more surprisingly—very little wool.

The 18th century was a time of great improvements, not only in industry but also in farming. The population was rising rapidly, and the demand for meat and wool was high. The time was ripe for the improvement of the Long sheep, and in the 20 years following 1760, a Cheviot hill farmer named Robson, and a few of his friends, perfected the breed to the stage where they produced a third more meat and wool. This was achieved by crossing the Long sheep; firstly with rams from the Wolds of Lincolnshire, and later by the use of rams of Spanish or Merino origin. The breed was further improved by the addition of Ryeland ewes and rams, which were highly regarded for producing the finest wool. By the end of the experiments the Long sheep was gone and the Cheviot had arrived.

There being little land available locally on which to expand the new breed, a few lowland farmers seeking their fortunes turned northwards to the Highlands of Scotland, where the Glens or Straths were eminently suitable for large sheep walks. There was, however, one problem, in that the Straths were already populated by the clans of the Highland Chiefs, who, having lived there for hundreds of years with their Black cattle and straggly poor quality sheep, had formed a deep attachment to the land, but because of Culloden and its aftermath—and the constant feuding among the Clans—the Chiefs had become impoverished and were more than eager to lease their land to the lowlanders for sheepwalks. They cared little for their people; where once their wealth was measured in the numbers of men they could raise for an army, now only money would satisfy their greed, and to their undying shame, in less than 100 years, the Straths were emptied of their human population.

Summer and winter the evictions continued, the houses torn down and burned. The clansmen were pushed further and further northward to the

*Highland Clearances by John Prebble; and Livestock on the Farm, Professor C. Bryner Jones and others.

inhospitable climate and the barren coasts, where, finding nothing to sustain them, were forced by starvation and misery to emigrate in their thousands to Canada and Australia, but, packed like sardines in the holds of ships, with little food, bad water, and no sanitation, it is little wonder that the dreaded cholera came and struck them down like flies and many who set out to begin a new life never reached their destination.

There can have been few worse cases of man's inhumanity to man than to deliberately remove virtually the whole of the rural population of the Highland Region, in order to replace them with a multitude of Cheviot sheep and a few lowland shepherds, for the sole benefit of the Highland Chiefs and a few fortunate flock owners.

This, of course, was not the case on Exmoor, where prior to 1820 the population was practically non-existant. Here the Cheviots were to provide useful employment and play a major role in the economy of the Moor, enabling an increasing population to be sustained there.

Once the decision had been made to begin sheep ranching on a large scale, Frederic Knight wasted little time in going north to make his purchases. This accomplished, he persuaded some of the Scottish and Northumberland shepherds to not only accompany their sheep down to Exmoor, but to bring their families with them to settle on the Moor.

A look at the Census for 1871 reveals that there were only two Scottish shepherds on Exmoor when it was taken early in the year. One was James Easeman, who was lodging at Simonsbath House, the other was John Scott, the son of William Scott who had run Frederic Knight's Estates as bailiff from the time of Robert Smith's departure in 1861 until 1866 when Frederick Loveband Smyth was appointed Agent. The Scott family resided at Winstitchen, where a flock of Exmoor Horn sheep had been kept, but here, as elsewhere, Cheviots were now being brought in to replace them. The only other shepherds from the North on Exmoor at this time were the Dunn brothers, William and Adam from Northumberland, but after Adam's untimely death at Larkbarrow in 1875 at the age of 32, William and his wife and family appear to have left Exmoor, and are believed to have moved to North Wales, where they are known to have been living in 1881.

The manner of Adam's death, which occurred on the 7th November 1875, caused the following paragraph to appear in the *North Devon Journal* on the 11th November:

Suspected Murder on Exmoor

"On Saturday night a young man named Dunn, who was a shepherd to Frederic Knight on the Forest of Exmoor, left the Gallon House Inn about 9 p.m. for his home at Larkburrough. The body of the unfortunate man was found on Sunday morning with skull fractured and extensive injuries, to all appearances as if death had come about by foul means."

A fortnight later—in the *North Devon Journal*—a report was given of the inquest into Adam's death, when evidence was given by the labourer who found him about 9 a.m. on Sunday morning. The labourer, who had been working near Larkburrough, was attracted by the yelping of a dog, and when he reached the spot from where the yelping came he found Adam Dunn in a sitting position, leaning against a hedge with his tongue protruding and his head on one side, speechless and apparently dying. Dunn was quickly removed to his brother's house where he was attended by Dr. Hartley of Lynton, but he did not regain consciousness and died about noon on the Sunday. There was a slight scratch on the back of his head and he also had a black eye. It appeared he had been drinking all the previous Friday afternoon at Gallon House, and about 9 p.m. set out for his home about four miles away at Larkburrough over a dismal moorland, being wet and dark. He carried a gallon of whisky with him, for which he had paid 18/-, and he was found about midway between Warren and Larkburrough.

The following facts were recorded at the inquest, where Frederic Knight was the foreman of the jury: The deceased had drunk a great deal at the Gallon House where he had played the fiddle. He was the worse for liquor when he left although he was not drunk. It was conjectured he had fallen when getting over a fence, thus receiving his injuries. He was probably partly disabled from his semi-drunken state, and leaned against the hedge in the hope of recovering himself, and became overcome with exhaustion.

Dr. Hartley's evidence revealed that Adam Dunn's wounds did not cause his death, but that the deceased was of weakly constitution and suffered from a weak heart. After the usual deliberations, the verdict arrived at by the jury was that Adam Dunn had died from exposure.

Two other shepherds, both of them from Scotland, were also working for Frederic Knight prior to the Census of 1871. Neither lived on Exmoor Proper but at the offlying herdings at Badgworthy and Hoar Oak. David Bryden and his wife and daughter lived at the former, where a shepherd's cottage had been erected for Frederic Knight in the mid 1860's by two local tradesmen, John Bale and John Lethaby,· who are said to have removed many of the stones from the old 'Doone Cott's'—which stood close by—in its construction.

It was on this herding that many of Frederic's Exmoor ponies had been living, but as they became less and less profitable the herd was gradually reduced until only 60 or so ponies remained. The number of sheep on the herding were correspondingly increased to replace them.

William Davidson—the other Scottish shepherd—and his wife were living in the Hoar Oak Cottage at this time, using it as a base for the Chains herding, which was centred on the sheepfold further up the same valley near to the lower end of Long Chains Combe, and close to where John Knight's earlier cottage is believed to have stood.

Until recently I could not understand quite where Hoar Oak Cottage and the land that went with it—which for the most part is in Lynton parish

---

*John Lethaby was to spend much of his life on building and repair work on the Exmoor and Brendon Estates, first for Frederic Knight and later for Lord Fortescue.

—fitted into the scheme of things, because despite the Knight family's long association with it there is not one reference to Hoar Oak in any of the documents held in the Kidderminster Library that relate to John and Frederic Knight's estates in Devon and Somerset, and it is now clear that Hoar Oak was never a part of these estates, but was either leased or rented.

According to the Tithe Apportionment for Lynton of 1839, Hoar Oak and 389 acres around it were owned and farmed by John Vellacott, who also owned North Furzehill and Ratsbury. The Hoar Oak land included two large blocks of 'Mountain', 140 acres and 146 acres in extent, which would of course have been suitable only for rough grazing.

Hoar Oak appears on the Census of 1841 for Lynton as Oar Oak, when James Bale, a farm labourer—presumably employed by John Vellacot—was living there with his wife and daughter. They were gone by 1851, when another farm worker, George Moule, was the occupier. He had moved on before 1861, when we find the owner was again in residence with his wife, six sons and a daughter, but their farming interest at Hoar Oak was reduced to 14 acres, so presumably the rest of the land there was let, possibly to Frederic Knight.

At some time after 1861 Hoar Oak farm was again let, the tenant on this occasion being a Mr. R. Taylor. He remained there until Michaelmas 1867, when, after selling his livestock—consisting of ten bullocks, 50 sheep and two horses—he retired from farming.

I believe that it was following Mr. Taylor's retirement that Frederic Knight took a lease for the Hoar Oak farm, and shortly afterwards William Davidson moved into the cottage, which now became the home of the shepherd in charge of the Chains herding, and remained so for the rest of Frederic's lifetime and for many years after.

That Hoar Oak was rented and not owned by the Knights is confirmed by a letter written to Viscount Ebrington on 25th November 1898, some 18 months after Sir Frederic Knight's death. In this letter, G.C. Smyth Richards—Agent for both—writes: 'I see Hoar Oak is rented by your Lordship for £54 per annum, and in addition there are three allotments on Exmoor for which you pay £6. 10. 0 a year, but these are a separate purchase and I am not sure if Mr. Jeune is prepared to sell them.' Two days later—in a second letter—G.C. Smyth Richards wrote that Mr. Jeune was prepared to sell Hoar Oak and 60 acres for £1,150 and was also ready to sell his two-thirds share in the Exmoor allotments, and that Mrs. Lock Roe was also willing to sell her one-third share. What final price was agreed on is not given, but the sale was completed, and in the spring of 1899 Viscount Ebrington was suggesting the addition of a dairy to the cottage.

Just when and how Hoar Oak had come into the possession of Mr. Jeune is not certain, but it was probably in 1866, when the reversion in fee of moiety of the Furzehill and Hoar Oak Estate was put up for sale. *(North Devon Journal 24.5.1866).*

This was not the only land in this area that had been rented by the

Hoar Oak — before

— and after being acquired by the Exmoor National Park Authority

Badgworthy Cottage built by Frederic Knight in the mid 1860's

Artists re-creation of sheepfold and shepherds' hut near Long Chains Combe

Knights, because a sale held on Friday 13th August 1897, for Sir Henry Palk Carew of Woolhanger (who was selling off part of his Manorial Estates) included an Exmoor allotment undivided from Ilkerton Common, 200 acres in extent, that was stated to have been formerly tenanted by Sir Frederic Knight, then by his executors.

Returning to 1871, we find that in the space of a few short months in the latter half of the year that the mass exodus of sheep and shepherds from Scotland and the North of England to Exmoor had been completed. Some of these flocks came down by rail, some by boat, or a combination of the two, others arrived after following the long weary miles of the old drovers trails, and by the end of the year the number of sheep on Exmoor had been increased by some 5,000. The last shepherd to arrive on Exmoor with his sheep is said to have been John Gourdie, who had brought his flock down by train as far as Williton, where they were unloaded and driven the rest of the way to Simonsbath. With their long journeys over, the shepherds with families were reunited, and at first accommodated wherever there was a vacant cottage or farmhouse, but as other farms came in hand the shepherds were moved into more permanent homes.

A list of these shepherds is given in the *Reclamation of Exmoor Forest*. There were the Davidsons, Grahams, Johnstones, MacDougals, Littles, Murrays and Gourdies, but at least two of the entries for this period are incorrect, because James Johnstone and Donald MacDougal did not come down to Exmoor until 1886 and 1894 respectively, and neither Thomas Graham or Peter Murray are believed to have been on Exmoor prior to Adam Dunn's death on 7th November 1875. Other shepherds probably arrived with the first group or soon after, but failed to settle and had returned home before the Census of 1881 was taken.

It was by following the old drovers trails that Robert Tait Little and his flock of sheep finally reached Exmoor. His epic journey began in the County of Dumfries and ended at Duredon Farm, which came in hand in 1868 and was now a sheep herding. Robert arrived about the 16th July 1871, and was joined there by his wife Jane, and their two sons, Robert and John. Within a few years a daughter, Ellen, and another son, Thomas, were added to the family.

It is strange to find that no mention of R.T. Little has been made in the *Reclamation of Exmoor Forest,* where as head shepherd to Frederic Knight, and later to Viscount Ebrington, one would expect to find some reference, but according to R.T. Little's grandson, Tom Little, there is a simple explanation for this: Two families of Littles arrived on Exmoor at about the same time, and though they were not related were always the best of friends. The other family of Little, with William at their head, came down by rail with his sheep and took the herding of Pinkery, where they remained until 1898, when they moved to Toms Hill to take the double sheepherding at Larkbarrow. They continued there until this land was requisitioned during the last war for an artillery range and training area, when Toms Hill and Larkbarrow—together with the shepherd's cottage at Badgworthy—were used as target practise by the big field guns, and practically blasted out of existence.

The Toms Hill Littles were the better known of the two families because for several generations they continued to produce shepherds of the highest quality, and when in recent years information was required about the shepherds and their way of life, it was to the Littles of Toms Hill that the inquirers turned.

Robert Tait Little had been less fortunate in this respect. His eldest son (also Robert) although a shepherd under his father at Duredon, and later in charge of the Simonsbath herding, emigrated to Australia in 1887/8: His second son, John, also tried shepherding, but was not a natural shepherd, and after his marriage spent the first few years of married life at North Molton, working as a farm labourer at South Radworthy and High Bullen farms; returning to Exmoor in 1910 when the present Tom Little was eight years old, to live at Driver Cott, where John was content to go on working as a general farmhand. Robert's daughter, Ellen, married Donald MacDougal, another of the Scottish shepherds, who after living for a while in Simonsbath moved to Wheal Eliza Cottage to take the Mines herding (formerly Winstitchen). Robert's youngest son, Thomas—not to be confused with the present Tom, was also under-shepherd to his father at Duredon, later taking over this herding, but his heart was set on farming, and long before the first edition of the *Reclamation of Exmoor Forest* was published he was farming; firstly the small holding that went with South View, and later at Cloven Rocks, and so, when Robert T. Little died in 1907, and Thomas Little gave up shepherding a few years later, there was not one male member of this family left with a sheepherding on Exmoor.

As head shepherd, Robert Little was responsible for keeping the flock records of all the herdings, and most of his notebooks have survived. One, for the years 1876-1884, is in the possession of his grandson, Tom Little. Three others, for the years 1885-91, 1891-99 and 1900-1907, are to be found among the Fortescue papers in the D.R.O. Exeter. It is possible there was an earlier notebook covering the years 1871-1875, but this is by no means certain, because a compilation of Robert Little's notebooks into one larger Stock Book (also in his hand) relates only to the years already mentioned, namely 1876-1907. These books are of some interest, because not only do they record the numbers of sheep, lambs, and sales and losses for each herding on Exmoor, but they also provide us with much other useful information.

There were seven herdings on Exmoor in 1876, with another just outside the Forest at Badgworthy. The number of ewes and ewe hogg replacements to each herding were as follows: Winstitchen 534 ewes, 122 ewe hoggs; South Forest 501 (130), Larkbarrow 751 (246), Oar Oak (Chains) 494 (130), Duredon 421 (—), Cornham 300 (41), Pinkery 427 (116), Badgworthy 594 (188), making a total of 4,039 ewes, plus 975 ewe hogg replacements. A list of Tups (rams) used in 1878, shows that there were 56 Cheviots, 10 Blackface, six South Downs, and one Dartmoor. These mature rams were assisted in their duties by 32 Cheviot, seven Blackface and six Oxford Down hogg rams. Throughout the years covered by Robert Little's first notebook (1876-84) a solitary Dartmoor ram kept his place, but it was not used thereafter.

In a report in the *North Devon Journal* on 1st March 1875—the year before Robert Little's records begin—one of the problems of feeding the large numbers of sheep on Exmoor during prolonged spells of bad weather is highlighted, when it was stated that 'For several days in the past week five wagons with two horses to each have been engaged in carrying hay from a few miles south of South Molton to Exmoor, where the sheep are starving on account of the inclement weather', but losses were not as great as in 1878, when after severe snowstorms during the night of March 28th—and the next morning—the following deaths were recorded by Robert Little for the eight herdings: Winstitchen 21, Simonsbath (South Forest) 28, Larkbarrow 40, Badgworthy 28, Chains 13, Cornham 40, Duredon 55, and Pinkery 57. A loss of 292 sheep in just 24 hours. The total losses for the period November 1st 1877-July 6th 1878 (including the blizzard) were 583, the equivalent of a complete herding wiped out.

In January 1881, Robert's records show that six hoggs were lost on Ashcombe in a great snowstorm. He comments that he had never seen so much snow. Ten years later on March 9th and 10th 1891, there was another great snow storm, when 150 sheep perished at Larkbarrow, but fortunately there were no losses on the other herdings. Another prolonged spell of bad weather occurred in 1895, when for eight weeks in January and February the land was frozen solid by a bitterly cold east wind. Once again food resources were stretched to the limit, but there was little snow and there were no more than the usual losses.

It was the custom on Exmoor to dispose of as many as possible of the draft ewes, fat lambs and hoggs by the autumn, in order to cut down on the number of mouths to be fed through the winter. Demand for Frederic Knight's prime sheep had greatly improved, and sales ranged from the small markets of Appledore and Bideford, to the larger markets of South Molton, Taunton, Bridgwater, Weston-super-Mare, Worcester and Birmingham. There was also a thriving local demand at Dunster Castle, where 274 lambs in 1876, and 384 in 1877 ended their days.

Robert Little's notebooks also clear up one mystery that in recent years has caused much discussion among those interested in the finer points of who did what on Exmoor. Two circular stells (shelters for sheep) were built on the Moor, and though their construction was correctly thought to have dated from Frederic Knight's time, little more was known about them. Not only can we now pinpoint accurately their construction date, but also whose idea it was, and the reasons for building them.

From the terrible sheep losses in 1878, it had become obvious that there was insufficient shelter provided for the sheep grazing on the open moor when caught in snow and blizzard conditions, and an entry in the earliest note book reveals that the work of building two stells was put in hand soon after. R.T. Little, coming as he did from Dumfries-shire, would have been fully aware of the benefits of such enclosures, which in that region are very plentiful and are built in a multitude of different styles. The type constructed on Exmoor is clearly based on that given in Captain Napier's book *'Practical Store Farming'*, published in Edinburgh in 1822, from which the following extracts had been recorded by R.T. Little. 'Captain Napier on Store farmering says that sheep without food and shelter is farming on mere chance, that is to say without stells and hay'. A description of a stell follows thus: 'A circular stell of dry stone ditch (wall) ten-twelve yards in diameter, with a three ft. open door and six ft. high including cope is the least expensive and most sure improvement that can possibly be adopted'. One further item recorded from Capt. Napier's book followed: 'A stone of good hay supports a score of sheep for a day, computing 24 lbs. to the stone, and they lose very little vigour or flesh.'

From the above notes it is clear that Robert Little was responsible for bringing the stell to Exmoor, but it was probably Frederic Knight's idea to improve them further by planting trees upon the perimeter wall: Hawthorn in the case of the Pinford Stell which lies about a mile west-south-west of Toms Hill Farm, and beech on the stell at Three Combes Foot, three-quarters of a mile north-north-east of Larkbarrow Farm, beside Chalk Water. In one of the beech trees here a pair of Ravens nested regularly for a number of years, but recently some vandal—using climbing irons—reached the nest, and illegal though it is, removed the eggs.

I know of no other stells on Exmoor, although there is a great similarity with some of the ancient circular enclosures, such as the one on the west side of Hoaroak Water—not far from the tree—and those outside the old Forest—on Badgworthy Hill. There are, however, two or three much larger enclosures that almost certainly date from Frederic Knight's time which could have been used for the same purpose, as well as the sheepfold at the junction of Long Chains Combe and Chains Valley Water.

The enclosure on Great Woolcombe measures about 50 yards by 50 yards and is topped by beech trees that have now reached their prime. In the hot summers of 1976 and '83 they also provided shade for the sheep in an otherwise treeless area. John Knight had done little in the way of planting trees on Exmoor, but Frederic soon realised that shelter and windbreaks were essential in this high moorland region, and for some years he employed a nursery man full time to grow trees. Many miles of his wall-bank fences were planted with young beech, and a few plantations of mixed trees—mainly fir—were also laid down.

The most fascinating of the enclosures on Exmoor is the one on Lanacombe, facing Trout Hill. This truly artistic piece of work suggests (at least it does to me) the influence of Frederic Knight's lovely wife, whose undoubted talents were a great blessing to her husband.

This enclosure measures approximately 130 yards by 80 yards. All the sides curve inwards, with the banks being carried on outwards beyond the corners of the enclosed area. On the extended corners beech trees have been planted, but apart from these trees the banks are bare. Four more trees were planted inside the enclosure; two near the centre of the north boundary, and two more, one each side of the west entrance. A small building was formerly attached to the north-west corner but this has long since disappeared.

Two hundred and twenty yards north-north-west of the north-east corner of the enclosure can be found relics of a much earlier date. Here, there are a group of nine irregularly placed stones that trend roughly in an east-west direction. They do not appear to have been recorded on any map, nor have I found them mentioned in any book, and on studying them closer, two of these stones were found to be deeply inscribed with the letters T D, so henceforth I should like to call this group the T D stones. We are now left with the problem of who was the mysterious T D, and after musing long and often over these initials I have come up with several alternatives, which are probably all wrong. The first that comes to mind is Thomas Darch, who was a lessee—with others—of the Forest from 1740-1750 (he also owned the tithes), but the style of lettering does not appear to be that old, which also rules out Thomas Dure who was a tenant at nearby Badgworthy in 1424; and any member of the Doone clan. Possibly the initials were carved by one of the labourers working on the enclosure near by, but more likely they belonged to one of the moorland shepherds and were cut to while away a few of his lonely hours. Should this be so, then Thomas Davidson is the likeliest candidate during the five years (1893-98) that he lived at Larkbarrow, which was not too far away. There is of course always the chance they were carved by one of the wartime soldiers training on the Moor. The possibilities are endless, and after a closer look at the T D stone nearest the enclosure revealed the less obvious initials of I B cut in its edge, I meekly withdraw from the guessing game and leave it to others to come to their own conclusions.

The stones, and the area around them suggest an ancient site, with in all probability a settlement close by, because just north-east of the central T D stone there is a small round barrow. Forty yards further out in the same direction is what appears to be a ruined cairn, or possibly the remains of a hut circle, and 220 yards beyond this, on the same line, is a much larger barrow.

I have wandered back into the distant past, which is very easy to do when musing alone among Exmoor's ancient relics, but it is time to return to reality, and to the more recent history of the shepherds, who, for the most part, lived far out on the lonely moorlands, and were to a large extent dependant on their own resourcefulness. For their efforts they received 20/- a week,· which compared very favourably with the ordinary farm worker, who was lucky to be paid 15/- a week, with 2/- deducted if living in an estate or farm cottage. The difference between the two wages reflects the importance of the shepherds contribution to the economy of the Moor,

---

·Wages paid early in Viscount Ebrington's time; probably little different from those paid by Frederic Knight, in his later years.

and also helped to compensate them for their lonely existence.

A look at the Census of 1881, in regards to Exmoor, shows that most of the early Scottish shepherds were still on the Moor. Peter Murray was at Toms Hill, Thomas Graham at Larkbarrow, Robert Tait Little at Duredon, with his son Robert as under shepherd. William Little at Pinkery, and John Gourdie was lodging in one of the old West Cottages at Simonsbath. William Davidson had been replaced by John Renwick at Hoar Oak, and was now at Winstitchen; David Bryden was gone from Badgworthy, his place having been taken by William Howeston and an assistant shepherd William Hepburn.

All of the new men were from Scotland, but there was one English shepherd, William Carey, who was in charge of the Cornham herding. This made a total of 11 shepherds on eight herdings at this time.

In the first of R.T. Little's sheep record books the names of the shepherds on Exmoor are not given, but in two of his later books they are, and with the aid of the Census Returns and the help of his grandson, Tom; William Little's grand-daughter Mrs. H. Prout, and especially Jack Buckingham, in regards to the more recent shepherds, it has been possible to compile a list of shepherds on each herding from 1871 to the present day with very few exceptions, which, for those interested, will be found in the appendix.

In the third of Robert Little's notebooks a memorandum reveals that in 1892, Peter Murray—who had for some time been living at Larkbarrow—had in some way blotted his copybook, having been apprehended on the 30th September and taken to Dulverton. On pursuing the matter further, it was discovered that he had been charged by Frederic Knight with stealing the two hindquarters of a sheep, and at his trial on 5th October he was found guilty and fined £2. 0. 0, with the alternative of one months imprisonment without hard labour. Naturally enough in the circumstances his employment was terminated, and as he did not leave Exmoor until the 9th November, it would appear that he chose the latter form of punishment. Murray's temporary replacement, John Blackmore, remained at Larkbarrow for only ten weeks until a shepherd arrived from Scotland to take over. His arrival is noted on a slip of paper in one of Robert Little's notebooks, and reads: 'Sir Frederic Winn Knight to John Hewitt; Railway fares from Dailly, Ayrshire, Scotland, to South Molton; four at £1. 18. 0, plus furniture expenses £3. 9. 6'. This is of some interest, because it is not only the one such record we have, but it is also one of the few instances where the place from which a Scottish shepherd came from is known, the Census Returns merely recording Scotland as the place of birth.[3]

The largest turnover of shepherds occurred at the offlying herding of Badgworthy, where, over a period of 27 years from 1871-1898, at least six shepherds came down from Scotland, remained for a short while, and then departed.

As we have already noted, it was customary to sell the culled ewes, fat lambs and hoggs not required for breeding at the end of the summer grazing season, thus keeping the numbers of sheep on Exmoor to a minimum during the long winter months, when it was often difficult to provide enough food for sustenance. With winter keep in short supply it became customary to send the young replacement ewe hoggs down to the lowland areas for the winter, thus maintaining them in good condition and improving their chances of survival. Farms where keep was taken varied from year to year, but areas around Ilfracombe, Combe Martin and at Cadeleigh near Tiverton, were much favoured. In 1886, the ewe hoggs from the Badgworthy, Chains, and Larkbarrow herdings were wintered at Georgeham. In the following year the Badgworthy and Larkbarrow young stock were sent to Ilfracombe. In 1889, the ewe hoggs from the Deer Park flock were taken down to Combe Martin. In 1891, keep was taken at Marwood and Cadeleigh, and in 1894, winter quarters included Grilstone near South Molton, Ilfracombe, Stoke Rivers, and Ash Farm Braunton. Some winter keep was still taken after Lord Fortescue took possession of the Exmoor and Brendon Estates, but many of the young moorland sheep were taken down to Castle Hill for the winter, and to Georgeham, where his Lordship also owned considerable property.

At the time of Frederic Knight's death in 1897, the numbers of sheep of all ages on the eight Exmoor herdings, plus Badgworthy, totalled 10,043. There were also 167 rams, all of which were taken over by Viscount Ebrington. In R.T. Little's records an inventory of the sheep on these herdings at this time is given in detail and they are worth recording in full because they show the full extent to which the sheep ranching enterprise had grown.

Herding	No. of Ewes	Hoggs	Lambs	Rams	Total
Winstitchen	594	157	550		1,301
Deer Park (South Forest)	474	129	459		1,062
Larkburrough	834	206	715		1,755
Badgworthy	610	136	472		1,218
Chains (Hoar Oak)	495	116	381		992
Cornham	334	83	344		761
Duredon	412	102	444	167	1,125
Pinkery	410	129	402		941
Wintershead	463	112	480		1,055
	4,626	1,170	4,347	167	10,210

The first two figures represent the breeding stock of 5,796 ewes and replacements. The 167 rams were kept at Duredon out of season.

It is a commonly held belief in the Exmoor Region that Frederic Knight employed only shepherds from Scotland and the North of England (or their descendants) during the period of his great sheep ranching enterprise (1871-1897), but there were exceptions to the rule. William Carey, who was born at Portsmouth, was for a number of years the shepherd in charge of the Cornham herding. He was followed in 1892 by Robert Cann, who began his working life on Exmoor as a labourer, graduated to shepherd at Cornham, and in his last year as a shepherd looked after a herding at Honeymead, before taking a farm of 130 acres there in 1899, to which he was able to add a considerable acreage in the following few years.

Another English shepherd employed by Frederic Knight was Richard Steer, the Exmoor born son of Joseph Steer, who had worked for both John and Frederic Knight before taking one of the Simonsbath smallholdings. Richard had also begun as a labourer, and was living in one of the Cornham Farm cottages in 1881, but for some years after Robert Little junior emigrated to Australia in 1887/8, he looked after the Deer Park herding, and it was not until 1894 that Donald MacDougal came down from Scotland to replace him.

Of the shepherds who had come down from Scotland prior to—or during the early 1870's, only four were left on Exmoor in 1898, and one of these—John Gourdie—had ended his employment as a shepherd, when, on Lady Day of the same year, he took the tenancy of Wintershead Farm and an allotment, which included the land that for many years past had been his herding. William Davidson, shepherd at Hoar Oak in 1871, and later at Winstitchen, was also still on the Moor, as was Robert Tait Little at Duredon, and William Little, who had just moved from Pinkery to Toms Hill to take charge of the double herding at Larkbarrow in an exchange with one of the later arrivals, John Hewitt, who replaced Peter Murray in 1892. Donald MacDougal, who took the Deer Park (S. Forest) herding in 1894, was also still around, and on the offlying herding of Badgworthy, Thomas Armstrong, who took over from Thomas Graham in 1893, was likewise still there. Descendants of the latter have lived on the fringe of the Moor ever since, farming at Wilsham in Countisbury parish, and at Parracombe. James Johnstone, the shepherd of the Hoar Oak herding since 1886, was still living at Hoar Oak. In fact, he remained there until his death a few years later in 1904.

It was not my intention when I began this chapter to continue it beyond Sir Frederic Knight's lifetime, but there is so much left unsaid about Robert T. Little, and the upheaval the shepherds were subjected to by the re-arrangement of the herdings and accommodation in the years immediately following Viscount Ebrington's accession to the Exmoor and Brendon Estates—when he reverted to Sir Frederic's earlier policy of letting as many farms and as much land as possible—that it seems pointless to end this chapter without at least pursuing the story of Sir Frederic Knight's shepherds to either their departure from the Moor, or in some cases, to their deaths.

The changeover had not been an easy one for Robert T. Little. There appears to have been a certain amount of friction between him and the Exmoor Agent, George Cobley Smyth Richards, which was not lessened when the latter went over his head in the re-arrangement of the shepherds at the Larkbarrow herding. This was shortly after William Little's transfer from Pinkery to Toms Hill in 1898, and no doubt the Agent believed it was a good idea to have William's son (also William) as undershepherd on the double herding.

There was, however, an ulterior motive in this arrangement, for in removing Thomas Davidson (who was the Larkbarrow shepherd) to Cornham in time to help with the lambing, it left Larkbarrow Big House—where he had been living—free to let. A letter written by G.C. Smyth Richards to Viscount Ebrington a little later, confirms that arrangements had been made to let the house as a hunting and shooting box, and from that time on until it was abandoned to the army as a training ground during the last war it was always let in this way.

There was also some bias shown in the Agent's early letters to Viscount Ebrington, in which his reports indicated that the sheep on the Home Farm at Castle Hill, Filleigh, were always doing or looking better than those on Exmoor, which, with far better keep available, they should have done, but after a while there appears to have been a growing awareness that Robert T. Little, and the shepherds under him, were extremely capable men and losses of sheep and lambs—apart from those in unforeseen blizzard conditions—were no worse than those on the better land of the Home Farm.

In December 1897, shortly after Viscount Ebrington took possession of the Exmoor and Brendon Estates, the first batch of ewe hoggs sent down to Castle Hill for the winter began to suffer losses from what was believed to be Braxy, a mysterious illness practically unheard of today, which strangely affected only young sheep, and then only from November to February when it was immediately gone. In the past, Sir Frederic Knight had on occasions called in the 'Vets' to treat these sheep, and they were drenched with we know not what, but were apparently cured. After similar treatment by Robert Little no further losses were reported.

The largest get-together or gathering of shepherds on Exmoor was at shearing time, and it must have been an impressive sight when the sheep were brought into the pens at Simonsbath, a flock at a time, to be sheared in the traditional Scottish style which considerably differ from our own.• It was the custom of the Scottish shepherds to sit on the narrow end of a wedge shaped form about four feet long, the shearers never leaving their seat, with the sheep brought to them, and after shearing taken away, marked, and the fleeces tied by other helpers. This was, of course, long before the days of mechanical clippers, all sheep being hand shorn, but this was not the slow operation one would expect it to be, and on one occasion for a wager, Donald MacDougal took on the challenge of shearing a sheep in under two and-a-half minutes. The bet was for a bottle of Whisky, and needless to say, with such a prize at stake, Donald completed his task within the stated time. To anyone familiar with shearing, even with modern shearing techniques and the latest equipment, this was no mean feat.

•Shearing also took place at Larkbarrow and Hoar Oak.

In 1898, the trade for fat lambs was in a very depressed state. The wool trade was no better, and it was not until January 1899 that Brintons of Kidderminster made an offer of 5½d. a pound to clear the lot, and to keep up old connections (implying that they had also been buyers of wool from Frederic Knight). Although this was probably the best offer they were prepared to make in the circumstances, it was refused. Approaches were made elsewhere, but with no better results, and the wool was eventually sold to Brintons for about the price first offered.

The loss of a few lambs at Larkbarrow in the summer of 1898 caused some concern. A dog was believed to be responsible, but G.C. Smyth Richards commented that it was a curious thing that once a fortnight we lose a lamb, then the killing seems to stop. A later comment was: 'It must be a dog as the torn skin and part of the sheep has been found on nearly every occasion', but the regularity of the killings suggest that a two legged animal was more likely to have been responsible. Several sheep were killed at Larkbarrow later the same year, but in this instance six or seven hounds lost by Mr. Amory were believed to have been responsible.

On Lady Day 1899, Cornham Farm was let to William Kingdom. Some of the ewes from this herding were added to other herdings, but the bulk of them—443 in all—were sent to Castle Hill.

The next farm to be let was Duredon (1901), where Robert T. Little had been living for the past 30 years, and it is doubtful if he was at all pleased with having to move into the Limecombe Cottage, which, although not far away, was not of the same dimensions or quality. An undated plan of a proposed conversion of two cottages at Limecombe into one, may have been carried out at this time, greatly improving the accommodation there and making it more habitable. With a certain amount of reshuffling of the herdings and spare land, the Duredon herding was retained. From that time on it was also known as the Limecombe herding.

Winstitchen was the next herding to suffer, when the farm and most of the improved land around it was let in 1903, but with certain adjustments, sufficient land was left to continue the herding. It was at this time that the old mine cottage at Wheal Eliza was utilised as a base for the shepherd. Thereafter, this herding has always been referred to as Mines. Thomas Elworthy junior, who had just given up this cottage, had been there for nearly 40 years, and there, he and his wife Ann had raised a large family, with Thomas working as a jobbing labourer, taking whatever work was available, and his wife taking in laundry to help make ends meet. For a time while he was working for Frederic Knight he had paid no rent, but later this was fixed at £4. 4. 0 per annum, reduced by Viscount Ebrington to £3. 12. 0. On his retirement Thomas Elworthy moved into a cottage adjoining Winstitchen, where he died in 1924, at the age of 85.

The uprooting of some of the Exmoor shepherds from their homes and herdings, to which they had become deeply attached, was solely due to Viscount Ebrington's decision to let as many of his farms as possible, and though this may have been necessary from the financial point of view, it had the immediate effect of undermining the morale of the remaining shepherds, who were left wondering as to just how secure was their own position, and it was around this time that some of the familiar shepherds names began to disappear from the Moor.

This was the case with William Davidson, who was first employed by Frederic Knight on the Hoar Oak herding, prior to 1870, and later at Winstitchen. At the time this herding was let as a farm in 1903, William was the longest serving shepherd on Exmoor, but neither he or any member of his large family remained on the Moor to take the newly created Mines herding. They either returned to Scotland, or took employment elsewhere. The first shepherd at Wheal Eliza, also from Scotland, was a man named Bain, who arrived in 1903 and returned to Scotland in 1910; his place was then taken by Donald MacDougal.

With much of the better land now let, an increased demand was put on the remaining herdings, which were for the most part rough moorlands. In an effort to improve the quality of the sheepkeep, grassland experiments were begun in 1903, and continued over a period of five years. Various types of fertilizer were used on six equal sized plots. Eight Cheviot wether hoggs were kept on each plot, being weighed in on 23rd May and weighed again on 10th October. The total weight gains on each plot were then recorded: Plot number one had no fertilizer dressing whatsoever, for comparison with the other five plots; the total weight gain here in 1903 was 191 lbs for the eight sheep. Plots five and six, dressed with 12½ cwt of Super Phosphate and 30 cwt of ground lime, and a straight 12¾ cwt of Super Phosphate respectively, showed no improvement at all: Plots two, three and four, received 12 tons of lime, 12¾ cwt of Super Phosphate, plus 150 lbs of Potash and 15 cwt of Basic Slag, respectively, benefitted to a much greater degree, showing total sheep weight gains of 234 lbs, 231 lbs and 230 lbs, but results over the five year period were inconclusive, and on Robert T. Little's death in 1907 the grassland trials ceased.

At the age of 65, Robert Little went into a London Hospital for an operation, and while he was undergoing surgery died on the operating table (17.9.1907). His body was brought home and interred at Simonsbath, in the midst of his beloved Exmoor sheepherdings that, for the past 36 years had been his life. He proved to have been a very prudent and careful man where money was concerned. Out of the 25/- he had been paid each week as head shepherd he had saved £1,350, a considerable fortune for a working man at that time. Because he had been so thrifty his widow was unable to draw a pension, as the interest on this money at two-and-a-half percent was considered quite adequate for her needs. This interest was paid twice yearly from the bank, and brought to her in sovereigns and half sovereigns at Limecombe, where she was still living with her son Tom.

While Robert Little was alive Tom had worked under him as a shepherd, for which he received the customary shepherd's wage of 20/- a week, from which his father deducted 8/- a week for his keep. This, with the 5/- Robert allowed his wife, made up the 13/- she was expected to keep house on, which, being fair, was no less than most households had to live on, and was further supplemented by keeping a couple of pigs and a few hens. The remaining 12/- of Tom's wages were set aside and banked for him by his father, and by the time of Robert's death Tom had £400 in his own account. Shortly after this, Tom married, but continued to live at Limecombe until after his mother's death in 1917, when, on the terms of his father's will, he inherited £600; the remainder of his father's money being shared between Tom's brothers and sisters. In 1920, with £1,000 in the bank, Tom took the tenancy of South View and the small-holding that went with it and there can have been few men who started farming on Exmoor with more capital than this, and later, when he moved to a larger holding at Cloven Rocks, success seemed assured, but there was little or no profit in farming in the 30's, and it is believed he finished farming with less money than he started with. Farming then, as now, requires more than an element of luck to be successful.

Robert T. Little was a remarkable man in many ways. He was educated far beyond the standard of the ordinary working man of his day and kept meticulous records of everything connected with the herdings under his control. He was a capable man in other respects as well, particularly in his treatment of wounds, both animal and human. On one such occasion, which happened before the present Tom Little was born, Robert's son John (Tom's father) was cutting out hay from a rick when the hay knife he was using slipped and badly cut his leg, taking with it a large slice of flesh which was not entirely cut off but rolled back. Robert, who was noted for his skill in this kind of emergency, gathered up the roll of flesh and neatly sewed it back in place. So good a job did he make of it, that after it had healed no scar whatever could be seen. This was not the only case of its kind, and later, when George Molland (the Estate bailiff since 1892) inadvertently got his thumb between a hoof of his pony and the road and it was badly mangled, it was to Robert he turned to have it tidied up and reshaped.

There is a tradition handed down in the Little family that Robert Tait Little had trained as a dental surgeon before coming south to Exmoor. There is no doubting his skill with a needle and the treatment of wounds, but if this was so, why did he foresake a profession of such high standing to tend sheep on the bleak and lonely hills of Exmoor? The answer to this question has not been found, and it is most unlikely now that it will ever be known.

At the time of Robert's death the number of sheep herdings had been reduced from a maximum of ten, with 11 or 12 shepherds, to seven herdings with eight shepherds (including Badgworthy and the double Larkbarrow herding). With fewer herdings to look after there was no longer any need to employ a full time head shepherd, and George Molland assumed responsibility for these duties.

Taking stock of the situation shortly after Pinkery was let in 1912, reveals that there were now only two of Frederic Knight's former shepherds still living and working on Exmoor. William Little, the sole survivor of the shepherds who came down from Scotland in the early 1870's; and Donald MacDougal, who arrived in 1894. William Little, who had moved to Toms Hill from Pinkery in 1898, continued there until September 1925 when he was well into his 70's. He retired to the Lodge at Castle Hill, Filleigh, and remained there until his death in 1939 at the age of 88. His body was then taken back to Simonsbath for interment among the moorland hills that for over 50 years had been his home and constant companion.

Donald MacDougal, who had taken the Deer Park—or South Forest herding as it was later known—in 1894, was almost certainly in lodgings prior to his marriage to Ellen Little in the late 1890's, when they moved into one of the newly built West Gate Cottages that were completed in March 1899. Shortly afterwards, Donald approached G.C. Smyth Richards, because as yet he had no facilities for keeping a cow, one of the perks enjoyed by the shepherds, but one that was needed—especially at lambing time—to provide milk for the orphan lambs and others whose mothers had little or no milk on which to feed them. Later in Lord Fortescue's time two cows were provided, one of them being freshly calved at the appropriate time, but for the present, Donald MacDougal had to content himself with an extra 2/- a week, until his new cowhouse was built.

In 1910, Donald moved into the old Wheal Eliza Cottage to take charge of the Mines herding, which had been re-arranged to include much of his former herding. He remained at Mines for about ten years until his employment was terminated abruptly by George Molland—the Farm and Estate bailiff—who for some unknown reason had taken a dislike to Donald, and had for some time past been seeking a chance to dismiss him, but though he had on several occasions complained to G.C. Smyth Richards about Donald and the state of his herding, the Agent could never find anything wrong and had refused to sack him. Donald was a quiet man with a long beard that he was in the habit of constantly stroking, and a grave injustice was done to this fine shepherd (who lived for his sheep) when he was taken ill one lambing time and the two men sent to help him out lost many lambs, which resulted in George Molland giving Donald the sack. William Little's son, William—who was under-shepherd to his father on the Larkbarrow herding—on hearing of Donald's dismissal raised 'merry hell' and really tore off a strip to Molland, telling him he had sacked the wrong man and better fit he had sacked the B.....s he had sent down to help him, but it was no use, George Molland had made up his mind, and Donald had to go, and it is a wonder that William too was not sacked on the spot.

On leaving Exmoor, Donald went to live at Sherracombe, not far from the Poltimore Arms, Yarde Down; where he looked after the sheep on the offlying farm for two Brayford farmers, Messrs. Prideaux and Huxtable. When shearing time came around Donald was asked to take down enough sheep to Brayford to keep two shearers busy all day, but when he went to collect the sheep in the evening he was told that 'he had given the shearers something to get on with' implying that he had taken down more than enough, to which Donald replied, 'no more than I could shear myself laddie, no more than I could shear myself'.

Donald MacDougal died on 2nd September 1933 at the age of 76, and he too lies buried in the little churchyard at Simonsbath.

With the deaths of William Little and Donald MacDougal, the last link between Frederic Knight and the shepherds who came down from Scotland at his behest was broken, and though William Little's sons and grandsons were to continue to uphold the finest traditions of shepherding for many years more, an era had ended, and Exmoor was never quite the same again.

Footnote: In 1983 Aza Pinney drove a flock of Cheviot sheep from Hawick down to Simonsbath using many of the old drovers trails. This journey was filmed for Television and appeared in a series of half hour programmes in 1985.

CHAPTER 8

MINING ON EXMOOR PRE 1900

LONG before recorded history, man was at work on Exmoor digging out metallic ores, but just how long ago and who were the first miners there has to be a matter of conjecture. Possibly the Beaker Folk or men of the later Bronze Age discovered and worked small veins of copper within our region, but more probably it was the Celts of the Iron Age, for they were certainly familiar with the iron ore deposits on and around the Moor.

The earliest method of extracting the ore was known as 'patching', and at places where the iron lay close to the surface it was dug out, smelted, and made into tools and weapons. There are several sites on Exmoor that show signs of having been worked at an early date, notably at Exe Head, Moles Chamber, Hangley Cleave and Burcombe, although the so called 'Roman Lode' working which can be traced for some distance across the latter is of a much later date. MacDermot suggests that this may have been the work of Michael Wynston in the middle of the 16th century, who claimed to have found 'divers mines of iron and steele' within the Forests of Dartmoor and Exmoor and was granted a licence by Edward VI to dig for the same in 1550, but there is no evidence to show that it was Wynston who carried on the mining there, nor has anything been found to support MacDermot's other suggestion that it was the work of James Boevey a century later.

In between, however, in Elizabeth Ist reign, there was a period of intense mining activity in this country when a number of German miners were brought over to work our mines. At the time, the Germans were far in advance of our own countrymen in mining technology, and some of them are known to have reached our area, where they worked the iron ore deposits on Ison—or Eissen—Hill, which lies about midway between Winsford and Luckwell Bridge.

According to tradition, the Germans were also mining iron on Tabor Hill in the parish of North Molton, so it is not improbable that they were also involved with mining on Exmoor. If this was so, then one of the most likely places to have attracted their attentions could well have been the so called 'Roman Lode' on Burcombe.

This openwork, some 600 yards long and up to 30 feet deep, is still quite impressive, and must have yielded considerable quantities of iron ore. In fact, we now know that this lode was worked much deeper, as Frederic Knight found when he and Robert Smith were exploring the former's domain for iron ore in the early 1850's: Roughly in the centre of the long openwork, Smith sank a shaft 48 feet deep through mining deads (waste) —left by the old time miners—before reaching the lode, which at that point was four to five feet wide.

If mining to that depth was continuous over the 600 yards extent of the surface workings, then to remove such vast quantities of ore from this depth would have required a competent working knowledge of mining methods that were in all probability beyond the capabilities of our own miners at that time, but not that of the Germans. We know too, from later records, that pillars of ore were left in place to keep these workings from collapsing, and this, I believe, adds further support to my belief that the Roman Lode was worked either by the German miners, or under their supervision.

Michael Wynston, however, was—as far as is known—the first miner recorded as working on Exmoor. He also obtained a patent for erecting furnaces and forges for the manufacture of iron and 'steele', using moor coal (peat), but no trace has been found on Exmoor Proper of any such industrial remains. The only furnace (smelter) known to have existed in our area, apart from the traditional one near Exford, was at Sherracombe Ford in the parish of High Bray, where large quantities of smelting slag containing a high proportion of iron can still be found.

It was not until 1798, when Billingsley wrote his *General View of the Agriculture of the County of Somerset,* that mining on Exmoor is again referred to. He records that 'veins of both copper and iron have been discovered (on Exmoor) that might be worked to advantage, considering how convenient the situation is for shipping off the produce; Porlock, Lynmouth and Combe Martin, all sea ports, being not more than nine miles distant from the centre of the Forest. From each of these places, and also from Ilfracombe and Barnstaple, vessels are every week passing to Wales where foundries have been long established, in ballast'.

Although the location of the copper and iron veins are not given, there is a distinct possibility that the former relates to the mine later known as Wheal Eliza, the only mine at work in the Forest during John Knight's lifetime, having been worked for copper from 1846-1855 by a local syndicate. It was from this spot—which lies about one mile below Simonsbath beside the River Barle—that John Knight believed iron ore had earlier been extracted, although an unreliable informant had told him it was a copper mine.

A prospectus was issued in 1845 for this mine, which was to be called Wheal Maria, the shares being in units of £2, of which 256 were taken up. Russel Riccard, a solicitor; and John Cock, a builder; both of South Molton, together with Oliver Matthews, a mining agent from Molland, took up some of the shares, but the majority were acquired by Richard Sleeman, a surgeon from Tavistock, who is said to have disliked the name Maria and had it changed to Eliza.

On behalf of his father (who was now retired and living in Rome) Frederic Knight granted the syndicate a lease of a mining sett comprising the whole of Honeymead Farm—which at that time included the land of Winstitchen, Picked Stones and Cloven Rocks—for a term of 21 years. Although no dead rent was paid, Frederic was entitled to receive one-fifteenth of the value of the ores raised, less the carriage costs to its destination. Copper was the main objective, but all other metallic ores were included. Among the conditions laid down in the lease it was stipulated that six miners were to be kept at work, and anyone caught molesting or killing the Red Deer was liable to a fine of £25 for each and every offence. A further stipulation was that after 200 tons or ore had been raised six cottages were to be erected to house the miners, but as only one was built, the conclusions are obvious.

The syndicate appointed Oliver Matthews as Mine Captain and work commenced in 1846 sinking a shaft on a lode 20 feet and more in width, which lay close to the north bank of the river. This east-west lode had been exposed at surface for upwards of 100 fathoms and was in the centre of the sett which was two and a half miles long and one mile wide. Towards the end of the year, when the shaft was down four fathoms, Captain Matthews left. He was replaced by Joseph Pryor (or Prior) at a salary of £7. 7s. 0d. a month (later reduced by one guinea). In sinking the shaft deeper, Pryor discovered some good stones of copper. When analysed, these were shown to contain between 14¼% and 19¼% copper, which was comparable with the best that the well known Bampfylde mine at Heasley Mill could produce, and prospects for the new mine—considering the shallow depth this ore was discovered—looked very promising.

In making a whim round, Captain Pryor discovered a second lode, nine feet wide, 30 feet north of the shaft, and to prove the lodes an exploratory adit level was driven northwards from a point 60 yards east of the shaft. Before the year was out both of the lodes had been cut and followed east and west for a short distance. Other work completed in 1846 included the Blacksmiths and Carpenters Shops and the Account House. Essential as these buildings were to the well-being of the mine, Captain Pryor had cause to complain about the lack of a shed over the shaft and tackle, without which it was impossible for the men to stand and work there in times of severe weather.

To facilitate pumping and winding operations at the mine a 25 foot waterwheel was installed on the opposite—or south—bank of the Barle; power to the machinery being supplied via flatrods across the river. This work, together with 600 fathoms of leat cut around the hillside to bring water to the wheel from further up the Barle, and 150 fathoms of ground levelled off below the wheelpit to take away the tail water, was completed and in use before the end of May 1847.

In levelling the latter, a six inch wide branch of a lode containing very pretty yellow coated and black copper was discovered, and men were put to work costeaning on the hillside 200 fathoms east of the engine shaft, to cut this and the other lodes they were working on. Like most other mines Wheal Eliza had its share of problems; good miners were hard to find, as very few were interested in working in such an isolated spot, although the Census of 1851, taken a few years later, records a miner and his wife, and four other miners and a blacksmith living in the mine cottage, with another miner and his wife lodging in Simonsbath. Incidentally, the mine was still called Wheal Maria on the Census Returns.

Sinking the engine—or main—shaft continued, always with the promise of untold wealth just a few feet away. An adit level was driven from the mouth of the shaft to drain the north lode, where a second shaft was being sunk. This shaft (now covered at surface) continued down to at least five fathoms below the adit level, but very little development is thought to have taken place, and thereafter, in order to reach the north lode, crosscut levels were driven from the main shaft.

In 1848, Joseph Pryor was replaced as Mine Captain by Richard Moore. He began badly, when, shortly after his arrival, work came to a standstill on no less than three occasions after heavy rains broke down the banks of the leat, stopping the wheel from pumping out the flooded workings. In the following year a vast influx of water from melting snow again flooded the mine, which had now reached a depth of 24 fathoms. After this, things ran reasonably smoothly although very little ore worth saving was coming to the surface. Early in 1852—soon after the shaft had reached the 36 fathom level—a rich pocket of ore was discovered in one of the lodes and 40 whim hubbles of good ore were quickly raised before a drought in April again brought mining to a standstill. Whilst the dry weather continued, floors for dressing the ore were prepared. When work underground was resumed a month later, production from the mine reached its peak, and by July a larger dressing floor was under construction.

Hopes of a dividend for the shareholders, however, were short lived. By the end of the year the pocket of ore was nearly exhausted and very little good ore was now being raised.

A mining journal report in January 1853, discloses that the mine was unproductive, although sometimes very rich. It also stated that the shaft must be sunk deeper than 50 fathoms to open up the ground where three large lodes were expected to join. The 50 fathom level was reached in February, but this was in fact as deep as the mine went.

A certain amount of exploratory work was still going on in other parts of the sett, and a new lode—which was described as 'the most important discovery on Exmoor' was cut 700 fathoms east of the engine shaft. This ties up neatly with a known adit on the west bank of White Water, which is believed to have been quite extensive but is now blocked at the entrance and by a roof fall 85 feet inside. The adit is believed to have been the work of the Wheal Eliza Company, even though in later mining reports the area in which it was driven is described as virgin ground: No records of production have been found.

Before 1853 was out the Mine Captain was once more replaced, this time it was William Dunstan's turn to try his luck, but he was no more successful than his predecessors. The lodes at the 50 fathom level had been disordered by a slide, and output, small as it was, declined still further. In December, the waterwheel froze solid and several miners left, and though replacements were sought none could be found.

S N

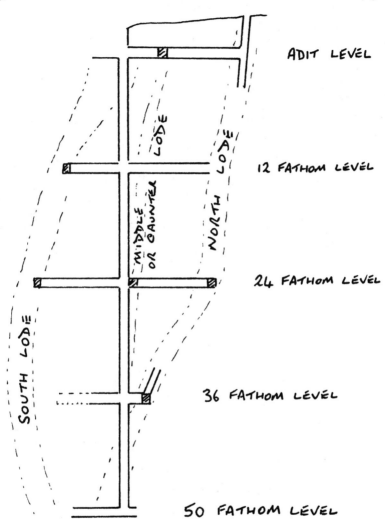

ADIT LEVEL

LODE

NORTH LODE

12 FATHOM LEVEL

MIDDLE OR GAUNTER

24 FATHOM LEVEL

SOUTH LODE

36 FATHOM LEVEL

50 FATHOM LEVEL

WHEAL ELIZA
CROSS SECTION OF MAIN SHAFT
PFC 1989

| 0 | 10 | FATHOMS |
| 0 | 60 | FEET |

Wheal Eliza Mine and ruined cottage

Honeymead Mine on Exe Cleave

In March 1854 a fine looking lode was discovered half a mile south of Wheal Eliza, probably where an adit was driven 60 feet into the hillside above the north bank of the River Barle, at a point opposite the mouth of the tributary stream coming down from Great Woolcombe, but from the appearance of the spoil heap it was sadly lacking in metallic ores.

The Adventurers hopes were temporarily raised, when, shortly after the above discovery, silver was found in one of the lodes in the Wheal Eliza mine, but as nothing more is heard of it we can assume it was either a very small pocket of this ore, or just as likely, planted there to revive the flagging interest of the shareholders; a not uncommon practice in similar circumstances in other such mines.

William Dunstan lasted only a year, and though another Mine Captain was appointed, time, money, and patience were running out, and when a further call on the shares was made in September 1854, many of the shareholders failed to respond and forfeited their shares. The end was in sight, and by June 1855 all operations by the mining syndicate had ceased. Altogether some £10,000 had been expended on the mine and the only results for nine years of hard labour were just a few tons of saleable ore. Throughout the mine's history it is apparent that copper ore was frequently met with in small quantities, but when the lode was followed it split into many small branches which were impossible to follow further.

On ceasing operations, Frederic Knight purchased (through a nominee) the remainder of the lease and all the mining machinery, in fact, everything at the mine, for the sum of £328. 17. 6.

Although a great deal is known about the Wheal Eliza mine during the nine year period of the mining syndicates existence, very little is known of the miners who worked there, who, for the most part, came from Cornwall. The maximum number employed underground at one time would appear to have been 11, and though it was a very wet mine, underground conditions were no worse than in many other mines, and probably the greatest hardship for the miners was the isolation and the distance from any large town or village where they could let their hair down and enjoy themselves.

It is hardly surprising, therefore, that when the miners did get the chance to get away from the Moor for a short period, they tended to make the most of it. Such was the case with Thomas Soper *(North Devon Journal* 29.6.1854), a young Cornish miner who was working on the Forest of Exmoor in 1854, who, after paying a visit to the watering places of the North Devon Golden Coast, calling at Combe Martin, Berrynarbor and Ilfracombe, he, like a million other fools before him, got drunk, and in that state went to Hele where he met a local man, Thomas Chugg, and soon a quarrel sprung up between the two men, followed by fisticuffs. A constable was sent for, who, in trying to arrest Soper, was kicked in the legs. At the Court hearing that followed, Soper was fined 10/- and ordered to pay £1. 17. 6 costs. He did not want for money, with a half sovereign in his watch and two more in his boots, and as he had the cash, the magistrate suggested that it would be as well if he could find the conscience to compensate the constable for the injury perpetrated on his legs, but after paying the fine and the costs, it is doubtful if Thomas Soper was inclined to agree.

On April 3rd 1856, Wheal Eliza was included in a mining sett leased to Messrs. Schneider and Hannay; a mining company from Ulverstone in Lancashire. They re-opened the mine and prospected it for iron for about 12 months without success, although some ir·ın ore was raised, but again, although the quality was good, it was not in sufficient quantity to justify the expense of getting it out.

One further event in the history of this mine occurred in 1858 when it was used by a cold blooded murderer to conceal the body of his unwanted daughter.

The story of William Burgess has been told and retold in practically every book written about Exmoor in the last 100 years, and with each retelling it has wandered further from the truth, until it has now reached such a level of absurdity that it needs to be related once more, this time sticking to the facts as given in contemporary newspaper reports of the day; and the story given by the Rev. Thornton, who was on the spot, and largely responsible for bringing Burgess to trial for his evil deed.

To get some insight into the character of William Burgess, it is necessary to go back to the Rev. Thornton's early days on Exmoor, when he was approached by Burgess with a hard luck story and asked to draw up a brief, which he could then take around the district to raise money to support his supposedly ill family. At this time he was living in a cottage beside White Water (Cow Castle Cottages), close to where the track from Winstitchen crosses the water en route for Picked Stones Farm. Although the Rev. Thornton refused to sign the brief, a friend of his was persuaded to do so, and later, both men suffered much discomfiture when accused of assisting a rogue to obtain money under false pretences, but by this time the damage was done, and Burgess was able to spend a week in South Molton on a drunken spree from the proceeds.

In January 1857, Burgess's wife died suddenly, and when the Reverend visited him shortly afterwards he had already made arrangements to place two of his children, Tom and Emma, into service with a Mr. Hayes, a North Molton farmer.[1] Burgess and his youngest daughter, Anna-Maria, where then going into lodgings in the village of Simonsbath.

It is at this point that most of the discrepancies in the stories since told, begin. Nearly all state that Anna-Maria was an only child, but the Rev. Thornton has already referred to two more, and shortly—as we shall see— another daughter turns up. In 1890, J.L.W. Page says that 'Burgess had but one child, a daughter, who it is said was obnoxious to the woman her father intended to marry, so the unnatural father determined on her destruction and the poor girl as murdered.'

Many writers have since drawn on this account for their own story, but there is no evidence to suggest that Burgess intended to marry again, and there was certainly no woman forthcoming, either before, during, or after his trial.

These stories are bad enough, but the one that really takes the biscuit is recorded in *Days of Renown* by J.M. Slader, in which Burgess is said to have objected to the one his daughter intended to marry. What, at six years of age! The original source of this story is unknown, but a little more was added to it in the 1983 AA publication *Discovering Britain,* which relates that Burgess was a widower who had but one daughter who he ruled possessively, and when she became engaged he objected strongly. She refused to break the engagement and in a fit of rage, Burgess killed her. Where will it end? The truth is—uninteresting as it may be—that she was murdered to save the 2s. 6d. a week it was costing Burgess to keep her.

For a few weeks prior to Anna-Maria's death she had been in lodgings with her father at the home of John and Sarah Marley, in one of the two cottages opposite the Gallon House Inn. It was a most unsatisfactory arrangement, with father and daughter sharing a bed with a fellow lodger, William Cockram of Exford, who was at that time an underground worker in the same mine as Burgess, who was employed on the surface.

On Saturday the 24th July 1858, Burgess asked Mrs. Marley to get all of Anna-Maria's clothes together as he intended to take her to Porlock on the following day to lodge with his sister, and at the ungodly hour of 3 o'clock on Sunday morning, Burgess and his daughter left the Marley's. It was about 3 o'clock in the afternoon when he returned to his lodgings, and, as expected, he returned alone. Soon after this, Burgess started to become restless and talked about leaving Exmoor. When he was asked if he proposed to take his daughter with him, he replied that he surely would take her to a better place. On the 10th August he left Exmoor for an unknown destination, although he left some of his belongings behind, and it was shortly after this that suspicions were first aroused that all was not as it should be, when John Mills, the son of the proprietor of Gallon House and farm, discovered the remnants of a fire, which was in the shape of a beehive, on an allotment about two fields away from the rear of the Inn. On running his foot through the mound he uncovered buttons, hooks and eyes, and pieces of partly burnt cotton print, which in colour and material were identical to Anna-Maria's spare pinafore. Word of this find soon reached the Rev. Thornton, and William Court, the Forester, quickly departed for Porlock to check out Burgess's story, which was soon found to be only partly true. He had certainly been there on the Sunday in question, but he arrived alone, and after staying only a short while, he had left alone.

By this time, Burgess had completely disappeared, and on William Court's return with the news, the vicar asked the local constable, William Fry, to go to Lynmouth, to see if Burgess had slipped across to Wales. On the following morning, the Rev. Thornton, now fully convinced that Burgess had done away with his daughter, set off on horseback at 3 a.m. heading for Taunton and Curry Rivel—about ten miles further east—to consult with the Chief Constable of Somerset who lived there. He arrived at 8 a.m. and in half an hour, his story told, the two men were in the saddle on the long journey back to Exmoor. On reaching Gallon House they were met by a number of people, who cried out that they had found the grave amongst the deads of an old mining trench, not far from the now deserted Wheal Eliza Mine. The search party had cleared it out, but the grave was empty.

On arriving back at Simonsbath the two men were met by Constable Fry, who reported that Burgess had indeed crossed to Wales, having been taken over to Swansea in old Ned Groves boat on Friday last.

(It should be noted here that in many details—including dates—the Rev. Thornton's account and the reports in the *North Devon Journal* conflict with one another, so, to a large extent I have used the reports in the *North Devon Journal* as a basis for this story. This is not because of any prejudice against the Rev. Thornton, but because his account was not written until some 40 years after the events, and as we know only too well, the memory plays strange tricks. This was certainly so when he wrote of his journey to Curry Rivel to see the Chief Constable, who he mistakenly believed was Superintendent Jeffs, but in fact, was a man named Goold or Gould.)

Superintendent Cresant Jeffs, the head of the Wiveliscombe Division of Police, was, however, in charge of the case, and he was the man who accompanied Constable Fry to Lynmouth and across to Swansea to apprehend Burgess and bring him back for questioning on suspicion of murder. Burgess was quickly found, working on the construction of the New Docks at Swansea. After his arrest he asked if they had found the little maid, and on hearing that by now they surely had, he broke down and said he wished to die as he would never be happy again. He then asked that his box—which was still on Exmoor—should be given to his daughter Emma, and the £2. 6. 0½ in his pocket to his son Tom, but no mention was made of his other children.

Despite a relentless search, the body of Anna-Maria had not been found when the trio returned to Exmoor, and Burgess flatly refused to answer when asked what he had done with her. With little if any progress being made—although the search was continuing—Superintendent Jeffs offered a reward of £10 to any person giving information that resulted in the finding of the body of the little girl. Burgess, who had been charged at Exford with 'wilful murder', was then taken to Dulverton where he found a large crowd assembled, among them his own daughter, a strong country girl of about 16 dressed in black. She had walked from Winsford where she was in service, but after telling her she had no business there, Burgess had nothing more to say to her.

In the *North Devon Journal* report on 2nd September, Burgess is described as a 'mild looking man of about 40, of middle height, light complexion, large blue eyes and light brown hair and short bushy whiskers. His facial expression betokes a spirit of reckless determination and cruelty, and there is a complete absence of that pleasing look of intelligence which is usually found in the glowing countenance of a sober, thrifty and industrious English peasant',

Week after week the search for the body of Anna-Maria went on, and the Dulverton magistrates were saying that as there was not sufficient evidence that a crime had been committed, they could not hold the prisoner much longer, but shortly after this came the breakthrough they had all been praying for, when a man came forward and said that he could throw some light on the matter, providing his own behaviour was overlooked. Having agreed to this, he told them that on the Tuesday night after the child disappeared he was on the hillside above the deserted Wheal Eliza mine, about half way between the grave and the mine. He admitted he was up to no good, and on hearing footsteps he had hidden and someone passed below him going towards the mine, but in the darkness he saw nothing.

With this clue as to the probable whereabouts of the girl's body, a diver named Holward, from an eminent London firm, was brought in to search the flooded mine *(North Devon Journal* 23.9.1858) but because of the peculiar construction of the shaft he was unable to descend far enough into the mine to conduct a proper search while such a vast body of water remained in the workings. On hearing this, the Dulverton magistrates said that they would have the mine pumped out. If nothing was found, they would foot the bill.

It was about this time that Burgess, aware that the game was up, attempted to commit suicide. PC Taylor of Exford, who knew the prisoner well, had gone to Dulverton Gaol and taken breakfast into Burgess's cell and temporarily removed his handcuffs. For a brief moment PC Taylor had turned his back on Burgess, and in the short time that his back was turned the prisoner had thrust the points of a pair of scissors into his throat and was attempting to open up the wound. He was quickly restrained from doing further damage to himself, his wounds were treated, and shortly afterwards he was removed to Taunton Gaol to await his trial.

Tenders to drain the mine had been invited by the Dulverton magistrates, and the lowest tender of £250 from Thomas Scuse (or Skewis) a mining engineer—who lived at Molland—and his partners was accepted. Pumping operations to dewater the mine were commenced on 16th October, but shortly after, the delapidated machinery broke down. After repair pumping continued steadily through the rest of October and into November. By the end of the month the mine was all but dry, but unfortunately the air in the workings was so foul it was impossible to climb down the shaft to see to the pumps and the mine began to flood again. This was quickly rectified, and on the 2nd December a large party gathered at the mine to assist with the next part of the operation.

Here again we have differing accounts of exactly what did happen that day, but as the Rev. Thornton's account is the more colourful we will give this first and point out the basic differences after.

The Reverend Thornton's Story
'I called for a volunteer to go down the mine and a young man stepped forward. We tied a rope under his arms and I told him to jerk on it if he was overcome by bad air. The old mine ladder was still in place down the shaft, rotten, green and mouldy, but down this he went while 20 of us held the rope. When he reached the bottom the rope slackened and we eased off. Presently he jerked the rope, and hand over hand, aided by the rope he climbed to the surface. I shall never forget that moment when his young face, ghastly with bad air and distorted with toil, appeared on the surface. In his arms he carried a large parcel wrapped in a seaman's tarpaulin coat and bound with tarred cord. I cut the cord, inside was a guano bag. I slit this and inside was another bag and inside this was the body. There was an old cottage beside the abandoned mine in which was one sound room. I locked the bundle in and sent a servant at full gallop to Dulverton with the news.'

In the report in the *North Devon Journal* of 9th December 1858 (in which no mention of the Rev. Thornton is made) it was Thomas Scuse and his partner John Moffat who went down into the mine; principally to check that the pumps were in proper order. On reaching the bottom of the shaft (which they give as 36 fathoms although mining journal reports of February 1853 and after give it as 50 fathoms) they discovered the bundle, and between them and the help of a windlass they brought the body to the surface, where PC Taylor was waiting with a large crowd. The bundle was opened and the body of the child and two large stones were revealed. The body was immediately placed into a box of water from the mine to prevent it from decomposing further; the lid of the box was nailed down, and box and contents placed in the Smith's shop close by and securely locked in, PC Taylor taking away the key.

In a short while the coroner arrived, accompanied by three doctors, several policemen and a magistrate. The body was examined and though the face was partly gone the remains were very little decomposed. The doctors stated that the body was a female child of about seven years old, and Mrs. Marley identified it as being Anna-Maria by her hair and the clothes she was wearing.

The Rev. Thornton was asked by the Coroner to remain during the Post Mortem and he was forced to watch this sickening spectacle. The result of the PM was that Anna-Maria Burgess had suffered a fractured skull but her death was probably due to suffocation.

With the cause of her death established, the mangled remains of the poor little mite were handed to the vicar for Christian burial, which was carried out as reverently as was possible.

A Jury of 12 men had been sworn in following the Post Mortem at the mine and they went off to Exford to hold the inquest; where a verdict of wilful murder was recorded against William Burgess, who was awaiting trial at the forthcoming Assizes at Taunton. The Rev. Thornton was subpoenaed to appear at the Assizes on 20th December 1858, and arrived there after a 30 mile ride over rough roads, only to find, after hanging about all day, that the trial was adjourned until Monday. It now being Saturday, and with his customary Sunday duties to perform, the vicar now had to travel all the way home again. At ten o'clock on Monday morning he was back in Taunton as requested for the trial, where, as expected, with all the damning evidence there was against him, Burgess was found guilty of the wilful murder of his daughter and sentenced to death. He was afterwards seen by the Rev. Thornton and immediately acknowledged his guilt, but when asked why he had done such a dreadful deed, he replied that she cost him 2s. 6d. a week and that when he did not pay, Marley's wife kept pestering him for the money. The child was in his way, in everybody's way, and he thought she would be better off out of it. His one request was to see his son Tom and his daughter Emma once more before his sentence was carried out.

After travelling home to Simonsbath, the Rev. Thornton dined, and then rode on to North Molton to see the Burgess children, who knew nothing of the death of their sister, but were not in the least surprised, and said that they considered their own lives were not safe from their father. It took all of the vicar's powers of persuasion to get them to go to Taunton, where Burgess saw them for the last time and wept. On the morning of January 7th 1859, he was hanged in front of the Somerset County Gaol. An attempt to keep the day and the time of his execution secret had been made, but word got about, and at 9 a.m. a large crowd had gathered to witness his end. An hour after the hanging, Burgess was cut down and his body buried within the precincts of Taunton Gaol.

Wheal Eliza Mine was never again reopened. It is doubtful if any miners —who are notably superstitious—would have been persuaded to set foot in the mine after that fateful day when little Anna-Maria was precipitated from this world into the next.

By August 1865 all hopes or reopening the mine had passed, and Mr. John Gould, the Barnstaple auctioneer, was instructed to auction off the whole of the mining plant, but in order to remove the pumps it would have been necessary to dewater the mine once more, so they were left in place, the top section still visible above the debris of the filled in shaft. Of the cottage that once housed the miners very little remains. Gone too are the mine buildings, but it is still possible to trace some of their sites. Sizeable spoil heaps surround the shaft and samples of Pyrites, Chalcopyrites, Chalcocite, Malachite, Manganese Oxide and other minerals can still be picked up. On the opposite bank of the river part of the wheel pit remains, and the leat that fed the wheel can still be easily traced back to its point of entry; not far below Simonsbath.

In following the history of the Wheal Eliza and the story of Burgess, we have gone ahead of events happening elsewhere on the mining scene, and it is necessary to go back to the early 1850's, when Frederic Knight, in a desperate effort to increase the revenue of his estate, turned to the mineral resources of his land. Spurred on by the success of the iron mines at work to the east of Exmoor on the Brendon Hills, and convinced that similar quantities of iron ore lay under his own property, Frederic and his Agent, Robert Smith, spent many a long day searching for the ore bearing lodes, with considerable success. In the late 1850's, the Rev. Thornton, in Frederic's company, continued the search for iron, exploring ground to the far corners of the old Forest.

Satisfied in his own mind that there were substantial reserves of iron ore on his estate, Frederic called in the experts, and in 1853 a Mr. Samuel Blackwell and his brother-in-law Ebeneezer Rogers (both of whom had been involved at the start of the mining boom in the Brendon Hills) arrived on the Moor. They quickly confirmed Frederic Knight's opinion that there were large iron ore reserves beneath the surface of his land, and on one of the lodes that had been exposed by exploratory costean trenches in a corner of the old Deer Park—adjoining the road from Bluegate to Simonsbath, and the road into Wintershead and Horsen—they sank a shaft 45 feet deep and raised 62 tons of ore, before a severe recession in the iron trade called a halt for the time being of all mining operations there.

The mine was still at this stage in its development when Schneider and Hannay took the large sett, which included the Deer Park and the Wheal Eliza, but did not extend as far as Honeymead. Also included was a large area north of the Simonsbath to Challacombe road, which extended as far as the Hoar Oak boundary. The lease for this sett was taken for a term of 43 years at a dead rent of £2,000 per annum, plus royalties of 1s. 3d. a ton for iron ore, and 8d. a ton for iron claystone. The company also offered to pay £7,000 towards the cost of a proposed railway to the coast.

Mining commenced at Blue Gate by deepening the shaft opened by Rogers, and three other shafts were sunk close by. A report in the *North Devon Journal* June 6th 1856, states that machinery and other requisites destined for the mine had been shipped over from Wales and was now being unloaded. In a further report on August 21st 1856, Messrs. Schneider and Hannay were said to be carrying on their operations with great spirit; the steam engines for raising the ore and for pumping out the mine were put to work last Saturday and were found to work perfectly and answered their purpose well.

Lying in a particularly wet area of Exmoor, water caused problems right from the start, and an adit driven from the valley below for drainage would have been a great advantage. According to the *Reclamation of Exmoor Forest* one was started but not completed. It was said to have been cut from close to the River Barle, but the only adit that I can find of this period—heading in the right direction—lies under the saddle of a spur of rock which protrudes from the east side of the lower part of Drybridge Combe, but as it has only been driven 16 feet southwards, it is unlikely to be the adit we are looking for. Another adit can be found at the head of the eastern branch of the same combe, just below Drybridge, where it was driven east-south-east on a lode for 130 feet, passing under the Simonsbath to South Molton road, but this was on a different lode and unconnected with the main workings, and was in fact the work of Henry Roberts for the Exmoor Mining Syndicate in 1910-1912.

About one mile roughly to the east of the Blue Gate Mine, lying between the enclosure on Great Woolcombe and the road from Blue Gate to Horsen, two long mining trenches 150 yards apart were cut from north to south, probably to find the extent of the lodes of the aforesaid mine. In the trench nearest Blue Gate a pit was sunk on a lode and samples of ore heavy with iron still lie there. Two hundred and twenty yards west of this trench a series of pits and mounds extending 100 yards in an east-west direction, are, I believe, of much earlier date, and this is probably one of the places where miners of old (the 'Ancients') patched the surface for iron.

In the northern part of their sett, Schneider and Hannay made little effort to find ore, but there is a trial adit about half way up Tangs Bottom (I hope it wasn't too painful) to the west of Duredon Farm. This adit, driven northwards through the side of a hill, ends in a deep pit where it comes out to daylight. It is now very wet and silted up for the whole of its length of 177 feet.[2] A little further up the same valley, samples of iron ore can be found in a spoil heap that has obviously come from the cut in the hillside nearby.[*]

The only other workings of note in the northern section of the sett are in the combe that runs from Hoar Oak Hill to Gammon Corner; west of the ancient circular enclosure. This working is probably a little more extensive than at first believed, for not only is there a sizable spoil heap beside the stream, but just above and to the east of where this spoil came from, a hole has recently appeared, suggesting that a sinkage has occurred into a level driven below. Three large pits east of this hole, and another trial a little way up the valley, complete the industrial remains in this area.

At the end of 12 months Schneider and Hannay had raised only 800 tons of iron ore, and they were now convinced that there were no large workable deposits of iron within their sett and accordingly gave notice of their intentions to quit. Frederic Knight, firmly convinced that there was, and believing the company had not given the mining a fair trial in accordance with the terms of their contract, promptly sued them for failing to meet their obligations, but even though he won the day, Schneider and Hannay opted to pay him £10,000 to be released from their contract, rather than to continue working the mines as had been hoped.

During this period, when the mining boom was at its height, two other companies were at work on Exmoor. A lease that had been granted to Anthony Hill of the Plymouth Iron Company (although they came from Merthyr Tydfil) on January 14th 1857, included most of the Honeymead land east of Wheal Eliza, and a further section north of the Simonsbath to Exford road; extending as far as Larkbarrow in the north-eastern part of the old Forest. The lease for this sett cost the company £500 dead rent per annum, with royalties the same as Schneider and Hannay. The main

---

[*]There was also an adit driven into the hillside west of Limecombe Water, between the plantation and the cottage.

workings of this company were at Picket—or Picked—Stones on the hillside east of White Water, about 450 yards north-east of Cow Castle.

Of all the mines on Exmoor this has proved the hardest to evaluate, owing to the difficulty in separating the mining work done there by the Plymouth Iron Co., from that done over 50 years later by the Exmoor Mining Syndicate. Records of the earlier period are particularly hard to come by, but by piecing together what we do know it is now believed that the Plymouth Iron Co. sank a shaft to a depth of 65 feet below the surface workings, which were in turn 15 feet below the level of the surrounding ground.

The company also commenced driving an adit level east of the shaft. A further adit level was begun beside White Water, some 300 yards away, this level being driven eastwards towards the shaft. We know nothing of the output of the mine at this time, but Mineral Statistics give a total of 1500 tons of Spathose ore produced on Exmoor in 1857, some of which could have come from this mine. According to an Exford farmer there was also an adit level behind a big rock higher up the White Water valley beyond the Picked Stones-Winstitchen track, and close to where the water divides. This too, was probably the work of the same company, but although this adit was known to be open in 1939, it cannot now be traced.

Housing accommodation for the miners working at Picked Stones was very limited, and farm buildings at the nearby Picked Stones and Winstitchen farms were converted into temporary sleeping quarters, with other miners lodging at Simonsbath or anywhere else they could find a room.

Shafts sunk in the field north of the Exford-Simonsbath road, opposite Gypsy Lane, and a possible adit driven northwards towards Red Deer Cottages from the lower part of the field in which they stand, are also believed to be the work of the Plymouth Iron Co., but neither the extent of the workings or the output are known.

On the steep slopes of Exe Cleave, in a very spectacular and lovely part of Exmoor, the Plymouth Iron Co. commenced work on a second mine, and from the Honeymead Mine—as is is believed to have been known— 500 tons of carbonated iron ore is said to have been raised in 1858. Mining on Exe Cleave was confined to a small surface working and a shaft close by, but like most of the Exmoor mines it was very wet, and an adit was driven south to the shaft for drainage. The entrance of this tunnel is finely arched with stone for a distance of 30 feet, but thereafter is in solid rock. About 115 feet from the adit mouth the level is blocked off at the point where it meets the shaft, which has been filled in. Outwardly there is little sign of any great mining activity here, but a stone building of some kind was erected, the ruins of which still remain.

According to F.J. Snell in his *Book of Exmoor,* the Plymouth Iron Co., in conjunction with the Abervale Co. (Ebbw Vale?) carried out some exploratory work in the North Forest at Sparcombe. Mining work in this area was mainly confined to the triangular section of land between Ramscombe, Sparcombe, and a later boundary formed by the bed of the railroad cut by Frederic Knight for his long dreamed of railway to the coast. A dream that was never to come true. If this railway had been completed and in use, a little more effort might have been put into the mining there, but as it was, the sum total of the work carried out amounted to no more than a few trial pits and trenches and an 85 foot long adit driven northwards from the gully inside Knight's boundary hedge adjoining Sparcombe Water. So ended the Plymouth Iron Co's. attempts to raise iron ore on Exmoor and they also faded from the scene.

The Dowlais Iron Co., also from Merthyr Tydfil, was the third mining company at work on Exmoor at this time: William Llewellyn, an independent mining consultant,· had, with confident assurance, given them a very high opinion of the prospects; an opinion that was soon confirmed by Dowlais's own managers, and shortly afterwards Dowlais followed their recommendations and leased 2,090 acres of mining ground to the east and south of the adjoining sett held by Schneider and Hannay. The lease was to run for 42 years, with a minimum dead rent of £500 payable for the first year, and £1,000 per annum thereafter, plus 1s. per ton on all iron ore raised.

On the whole of Exmoor there was no more promising area for mining than that now held by Dowlais, where a number of important lodes outcropped, including Hangley Cleave and the 'Roman Lode' on Burcombe, where there was every reason to believe considerable iron ore reserves lay beneath the surface workings of the 'Ancients'.

The arrival of Dowlais on Exmoor was dutifully recorded in the *North Devon Journal* of 29th November 1855, where it was seen as a welcome move towards increasing the prosperity of the whole district; 40 tons of mining plant had arrived the previous week and was awaiting conveyance to the Forest, and though the lease did not officially come into force until 1st January 1856, a number of miners and engineers had arrived with the plant.

Surveyors employed by Frederic Knight were busy in the surrounding district, with a view to laying down a light railway to the coast, either to Lynmouth or Porlock Weir, because it was quickly realised by all the parties concerned with mining on Exmoor, that unless they could quickly overcome the problems of transporting the large quantities of iron ore they were shortly expecting to raise, to a port on the north coast for shipment to the furnaces and foundries in South Wales,·· then there was going to be little point in mining this iron ore.

Frederic Knight—because of the protracted Chancery Court actions with his brothers and sisters—was in no position to finance the construction of the railway himself, and Dowlais had agreed to supply such rails and iron work as were needed, and with the help of the £7,000 promised by Schneider and Hannay it was hoped that the railway would be

---

·Brought in by Frederic Knight, and also acted as his mining agent, handling both Dowlais and Schneider and Hannay's agreements.
··And Staffordshire.

soon built. So confident were Dowlais at this time of quickly extracting a large and continuous supply of iron ore, that they declined to renew or make fresh contracts for the future supply of iron to their foundries, and by the end of November 1855 they were hard at work on Exmoor.

The first lode to attract their attentions was the Cornham Vein, which outcropped at a point 85 yards south-east of Cornham Ford, where an adit level was driven and a shaft sunk on the lode. By June 1856, 100 tons of ore were stacked on the surface to await transport to Lynmouth, and by August 12th, 15 tons of iron ore a day was leaving the mine, but after 175 tons of ore had been brought out the vein became too narrow to work, and shortly after, it was abandoned. Another attempt to find ore was made a little nearer the ford, but it was not productive. A third level on the south side of the river—just below the footbridge across the Barle—also yielded nothing of value, and after being driven 35 feet, it too was abandoned. North of the river a very short tunnel driven into the steep hillside above the trackway to Cornham Farm also came to nothing, but great things were expected of the Main Drift which was begun on Christmas Eve, at a point 170 yards north-east of the ford.

This drift, a very ambitious undertaking, was to be driven southwards through the sett for a distance of nearly two thirds of a mile, in order to prove at depth a number of iron veins, including the Roman Lode and Rogers Lode —which had first been opened up by Ebeneezer Rogers in 1853 in the adjoining sett; afterwards worked by Schneider and Hannay.

Because of the extremely hard rock, progress in the drift was painfully slow, and though it had been anticipated that it would take 18 months to complete, this proved to be totally unrealistic, even though three teams of miners worked in shifts around the clock. Only 413 yards of the tunnel had been completed at the end of two and a half years, less than half the distance required to prove the worth of the sett.

To speed up operations, and at the same time ventilate the mine, a shaft was sunk in the Burcombe Valley floor on the line of the Main Drift, at a point a little to the south of where the Roman Lode outcropped. The intentions were to drive levels north and south from the bottom of the shaft (at 150 feet), to join with the Main Drift and extend it at the same time. Theoretically, this shaft should have passed through the Roman Lode, which dipped steeply southwards towards it, but no sign of it was discovered by the time it had reached the level of the Main Drift.

In sinking the shaft in the valley floor problems arose from the amount of water running into it from the surrounding catchment area, even though a channel was cut around it to take off the surface water and that coming from further up the same valley. In order to keep the workings dry, an eight inch pump was fixed in the shaft; this being worked by a series of flatrods from a water wheel installed over a quarter of a mile away, near the junction of the Burcombe Valley Water and the River Barle. No ore was found in the shaft workings or in the Main Drift and before the two were connected the project was abandoned. A complete waste of time, manpower and money.

In the meantime, Dowlais were making great efforts to find workable deposits of iron ore in other parts of their sett, and before the year 1856 was out at least five other adit levels had been started. The first of these, Comers, was named after the Mine Captain of the first team of miners to work for Dowlais on Exmoor. This level was driven 150 yards into the western hillside of the Burcombe Valley, at a point about 300 yards up stream from the shaft, where it was expected to cut Rogers Lode, now being worked by Schneider and Hannay a half mile to the east; and had also been surface worked on their own sett close to where they were driving the level. After passing through the expected line of the lode without finding any trace of it, and continuing for some distance beyond through barren ground, the level was abandoned. A second adit (named after William Llewellyn) was commenced about the same time. This level was about 200 yards from Valley Shaft, a short distance up the western tributary of the Burcombe Water, and was driven to intersect Llewellyn Lode, which was reached about the middle of August 1856. The *North Devon Journal* of August 21st recorded the event, which was celebrated in Simonsbath with a great rejoicing; the lode was eight feet six inches big and the south wall of it had not yet been reached. The celebrations, however, were a little premature, because the ore was too mixed with quartz to be of any value, and after continuing the level to a distance of 212 yards, with nothing better discovered, this level was also abandoned.

This was to be the pattern of things to come, but in the June of 1856 all of the three mining companies at work on Exmoor were in a highly expectant mood and were anticipating a total annual production of ore in the region of 200,000-300,000 tons; with the smallest of these, the Plymouth Iron Co. expecting to produce 40,000 tons annually.

The most promising lode in the Burcombe area was, of course, the Roman Lode, which neither the shaft workings or the Main Drift had encountered, and to find this lode an adit level was begun from the east bank of Burcombe Water, about 30 yards north of the line of the outcrop of the lode. After driving 86 yards the vein was cut, and followed east and west for some distance, but in the two years it was worked only 640 tons of ore were brought out before the vein was exhausted, and one more disappointment was added to Dowlais's growing list.

Meanwhile, work had begun on Hangley Cleave, one of the places favoured by the 'Ancients'. Here, an adit was driven 125 yards southwards to a lode, which on the surface was 15 feet wide, but where it was cut 40 feet below the surface had narrowed to six feet. A shaft was sunk at this point and 1,200 tons of rich brown Hematite was raised before the vein petered out and work there ceased in August 1857.

Late in 1856, another level was begun in the Burcombe Valley. This time it was into the western hillside about 250 yards down stream from Valley Shaft. This was on a very narrow vein of iron, which disappeared completely 33 feet in, and was not driven on further.

The height of the mining boom came in late 1856, and for 12 months or so every spare room for miles around had its full quota of miners. On the north bank of the Barle below Cornham Ford, a terrace of six cottages were built to provide housing for some of the Dowlais miners and their families. So far as is known they were the only cottages (apart from the one at Wheal Eliza) to be built specifically for this purpose. The *North Devon Journal* of November 13th 1856, says that the first stone of seven miners cottages was laid last week at Cornham Ford mines. Seven cottages were certainly proposed, as a site plan in the Fortescue papers shows, and the ruins of seven can be traced on the ground, but one of these was the mine office, which was erected at the same time. The only other building in the immediate area was the Blacksmith's Shop, which stood close to the Cornham track between the cottages and the ford.

Although it was essential to keep the cost of building these cottages to the minimum they were not built to the traditional terrace design, but alternatively protruded four feet six inches, first to the front, and then to the rear. Not the cheapest form of building even if it was more attractive. Nevertheless, the cottages were of a reasonable size, with the two ground floor rooms measuring 14 feet by 12 feet, and 10 feet by 12 feet; no smaller than many houses built today.

Transporting the ore away from the mines had always been a problem— as we stated earlier. It was agreed at the outset that Dowlais would supply the rails and ironwork for a railway, either to Lynmouth—where they were already carting their ore—or to Porlock Weir. Schneider and Hannay had promised to help the project with money, and it was this agreement that cost them dearly when they broke their contract, and later also cost Dowlais a great deal of money. In November 1856, however, all of this was in the unforeseeable future, and the *North Devon Journal* of 13th November reported that the mines on the mountain were making satisfactory progress and that Dowlais were contemplating building a regular station at Cornham Ford to link the branch tramways from their mines to the proposed West Gate Station (on the Simonsbath Challacombe road), at the foot of the main incline leading to the coast.

Although their intentions were unquestionably sincere, Dowlais were hesitant in rushing into the project until they had found sufficient quantities of iron ore to warrant it, and though their own managers were still confident that this would soon be found, the depression in the iron trade which caused a lay off of workers early in the winter of 1857-1858— when all work at the mines ceased for 15 weeks—did little to reassure them. As a precaution, Dowlais gave Frederic Knight 12 months notice of their intentions to quit, but in March 1858, prospects were a little brighter and mining was resumed, but still that large body of iron ore eluded them.

It was at this time that Henry Scale—who had been the Superintendent of the Dowlais operations on Exmoor since June 1856—was replaced by William Dunstan, who had previously been one of the Mine Captains at Wheal Eliza, and had worked for Ebeneezer Rogers, sinking the first shaft in the Deer Park. He had also been connected with other mines in the

North Devon area. Dunstan was to have no more success for Dowlais than he had at Wheal Eliza, and on June 8th 1858 all work ceased at the mines.

During the early part of 1858, while operations were suspended at the mines for 15 weeks, Henry Scale was sued by four of the miners who had been working for Dowlais, for the payment of wages owed them. The principal claimant was a George Jewell, who claimed 30/- due to him for nine days work as a miner *(North Devon Journal* 11.2.1858). When first employed by Scale he had agreed to take a house to live near the works (Cornham Ford?), but soon afterwards he had left, without giving notice, to better himself at Dulverton. Because of the alleged breach of regulations, Scale had refused to meet him to settle his account. The action was heard in the South Molton County Court, where the judge, after hearing the evidence, said that he was not satisfied that it was customary for notice to be given as Scale claimed, and he would have been wiser to have stuck up a notice of the required regulations. Jewell was also at fault, being most unwise in leaving without prior notice, but he thought he was entitled to his wages. Judgement was given accordingly, but not for costs, and the same applied for the three other cases.

With the departure of Schneider and Hannay from the mining scene; later followed by Anthony Hill and the Plymouth Iron Company, Dowlais alone were left on Exmoor, but the terms of their original mining agreement were now proving too restrictive and punitive for their liking, and they were not prepared to resume mining unless certain conditions were changed. To begin with, they were most unhappy about paying £1,000 per annum dead rent, with little to show for it in return, and Frederic Knight's insistence that they confine their workings to driving specific underground levels, particularly the Main Drift at Cornham Ford, had proved disastrous, and led them to request permission to follow and work the known lodes from the surface. Frederic Knight on the other hand, even if he was prepared to grant the Dowlais requests, could do nothing without the agreement of the Chancery Court and his brothers and sisters, who had not yet received all of their inheritance, and so, the whole issue became deadlocked and negotiations were to all intents and purposes at an end.

With the express purpose and hope that he could still persuade Dowlais to resume mining on their sett, Frederic Knight now took action against them, and at about the same time obtained the long awaited agreement with Colonel Blathwayt for the land he required across Porlock Common and at Porlock Weir to complete the proposed railway from Simonsbath. He them approached Dowlais for the supply of rails etc., as promised in their agreement, and to hurry them along, several sections of the bed for the railroad were cut (a particularly long stretch over Porlock Common and Elsworthy, running to near Warren Farm still remains today much as it was cut), but by this time, Dowlais, thoroughly disheartened by their inability to find ore in commercial quantity, had given up the struggle, and despite the efforts of Frederic Knight and the Court action brought against them, they preferred to pay him £7,000 (paid in five annual instalments commencing 1st January 1863) with all the buildings and mining equipment thrown in, rather than continue with a lost cause. The total cost of their involvement on Exmoor could not have been less than £17,000. A very costly venture for the meagre 2,000 tons or so of iron ore raised.

This was the end of any major attempt to mine iron ore on Exmoor during Frederic Knight's life-time, but a certain amount of prospecting was carried on. The *North Devon Journal* of February 10th 1859, carried the following advertisement: 'To miners: to be let by tender, the driving of an underground level of full size and about 75 fathoms in length. Specifications may be seen at the office and tenders will be received at Simonsbath on Saturday 12th February at 12 o'clock. Signed Robert Smith of Emmetts Grange, Exmoor'. It is not known who undertook the task of driving this adit level, but we do know that it was situated on the south bank of Kinsford Water, about half a mile east-south-east of Emmetts Grange—in what is now a fir plantation—and that it was driven on a lode that had been exposed on the surface for 100 yards. The result of this trial are also unknown, but the spoil heaps do not reveal a large iron content, and no further development appears to have taken place there.

In August 1874, a mining journal reported that a strong and powerful company of adventurers contemplated taking for a long term the Exmoor and Brendon properties of Frederic Knight, with a view of effectively working on a large scale the rich and most extensive lodes of iron ore which lie under this gentleman's domain. As nothing further developed, it would seem that a closer investigation of the property, and the poor results of previous companies working there, were enough to deter this company from risking their capital, and it was not until after Frederic's death that the next serious attempt was made to get the iron mines going again, but this is another story, in another era of Exmoor's history, which will find its proper place later in this book.

CHAPTER 9

THE OTHER FARMS AND ALLOTMENTS ON EXMOOR

WHILE it has been comparatively easy to compile a brief history of the Knight family and their doings on Exmoor, from the many and readily available documents they have left behind, it has proved a little more difficult to gather information concerning the individual farms on the remaining 4,000 acres of Exmoor Proper that was not in their possession. This was due not only to frequent changes of ownership and occupants, but also to the odd habit of changing the names of some of the farms and cottages at irregular intervals; thus creating a situation that has taken some sorting out, and one that has not been helped by inaccuracies in the Census Returns, particularly those of 1851, which, among other errors, gives the tenants of Higher and Lower Sherdon in the wrong places.

We will begin our investigations in the south-eastern corner of Exmoor, for it was here, and here alone, that any real effort was made to establish a second farming community within the old Forest boundaries. When we last looked at this area there were (according to the Census of 1841) only four farms; Ferny Ball, Holes Allotment, Burcombe and Greenbarrow, but here, as on the Knight Estate, great progress had been made in the decade that followed. In addition to the original farms, there were now the new farms of Higher and Lower Sherdon, Kingsland Pits, Lyddons and Sandyway, as well as an inn and a number of cottages.

William Balmond, who is given as the tenant of Higher Sherdon in the Census of 1851, was in fact renting and living at Lower Sherdon; this farm having been created out of the allotments awarded to Thomas Thornton, esq. in respect of Higher, Middle and Lower Brightworthy, Withypool. A year later, Balmond purchased the freehold of the 112 acre farm for £700, all of which appears to have been borrowed money.[*] Eighteen months later he had paid nothing off his mortgage and owed a further sum of £60 in interest. In 1856, before he had time to repay his debts, he died at the early age of 41, leaving behind a widow and four children, the eldest, a son named Joseph who was just 15 years old. The chief creditors were a Lucy Brook of Stoke-on-Trent, Staffordshire, and a local man, William Moule, the latter being owed £163. 7s. 0d., a sum that was partly secured by a bond on the title deeds of a dwelling house and premises in Exford which had belonged to the deceased. Moule promptly sold the property towards the discharge of the debt, but this money being insufficient to clear it, he filed a claim in the High Court of Chancery on behalf of himself and other unsatisfied creditors, to have the real and personal estate of the late

---

*Deeds of Sherdon, S.R.O. Taunton

151

William Balmond administered by the Court. An order was granted by the Master of the Rolls on 14th November 1857, to sell sufficient of the farm to meet the repayment of the debt. On the 1st July 1858, the whole of the farm was put up for sale at the Red Lion, Dulverton, and sold to Robert Baker of Hawkridge for £1,270.

On looking back to the Census of 1851, we find that Ann Balmond's father-in-law Joseph and his wife were also living at Lower Sherdon, together with her brother-in-law John, but whether they were still there at the time of William's death is not known. We do know, however, that at the time of the 1861 Census, Joseph Balmond senior, who was now described as a widower, was living in one of the Horsen Farm cottages, where, although now 72 years of age, he was employed as a farm labourer. Living there also was his daughter-in-law and her family. Shortly afterwards, Joseph became the landlord of the Sportsmans Inn at Sandyway, and it is likely that his late son's family accompanied him there, but after a couple of years they moved again, probably to Hawkridge, because this was the address given in May 1864, when John Blake, their former neighbour at Higher Sherdon, brought a court action against Joseph Balmond junior and his Uncle John, who were both labourers of that place.

Blake was seeking the repayment of a promissory note, value £10. 18. 6 including interest and the cost of a former court summons. He won his claim and the defendants were given one month in which to pay. How many similar tales there are of self sacrifice and hardship, and for every man who succeeded on Exmoor, another on the threshold of making good was struck down and all that he had worked and striven for was lost.

After purchasing Lower Sherdon, the new owner, Robert Baker, did not immediately move into his farm, and for a while, Henry Baker—who was probably a relative—was employed there as a herdsman cum shepherd. Robert and a sister were in residence and farming 190 acres there before 1871, but both were gone by 1881, when Lower Sherdon was occupied by a Benjamin Buckingham, and for close on 60 years, the name of Buckingham was synonymous with the farm.

Two hundred yards to the east of Lower Sherdon Farm, beside an old track to its higher fields, lie the ruins of an earlier farm, complete with a badly silted up pond that was fed by a spring on the hillside above. It was not until quite recently that I was made aware of the existence of this old farm, and I am grateful to Jack Buckingham (of Rose Cottage, Simonsbath) who was born at Lower Sherdon, for pointing out its whereabouts. This has helped to clear up a small mystery that had been bothering me concerning the Census Returns of 1861 and 71, when for those two Returns only, an additional cottage (uninhabited) appears in the Sherdon area. With the whereabouts of this cottage-cum-farmhouse confirmed, it is safe to assume that when Robert Baker moved to Lower Sherdon at some time prior to 1871, it was into his new farmhouse, and that by this time the old farmhouse, first occupied by William Balmond

Higher Sherdon

Woolcombe

Site of Kingsland Pits Farm

Kinsford

and his family, and for a short time after by Henry Baker and his wife, had gone out of use.

This being so, a thought has just struck me concerning the Acland Arms at Moles Chamber, where exactly the same thing happened in 1851, when an additional house (uninhabited) is recorded in the Census of that year only.

It would therefore appear that the scant ruins of the building still to be seen at Moles Chamber, are not the ruins of the original inn, but its replacement, which would have been built by George Chapple (the innkeeper) at some time between 1841 and 1851. At this late date we cannot now be sure of the location of the earlier inn at Moles Chamber, but there are some indications that it may have been closer to the road, on the plot of ground between the old drovers trail and the stream.

The story of Higher Sherdon is no less interesting, and in its early years illustrate the long struggle of John Blake, who began his working life as a labourer, and progressed steadily up the farming ladder to become, by 1871, the successful farmer of 438 acres, 160 of which he owned. Successful he certainly was, but he had very little time left in which to enjoy the fruits of his labours and a well earned retirement, for shortly after, he died, leaving his daughter Ellen and her husband George Thomas Brook to carry on. George, who had formerly been farming at Upcott Farm, Bideford, had for a number of years been renting an allotment on Long Holcombe, the property of Frederic Knight. In October 1870, he had the misfortune to lose one of his bullocks, when it fell about seven or eight feet into an unfenced quarry on the allotment and broke its neck. When George Brook approached Frederic Knight and asked him for compensation, he was told to take it up with his Agent, but he was not at all helpful and refused to pay him a penny.

In a subsequent claim for compensation brought at Bideford· Brook stated that the bullock was valued at £10, but he was only asking £9. 8. 9 as he had been able to sell the hide for 11s. 3d. The judge was totally unsympathetic to Brook, even though it was made perfectly clear that in a similar case brought by Frederic Knight against a mining company some years before, for the loss of bullocks falling down a mine shaft, damages had been awarded. The long and short of the story is that although it was apparently quite alright for the landowner to receive compensation for the loss of his bullocks, the rules were changed when it was the tenant who suffered a similar loss and the judge dismissed the case. Frederic Knight's solicitor then asked for costs, but the judge did at least have the decency to refuse them, the very least he could do in the circumstances. A little later, in 1873, George Brook and his wife again fell foul of Frederic Knight over an unspecified breach of covenant in respect of Middle Long Holcombe (on which they held a lease), but after three Court hearings he again lost his case, and Frederic was awarded £15. 8. 2, plus the costs of the actions.

North Devon Journal 24.11.1870, 20.7.1871.

The Brook family continued to farm Higher Sherdon until the death of Tom Brook in the late 1930's. Tom, the last of the male line of the family to live there, was killed in a riding accident on 13.12.1937, when he was only 33 years old. He was a big man of about 18 stones, and whilst riding down Sheepwash Hill* a stirrup leather broke. He was precipitated from the saddle and fell heavily, breaking his neck in the process.

Higher Sherdon was not sold after Tom Brook's death, but came into the possession of his eldest sister Maggie, who married Frank Hill of Burch Farm, Twitchen. She retained it until her death, letting the grass annually. The farm then passed to her grand-daughter, who does likewise. It is of interest to note here that Higher Sherdon has not been on the market for at least 135 years, the longest time, I believe, that any one farm has been retained in this way on Exmoor Proper.

An allotment of land, once known as Bincombe, but shown on the present 2½ " OS map as Barcombe; situated on the Sandyway side of Littons (opposite the farm lane entrance), was also in the possession of the Brook family until the 1970's, when Daisy Gough (née Brook) sold it to Mr. Sanders of Pulham Farm, Twitchen. The lower fields of this allotment were first reclaimed many years ago, probably by John Blake, who is believed to have purchased it when it came on the market in 1856 *(North Devon Journal* 14.2.1856). The top field remained unbroken until after Mr. Sanders drained it in the 1970's.

Kingsland Pits,** has, since 1815, been the name of a part of Withypool Common that adjoins the Forest boundary on the hillside east of Sherdon Water, opposite Ferny Ball. Included in this area is a large level topped mound, all but surrounded on three sides by a deep, wide, and apparently natural valley, which curves around it, with both ends opening out to face Sherdon Water—access from this side being very steep. The only place where it is possible to gain a reasonably easy entry to the mound is on its western side, where the valley is bridged by a natural ridge that crosses it from the adjacent hillside. From the top of the mound fine views are held of the lower part of Sherdon Water and Ferny Ball, also of the River Barle and the moorlands around and beyond. There is nothing to suggest that this natural site for defensive purposes was ever used in times of trouble, neither was it the site of the farm known as Kingsland Pits, which first appeared on the Census of Exmoor in 1851; nor is the farm to be found on the hillside above and around this place, where much of the land has at some time been enclosed, and though now let back still provides good grazing.

Very few people (even locals) have ever heard of the farm known as Kingsland Pits, which is not altogether surprising, as the name of the farm was changed on several occasions later. Kingsland Pits was, in fact, located on the allotment awarded to Federata Cutcliff in the northern part of the triangular piece of land bordered on two sides by the roads leading

*Molland.
**Formerly Kingbourne Pits.

from Withypool Cross to Lanacre, and from the same Cross to Withypool; the third boundary corresponding with that of Withypool Common.

The first occupant of Kingsland Pits that we know of was John Buckingham, who was farming 80 acres in 1851, and at that time, William Carter—who had been living and farming at Holes Allotment in 1841—was recorded as being a visitor there with his wife and family. Visitors they may have been, but probably long staying ones, because his former home was now occupied by James Stenner, and all other properties in the area were also inhabited. John Buckingham was still living at Kingsland Pits in 1861, under its new name of Cottage Farmhouse, but he was now 71 and retired from farming. The name of the farm had changed again by 1871 to Lotmint, when we find John's son, James, living there and farming 100 acres. Ten years later the mis-spelt 'Lotmint' had changed to Allotment, and the farm had grown to 140 acres, but at some time before 1888, the old farmhouse was let down and Woolcombe built to replace it on a more sheltered site below the road to Lanacre, on land that also once belonged to Federata Cutcliff. All that now remains of the old homestead of Kingsland Pits is a stone barn and the windbreak of beech trees planted around for shelter.

It was James Buckingham who became the first occupant of Woolcombe. He was followed by his son William, who, for a few years from Lady Day 1899, also farmed Lower Sherdon. William gave up both farms prior to 1910 and moved to Higher Fyldon on the North Molton Estate. He was the last of the Buckingham family to farm at Woolcombe, but not the last at Lower Sherdon, because in 1929, William James Buckingham (Jim), who had been renting it since 1919, purchased it from a Mrs. Hill of Keynsham, Bristol. He remained there until his death in 1936 at the age of 49. Lower Sherdon was then let to Stan Little for a number of years and in 1950 he bought it.

Sandyway farm was also established during the progressive 1840's, and for more than 70 years it was farmed by three successive generations of the Gillard family. What is less well known about the Gillards is that for some years prior to 1859 they were also the tenants of the neighbouring farm of Barkham. Both farms at that time were the property of John Cock, a well known South Molton builder. He also owned the adjoining small farm known as Coles Cross and a little fir plantation; some 216 acres in all.

After the death of George Gillard senior in 1859, the whole of this estate was put up for sale in four lots, but only Sandyway Farm and 82 acres were sold, and George Gillard junior was the purchaser. He remained there until his death in 1904, and was succeeded by his son Seymour, and though he too had a son, the farm was sold to Dick French senior, when the lad was only 11 years old, and the Gillards then moved off the Moor.

One memorable occasion in the life of George Gillard junior is recorded in the *North Devon Journal* of 31st August 1876, which describes a very pleasant religious gathering held at Sandyway Farm. It was a large meeting, and after the service there was a public tea, of which about 100 people partook.

By the end of the 1840's, a sufficient number of farms and cottages had been built in the Sandyway area to warrant an Inn, and at some time before 1851, one of two adjoining cottages at Sandyway became a Public House, when a licence was granted to Richard Barrow; the other cottage being occupied by Edward Cockram. There were still two cottages there in 1861, when the licensed premises were now known as the Sportsman; the two respective occupants being Isaac Barrow and Joseph Milton, neither of whom were listed as an innkeeper, and on 24th July the same year, the licence was transferred to Joseph Balmond.

In 1863, the licence passed to William Dalling, and a year later to Robert Holcombe. It was about this time that the two cottages were merged into one, making the premises much larger. Robert, who had previously been one of Frederic Knight's tenants at Simonsbath, renting a house, garden and shop, as well as 32 acres of land, was certainly an industrious man, and after taking the tenancy of the Inn combined his duties there with his trade as a mason, and also farmed 25 acres. Robert was still the tenant in 1875 when the Inn was sold, *(North Devon Journal* 22.7.1875) probably to a John Buckingham, who was certainly in occupation in 1878,* when he provided an excellent luncheon at a very moderate cost to spectators of a horse race meeting held close by. It was quite a day, with over 200 people in attendance. After the racing was over there was dancing at the Inn to the strains of a violin, and wrestling matches were also being carried on in good style. John Buckingham continued as the landlord of the Sportmans Inn for the remaining years of the 19th century. In fact, he was still living there at the time of his death on December 8th 1903, at the age of 76.

The next landlord of the Inn was John Buckingham's son James, One story about this man was recalled by his son-in-law, the Jack Buckingham who for many years ran the saw mill and carpenters business at Bottreaux Mill, Molland. Jack, who is now in his late 90's,** told me that on at least one occasion his father-in-law drove his horse and cart from the Sportsmans Inn to Plymouth to meet a boat; a remarkable achievement in the days when few people ventured beyond their nearest market town. Unfortunately, Jack does not remember who or what was collected at Plymouth, or how long the journey took.

We now come to the last of the farms listed in the Census of 1851 for the south-eastern part of Exmoor; Lyddons, or Litton as it is now known. This farm was created out of the allotment of land that John Knight purchased from Lord Carnarvon in 1829, some 246 acres in extent, which was enlarged upon by further purchases in the area to about 350 acres, and though there was no house recorded there in 1841, one must have been built shortly after, when James Coombes became its tenant in 1844, taking most of the 350 acres for a farm. Coombes struggled on until 1851,

---

North Devon Journal 8.8.1878.
**100 years old in June 1988.

when he ran out of time and money and departed from the Moor.

According to Hannam's diary *(Reclamation of Exmoor Forest)* Coombes did not improve his position when he bought 500 sheep at a stock sale at Warren Farm in 1846. These sheep had wintered badly and some could hardly walk. Furthermore, Coombes had not an acre of cultivated or suitable land for this class of sheep and 60 of them died shortly after he got them home. He could not be persuaded to put the rest out to better keep and in the next five years Coombes continued on his downhill path until he lost all that he possessed. The Census of 1851 reveals that five labourers were employed on Lyddons Farm, but in the light of Hannam's story one wonders what they had been doing there.

Following the departure of James Coombes, the farm remained in hand for three years until 1854, when it was let with 275 acres to Richard Sharpe, who, after only 12 months, did a moonlight flit, leaving behind a pile of unpaid bills, and from then until William Carter took the tenancy of the farm in 1861, the land was let off in allotments.

From the time James Coombes rented this farm in 1844, and for many years after, Lyddons Farm is constantly referred to as Crooked Post Farm, but why this should be so is difficult to determine, because the only mention of Crooked Post in Frederic Knight's rent books for the years 1864-1875 is in the first year, when William Carter is recorded as renting part of Litton—late Buckingham's—and Crooked Post Cottage and land —late Barrow's, the total rent being £90 per annum. In 1865, the same rental was paid for what was now described as Litton Farm and buildings: Thus we have Frederic Knight's rent books and four consecutive Census Returns, 1851-1881, giving the name of the farm as Litton or Lyddons, yet all of the *Kelly's Directories* for Somerset prior to 1914; the 6″ and 25″ OS maps of this area for 1888, and later maps to the 1930's, showing Crooked Post Farm in the exact position that Litton Farm stood, and still stands.

In the circumstances this would appear to prove once and for all that Lyddons—or Litton—and Crooked Post are one and the same farm, but what of the other holders of the latter name that appear on other records and on the Census of 1851 and 1861, none of which relate to Litton Farm.

The origin of the name Crooked Post is lost in the mists of time. The earliest known reference is in the Forest Book for Exmoor of 1719, where there is an entry for sheep pastured there. It is included again from time to time in later Forest Books, and is mentioned by Collyns in *The Wild Red Deer,* when the hunt passed close by in 1790. On the 1″ OS map of Exmoor of 1809, Crooked Post is shown in the triangular section of land formed by the junction of the Sandyway-Lanacre road and the former road leading to Withypool, roughly where the Withypool Cross sign post now stands, which implies that the original Crooked Post was an earlier marker for the same parting of the ways.

So far, so good: We have established the location of the first known Crooked Post, and examined the link between Litton and Crooked Post; now for a look at the other contenders. In 1851, Crooked Post was the name given to Greenbarrow Farm, which reverted to its former name again shortly after. In 1861, Crooked Post had moved westwards to the entrance of Litton Lane, where in the corner of the field east of the lane, adjoining the main road, a cottage once stood. In 1851, this cottage was one of three listed under the name of Sandyway, and, like Greenbarrow, it held the name of Crooked Post for only a few short years before reverting to Sandyway. We can be sure that this Crooked Post and the Sandyway cottage were one and the same, because James Crocker lived there for over 30 years through the three relevant Census Returns, and though this cottage was uninhabited, and possibly already demolished before 1881, the field in which it stood is still known locally as Crockers field.

Crooked Post crops up once more as the name of an allotment of 36 acres that John Knight purchased from Francis Hooper in 1828 for £80. This strip of land, adjacent to the Sandyway-Withypool Cross highway, opposite Litton Lane, extended as far as Sherdon Water.

These, then, are the known Crooked Posts, and if a choice has to be made, as to the location of the cottage with the foremost claim to the name, then it has to be Litton, where a small cottage was built about 1841, even though this cottage is recorded as Lyddons Cottage in 1851 when James Venting—a mason—was living there, presumably either putting the finishing touches to Litton Farmhouse, which was added on to the old cottage, or working on repairs or the construction of new farm buildings.

We have almost completed our tour of inspection of the new farms and cottages in the south-east corner of Exmoor, and only two more cottages, one dating prior to 1851, the other first appears in the Census of 1871, remain to be looked at.

The cottage known as Coles Cross was situated beside the Green Lane that runs down towards Sherdon Water from the Sandyway-Kinsford Gate road, on land that once adjoined Barkham, but has for many years been part of that farm. The first known occupant was a farm labourer, Henry Roberts, who was living there with his family in 1851. When Sandyway, Barkham and Coles Cross came on the market in 1859,[1] the latter was listed as a small farm of 24 acres in the occupation of James Hernamen, a man who had spent most of his early life labouring on Exmoor. As neither Barkham or Coles Cross were sold, they were advertised the following year to let. Together, the two farms totalled about 115 acres, and the Census of 1861 shows that Samuel Shapland (who we dealt with in Chapter 5) was living at Barkham and farming the whole of this land. Coles Cross does not appear on this Census, but a Cottage with the name 'Private House' is listed in the appropriate place; occupied by one James Berry, a farm labourer. In 1871, 'Private House' had disappeared from the Census, and Coles Cross was restored to its rightful place, with another farm worker— James Elworthy—in residence. By 1881, there had been yet another change of resident, when a molecatcher named George May was living there. After his departure—and until the demise of the Cottage in the 1920's—it housed a farmworker employed on Barkham Farm.

Lower down Sherdon Water, and close to the lovely three arched stone bridge that carries the farm road into Higher Sherdon, the last of the cottages built in this area during the period under review, was completed at some time between 1861-71. On the latter date, a William Dallyn (who was also a farmworker) was living there, but in the Census of 1881 the cottage was uninhabited. It should be stressed here that it was unlikely that it was empty for very long as the ten year gap between each Census does allow for more frequent changes of occupants than are recorded, and unlike the farms of Exmoor, the cottages are not included in the intermediate Kelly's or other Directories of Somerset.

Only one other cottage or farmhouse was built on Exmoor prior to 1851. This small farm, then known as Kingsford Water, was located midway between Kinsford Cross and the entrance to Emmetts Grange, just to the west of the South Molton-Simonsbath highway. In 1851, Thomas Collins was the occupant and farmer of 35 acres, but at some time before 1861, Anthony Huxtable (who we last met up with at Driver Cottages) had taken over what was now known as Centsford Farmhouse and 20 acres. Before Kentsford Tenement (same place) came on the market in 1864, Anthony had moved back on to the Knight Estate and was renting Cloven Rocks Cottage and a little land for £5 10. 0 per annum, and there he remained until about 1875, when he moved into lodgings at one of the Limecombe cottages.

On the 2nd August 1864, Kentsford Tenement and 18 acres of good arable and meadow land was put up for Auction *(North Devon Journal* 21.7.1864). The smallholding was subdivided by substantial ditch bank fences into five enclosures and a garden, with a new house and buildings erected thereon; which tells us that the original cottage had either been replaced or completely refurbished. It was suggested that being so close to the public road, the property would answer well as an Inn and was sure to pay well, as outgoings of all kinds were only about £1 a year. The sale of the property was to be followed by the auction of the livestock, corn, roots, implements, and the household furniture and effects, as the owner, William Court, was about to emigrate. Presumably, everything was sold and William left the country, and though there may have been other farmers on Exmoor who did likewise, he is the only one known, which was a far cry indeed from the situation in other parts of Great Britain, where farmers and farmworkers were emigrating in their thousands.

The new owner of Kentsford was a Challacombe born man called Walter Fry, who continued to farm the smallholding in the traditional manner until his death in 1885, but as far as is known it never became an Inn. On the terms of his will, Kentsford was left jointly between his brothers, but on 24.12.1896, James Fry took possession of the farm, having acquired the other shares.[2]

So far, this chapter has been concerned only with the farms and cottages created on Exmoor Proper that were outside the Knight Estate, and though one or two items of interest have been held over for inclusion later, the known history of these early habitations has been completed to the end of the 19th century, and in some cases beyond. There is, however, still some ground left to cover in regards to the remaining Exmoor allotments, where even though no attempt had been made to erect farmhouses or cottages, some work may have been done on their improvement, and by comparing the allotment award of Exmoor (1819) with later editions of the 6" OS maps, followed by a visual check of the area in question—and a look at the documents concerning them that are available—certain observations can be made.

In the first place, some of the holders of the smaller allotments did not even go to the trouble of enclosing the land they had been granted, but whether these allotments were sold or exchanged for certain specified grazing rights on a larger enclosed portion of the old Forest is not easy to ascertain, and though it has been possible to trace a few of the transactions relating to some of these allotments, all but two were straightforward sales.

The south-eastern corner of Exmoor, where this chapter began, is as good a place to start from as any, and by working our way around the fringe of the old Forest in a clockwise direction, we can deal with any points of interest concerning the remaining allotments as we come to them.

The first two allotments to fall into this category after leaving Sandyway Cross in the direction of Kinsford Gate and Moles Chamber, lie between Barkham Farm and Long Holcombe. One enclosure of 15 acres, first awarded to James Gould, is reached by the Green Lane that runs down past the site of Coles Cross Cottage. The other allotment of 29 acres which adjoins it, was shared by D. Purchase of C.W. Avery;* all three men being farmers from Bishops Nympton. The state of the allotments at the turn of the century is not known, but the natural moorland has at some time been ploughed (where possible) and greatly improved.

Long Holcombe and Hangley Cleave formed part of the 1,880 acres awarded to Sir C.W. Bampfylde, purchased shortly after by John Knight, does not concern us here, but it is still very much in its earlier moorland state.

On the other side of the South Molton-Simonsbath highway, adjoining the road from Kinsford Gate to Moles Chamber, is the allotment awarded to Lord Morley** in respect of his North Molton properties. This allotment of 183 acres was surrounded by a ring fence into just one enclosure, and though it is shown on the OS map as Comerslade, it is more usually referred to locally as Strangers Allotment, after a one time tenant. Little time or money has been spent on its improvement, and for the most part it is wet and rushy and not very productive.

Between Comerslade and Moles Chamber a number of small allotments awarded in respect of tenements in High Bray and Charles, are of a little more interest, because here at least we do know something of their history.***

---

*Still known as Avery's Allotment.
**Purchased by Lord Poltimore in 1841.
***Acland Archive.

Out of a total of ten allotments on Squallacombe, five were incorporated into one enclosure of about 190 acres. Two of these allotments were awarded to H.A. Bryant, esq. in respect of Whitefield and Kedworthy in the parish of High Bray, and though we cannot be certain that he owned all five at the time of enclosure, he assuredly did later, because after his death they were left to his brothers and other members of his family. The position under the divided ownership is a bit involved, but on 24.9.1888, Sir Thomas Acland purchased the lot to add to the Acland Allotment which adjoined it.

I would like to make one comment here regarding Setta Barrow, in order to correct an erroneous and misleading statement in a recent book concerning Exmoor's past, in which the Author holds John Knight responsible for the desecration of this fine barrow by building the Forest boundary wall through and across the centre of it: John Knight was responsible for doing many things on Exmoor, but this was not one of them, because the boundary of his estate did not come within half a mile of Setta Barrow, and the man to blame for this act of vandalism was almost certainly H.A. Bryant, whose allotment adjoined the Barrow and the Forest boundary.

Of the other five allotments on Squallacombe, only two were ever enclosed. One, awarded to John Smith, who was the tenant of a small farm at Charles, the property of T.P. Acland, esq. of Little Bray, was assigned to the latter on 12th May 1819 by Salome Smith, following her husband's death. In return, Salome retained the tenancy of the small-holding and the allotment for a yearly rent of £2. Mary Leworthy's adjoining allotment also came into the possession of the Aclands, probably in much the same way, but when this happened is not known.

The holders of two of the three remaining allotments on Squallacombe died before they could take possession. If, as believed, they were tenants of T.P. Acland, then these allotments would have automatically passed to their landlord, either on their death, or the termination of their lease. For some other reason, the allotment awarded to the Rev. Bent of High Bray Parsonage was not fenced either, even though it was not purchased by Sir T.D. Acland until 1875, when a later vicar of High Bray, the Rev. Walter John Edmonds, sold it for £353. 15s. 0d, an exceptional price for 46 acres of rough unenclosed pasture, but one possibly justified by the thought that the proceeds were going to the benefit of the living of High Bray. Incidentally, not one of the Squallacombe allotments show any sign of improvement.

The largest single allotment on Exmoor outside of those in the possession of John and Frederic Knight, was that of 560 acres awarded to T.P. Acland in respect of his properties in Little Bray, High Bray and Charles. The allotment was subsequently enlarged by the acquisition of the Sqallacombe allotments and another on Black Hill, to just under 800 acres, and apart from the land around Moles Chamber improved by Jeremiah Smyth—when he was living at the Acland Arms—the remainder was all virgin moorland prior to the second decade of the 20th century.

For many years, Jeremiah Smyth had tended the stock taken in to keep on the Acland Allotment,[3] but in 1874 an agreement was made between Sir T.D. Acland and William Trix of Great Hele, South Molton; granting the latter a year by year tenancy of 600 acres or thereabouts of the allotment, at an annual rent of £40. The agreement was principally granted with a view to a joint stocking of the allotment, subject to certain conditions. The landlord could keep such horses, cattle and other stock as he required upon the allotment, but had to pay according to the schedule of charges set for the grazing season, which, in effect, were practically identical to those set by Frederic Knight on his estate in 1862. William Trix, as tenant of the allotment, had to debit himself likewise for any animals he placed there, but he was allowed to take in other stock to keep, either on a weekly basis or for the grazing season. Proper accounts had to be kept of all receipts and expenditure, which were presented monthly, either to Sir T.D. Acland, or his Agent. The profits from the venture were then divided equally between tenant and landlord.*

From advertisements in the *North Devon Journal,* we know that Jeremiah Smyth continued to look after the stock, and we know also that the agreement did not last long, because in 1877 the land was again in hand, with Sir Thomas Acland's Agent at Little Bray and Jeremiah Smyth taking the bookings.

The area around Moles Chamber had (as we have already noted) been much improved by Jeremiah Smyth, but of the three allotments that lie to the north of Roostitchen (between Moles Chamber and the Challacombe-Simonsbath highway) awarded to Richard Harding of Gratton, High Bray; J.D. Basset in respect of Wallover, Challacombe; and Lord Fortescue in respect of some of his Challacombe properties, only Richard Harding's allotment of some 77 acres adjoining the tributary of the River Barle shows sign of improvement, having been ploughed and reseeded where possible by the late William Tucker of The Grange, Bratton Fleming, who farmed it for many years, first with Muxworthy, High Bray; and later from The Grange.

At the southernmost point of Challacombe's South Regis Common, where it meets Gratton Common (now known as Castle Common) and the old Forest boundary, stands a stone which on the OS map is shown incorrectly as the Sloley stone. Cut in its northern face is the name Earl Fortescue; on the reverse a bench mark. MacDermot refers to this stone as the Hore or Lewcombe Stone, but this is not the original stone that stood at this spot. The earlier stone, has in recent years been recovered from the mud close by into which it had sunk, and figures carved on its face would appear to be a date, but are now so badly worn away that it is impossible to state when.

Lord Fortescue's Allotment on Roostitchen was not enclosed by itself, but for many years lay open to Challacombe's South Regis Common to the west, and J.D. Bassetts Allotment to the east. The Enclosure award for

_____

*Acland Archive.

South Regis Common of 1861, shows Lord Fortescue's Allotment as 107 acres, which were incorporated with his Exmoor Allotment into one large enclosure at some time before 1868. The boundary hedge between his property and J.D. Bassett's Allotment is believed to have been erected about the same time.

Because Earl Fortescue enclosed his two allotments as one, the old Forest boundary across Roostitchen to the Edgerley Stone (beside the Challacombe-Simonsbath highway) remained unfenced. This old boundary stone, marks not only the Devon-Somerset boundary, but also the division of Challacombe's North and South Regis Commons from one another and the old Forest.

North of the main road, on Bill Hill and Broadmead, were the other allotments awarded to the Challacombe landowners, including once again, Lord Fortescue, who altogether gained 218 acres under the Exmoor enclosure award, which, incidentally, was considerably less than he had claimed. This was not really surprising, for it was not un-natural to find that when the original claims were sent to the Commissioners acting on behalf of the Crown, prior to the allotment award of 1819, that the Freeholders of land around the Forest, and their lessees, who had been regularly sending sheep to Exmoor for the summer grazing, had tried to maximise the number of sheep depastured there in order to gain a larger allotment of land. In the case of Lord Fortescue and his 23 Challacombe tenants with such rights, one suspects that every sheep they owned were included in the claim, regardless of whether or not they ever pastured on the Forest. Some 3,000 sheep in all were claimed for, and on this basis, Lord Fortescue and his tenants should have received 750 acres by way of compensation for their loss of grazing rights, but unfortunately for them, the Commissioners were fully aware of what was going on, and as some of Lord Fortescue's tenants had, over the past 12-13 years, also been neglecting to pay the customary Forest Court rents, the total acreage finally agreed upon was just 218.

Lord Fortescue also purchased two small allotments on Bill Hill—ten acres in all—belonging to two Challacombe freeholders, Edward Webber and I.P. Chichester, but these were given over later to William Crang of Whitefield Barton, in exchange for his allotment on North Regis Common.

He included them with his own Exmoor Allotment which adjoined, surrounding the whole with a ring fence, but there are no signs today of any further improvements, and the land provides no more than limited rough grazing.

Adjoining the western boundary of William Crang's Allotment, were the 19 acres awarded to Ann Ridd, which were enclosed into three or four fields and reclaimed where possible into useful pasture land. At some time, a barn or some other building was erected there, making it one of the very few allotments on Exmoor outside the main farming areas to be equipped in this way. It is also of interest to find that this land is still in the possession of a member of the same family, David Ridd, whose father purchased it some years ago to ensure that it remained in the family, thus making it one of the last remaining Exmoor allotments still held by a descendant of the original holder.

Lord Fortescue's Allotment north of the Challacombe highway—which extended as far as Saddle Gate—was divided into three enclosures. The first, known as Broadmead, adjoining the main road, was situated between Ann Ridd's Allotment and North Regis Common, which also belonged to Lord Fortescue. Part of the latter was incorporated with Broadmead to square it up when it was enclosed in 1858, leaving a number of mere stones to mark the route of the old Forest boundary, which runs diagonally across it from the Edgerley Stone to the Bill Hill Stone, where it turned northwards side by side with the enclosure hedge. It was not until 1861 that an agreement was made between Earl Fortescue and some of his tenants for the enclosure of North Regis Common, and it was probably around that date that the second part of his Exmoor Allotment was enclosed. The boundary hedge between the allotment and North Regis Common has, in recent years, been breached in several places, allowing stock to wander at will between it and the rough moorlands north of Yarbury Combe.

Northwards again, the third and last part of Lord Fortescue's Allotment, 74 acres in extent, was first enclosed with 390 acres of Challacombe's North Common, which also belonged to his Lordship, but some time around 1858 a fence was erected across the common, reducing the Exmoor Allotment and the adjoining part of the common to a more manageable 214 acres, centred roughly on Woodbarrow Hangings.

The old Forest boundary across this open moorland from Woodbarrow Gate to Saddle Gate is not now easy to find, but is best done by following the old Lynton track which approximates closely with it. Included in this area of rough moorlands was the small allotment awarded to the Rev. John Blackmore, the grandfather of the celebrated novelist R.D. Blackmore of *Lorna Doone* fame. This allotment, awarded in respect of Bodley, Parracombe; the only one granted to a Parracombe man, was not enclosed separately, but was subsequently sold to Lord Fortescue who incorporated it with his own.

The Fortescue Allotments are today still very much in their original state although a little drainage work has been carried out in the past few years.

Along the northern slopes of Exmoor, between Saddle Gate and the Hoar Oak enclosures, lie the allotments awarded to John Lock in respect of Woolhanger, Ilkerton, New Mill, Dean and other tenements in the parish of Lynton that he owned. For much of its length this 163 acre allotment lies between the Chains and Ilkerton Common, and though perhaps not of the greatest historical importance, there is no other area within the boundaries of Exmoor Proper where the line between two quite distinct and different types of moorland vegetation is more plainly defined. Walking beside the wall erected to part the Chains (Knight property) from John Lock's Allotment, one can be forgiven for believing that this is both the natural and real boundary of the Forest. The dominant Molinia grass on the Chains side of the wall contrasts so completely with the mixture of heather and bracken on the other, which, to all intents and purposes, is part and parcel of Ilkerton Common, but in fact is merely an extension of it.

This land remained unfenced and undivided from the common for many years; this being the allotment included in Sir Henry Carew's* sale of manorial properties in 1898, that was rented by Sir Frederic Knight for some years prior to his death in 1897. In fact, it was not until the latter half of this century that a wire fence was erected to part it from the common. This method of fencing has left the mere stones of the Forest boundary undisturbed, but the wire has since rusted away in many places and the allotment is once more open to the common.

East of John Lock's Allotment lies that of 15 acres awarded to Charles Chichester of Hall, Bishops Tawton; in respect of South Furzehill. This allotment was purchased by John Knight in 1839 and enclosed by him with a small part of Furzehill Common, and like the allotments adjoining, granted to John Vellacott in respect of North Furzehill, Ratsbury and other Lynton tenements, it has been reclaimed and much improved. The former allotment came into the possession of Lord Fortescue on Frederic Knight's death; the latter were purchased with Hoar Oak in 1898.

From Hoar Oak to Manor Allotment the Forest boundary and that of the Knight Estate were one and the same, but Manor Allotment—misappropriated from the Crown by the men of Oare prior to the Survey of the Forest in 1815—still provides useful rough grazing, as it has done since time immemorial, although it is no longer the home of the Blackgame. East of Manor Allotment was again Knight property, and continued so until it reached a point almost halfway between Chalk Water and Black Barrow, where the boundary fence of John Knight's Estate turns abruptly southward. This south bound wall meets the lane into Larkbarrow Farm and continues beside it to its entrance on the road from Lucott Cross to Wellshead Farm.

Between the Larkbarrow boundary wall of John Knight's Estate and Porlock Common lies the 365 acre allotment awarded to Mrs. Blathwayt in respect of her numerous properties in the parishes of Porlock and Luccombe. Adjoining the northern edge of this allotment was the 28 acres granted to Lord King for his tenements of Yearnor and Wear Wood** in the parishes of Culborne and Porlock, and beside the road in the southeast corner adjoining Alderman's Barrow was the 25 acres awarded to John Tamlyn of Lucott, Stoke Pero. This latter allotment was exchanged in an agreement with Sir Thomas Acland (8th July 1819) for a smaller piece of land closer to home, but Sir Thomas's motives for acquiring this land are not clear as he had already sold all but 15 acres of his own 3,300

*A later owner of Woolhanger, Ilkerton, etc.
**Also known as Weir Wood.

acre concession on Exmoor to John Knight. What ultimately happened to these two small allotments is not known, but neither were enclosed and so presumably became part of John Knight's and Mrs. Blathwayt's estates.

Lord King's Allotment also seems to have at some time come into the possession of the Blathwayt family, as this too was never fenced. In point of fact there were no enclosures whatever made from the 420 acres of allotments in this area; the whole of it being incorporated with a major part of Porlock Common into one large enclosure in or about the year 1867; the mere stones of the old Forest bounds from Black Barrow to Alderman's Barrow being the only indication as to where the dividing line between Forest and common lie, as the heather from Porlock Common has spread over practically the whole of the allotment, gaining such a strong foothold that it has become the predominant species of vegetation; one of the very few places on Exmoor Proper where heather has taken over from the natural grasses of the old Forest.

Very little documentation has been found concerning the allotments awarded to the owners of the 23 Exford Tenements who succeeded with their claims and were granted about 250 acres in all from the old Forest. This is probably because they were for the most part small farmers and their allotments were correspondingly small. What is certain, however, is that on the whole the Exford farmers were very industrious, and apart from an area of rough moorlands on Red Stone Hill very little of the land on their allotments escaped the plough.

The Exford allotments can be divided into three groups; the first, from Larkbarrow Corner to the head of Sparcombe, was awarded in respect of Hill Farm. It still goes with the farm and has for the most part been much improved.

On the steep hillside to the west of Sparcombe Water, four small allotments were individually enclosed by their owners with wall and bank hedges topped with beech trees, and though three of these fields have been let back and bracken has taken over, they do, nonetheless, reveal the unmistakeable signs of having once been lovingly tended and cared for. All four of these fields are now in the possession of Mr. Edwards of Westermill Farm; the top two fields formerly belonged to Mrs. Beaumont of Luccesses Farm, Exford.

Across the River Exe on Red Stone Hill lie the second group of allotments awarded to the Exford farmers. On the steep hillside above the river the land awarded to John Smith (now shown on the OS map as Penn Allotment) has in part been recently reclaimed and laid down to permanent pasture. Above and to the south of this allotment is the 77 acres awarded to I.H. Bevett, esq.; the largest award granted to an Exford landowner, but apart from a small plantation of fir trees in one corner, and the section of land lying west of the 22 acres awarded to Mary Greenslade (alongside the Exford-Simonsbath road) with which it was combined to form one enclosure and reclaimed, the remainder of I.H. Bevett's Allotment was left in its natural and very rough moorland state. Two other allotments in this group were purchased by John Knight from Philip Hancock in 1828 and 1841, along with the Gallon House Inn (Red Deer Farm).

The third and last group of allotments awarded to the Exford men lie along the west side of Gypsy Lane. All were enclosed and reclaimed and now provide some of the best grassland in the area.* Between these allotments and the River Barle the Knight Estate again took over, and after leaving this behind and crossing the river, we are back in the south-eastern corner of Exmoor where our journey began, and though we have already dealt with the farms and cottages in this area and some of the allotments, a few others remain to be considered.

On the north side of the road from Withypool Cross to the Greenbarrow cattle grid, two allotments of 26 and 45 acres were awarded to the Rev. W.M. Stawell in respect of Lower Blacklands Farm; and Stephen Crocker in respect of Higher Lanacre. These allotments were enclosed in their entirety into two separate fields. The smaller field nearest Withypool Cross was partly reclaimed many years ago, and at a later date when it was rented by Tom Carter (grandson of the first William Carter of Litton), it was tilled to corn. It has been broken on a number of occasions since, but is now down to permanent grass.

The other allotment, known as Higher Lanacre Common, was one of the places in the old Forest where spine turf (peat) was formerly dug. It was first reclaimed during the last war, and again during the 1960's, when George Thorne—who was then farming it with Sandyway Farm— renewed the pasture there.

Stephen Crocker was awarded a second allotment on Exmoor, in respect of Lower Lanacre. This allotment of 31 acres, known as Lower Lanacre Common, is situated on the south side of the Greenbarrow road, adjoining it and the Forest boundary (opposite the eastern end of Higher Lanacre Common), and like this common it was broken up for the first time during the last war. Before its reclamation it was one of the places on Exmoor Proper where Whortleberries grew in profusion, and it was here that Bert Carter (who we will come to again in the next chapter) recalls picking a peck of 'worts' in six hours, about the time of the First World War, no mean achievement, as anyone who has taken part in this somewhat tedious business will tell you.

The link between Lanacre and the commons of the same name on Exmoor must surely go back to the very dawn of Forest history, when its evolvement as summer grazing pastures began, and the body of Officials, Free Suitors and Suitors at Large were established to enforce the Forest Laws and keep it in good order. Of all the manors and tenements around Exmoor, Lanacre alone has carried its name into the Forest, probably because of the special place it held in Exmoor's history, for it was there that the first of the two Swainmote Courts were held each year. Sadly, the link between Lanacre and its commons has been broken, as both Higher

---

*Later purchased by Sir Robert Waley Cohen of Honeymead.

and Lower Lanacre Commons have in recent years been sold off.

Between Lower Lanacre Common and Greenbarrow Farm lies the allotment of 31 acres awarded to the Trustees of the Pincombe Charity in respect of Garlicombe Mill, Withypool. This allotment, known locally as 'Bakers Ground'—after a one time owner or tenant—came at a later date into the possession of Messrs. Phillips, the Auctioneers of Minehead, who retained it for many years. In more recent times it was sold to Mr. Rawle of Little Nurcot Farm, Winsford; and his son-in-law Ken Pook is the present owner. The allotment was divided into two fields; that against the road has been broken many times, the lower one only by Mr. Pook.

South of Willingford Farm, between it and Litton Water, is the allotment of 84 acres awarded to the Hon. George Courtenay, owner of the large Molland Estate, which, at the time, took in nearly the whole of the parish of Molland. The allotment still belongs to the estate and has for many years been run in conjunction with Sheepwash Farm.

Between Litton Farm and Litton Water, and adjoining the western boundary of the Molland Allotment, lies the last of the allotments under review. This allotment of 183 acres was granted to Lord Clinton in respect of his West Anstey properties, but has for many years been in the possession of the Thorne family of Higher House Farm, Twitchen. Once predominantly wet and rushy, it has been reclaimed where possible and the grassland much improved, but rushes are again taking over in places, a not uncommon occurrence on this type of land no matter how well drained.

CHAPTER 10

LORD FORTESCUE AND EXMOOR AFFAIRS

FOR the last 25 years or so of Sir Frederic Knight's lifetime, the greater part of his Exmoor Estate had been given over to supporting his vast sheep ranching enterprise; the letting of his farms assuming a less important role than in earlier years. This trend was reversed shortly after Earl Fortescue and his son Viscount Ebrington took possession after Sir Frederic's death in 1897, when, in quick succession, Wintershead, part of Honeymead, Cornham, Duredon and Winstitchen farms were let, followed a few years later by Pinkery.

The disruption to the shepherds and sheepherdings that had been based on these farms has already been noted in Chapter 7, but for all that, the traditional style of estate management of landlord and tenant farmer relationship had much to commend it, not only in the way it provided a regular known annual income to the landlord, but because it gave the would-be farmers of the Nation, who lacked the means to purchase their own farms, the only alternative opportunity to begin farming on their own account. Never was this more true than on Exmoor.

For some years, farming in general had been going through one of its periodic depressions, which in turn was reflected in the amount of rent Viscount Ebrington's tenant farmers could afford to pay him, and a comparison of the Exmoor rent rolls of 1886 and 1898, reveal that in many instances—where it is possible to cross check individual farms—the rents paid in 1898 were some £30-£50 less than in 1886 for the larger farms, with a corresponding decrease for the smaller holdings, and one cannot help thinking that if Sir Frederic Knight had had his share of financial worries, Viscount Ebrington's start was no more promising. Nevertheless, despite the declining revenue of the Exmoor Estate, work went ahead on renovating farmhouses, buildings and cottages, and some new cottages were also built. A certain amount of reclamation work was also done, and some of the woods and plantations planted by Sir Frederic Knight were extended, and a few new plantations created.

Another project put in hand, was the complete reconstruction of the estate buildings near Simonsbath Bridge, where John or Frederic Knight had installed a waterwheel to drive barn and other machinery. A letter from G.C. Smyth Richards in September, 1897, comments that unless something is done quickly to repair the waterwheel, they would be unable to use it in the autumn for sawing or for chaffcutting. Presumably, temporary repairs were carried out, because although only a month later a proposal was put forward for a complete new range of buildings to be erected on precisely the same site, it was a year or two before this work was completed.

169

The new buildings ranged from a sawmill and carpenters shop, to a chaff millhouse, and provision was also made for a dynamo and accumulators for electric light. The waterwheel was dispensed with, and a turbine fixed instead. This remained in use until the time of the Lynmouth Flood Disaster of 1952, when, like many similar installations close to the rivers of Exmoor, it suffered extensive damage when the leat providing water to the turbine became badly choked with debris carried down by the flood. Although it would not have been an impossible task to clear it, this was decided against, and the turbine was replaced by a large oil engine—a Ruston Hornsby—which continued to generate electricity until the mains arrived at Simonsbath in 1962. The same engine is still in use, providing power for the sawmill equipment. How large a part of Simonsbath was served by the old electric plant is not certainly known, but Simonsbath House and the stables, the Exmoor Forest Hotel, the Parsonage and Rose Cottage, were connected.

By 1905, the electricity supply had been extended to include the cart shed west of the courtyard of Simonsbath House, to provide illumination to both the target area and firing point of an indoor rifle range. The target holder was fixed high up on the south wall of the building, the firing point was from a hatchway in the Estate Office, which adjoined the Reading Room. These buildings, which were reached via a flight of stone steps on the northside of the courtyard, were also connected to the electricity supply. The targets were pulled fore and back on a wire rope and pulley system, the remained in use until 1968, when the rifle club was disbanded. The wire rope and light fittings have disappeared, but the pulley attachments and target frame are still there.

In the closing years of the last century alterations were made to Boevey's old house at Simonsbath, or the Lodge as it was now known. Hitherto, the house and the woolstore to the west had been separate buildings, but the gap in between was now filled in by extending the existing house. It was around this time that the demolition of John Knight's unfinished mansion is said to have taken place. A part of it was certainly removed, but the remaining walls were merly lowered to more acceptable proportions and then roofed over by the firm of contractors brought in from away.

The building we are left with, adjoins the rear of Simonsbath House, and forms the east wing. When Jack Buckington came to Simonsbath over 48 years ago to work on the Exmoor Estate, there were still a few of the older inhabitants who could remember the roofless building, and the roof being put on. The conversion of the mansion to a house of more sensible proportions was begun towards the end of 1897. G.C. Smyth Richards records in his diary that 'in cutting open the walls of the old house (mansion) the mortar was found to be harder than the stone'. According to Sir Frederic Knight (memo) this mortar had been made with lime from the Newlands Quarry, which needed very little sand, but set harder than cement and made the strongest mortar in the neighbourhood. G.C.

Smyth Richards fully recommended using Newland's lime for the new work.

In 1898, the westernmost of John Knight's original cottages at Cornham Farm was taken down. It had deteriorated into a tumbledown ragged old place, and after removing the slates it was demolished.

In such difficult times, every possible source of income was looked at. Honeymead House and Larkbarrow Big House were let as Hunting and Shooting Boxes, and shooting and fishing rights on other large blocks of land were also let. Rabbits were trapped and sold, 6d apiece being the normal price received, but there was more profit in letting the trapping and shooting rights than in trapping by the estate, as the carriage charges and commission on at least one occasion (to Birmingham) swallowed up nearly all the profits made.

Another source of revenue, which does not appear to have been followed up, was the sale of sphagnum moss, of which there is a virtually unlimited supply on Exmoor. A letter from a nurseryman, Mr. Thomas Rockford, of Turnford Hall, Broxbourne, Herts; reveals that he was in receipt of a quantity, but had not received a quote and wished to know the price. The outcome is not recorded, but, presumably, the usual problems of transportation—and the cost of—outweighed any monetary advantages, and nothing came of it.

The Telegraph reached Simonsbath in 1898, and William Kingdom, the Postmaster, is believed to have received the modest sum of 1d. for every message delivered within three miles. Viscount Ebrington may have done a little better out of the deal, as he was paid 6s. 4d. per annum by the Postmaster General for the telegraph poles placed in his hedgebanks beside the road from Exford to Simonsbath, and for the cutting of small branches from his trees to clear the wires.

One relic of Viscount Ebrington's early years on Exmoor, still in its original setting, is the small 30 hundredweight Avery cattle weightbridge installed on the east side of the Simonsbath-Lynton road, opposite the Challacombe turning, and though no longer in use there can be few such weighbridges left in this country and I trust it will be preserved.

Other relics of this period are the gorse bushes growing along the eastern hillside of Lower Limecombe, which, strange to say, are the product of a packet of gorse seeds purchased in 1898 for 6s. 8d. The sowing of these seeds is recorded in G.C. Smyth Richards diary, but he does not reveal its intended use.[1]

In was about this time that a number of enquiries were made concerning the dormant iron mines on Exmoor, but it was not until 1908 that mining was restarted on the Moor. Very little of the history of mining during this period has been recorded, and the next chapter will, I trust, help put this right.

In 1910, an agreement was drawn up between the 4th Earl Fortescue (Viscount Ebrington—who had succeeded to the title on his father's death in 1905) and the International Carbonising Co. Ltd., but never completed.

On the terms of this agreement, Lord Fortescue, as owner of large deposits of peat on and about Exmoor, gave the Carbonising Co.—who had an exclusive licence to use a certain wet carbonising process to produce peat coal and other products—three months in which to determine the suitability of the peat for the process, after which £10 per acre was to be paid for every acre used; Lord Fortescue to provide a site or sites near the deposits for the purpose of treating the peat.

Although initially three months had been allowed in which to prove the product, negotiations were still being carried on three years later, but on the 23rd September 1913 the agreement was all but completed. Three days later, G.C. Smyth Richards accompanied Lord Fortescue to a meeting with the managing director of the Carbonising Co., Mr. Testrup, and his solicitor, to finalise the deal, but after a long discussion two matters were still unresolved. One, was over the first spit of land taken off,[2] the other concerned the dead rent of £750 asked for by Lord Fortescue, and on these two points the talks were temporarily abandoned. Nevertheless, the surveying of a route for a railway to take the peat products off the Moor went ahead, the route proposed being to the north of Pinkery Pond, running from the Chains to Westland, where a small station would be built beside the Lynton-Barnstaple railway near the old slate quarry. Mr. Lund, the surveyor, could forsee no difficulties in regards to the construction of this railway, which would have been relatively cheap to build, but like earlier, and later proposals for a railway on Exmoor, it was not to be, and though talks with the Carbonising Co. drifted on until well into 1914, no agreement was ever signed. It is possible that the advent of the First World War caused the final breakdown in negotiations, and thus Lord Fortescue was denied the opportunity of reaping what would undoubtedly have been a very profitable source of revenue, but to Conservationists it has been a blessing in disguise, for the inevitable result of such an undertaking on Exmoor would have been the destruction of its finest wetlands.

In a breakdown of accounts for the period 1898-1908 (the first ten years of the 4th Earl Fortescue's ownership of the Exmoor and Brendon Estates), the Exmoor Estate farm made profits of £26,847 after allowance was made for a fall in stock value of £1,123. A comparison with the last ten years of Frederic Knight's lifetime reveals that this was an average of £143 per annum less than he received, but this was more than offset by a corresponding increase in rents received from the Exmoor and Brendon Estates, which, with the letting of several more farms, had risen from £2,598 to £3,426 per annum.

In the following decade (which includes the 1914-18 War), the prices obtained from the sale of sheep and cattle rose dramatically, as farming in general entered one of its more prosperous phases. There is little doubt that at this time some of the tenant farmers on Exmoor—who for the most part employed little labour outside the family circle—made considerable fortunes, but on the estate farm, which was wholly dependant on hired help, large wage increases and rising costs cut deeply into the profits, and

Exmoor shepherds and other helpers at shearing time (c1905)

Left to right, back row: Unknown, Jack Jones sen. (Estate Worker), Archie Jackson (Hoar Oak), Jack Little (Pinkery), Robert Tait Little (Limecombe), William Little jun. (Larkbarrow), William Little sen. (Tomshill), William Blythe (Badgworthy), Lady Fortescue (4th Earl's wife). front row: Friend of the Fortescues, Thomas Little (Limecombe), William Bain (Mines), Willie Welsh (sheep marker), Unknown, Dick Jones (Estate Worker).

Donald MacDougal (South Forest) who for some unknown reason was missing from the group above.

Robert Tait Little (head shepherd) and his wife Jane.

Titchcombe Bungalow (shepherds) built about 1910

though the total income from the rent roll and estate farm reached £14,679 in 1918, expenses of £12,068 left a profit of only £2,611, as against a profit of £5,787 in 1913, on gross returns of just £12,405.

Comparisons of stock prices obtained in 1913-14 and 1917-18, reveal that the average price of cattle sold had risen from about £15 a head to £25. Average prices obtained for sheep rose from a little over 22/- to about 37/-; wool from 10d. a pound to 15d.

Like many other landlords at this time, Earl Fortescue was under considerable financial pressure as a result of increasing costs, taxes, rates and interest charges, and because of the nature of the Exmoor and Brendon Estates, rents obtained were much less than for a corresponding acreage on the more productive low lying farms around the Moor. The cost of maintaining the moorland farmhouses, cottages and other buildings, subjected as they were to the worst gales and weather conditions, was always high, and in an effort to reduce costs and improve the financial position of the estate it was decided to sell off three of the offlying Brendon farms, Slocombeslade, Cranscombe and Malmsmead, but before Slocombeslade was put on the market, a new tenant was found for it. Cranscombe was advertised in the local papers, and Malmsmead was offered to the sitting tenant—Mr. French—for £800, but whether his offer of £700 was accepted is not at present known.

A year later, on 16th August 1915, G.C. Smyth Richards showed Sir Edward Mortimer Mountain* around Brendon Manor House, and some time later took him on a tour of inspection of the Brendon Estate; all of which he purchased—subject to contract—on 7th December 1915, for £30,250, with possession in 1916. According to this agreement the amount of land purchased was 5,353 acres, which would tend to confirm that part of the Brendon Estate had already been sold off, as the total acreage taken over by Lord Fortescue in 1897 was 5,664 acres, but in a sworn declaration just prior to the completion of the sale, G.C. Smyth Richards gives the Brendon acreage as 5,774 (most confusing). What is more certain, is that Lord Fortescue did not show a profit on this deal, because the sum realised, was no more than John Knight had given for the Brendon Estate in 1820, plus John and Frederic's later purchases in the Brendon area.

After the sale of the Brendon Estate, Badgworthy herding was given up, and because of the War, a proposed new bungalow for a shepherd at Prayway (Blackpits) had to be postponed for a time, and it was not until 1920 that a bungalow was built there to serve the herding created around it.

This policy of creating new herdings by rearranging the available moorlands left over when former—or parts of former—herdings were let off as farms, had already proved successful elsewhere, but Titchcombe, once a part of Duredon herding, did not become a herding in its own right

---

*Sir Edward Mountain also purchased the Oare Manor Estate around the same time, following Nicholas Snow's death.

until shortly after Robert Tait Little's death in 1907, and it was not until 1910 that a bungalow was built there to serve it.

A memorandum in G.C. Smyth Richards diary for 1915, reveals that the Brendon farmers had been accustomed to grazing rights on Exmoor's North Forest, but these rights were terminated after the sale of the Brendon Estate, although they still retained their full rights on Brendon Common.

Soon after the First World War began, orders from the County Agricultural Committee arrived on the doorstep of Lord Fortescue and his tenant farmers, to plough up parts of the better land on Exmoor and till corn. Because of its height above sea level the chances of successfully harvesting corn crops grown on Exmoor had always been a problem, and was the main reason why very little corn had been grown there in recent years. It was to prove no different during the War years, and though 60 acres of corn tilled at Limecombe in 1916 gave a reasonable return, Dyers field at Winstitchen in 1918 was a complete failure, and as soon as possible after the War was over corn growing was given up, as the greatly increased costs of labour, manure and seeds, precluded any chance of profit being made by its continued growth.

Early in 1918, some of the Spruce and Larch plantations created on Exmoor by Frederic Knight (which had now reached maturity) were sold to the Government timber buying department, but it was late in the year before a gang of Portuguese timber fellers, who were temporarily housed in accommodation huts placed at Simonsbath, began felling the timber on the Halscombe and Cornham plantations, and it was not until the latter half of 1919 that work started on clearing the Flexbarrow plantation near the old Wheal Eliza mine. Woodland accounts show that prior to 1918, the sale of timber had contributed an insignificant amount to the estate income, but in the years 1918-19, and 1919-20, £1,300 and £2,303, was received from the Government for the Exmoor timber. Thereafter, the income from the woodlands was again negligible.

A lesser known fact about the felling and removal of the Flexbarrow timber is that it involved the construction of a rail or tramway to Simonsbath, about a mile away. The rolling stock of this little railway was comprised of just two flat bottom timber wagons, capable of taking 20 foot lengths of timber, and a small petrol driven engine. It was, nevertheless, unique on Exmoor Proper, in that it was the only one of the many proposed railway schemes (apart from the horse powered tramway at Picked Stones Mine—see Chapter 11)—that was ever completed and working. Even more remarkably, the engine driver, William Grant, is still alive and though he is now 91,* can still recall many of the details of its construction and short working life.

William Grant was born at Limecombe in 1896, but left Exmoor with his parents when he was only a few months old; his father having taken

---

*1987. Died 9.2.1988.

employment in a coalmine at Merthyr Tydfil, South Wales. When William was 13 years old he followed his father down the pit, earning 10/- a week, of which 3/- were spent on fares getting to work, and another 1/- in Union dues. He joined the Navy during the First World War, and having no desire to return to the pits when the War ended, sought employment elsewhere. William Grant still had two uncles living on Exmoor, farming at Balewater and Cloven Rocks. He wrote to them, but they had nothing to offer. There was, however, a vacancy working the circular saw placed at Cornham Brake by the Fortescue Estate, to deal with the felled timber from the Cornham and Halscombe Plantations. He applied for the job, was successful, and came back to Simonsbath, but the noise made by the saw became more and more unbearable, and when it was decided to construct the railway from Simonsbath to Flexbarrow, he volunteered his services to help lay down the line. On its completion he became the driver of the engine, which he believes was purchased by Lord Fortescue in Somerset

The route of the little Exmoor railway can still be traced for much of its length. It began by the road near Simonsbath Bridge, crossed over Ashcombe Water into the meadow where the Simonsbath Pound once stood, and then followed close to the northern boundary fence of the small fields—lying under Birch Cleave Wood—that were for many years part of the Lower House smallholding. At a point just beyond the far end of these fields (roughly opposite the junction of the Water coming down from Halscombe, with the Barle), the railway crossed the river and followed the south bank down to Flexbarrow, where the timber was dragged across the river and loaded on to the railway wagons.

When Mrs. Harry Prout (née Maggie Little) was a young girl, she and some of the other village children used to ride down to Flexbarrow on the empty wagons, and walk up behind them when they were loaded. A boy was also employed on the engine; his job was to look after the sand boxes, running sand on to the lines to keep the engine moving when it made the return journey pulling the loaded trucks. A sharp look out had to be kept on the track ahead to avoid running down John Elworthy's sheep and lambs, which were in the habit of lying between the rails where it was nice and warm, but despite the care taken, an occasional sheep or lamb was killed. On a good day it was possible to haul 11 full loads from Flexbarrow. Loading went on six days a week; maintenance being carried out by William Grant on Sundays. Eleven gallons of petrol were delivered every Monday morning and five gallons later in the week. Most of the timber from the Exmoor plantations was transported to South Molton and sent away by rail. By the end of 1922 the last of the trees on Flexbarrow had been felled and removed. The line was then taken up and sold with the engine and wagons to a Brickyard Company in the Birmingham area. The new owners offered William the job of driving the engine, but he declined. With the timber felling contract completed, William was out of a job and he moved off the Moor, taking work where he could find it, eventually settling down in a cottage at Leary Barton, West Buckland, where he worked on the farm for Mr. Thomas for over 25 years.

For the first time in the early part of 1918, a tractor was hired in to plough the Limecombe corn ground. The success of this operation led shortly afterwards to Lord Fortescue purchasing a new Fordson tractor from the works for £250. It was not placed on Exmoor, however, but at Townhouse, one of the farms in hand on the Castle Hill Estate, and it was some years before the Exmoor Estate had their own tractor.*

The sale of the Brendon Estate in 1916, had reduced the number of sheepherdings on Exmoor to six, and when the Acland Allotment came on the market in 1919, following the death of Sir C.T.D. Acland (when the whole of the Little Bray Estate of some 7,000 acres was sold off to pay death duties), Lord Fortescue had his Agent bid for this land; which, being nearly all virgin moorland, would have made an excellent herding. G.C. Smyth Richards bid up to £1,450 for the 815 acre allotment, which included part of High Bray Common, but he was not successful, and the allotment was eventually knocked down to W.J. May, a farmer and cattle dealer of Barnstaple, for £1,800, and this family have owned it ever since. Part of the Acland Allotment has since been reclaimed, and a house for a resident stockman was built there in 1925-26.

Amongst the other lots sold off following Sir C.T.D. Acland's death, was 31 acres of land at Moles Chamber, which had been reclaimed and much improved by Jeremiah Smyth whilst living at the Acland Arms. His son, Charlie Smyth of Natsley, was still renting this land at the time of the sale, but it was not he who purchased it (at £200), but John Marsh, who had for some years been farming at Kinsford. How long it remained in his possession is not known, but about 12-14 years ago the Moles Chamber land also came into the possession of the May family.

In 1898, the number of sheep including ewe hogg replacements on the seven Exmoor herdings, plus Badgworthy, was 6,416, but with the reduction of herdings to six, the numbers of sheep and followers were correspondingly reduced to 4,285 in 1916. Despite this drop in sheep numbers, the cattle herd was on the increase. The policy here was to buy young Shorthorn bullocks in the spring of the year at Bristol, which after arrival on Exmoor were spread around the sheepherdings. The bullocks were kept for two summers, but only one winter, in order to keep supplementary feed requirements to a minimum. After the second summer's grazing was over they were sold off, and replacements purchased the following spring.

In the ten year period 1898-1908 the average number of bullocks sold each year was 80, but in the next decade the average annual output had risen to 173. In addition, about 150 heifers, mostly Shorthorns, were brought up from Castle Hill each year, and after summering on the Moor were sold in the autumn as down-calvers. A limited number of cattle from

---

*1939.

around the Moor were also taken into keep each summer, and it was a fairly common practice among the Exmoor tenantry to do likewise. Basically, it was a question of economics, it being far more practical and profitable to take in stock to keep for the summer, when it was almost impossible to overstock, rather than increase their own herds of sheep and cattle, and then have to purchase expensive feeding stuffs to see them through the long winter months.

It was during the period under review that one of the more intriguing—if morbid—incidents in Exmoor's history occurred, when, in the early part of 1913, after a search for a missing Exford man, William Stenner, had been carried on for nearly six months, with neither the man or his body discovered, and with rumours circulating that he had last been seen near Pinkery Pond, it was decided to empty it of its contents, in order to confirm whether or not William Stenner's body was in the pond.

For some years prior to the draining of the pond the fishing rights had been let to Mr. W.E. Arthur and his friend, F.G. Richmond, for £4 per annum. The former gentleman also rented in succession, Honeymead House and Larkbarrow Big House, together with extensive sporting rights on Exmoor, at a rental of about £60 a year. Pinkery Pond was said to have been well stocked with trout, and the fishing there excellent, but once the water was drained off the Herons for miles around flocked there and had good sport. No body was found, and after lying empty for a few days the outlet was blocked again and the pond refilled, but it was not restocked with fish.

Only twice in the 160 years or so since Pinkery Pond was constructed by Irish labourers working for John Knight in the 1820's, has it been emptied. On the first occasion, in 1889, the body of a Parracombe farmer, Richard Gammin, was recovered, but the second—as we have just seen—drew a blank.

A little of the story of these two men, whose lives were ended by their own hand, has been told in *Murder and Mystery on Exmoor* by Jack Hurley,* but many of what I consider to be relevant and important details have been omitted, and by consulting the *North Devon Journals* for the periods when these sad occurrences took place, it has been possible to put together a more complete account of the two incidents; which are as follows:

Prior to his death, Richard Gammin had lived at Rowley Barton, Parracombe. He was a well known and respected farmer of over 1,000 acres, and though he did not go in for prizes or pedigrees, he had a splendid lot of stock of the rent paying kind. Richard was of a rather excitable nature; of slight build but very strong, and in his younger days excelled in all manly pursuits. Lithe and active, he was as conspicuous on the cricket field as he was capable in the shearing sheds, where he had few equals. In his time he held most of the parish offices, but owing to

---

*Also briefly recorded in S.H. Burton's *Exmoor* and other books.

increasing deafness he devoted more and more of his time to his thriving farming business.

The events that led to his death in Pinkery Pond on the afternoon of Wednesday the 13th March 1889, at the age of only 48, began with the loss of his dear wife six years earlier, when he was left a widower with ten children to raise. Of late, he had been paying his attentions to a young woman in Parracombe, but she declined his advances. On the day that he went to his death he received a letter from her, to the effect that she did not wish to see him again. Later the same day he called at the Fox and Goose Inn at Parracombe, where he was heard to express a determination to drown himself in Pinkery Pond. He left the inn at 3 p.m., and just two hours later, William Little, one of Sir Frederic Knight's shepherds, who was at that time living at Pinkery Farm, discovered Mr. Gammins pony secured near the pond, with his coat, vest (waistcoat) and hat lying nearby, and close to the edge of the pond was his collar and shirt front. In the pocket of the waistcoat was the letter Richard had received earlier in the day, and William Little, convinced that he had done away with himself, lost no time in contacting his nearest neighbour, Alex Kingdom of Driver Farm, who immediately saddled his horse and rode off to Holwell Farm, Parracombe, to inform Mr. Joseph Gammin of his discovery.

A search party was quickly organised, and an intensive search of a wide area carried out, without finding the missing man, and with sinking feelings in their hearts they now feared the worst. On the following morning the Captain of the Lifeboat at Lynmouth, John Crocombe, was contacted, and a boat was conveyed to Pinkery Pond, which was then carefully dragged, but the search was fruitless and on Sunday it was called off. A diver by the name of Binding who lived at Cardiff was called in. The next day, he and his son came down to Exmoor.

News of what was happening at Pinkery Pond travelled quickly around the district. On Sunday, over 1,000 people visited the spot, many with genuine desire to help in any way they could, others out of morbid curiosity. On Monday and Tuesday, 600-700 people turned up to watch the diving operations, the progress of which could be easily followed by the trail of bubbles arising on the pond. Still no body was found. Dynamite was sent for, but not to blast a hole in the dam as an over-enthusiastic reporter of the *North Devon Journal* stated, but to place in cannisters and explode under water, in the hope that the body would be dislodged and raised to the surface. This, too, failed to achieve the desired result, and the divers efforts were now concentrated on locating the two 12″ pipes placed in the dam wall during its construction, where, by removing the plugs placed in the end of the pipes, the pond could be emptied.

Throughout the diving operations and the subsequent work entailed in removing these plugs, large numbers of people continued to visit the pond daily, and on one occasion Sir Frederic Knight paid a personal call. The problem now, was that having decided on the course of action, could it be done?

John Knight's original plan of campaign to empty the pond as required was in theory a simple system, whereby on pulling on the chaims that had been connected to the plugs in the pipes, presumably with the aid of some horse-power, the bungs would be easily removed, but he had not reckoned on the tremendous pressure exerted against them by a pond full of water, and when he tried his system out, the chains, strong as they were, broke. In one of the *North Devon Journal* reports at this time it was said that Squire Knight afterwards offered £50 to the man who was able to overcome this problem, but this money was never claimed. As the iron ring on one of the plugs was still intact, a chain was again attached, but in trying to extract the plug the ring was wrenched off, and with it, any chance of removing the plug in this way was ended.

Mr. Binding, having done all that was humanly possible in the murky depths of the pond, returned home, and the Jones brothers, builders by trade of Lynton, but better known for the famous cliff railway that Bob Jones designed and constructed (it was nearing completion), were consulted and the matter left in their capable hands. Bob wasted no time in getting to grips with the situation and on the same day visited the pond for a visual inspection of the problems involved. He decided that as there was no way that the plugs could now be pulled, then they would have to be forced out. This was to be no easy task either. First there was a long drainage tunnel to be cleared of mud and slush accumulations of some 60 years. This tunnel, cut through solid rock, was afterwards measured and found to be 170 feet long, four feet six inches high, and two foot six inches wide, and at its far end joined on to a culvert some 25 feet long, but reduced in size to three feet six inches high and two feet four inches wide. The culvert, constructed of brick, lay under the dam and contained the two 12 inch iron pipes, one above the other, and by using a pointed iron rod, Bob probed for and found the plug.

In order to force the plug out it was necessary to get a strong spar of at least 23 feet in length into the pipe, and therein lay a problem, for owing to the crooked nature of the main tunnel, nothing longer than nine feet could be brought in. This difficulty was overcome by joining together three six inch iron pipes, inserting them one at a time into the 12 inch pipe, one end against the plug, the other against a ten ton hydraulic jack fixed against a baulk of timber notched into the rock on each side of the tunnel. Other machinery was set to work the jack, the whole operation being controlled by lines of chains and wire ropes from the mouth of the tunnel. At 3 p.m. on Wednesday 27th March, the machinery was put in motion. After about ten minutes, with eight tons of pressure applied, the plug was forced out and some 2,000 gallons of water a minute poured in a muddy stream from the tunnel.

By Thursday morning the pond was sufficiently empty to expose to view the body of Richard Gammin, which was found by Alex Kingdom in a part of the pond that was only six feet deep, and close to where he had left his clothes. The body was removed to Simonsbath to await the inquest; the pond continued to drain. By Friday afternoon Pinkery Pond was nearly empty, revealing a black dismal gorge some 900 feet in length, 150 feet in width and 40 feet deep in its deepest part. At this point, Bob Jones removed the hydraulic jack and machinery from the tunnel, replaced the plug in the pipe, and the pond was allowed to fill up again.

At the inquest that followed on Saturday, the jury returned a verdict of suicide, committed while in a state of temporary insanity. The mortal remains of Richard Gammin were then removed to Parracombe, where they were interred in the family vault in the presence of a large gathering of relations and friends.

The circumstances surrounding the disappearance of William Stenner from his home at Riscombe on the night of August 9th 1912, were completely different, for until that moment there had been not the slightest suspicion that he intended to do away with himself.

William was a quiet man of 36, happily married with six children, and no known problems. He was in the employ of Mr. F.G. Heal of Riscombe Farm, who was also the Exford Parish representative on the Dulverton District Council. William was an industrious worker and completely trustworthy, and for a time in the spring of 1912, he took charge of the farm while his employer was on a vacation in California. For some time prior to his disappearance, William had been having sleepless nights, and in consequence had become very low and dispirited. Doctor Molony of Porlock had been called in and he advised a complete rest for a few days. The doctor was obviously concerned about William's state of health, because he paid a further two or three visits to the Stenner household within a week.

On the evening of the 9th August, William, who was in bed, asked his wife for something hot, and while she was in the kitchen preparing it, he got out of bed and jumped out of the bedroom window on to the garden below, and wearing only his nightshirt slipped away into a wild and rain lashed night. It was only moments later that Mrs. Stenner returned upstairs to find her husband gone. She quickly alerted her neighbours and a search was immediately begun, but no trace of the missing man was to be found. On the following day, 50 men searched the countryside for a radius of ten miles, but with the same negative results.

The mystery surrounding William Stenner's disappearance, and the steps taken to discover what had become of him, was to last for six months before his body was eventually found, but high on the list of likely places where he could have done away with himself, if he so desired, was John and Frederic Knight's old lime quarry at Newlands; long disused, and now full of water; this being only a couple of miles from his home, and at a cost of nearly £40 this was pumped out.

At this point I would like to put the record straight regarding the photograph of a pumping operation in the 1973 *Exmoor Review,* allegedly taken at Pinkery Pond. In no report in the *North Devon Journal,* or elsewhere that I have read concerning the draining of the pond, either in

1889 or 1912-13, was anything said about a pump being used there; both operations being carried out by the removal of a plug or plugs from the drainage pipes. Having said that, there is every reason to believe that the photograph shown is that of the pumping operation at Newlands Pond. Although no body was recovered, the occasion was well remembered by the late Mr. F.J. Westcott, father of Mr. Reg Westcott of West Ley Farm, Exford, who worked for some years in the adjoining Newlands Lime Quarry, because when the old pit was pumped dry he had his lunch on the quarry floor.

The decision to drain Pinkery Pond in January 1913, was more or less a last resort, all else having failed to find the missing man. It was partly brought about by unsubstantiated rumours that William Stenner had been seen in the area of the pond soon after he disappeared, and partly because Mr. J. Kingdom of Driver Farm, enthused no doubt by the story of the earlier draining of the pond in which his father played a major role, was all for draining it a second time.

When Bob Jones and his team of willing helpers had drained the pond in 1889, the operation was set up and completed in less than a week, but the efforts of Mr. Kingdom and his bunch of staunch followers were to last a month. Time and again the plug was forced out, only to slip back into place, but eventually, by using a similar technique to that used by Bob Jones, the plug was forced out by the use of a hydraulic jack, and by the end of January the pond was completely emptied. The Kingdom team were, however, considerably bolder than their predecessors, because all of their operations were carried out within the confines of the tunnel, which considerably increased the risk of danger to themselves. Nobody really expected to find William Stenner's body in the pond, as indeed it was not. Nevertheless, numerous spectators had again been turning up at the spot day after day. A black morass of peaty constitution was revealed on the completion of the drainage operation, which was left exposed for the world to see for about a fortnight, after which the plugs were replaced[3] and the pond filled up once more. The herons had cleared the trout and the pond was not restocked.

For some time, rumours had been circulating in the district that William Stenner was still alive and had been seen in Canada. That the Dulverton Board of Guardians—who since William Stenner's disappearance had been paying Mrs. Stenner 12s. 6d. a week parish relief in respect of herself and six children—believed this rumour, is evidenced by the fact that they offered a reward of £5 for information leading to the arrest of the missing man, and a warrant was still in force when his body was eventually discovered. About the time the reward was offered, Mrs. Stenner's parish relief was stopped. This may or may not have been a coincidence, but was probably because she had moved from Exford, and had for some time past been living in South Molton.

It was as dusk was falling on Tuesday 25th February 1913, that the **mystery of what had become of William Stenner was finally solved, with** the discovery of his body in an abandoned mine tunnel, in the side of the valley west of the ruined farm of Muddicombe, less than a quarter mile from his home, and, ironically, in an area that had been scoured in the first search. The tragic discovery was made by Reginald Hosking, one of the missing man's former workmates, after he had noticed that for some time bullocks had been refusing to drink near a stone drain that was in part fed by water from the mine. The entrance to the mine was all but obscured by the build up of silt around its mouth, where the surface of the water was covered by a green slime. Reginald pushed this away and suddenly caught sight of a naked foot some 20 inches inside the adit mouth. Closer examination revealed a second foot, and, greatly frightened by his discovery, he ran to Exford to communicate his gruesome find to the Police. Unfortunately, PC Padfield was at that time on duty some miles away, and was unable to visit the spot until the early hours of the next morning. He was just able to reach through the water to the nearest foot, to which he attached a rope. The rest was simple, and the man's body was drawn out of the shaft-like adit with ease. With the exception of his nightshirt, William Stenner's body was quite naked, but in a remarkable state of preservation seeing it had lain in the tunnel for over six months; the features of the dead man were easily recognised by those present at the time.

The body was removed to the Crown Hotel, Exford, and on Thursday afternoon a Coroner's inquest was held. Evidence given by the widow stated that there was absolutely no reason for her husband to leave home. There had been no quarrel, and apart from his inability to get his proper sleep, which had left him low and dispirited, he had no known problems, and had certainly given no indication that he intended to take his life. Dr. Molony stated that death was due to drowning, and the jury recorded a verdict to that effect, adding that the deceased had committed suicide while of unsound mind.

Having recorded in some detail the sad departures from this world of Richard Gammin and William Stenner, it is time to return to the primary objective of this chapter, namely the affairs of the Exmoor Estate and farm from the time of Sir Frederic Knight's death in 1897, to the beginning of the Second World War in 1939.

Despite careful and very efficient management, the sale of the Brendon Estate did not solve all of Lord Fortescue's problems, and in January 1920, the smallholding at Newlands in the parish of Exford, which included the cottage, 19 acres of land and John and Frederic Knight's old lime quarry, were sold to the tenant, Mr. J.F. Westcott for £350, and a year later the first sale of any part of the Exmoor Estate since it was purchased by John Knight, took place, when the offlying farm of Litton was sold to the tenant, William Carter (the grandson of William who took the tenancy of the farm in 1861), for £3,000, which, incidentally, was £400 less than the asking price in 1919.

The Carters continued to farm at Litton until 1945, and with the considerable help of two of William's sons, Bert and Leslie Carter, it has been possible to put together at least a part of this family's history, which is included here because in many ways it was typical of the evolvement of a new breed of farmers on Exmoor; local men with similar backgrounds.

According to the *Reclamation of Exmoor Forest* William Carter—who was born at Bishops Nympton—'began his working life on Exmoor as an Ox boy at Honeymead, and later became postillion in John Knight's stables at Simonsbath'. By the time he was 30 (1841) he was married with two children and farming Holes Allotment (now Willingford). In 1861, he took the tenancy of part of Litton Farm and Crooked Post Cottage and a small allotment, for which he paid a total annual rent of £90 to Frederic Knight. In 1865, the same rental was paid for what was now described as Litton Farm and buildings, and it is at this point that I would like to pause for a moment to take a closer look at Litton Farm and Crooked Post Cottage, for the latter building was, I believe, unique on Exmoor Proper, and bore no resemblance whatever to any other farmhouse or cottage built upon the Moor. This cottage was first recorded in the Census of 1851, but was assuredly built a long time before Frederic Knight built Litton Farmhouse, which was attached to it in 1848, and though the cottage was not recorded in the Census of 1841, I would suggest that it may have predated that year.

Bert Carter describes this old cottage as being of two storey construction, with one room down and one room up. At the centre of the long wall at the rear was a huge round stone built—but plastered—chimney which towered some 15 feet above the roof and was out of all proportion to the rest of the building. It was, as Bert described it, a real landmark and could be seen for miles around. The roof was also unusual for the date it was supposedly built, in that it consisted of huge rag slates two feet square, which was more in keeping with the roofing of John Knight's earliest cottages around Simonsbath, and there the similarity ends. So did he build it? or was it erected by the former owner of the Litton land, Lord Carnarvon? This is not unlikely, as the chimney bore a strong resemblance to the cottage chimneys of Porlock Vale, which in turn suggests the influence of Lord Carnarvon's wife, who was an Acland heiress.

Until the 1940's, the single room downstairs was always used as the kitchen, and was by far the warmest room in the two habitations. The pump supplying water to the household was conveniently at hand in the same room; the upper room being used as a store. The Carter family always referred to this old cottage as 'Crofters' and it is believed that it was originally built to house a shepherd-cum-herdsman tending the stock on the rough and lonely moorlands around it.

Alas! this cottage is no longer with us, having been demolished in the mid 1970's. So much for the preservation of our heritage. Exmoor, least of all, can afford to lose such places. The links with the past are disappearing at an all too rapid and alarming rate, and it is sad to think that in this so called enlightened day and age, that this unique building has disappeared without trace, with not one protest made, or one voice raised in its defence.

When William Carter took the tenancy of Litton Farm in 1861, it was still virgin moorland, and apart from an allotment on the northside of the Sandyway-Withypool road (opposite Litton Lane), the whole farm was in a single enclosure, surrounded by a drystone wall, with not one field enclosed within its boundaries. A formidable task lay ahead; two farmers had already failed, but with the help of his two sons, Tom and Henry, and his daughter Maria—who worked as hard as any man—fields were enclosed and much of the land successfuly reclaimed. Sadly, Tom Groves Carter did not live to reap the benefit of his labours, for he died at the early age of 28; his resting place among the three generations of the Carter family buried in Twitchen Churchyard.

By 1870, William Carter and his son Henry were farming 363 acres, for which a rent of £125 per annum was paid. Together, father and son had become noted breeders of the North Devon Cattle (Red Rubies), which did very well there. A flock of Exmoor Horn sheep were also kept, and by the time of William's death in 1886 at the age of 78, the Carter family were firmly established and the farm was prospering.

Henry married into the well known and respected Delbridge family (who have farmed at Blindwell, Twitchen, for many generations). They had three sons, Tom, William and Jim (who died as a baby), and four daughters. The improvement of the farm went on, and when lime was needed to sweeten the acid soil, it was fetched from Newlands quarry; two loads one day and one the next, with a team of three horses hauling approximately two tons at a time to the field where it was required, where, after being dumped into heaps and given time to slack (or slight), it was spread.

The Carters were one of the few tenants on the Exmoor Estate who neither asked for—or received—a reduction in their rent during the depression in the latter part of the 19th century. They tightened their belts and carried on.

Time passed; Henry's sons and daughters grew up and married, and when Henry died at the age of 75 in 1913, his two sons went into partnership and continued with the farm. About six months later the partnership was dissolved, when Tom Carter and his wife moved to Lower Lanacre to take the tenancy of the 233 acre farm, at an annual rent of £140. William remained at Litton, and a new agreement dated 25.3.1915 reveals that he was now farming a slightly reduced acreage (351) and paying a little more rent at £150. The fine herd of Devon cattle and the flock of Exmoor Horn sheep had been maintained, and some corn in the form of oats was also grown for consumption on the farm. There is reason to believe that this had been the practice for many years, as Litton had been equipped with a Round House and a barn thresher, which was worked in the traditional manner, with three horses providing the motive power. A chaffcutter was powered in the same way, but only one horse was required for this operation. Horse power later gave way to engine power when William Carter installed a Lister engine—towards the end of the First World War. The engine house was built with stone taken from the farm boundary wall, which was replaced by an earth and turf bank. When the original barn thresher disintegrated from the combined efforts of woodworm and fair wear and tear, a replacement was purchased from a manufacturer of farm machinery at Knowstone. Corn growing was eventually given up when only one harvest in three was gathered in successfully, and though other farms in the south-east corner of Exmoor Proper probably also grew a little corn, Litton alone had been equipped with the necessary barn machinery to deal with it.

In 1921, William Carter was able to purchase Litton Farm for £3,000, which was some £300 less than he offered for it in 1919, when G.C. Smyth Richards first approached him in regard to its sale, but what with the split with his brother a few years earlier, and a growing family of four sons and four daughters to feed and clothe, he was hard pressed to raise the money required, and the only way in which he could complete the purchase was to hold a disposal sale of all his livestock. William was now 40 years old, and he knew that with this sale, all the fine stock that he and his forebears had built up, would be gone for ever and he would have to begin again from scratch. Nevertheless, the sale went ahead, and the farm was his.

Leslie Carter (William's youngest son) still has a newspaper report of this sale, which was conducted by Mr. Edwin Cockram of South Molton, and attracted buyers from a very wide area. Stock prices included: Registered Exmoor Horn ewes with single lambs made up to £7 2. 5. Double couples to £6 2. 6. Ewe hoggs 75½s,—97s. Fifty seven Wether hoggs to 75s. and Registered rams 3½-14 guineas. The Devon cattle made £26 10.-£40 10. Heifers £20 1. 6d.-£40. Young heifers £11 5, and young steers £28 5, which were all exceptionally good prices at the time.

For two years after his livestock sale, William let the grass keep of his farm, but by 1924 he had again built up a small flock of Exmoor sheep. Among a number of mementoes that Leslie Carter has kept, are the wool sale records of Litton from 1921-1942, excluding, of course, the two years following the purchase of the farm. All the sales, 1924 and after, are for yolk wool (wool in its natural state), but in 1921, the wool sold was washed wool. Leslie explained that it had once been common practice to wash the sheep a few days prior to shearing, because washed wool fetched a little more money. The chosen spot where the sheep washing took place was about 150 yards up river from Lanacre Bridge, where the water level was just right for the purpose. Tom Little has since told me that the Kingdom brothers of Driver and Cornham farms used to do likewise, in the stream that runs down beside the lane from Driver Farm, where it adjoins the bridge carrying the main Challacombe-Simonsbath road. Barn doors from the farm were used to pond back the water, but this was not the best of places for the purpose, because the sheep, with their fleeces saturated with water, sometimes had difficulty in climbing out of the steep sided valley, and later, when a sheep dip was built about midway between Driver Cottages and Driver Farm, beside the lane, this was used instead.

Prices for wool fluctuated widely in the 1920's and 30's, reaching a top price of 1s. 8d. in 1928, when William Carter sold 1,570 pounds of wool and 15 pounds of 'locks' for £131 10, but the depression in the 1930's brought a sharp drop in prices, and though William sold 100 pounds more wool in 1932, the whole batch produced only £28 2. 6—just 4d. a pound. It is little wonder that so many farmers went bankrupt at this time, and many of the derelict farms around the Moor today are the result of this depression, but the Carters, like most Exmoor farmers, took in their belts another notch and weathered the storm.

Shortly after William Carter bought Litton Farm he purchased the adjoining small farm of Greenbarrow (from Mr. Fisher of Nurcot Farm, Winsford, for £520), which the family had been renting since 1889— although they did not at that time rent the house. This farm consisted of a four room cottage, the usual buildings, and 27 acres of land in seven fields, for which a rent of £26 per annum was formerly paid. Shortly after Greenbarrow was purchased, two lots of Litton land were sold. The first, in the mid 1920's, was 24 acres opposite the Sportsman's Inn, which William Carter sold to his brother Tom soon after he moved to the Inn following the sale of Lower Lanacre Farm where he had been the tenant. Only five acres of land went with the Inn, but with the 24 acres now acquired, and a further 18 acres rented, the combined business gave him a living.

In 1933, 37 acres of land called 'Northside'—opposite Litton Lane—was sold to Ned Bulled for an undisclosed sum. It was later sold to a man named Watts, who in turn sold it to Joe Sinkins for £600. Joe, who was employed by William Carter for a number of years, was lent the money for its purchase by old John Thorne of Bentwitchen in North Molton parish, who was a sheep farmer on the grand scale, renting many farms and other land in the North Molton-Exmoor area. It was not a bad deal from Joe's point of view, because when he sold his land a few years ago to Mr. Matthews of the adjoining Woolcombe farm, the sum realised was £26,000.

In 1927, a near fatal tragedy struck the Carter family when Bert Carter was out with two of his brothers, Jim and Leslie, shooting crows. They were about a mile from the farm and Jim was climbing a tree to see if a crows nest there was in use. The tree was wet and slippery and Bert went to his assistance, giving him a shove up, placing his gun in the normally safe position of half cock beside the hedge they were standing on. The gun started to slip away and Bert reached down to grab it, but the trigger snagged, either on a tree root or a twig, and there was a tremendous explosion, with Bert catching the full blast, which almost severed his hand from his arm, only a sliver of skin still holding it, which, according to Leslie, was easily snipped off with a pair of scissors. Bert's face was also peppered and he lost the use of an eye, but there is no doubt that the loss of his hand was the price he paid for his life.

If you can for a moment pause and try to visualise what life on Exmoor was like in 1927, when it was virtually carless and still very much in the days of the horse, you will realise the terrible predicament that Bert was in. The first problem was to get him home, and by the time they arrived he was weak from the loss of blood and the shock. It seemed impossible that he would live, but despite his terrible injuries, fortune smiled on him that day. Dick French of Sandyway Farm, mounted on George Brooks' (of Sherdon) pony, was sent post haste to fetch the nearest doctor from South Molton, eight miles away. By the time he was halfway to North Molton he was caught up and passed by Alec Chanter, chauffeur to the two Miss Abbott's of Dulverton, who were out for a drive and had heard the news at the Sportsman's Inn. The doctor quickly arrived, and Bert was made as comfortable as possible to await transportation to the Infirmary at Barnstaple. The Ambulance arrived in the shape of Mr. Crang's (Baker and Corn Merchant of North Molton) delivery van, which had been rapidly cleared out for the purpose, and Bert was taken as quickly as possible to the hospital.

For five days Bert lay unconscious, his life in the balance, and it was only his youth and strong constitution that saved him, and despite the loss of a hand and an eye he has led a very full life and there is little he cannot do. He was a fine shot before the accident, and remained so after. In 1931, Bert married a Molland girl, and for a year lived in Sherdon Cottage, in a sheltered spot beside Sherdon Water, close to the stone bridge. This cottage belies its position on the Moor, for it is much warmer here than the surrounding countryside. The following year was spent at West Port Farm, Bishops Nympton, working for his wife's uncle. A year later, Bert took the tenancy of East Lee, a small farm on the Molland Estate, and by combining the farm with contract work for the estate he was able—after a few years—to take the nearby and larger farm of Middle Lee, where he remained until his retirement to South Molton in 1974.[*]

In 1928, just a year after Bert's accident, William Carter bought a car, the first in that part of Exmoor, although there were already three at Simonsbath. George Molland, the Exmoor Estate bailiff, is believed to have been the earliest car owner on Exmoor Proper (early in 1917). Mary Elworthy, who was the tenant of the Exmoor Forest Hotel, had two more, which were used as taxis. All were Overland's, or Overland Whippets, made by Willys (the jeep firm), and they appear to have been the ideal car for the rough moorland roads.

One by one, William Carter's children had grown up, married, and moved away from home, until only Leslie was left to help his father run the farm, where it was expected he would one day carry on, but when his father reached retirement age, Leslie, who was a bachelor, could see little point in carrying on alone, and so, after 84 years and four generations of the Carter family had lived and farmed at Litton, the farm was sold in

---

*Forty years a tenant of Molland Estate. Bert Carter died 28th May, 1987, aged 78.

1945 to Major Worthington (the beer people), who nine months later sold it again, and it has changed hands several times since.

Greenbarrow, however, was not sold at this time as Leslie was particularly fond of it, and after moving with his parents to a small holding at Lower House, Twitchen, he continued to farm it for a number of years, later letting it, and finally selling it in 1971 to Chris Thorne of Eastern Ball, Twitchen, William Carter, his wife and Leslie remained at Lower House for about 11-12 years, but shortly after their Golden Wedding in 1956, they moved to North Molton, where, in 1966, they celebrated their Diamond Wedding. William died in 1968, at the grand age of 87, and was laid to rest in Twitchen Churchyard, where he was rejoined by his wife two years later.

The cottage farmhouse at Greenbarrow was let down in the 1920's. The last to live there was William Carter's sister, Mary Stenner, and her husband, but after Mary died her husband moved away. The slates were then taken off the roof and used on the end wall of Litton Farmhouse which was very damp, and shortly after, the cottage was taken down. The main problem at Greenbarrow had been the lack of a suitable water supply close at hand; the nearest reliable source being two fields away, and this in the end was to be its undoing.

In recent years there has been talk of an inn called the Cork and Bottle, which is said to have been situated somewhere along the same stretch of road as Greenbarrow, but as nothing can be found either on the ground or in any records, I came to the conclusion that its most likely site had to be the Greenbarrow farmhouse, where it would have provided a useful additional source of income. Bert and Leslie Carter are of the same opinion. They believe it was not a Public House with a full licence, but a cider or ale house.

These were not the only premises of this kind in the locality. Sandyway Farm is also known to have had a bar, which was served through a hatch from the kitchen. This bar was still there when Dick French senior purchased the farm from Seymour Gillard in 1920. It remained there—but not in use—until after Dick French junior, who married one of Bert and Leslie Carter's sisters, took over the farm in 1927. A trade sign with the Gillards name on it was also found, but which generation of the family is not known.

It seems a little strange that within a distance of a mile or so on the same road, three houses served strong liquid refreshment, and one is left to wonder where all the customers came from considering the sparcity of population. Moreover, many of the Exmoor farmers brewed their own beer, William Carter among them. Only one strong ale was taken off his brew, but in some instances several batches of ale of declining strengths were taken off before the brew was exhausted.

While we are still in the southeastern corner of Exmoor it would be as well to include one or two items of interest (for the record) which might otherwise be forgotten.*

---

*From conversations with Bert and Leslie Carter.

Some years ago, before Litton Farm was given up, Leslie Carter was ploughing the field known as Crockers which lies east of Litton Lane. In the corner, where the field adjoins the lane and the main road, he uncovered a cobbled floor, the last remnants of the cottage occupied by James Crocker for over 30 years; later pulled down by Frederic Knight. For well over 100 years Redcurrant bushes have flourished in the hedgerow against the lane, and as far as is known, still yield an annual harvest of fruit.

The triangular piece of open land lying between the Withypool Cross-Lanacre road, and the same Cross-Withypool, has for some years been held by the Somerset County Council, but in earlier years William Carter regularly cut the rough herbage there for bedding for his farm animals. It was also a favourite spot for the Gypsy caravans, once a familiar sight on Exmoor, to set up camp for a time while going about their business in the area.

The Sandyway Longstone, one of the well known Forest boundary markers of ancient times, disappeared around the time of the enclosure of the Forest, but according to Bert and Leslie Carter it is not far away from its original position close to Sandyway Cross, and is believed to lie under the North Molton-Sandyway road, where it forms part of the culvert carrying Litton Water from one side of the road to the other.

Coles Cross Cottage, later known as Barkham Cottage, was—as we have already seen—principally a farmworker's cottage, and for a few years a smallholding. It was still standing in the 1920's, but was in a derelict state the last time that Bert Carter went there. He remembers the occasion well because a badger was dug out from under the lime-ash floor. Nothing whatever now remains of this old cottage, which disappeared off the face of the earth when a bulldozer was brought in a few years ago, and the site levelled.*

For a few years following the end of the First World War, farming on Exmoor held its own against the post war depression of the Country as a whole, but there was little or no money to be spared for further reclamation or improvements. On the Exmoor Estate farm, exceptional profits of £5,171 were made in the year ending 31st March 1921, on gross receipts of £18,869; the highest farm receipts recorded during the period 1900-1932, but in the next year farm income dropped to only £10,321, and for the first time since Lord Fortescue took possession in 1897, the estate farm sustained a loss (£2,022). For the next three years profits again rose steadily from about £2,172 in 1923, to £4,076 in 1925, on gross returns ranging from about £11,500-£12,500, but in the year ending 31st March 1927, profits slumped to a mere £17. This last figure, however, was partly due to a change in accountancy procedure, and though prior to this date farm profits had always gone towards paying some kind of rent for the land in hand and interest charges, this rent did not appear on the estate

---

*Last to live there, a Mr. Leeworthy.

rent book. This was rectified in 1927, when a sum of £1,310 was transferred from the farm profits to the estate rents, and thereafter, depending on the acreage of land in hand, rent was paid in this way. In practical terms this meant that from 1927 on, farm profts shown were more accurate, though of course, considerably less.

An additional expense in 1926, was the renting back of Badgworthy, which had been sold off with the Brendon Estate in 1916, plus the cost of restocking it with sheep. Two years later in 1928, Honeymead and some 1,743 acres of land, including the farms of Picked Stones, Winstitchen, Red Deer and Cloven Rocks, plus a part of Winstitchen Allotment and Exe Cleave, were sold to Sir Robert Waley Cohen, who had been renting Honeymead House since 1924, and had for some time been seeking a large country estate on which to relax from the high pressure of a successful business career; he being second in command of the huge Shell group of companies. The price paid for the Honeymead Estate was £14,500; the equivalent of £8. 7s. 0d. an acre, which was less than Lord Fortescue had paid for it in 1886, and only £3 per acre more than John Knight had given on average for the Exmoor Estate in 1818, when it was virgin moorland.

At the time of Sir Robert's purchase, most of the Honeymead Estate was let, and it was not until 1939, when the tenant of Honeymead Farm retired and 550 acres came in hand, that Sir Robert set about maximising the potential of his property. As other land came in hand he improved this also, and by the end of the Second World War most of the land suitable for reclamation had been dealt with, and productivity greatly increased.

I do not intend to go into a more detailed account concerning Honeymead Estate, suffice to say that this has been excellently covered in the *Reclamation of Exmoor Forest,* but before returning to the affairs of the Exmoor Estate, I would like to add a comment or two to the story of Robert Cann, the last but one tenant of Honeymead Farm, who was one of the prime examples of a successful graduation from farmworker to large tenant farmer on Exmoor, and when he gave up the tenancy in 1927, it was to move to a farm he had purchased at Stoodleigh near Tiverton.

Robert Cann, the son of a small farmer at Exford (and grandson of Robert Cann, who was first recorded as a shepherd on Exmoor in 1821, employed by John Knight), came to the Moor in the 1880's when he was a young man, to take a position as a farm labourer working for Frederic Knight. By 1892, he had graduated to shepherd in charge of the Cornham herding, no mean feat, when considering Sir Frederic's preference for— and the competition from—the Scottish shepherds. Robert moved from the Cornham herding about 1897, to take a herding at Honeymead, and on Ladyday 1898, took the tenancy of his cottage there and 132 acres of land at a rental of £95 per annum. By adding to it in stages over the next few years he was farming nearly 550 acres by 1910, for which he was paying £204 a year; increased without objection to £220 in 1920. In that same year, his son William took the tenancy of Picked Stones Farm and 250 acres, but not in quite the way the *Reclamation of Exmoor Forest* describes it, as the main help in this direction came from William's choice of wife, who was the daughter of the outgoing tenant there.

There were few men on Exmoor who made the transition from rags to riches more successfully than John Gourdie, the last of the original band of Scottish shepherds brought down by Frederic Knight. When John Gourdie arrived on the Moor with his sheep in the latter part of 1871, he had just 2s. 6d. in his pocket, which was all the money he possessed.

For the first ten years or so after he arrived on Exmoor, John Gourdie was in lodgings at one of the West Cottages on the Simonsbath-Challacombe road. At this time, he was the shepherd of the Simonsbath herding, the extremities of which were not far from the Acland Arms at Moles Chamber in one direction, and Gallon House on the Exford road, in the other. It was his custom to call at both inns in the course of his daily shepherding routine, but after his marriage to Selina Tucker on Christmas Day 1882, John Gourdie no longer stopped off at the inns, although he did retain the habit of smoking an ounce of tobacco a day. Whilst I do not believe for a moment that it was his custom alone that had kept the Acland Arms and Gallon House going, it is strange but true, that both of these inns had given up their licences before the end of 1883. Fifteen years later, when Lord Fortescue renewed Frederic Knight's earlier policy of letting as many farms and as much land as possible, he was able to take the tenancy of Wintershead Farm and 736 acres, at a rental of £220 per annum. The farm comprised of 294 acres of enclosed improved land, for which John Gourdie paid 10/- an acre per annum. The remainder was in one large allotment of 442 acres of rough grazing on Great Woolcombe, which he rented for 3/- an acre. He was well acquainted with this allotment, for it had been a part of the Wintershead herding, where he had been the shepherd from 1885, until he took it with the farm in 1898.

It is interesting to note that although John Gourdie had been looking after a flock of Cheviot sheep for the past 27 years, he did not choose this breed for his own requirements, but followed local custom and purchased a flock of Exmoor Horn sheep, and though he did not go in for prizes for individual sheep in the local show rings, it was no idle boast when he claimed his flock would hold its own against any other flock of Exmoor sheep, on or around the Moor.

John Gourdie remained at Wintershead until his death in 1931, at the age of 81, and it came as some surprise when his Will was read, to find that he had accumulated the considerable fortune of £20,000; £8,000 of which was left to his wife, and £6,000 to each of his two daughters. Not a bad effort for a man who arrived on Exmoor with just 2s. 6d. in his pocket.

The General Strike, which began in 1926, and the decade of depression that followed, affected landlord and tenant farmer alike. On the Exmoor Estate farm, receipts dropped from £11,526 in 1925-6, to £9,732 the following year, and remained at about this level until 1931-2, when they slumped still further to only £7,972, resulting in the small profit of previous years being turned into a loss of £1,775 and shortly before his death in August 1932, the 4th Earl Fortescue commented to his Agent that 'though to a certain extent outgoings could be controlled, there seems to be little that can be done to improve receipts, as the nature of the land and climate makes it impossible to make any but small changes in management or system'.

One of the casualties of the General Strike was the Exmoor pony herd on the estate farm. When Lord Fortescue took over this herd in 1897, following Sir Frederic Knight's death, it consisted of three stallions, 26 brood mares, six yearling mares and a gelding, which were reduced in number in the same year by one stallion and seven mares. It remained at this strength until about 1910, when the herd was further reduced to 14-15 brood mares and a stallion. Average prices received for suckers sold at Bampton Fair for the years 1897-1931 inclusive, was £4. 11. 7, but demand during the First World War, and for a couple of years after, was exceptionally keen, with sucker prices for this seven year period averaging £8. 17. 6, with top prices of £11. 3. 4 apiece for nine suckers in 1918. Thereafter, prices again dropped to £4 3. 4 apiece in 1921, and to under £2 in 1925. Nineteen twenty six and 1927 were even worse, when returns averaged only £1. 3. 4, almost exactly the same price as draft lambs were making, and as more sheep and lambs than ponies could be kept on the same acreage, the herd was cut from 14 Brood mares and a stallion in 1925, to three in 1928, and by the end of 1930 not one Exmoor pony remained on the estate farm. In the final entry in the Pony Book, that of 1928, it is recorded that ponies at Bampton Fair again sold for nothing, 10/- being a rather exceptional price. A number of ponies of all ages were sold to a slaughterman at Barnstaple for export as dead meat to Belgium, and Mr. French of Brendon sold 50 ponies of all ages for one pound apiece.

An undated newspaper cutting, probably of 1927 or 1928, found in the Pony Book, puts the lack of interest in the Exmoor ponies on offer at Bampton Fair down to the prolongation of the Coal Strike, which had resulted in a large number of pit ponies being brought to the surface and sold off. There was, therefore, no demand for the Exmoor ponies in one of their customary markets, and Ireland, which was normally another good customer, was refusing to admit any ponies into the country without a Veterinary Certificate after examination for foot and mouth disease, which, on the prices offered, farmers could not afford to obtain.

In 1929, George Cobley Smyth Richards, who had taken over the duties of Agent of the Exmoor Estate on the death of his father in 1887, died, and was in turn succeeded by his son Frederick. That G.C. Smyth Richards had a love of Exmoor far beyond the call of duty, is made abundantly clear in his diaries, and there was nothing he enjoyed better than to mount a horse and ride around the estate, taking in all that was going on around him, and missing very little. Without a shadow of doubt, had it not been for his astute business brain and capable management of the Exmoor Estate and farming enterprise, even more of this property would have had to have been sold off. His death, was followed by that of the 4th Earl Fortescue in 1932, and only four years later on the 16th December 1936, George Molland, the farm bailiff for the past 44 years, died in harness at the age of 75, just six days after the death of his wife, Agnes. He was succeeded by Mr. John Purchase.

In the early 1930's, when the agricultural depression was at its worst, many landlords, Lord Fortescue among them, chose to reduce the rents due them from their less well off tenantry, rather than lose them, as the last thing they desired at this time was more vacant farms, for no one in their right senses was now entering farming. In the year 1932-3, the rents of some of the Exmoor smallholdings were reduced by about ten per cent, and in 1933-4, Mr. Hooper, who had succeeded the Kingdom family at Driver, had his rent for the 453 acre farm reduced from £200 to £184. In the same year, the tenants of Duredon and an allotment on Hangley Cleave, also received some relief, and from Ladyday 1934, a permanent reduction in rental was granted to Mr. W.J. Buckingham, the tenant of Pinkery, whose rent was reduced from £130 per annum to £100. At the same time, the rents of two allotments, Kinsford and Emmetts, were reduced from £45 to £30, and £38 to £30 respectively.

It was around this time that wages paid to agricultural workers and shepherds were also cut. General farmworkers, who had been accustomed to receiving 32/- for a six day week, were reduced to 30/6d., and shepherds from 37/- a week to 36/-. It is of some interest to note that in 1933, no less than five of the seven shepherds on the Exmoor Estate farm were from one family, these being descendants of William Little of Pinkery and Toms Hill.

In 1935, there was a shift in policy concerning the cattle raised on the Exmoor farm, when a small herd of pure-bred Galloway heifers, 18 in all, and a bull of the same breed were purchased. As the herd flourished, the annual number of young Shorthorn bullocks purchased at Bristol declined, and eventually ceased. In 1937, a white Shorthorn bull was purchased to run with some of the Galloway cows, this cross resulting in the famous Blue Greys, still to be seen on the Moor, but the first Shorthorn bull was not a great success, his progeny were poor, and he developed Tuberculosis. Later, a Devon and a Hereford bull were used with better results, the former adding a measure of tranquility to what was always a nervous and easily excitable breed. The crossbred cattle were equally as hardy as the pure bred Galloways, and for the best part of the year have the run of the sheepherdings, requiring only a minimum of additional feed to see them through the winter months.

The number of sheep on the six herdings prior to the renting back of Badgworthy in 1926, averaged about 4,250, a figure that was afterwards increased to about 4,750, falling a little after 1936, when the numbers of cattle were increased.

By 1935 the worst of the depression was over, and farming was beginning to pick up again. Government subsidies on lime and slag, introduced in 1937, were used to good effect, and a considerable acreage of grassland was improved, and by the beginning of the Second World War, Exmoor was reasonably well prepared to meet the demands about to be made upon it.

Before we move on to 20th century mining, and conclude this book by taking a look at Exmoor during Wartime and events that have happened since, I would like to include a short résumé on one of the most controversial characters to set foot on Exmoor in recent times, namely the Rev. George Wardropper Surtees, Vicar of the parish from 1918-1945, who, as a result of his actions over two relatively minor matters concerning the school at Simonsbath in the 1920's, managed to antagonise considerably more than half of the local inhabitants. The amount of paperwork that evolved at this time has to be seen to be believed, for not only are there a number of bulky files in the Fortescue deposit of documents at the D.R.O. Exeter, but a similiar quantity has also been deposited at the S.R.O. Taunton.

The first of the two issues came to a head shortly after Earl Fortescue handed Simonsbath School over to the Somerset County education authorities in 1925, when the old Board of Managers ceased to exist, and a new Board was elected. The problem arose over what was to be done with the funds left over from the former administration, and it was on this issue that the former Board of Managers were split down the middle, with the Rev. Surtees and his Church Wardens insisting that this money belonged to the Church, and the three other managers adament that it should go to the newly elected Board of Managers, for the future benefit of the school.

In order to determine who was rightfully entitled to this money, it is necessary to go back to 1857, when, on the completion of the new school at Simonsbath, built entirely at the expense of Frederic Knight, a fund was set up to finance the education of the children, and was contributed to by the local inhabitants on an entirely voluntary basis. A system that continued until the School Board Act of 1870, when each parish was given the right to determine whether the school continued on the voluntary system or become a Board School. Simonsbath chose to continue as they were, and the school funds continued to be administered by the Board of Managers.

After Sir Frederic Knight's death, Viscount Ebrington (4th Earl of Fortescue), was elected in his place as a school manager, and in 1903 it was decided to let the school premises to the Vicar and Church Wardens, for a nominal rent of £4 per annum, but though the school was run by the Church from 1903-1925, it was not officially a Church School as the Rev. Surtees believed.

At the time the school was handed over to the Somerset County Authorities, there was approximately £83 in hand. A year later the situation in regards to the surplus money was still unresolved, at least not to the satisfaction of the Rev. Surtees and his Church Wardens, because in the meantime, G.C. Smyth Richards, the treasurer to both the old and new Board of Managers, had handed the money over to the new managers.

The Rev. Surtees certainly left no stone unturned in his efforts to get hold of this cash for the Church. Letters appeared in the Press and Parish Magazine, and when this failed to achieve the desired result he took legal action against G.C. Smyth Richards, but in this too he was unsuccessful, and costs were awarded against him. The school fund remained where it was, in the hands of the new Board of Managers, who decided it should be used for getting special subjects to Simonsbath, such as gardening, dairy work, cooking and sewing, as the County Council would not send special instructors to the school unless their travelling expenses were met.

For a short time following the Somerset County Council's take-over of the school in 1925, the Rev. Surtees continued to give religious instruction at the school, but after his defeat in the Law Courts, he declined to continue.

In 1927, the County Education Authorities decided—in all their wisdom —that Mrs. Lena White, the headmistress of Simonsbath School, should be given three months notice to leave, and her assistant, Miss Wilminhurst, one months notice, as they wished to replace them with a qualified teacher.

In the case of Miss Wilminhurst this was understandable, as she had been taken on in 1922, when the number of pupils had risen to 35, and as there was now only 17, there was no need for a second teacher; but a storm of protest greeted the unwarranted attack on Mrs. White's reputation. Unqualified she may have been, but for nearly 30 years her teaching methods had given every satisfaction, both to the school managers and her pupils, and the present managers were prepared to pass a resolution for the decision to be reconsidered by the County Council. This proved to be unnecessary, as Mrs. White and her husband had decided to leave Simonsbath at the end of March of the following year, and the Manager's request that she could continue teaching until then was granted.

It was not the retirement of Mrs. White, but the presentation that followed, that brought the Rev. Surtees back on the offensive, when some of the Parishioners thought it desirable—as a token of their appreciation— to give her as a parting gift, the furniture of the School House that she had long enjoyed. Lord Fortescue proposed that this should be done, and it was agreed by the school managers. A Parish meeting was called to endorse the decision, which was approved, despite a letter received from the Rev. Surtees and read at the meeting, in which he claimed that the furniture belonged to the Church and was therefore neither Lord Fortescue's or the school managers to give, but the content of this letter was completely ignored and Mrs. White was informed that she might have the furniture to sell or retain as she thought best. She decided to sell, and the Rev. Surtees felt that he now had no alternative but to instruct his solicitors to take whatever action was necessary to ensure that the furniture was either replaced, or its value recovered from Mrs. White and Mr. George Molland, the co-defendant in the case. The relevant documents were examined by the solicitors, and it was proved that the furniture did belong to the Church Trustees, and not to Lord Fortescue as he believed, but it should be made clear here, that although the allegations in the Rev. Surtees letter to the parish meeting should have been checked before the school house contents were given to Mrs. White, there is no suggestion whatever that anything underhand was going on, because Lord Fortescue was of the genuine, if mistaken belief, that as he had purchased the whole of Frederic Knight's Exmoor and Brendon Estates, that this included the contents of the school and school house which Frederic had built.

A Court hearing planned for the 10th and 11th September 1928, at Exeter, did not materialise, as the case was settled out of Court when the Rev. Surtees agreed to accept payment of £25 from Mr. Molland and Mrs. White, in respect of the value of the house contents and the cost of the action.

It his all too obvious attempt to put one over Lord Fortescue and his fellow school managers, the Rev. Surtees had shown little concern for the feelings of Mrs. White, who was the innocent victim of his actions, and recipient of the well intentioned if unfortunate choice of gift in recognition of the fine work she had done over the past 30 years. The threat of legal action against her, and a demand he sent for the repayment of the money raised by the sale of the furniture, shows a complete lack of sensitivity on the part of the Vicar to what should have been a happy and memorable occasion. In one of his parish magazines he did possibly try to make amends, but even here he could not resist the temptation to cause further embarrassment, when he suggested that Lord Fortescue and Mr. Gammin, another of the school managers, called a further meeting; not to pass resolutions, but to open a subscription fund on Mrs. White's behalf to pay her costs, where it was hoped that all who so readily attended the earlier parish meeting, will bring with them substantial contributions, worthy of repentance.

There is no doubt whatever, that in the course of his long sojourn on Exmoor, the Rev. Surtees upset not only Lord Fortescue, but many of the local inhabitants. How and when the first troubles started is not known, but as early as 1923, Lord Fortescue had cause to cut off the electricity supply to the vicarage: Exactly when the supply was reconnected is also unclear, but the Rev. Surtees comments in the parish magazine on 7th October 1926, indicate that the trouble arose over a disagreement on the price charged for the electricity used. He states that the amount paid for the electric current used for the 12 month period to Michaelmas was £3. 10. 11, which was considerably less than the £5 paid annually prior to the installation of the meter. He follows this up by saying, 'This important piece of information is intended for those determined on making mischief'.

There can also be no doubt that it was largely due to the way the Rev. Surtees had been conducting himself on Exmoor, that led to Lord Fortescue's decision to hand over the school to the Somerset County authorities, and though we know from other documents that there was no suggestion that the Vicar had done anything illegal or immoral, he had not carried out his duties in the manner expected from a man of the cloth. He had neglected to visit many of his parishioners, but this was not an offence in the eyes of the Church unless he refused to visit a particular person when asked, and because he had kept within these limits, there was little that could be done—as was certainly desired—to remove him from his office.

By the time the school was handed over to the Somerset County Council, the gap between the vicar and many of his parishioners had widened to unresolvable proportions, and at this point there was a large breakaway movement from the Church. At first, this body of people held services in the open air, but later services were held in Frank Vigar's large kitchen at the Post Office. On special occasions, Lord Fortescue allowed them the use of his racquets court at his summer residence at Simonsbath Lodge (House). Later still, he provided a site adjoining the lane into Simonsbath school and the present car park, on which to build a Gospel Hall.

A report in the *Western Times* 19.4.1929, reveals that an Undenominational Church has been opened at Simonsbath, due to the unfortunate difficulties between the Rev. Surtees and a number of his parishioners. The new Church has accommodation for 50 worshippers, and was completed at a cost of £150, including furnishings; Most of this sum being raised prior to the opening ceremony. This was performed by Mrs. Annie Goaman, ex mayoress of Bideford, and a short service was led by the Rev. W. Houghton, Wesleyan Minister of Minehead. A public tea followed, and the £60 outstanding on the Church was loaned free of interest by Mrs. Gammin. Claims that the Rev. Surtees congregation at the Parish Church had dropped to six, were hotly disputed by the Vicar, but there is no doubt that the majority of church going people were now attending the new church, and thus it remained until it was taken over as an evacuee school in 1940.

It is sad to think that a man in his position, who should have fostered a happy community spirit on Exmoor, should be the one to divide a parish against itself and cause such feelings of resentment, but it did happen, and there must have been a feeling of intense relief when the Rev. George Wardropper Surtees finally packed his bags and moved on.

One mystery concerning some of the contents of the Parish Church that went missing, and were later mysteriously returned—while the Rev. Surtees held the living—remains unsolved to this day. The Vicar, in his usual forthright manner, recorded it in the *Parish Magazine* (6.3.1931) as follows: 'About six months ago an altar cloth of fine linen marked St. Luke, Exmoor, 1856, was found carefully wrapped in a brown paper parcel on the vestry table. About three months later another cloth, similarly marked but smaller in size was put there, we may assume by the same person, who prompted by the working of a good or bad conscience seems to wish to restore these articles, but to do so without being known. It will be noted that the cloths are of the date of consecration of the Church and are 75 years old. They are in excellent condition and we are very glad to have them returned. There is, however, more to the mystery than at present appears, and we hope this good deed may be the means of suggesting the restoration of some other properties belonging to the Church, concerning which so far there is no sign of any awakening of conscience, good or bad!

Who the mystery person—or persons—that first removed, and later returned the Church property, has never been discovered, but one is left to wonder if at any time while the Rev. Surtees was the Vicar of Exmoor, he had the slightest twinge of conscience that it might just possibly have been as a consequence of his own actions, that led to their removal in the first place.

CHAPTER 11

20th CENTURY MINING ON EXMOOR

FOR close on 40 years the iron mines of Exmoor had been idle, but early in 1899, Viscount Ebrington's Agent, G.C. Smyth Richards, was approached by a William Huxtable with a proposition, which, if carried to a satisfactory conclusion, would result in some 12-15,000 acres of the Exmoor Estate being let as one large mining sett, to one large mining company.

Huxtable, an accountant by profession, with offices at 17 Joy Street, Barnstaple; was also in business with Joseph Pope (lately the Mine Captain of Bampfylde Mine at Heasley Mill) and another partner as 'Mine Agents', and a deposit of letters recently found in the Athenaeum, Barnstaple, relating to setting up—or attempts to set up—mining concerns by these three men are an education in themselves, but none more so than the attempts made to get mining restarted on Exmoor, and even though they were unsuccessful, it is worth recording a little of the content of the letters passing between Huxtable and a William Chappell of Grantham (who was also a Mine Agent), because they show quite clearly the problems involved, and just how easy it was for the delicate negotiations to break down, and why nothing came of the intended venture.

As main agents, Huxtable and Pope were to receive £300 if their endeavours resulted in securing a lease for the proposed mining sett, but out of this money they had to pay solicitors and other agents fees, plus any other expenses incurred in the transaction. The terms of the mining lease were to be for an initial period of 12 months, with an option for 21 years, at a dead rent of £300 per annum, plus 6d. a ton for white iron, and one twenty fourth for all other minerals raised.

William Chappell's part in the operation was to persuade one or more of his wealthy contacts in the North of England to form a company to work the iron ore deposits of Exmoor. If successful, he would not only have received a commission from Huxtable and Pope, but could expect to be retained by the new company as their Agent. Not that this was necessarily all profit, because in this capacity he would also be held responsible for the loss of cattle—or other livestock—which fell into the mine shafts or pits opened up by the company, for which compensation was to be paid if the shafts and pits were not properly fenced.

By June 1899, negotiations were well under way, and Chappell—who was decidedly keen to do business—stated that no money would be spared in the development of the mines if the property was considered to justify it, but soon after, the first of many problems arose when G.C. Smyth Richards flatly refused to allow any prospecting on the Exmoor Estate before a deposit of £200 was paid. This, Chappell refused to pay, until he was sure the expense was justified, and on this point negotiations came to a halt.

In order to try to break the deadlock, Smyth Richards suggested to Huxtable that if he was prepared to take out a six months mining licence, 'we might get some mining done at once', but Huxtable, fully aware of the risk involved, was not prepared to part with any of his money.

In the meantime, samples of iron ore had been sent to Chappell, who wrote back that they contained too much Sulphur and Phosphorous to make the property easily handled. He also complained that the suggested working capital of £75,000 was too much. Letters continued to pass to and fro, with little headway being made, but on 25th November, Huxtable received news from Chappell 'that without a shadow of doubt I will have it through all right'. Less than a week later, he wrote about building a railway from Exmoor to Blackmoor (Gate) Station, which, he presumed, would run over Lord Fortescue's property the whole of the way, as permission to lay a line was essential to the working of the property.

After this sudden burst of enthusiasm, negotiations again slowed down, and it was not until September 6th 1900, some 16 months after talks were first begun, that Chapplell wrote to Huxtable with the news 'that the promotor he had spoken to was now prepared to form a company to work the iron ore deposits on Exmoor, providing the expert they are sending down gives a satisfactory report'. This caused further problems, because the expert could not examine the mining sett until Chappell had an option on it, and, 'because this man was costing him a great deal of money, it would be foolish on his part to pay him, and then perhaps be told afterwards that he could not have the property'. Chappell concludes with 'you will no doubt know that several big iron people have refused the property, who have been down at the Agents' invitation'.

This, unfortunately, was the last letter relating to Exmoor in the Athenaeum depository, which leaves everything very inconclusive, but it appears that by this time, Chappell, or his associates, were getting cold feet and the whole business was called off.

Other enquiries from mining agents were received by G.C. Smyth Richards around this time, including one from the Consett Ironworks, who asked for samples of the iron ore. Two were sent; one from Simonsbath, the other from Hoar Oak, but though they were both of excellent quality there were no further developments.

The Barrow Hematite Steel Company went a little further, asking for plans and sections of the property, and arrangements were made for a mining engineer to come to Exmoor to inspect the property, but once again nothing came of it.

A retired civil engineer, William Shaw, who lived at Deercombe*—one of Viscount Ebrington's properties—also showed some interest, and a

---

*Brendon.

report on an assay of three samples of iron and copper ore that he sent away for analysis, were said to have contained a considerable proportion of Gold, but though Shaw was hoping to form a syndicate to work it, he was not successful.

By now, it is clear that Viscount Ebrington was just as keen as Frederic Knight had been to exploit the mineral resources of Exmoor, but it was not until 1908 that any real effort was made to re-open the mines on the Moor. On October 18th 1908, Henry Roberts of West Bromwich—who also had an interest in the Blackland Mine in the parish of Withypool—was granted a licence to search for minerals on the Exmoor Estate until 25th March 1911, on condition that he spent £2,000 on the search. In the same month (October), he was seeking a buyer for 400 tons of iron ore lying at Rogers Lode at Bluegate. Roberts had hardly had time to unpack his bags, let alone raise 400 tons of ore, but in a letter written later (7th January 1914), the source of this ore is explained thus: 'Before we commenced mining work at Rogers Shaft, 700 tons of iron ore brought out by the previous company (Schneider and Hannay) still lay around the shaft. In 1907, Mr. John Brailey of Withypool (former Mine Captain of Bremley Iron Mine, Molland, in the 1880's, and Blackland Mine, Withypool, in 1895), took a sample from the heap, which was found to contain 59.02% iron: Presumably, some of the ore had already been sold, and by the time Alex Tucker was called in to report on the mining prospects in 1909, several large consignments of the remaining 400 tons had been sold to a number of different firms.

Henry Roberts had no intention of carrying the burden of the exploratory mining work on Exmoor alone, but his first attempt to form a company ended in failure, when the firm he was negotiating with, J. Wilde and Co., of London, found the terms of Lord Fortescue's lease unacceptable. Roberts was more fortunate in his second choice, when he was able to get together a small syndicate of men who were all familiar with the iron trade and its problems, and on February 3rd 1910, he made an agreement with Sir George Hingley of the Dudley Ironworks, Joseph Ellis of Workington and Edward Prosser Davis of the Bennerly Furnaces, Ilkeston, whereby these three gentlemen agreed to pay the costs of the search, with Roberts appointed the manager of the mines.

Most of the preliminary work carried out by Henry Roberts had consisted of clearing out the earlier workings of the three mining companies who had been at work on Exmoor in the 1850's, but in 1909, Alex Tucker recorded there was 200 tons of iron ore lying at the Picked Stones Mine, which was either lying there when Roberts took over, or had been raised by him since.

One of the most interesting items to come out of Alex Tucker's report, concerns Frederic Knight's exploratory mining work in the early 1850's, which, although known to have been extensive, very few people realise to what lengths he went to prove the lodes on his property. Tucker records that Frederic cut a 12-15 feet deep trench two miles long across the South

Forest from Hangley Cleave to Simonsbath, to intersect the outcrop of the east-west lodes. In 1909, much of this trench and the outcrop of the lodes were still to be seen, although already badly overgrown.

After a thorough investigation, the new company—known as the Exmoor Mining Syndicate—decided to concentrate their efforts on opening up three or four separate mines, in areas where the chances of quickly getting into production were greatest, namely Burcombe—where the Roman Lode outcrops; Deer Park—which included Rogers and Double Lodes, and Picked Stones, where a large iron vein, believed to be an eastern extension of Rogers Lode, was waiting to be tapped. These, then, were the principal mining areas; in fact, the self same areas worked by the previous mining companies. It was also proposed to extend Llewellyn's Drift to cut the assumed westward extension of Rogers Lode, thus proving it over a distance of nearly four miles.

With the prospect of quickly bringing the mines into production, a great deal of thought was given to the problem of transporting the ore away. Like Frederic Knight, the syndicate recognised the necessity of economic transport to the coast, and like him, they lacked the capital to finance the project. Nevertheless, by the end of August 1910, with less than a year to run on their current agreement, several schemes for a railway or an aerial ropeway had been looked at, and some survey work on the routes carried out.

The first of the proposed railways*—from Cornham Ford to Blackmoor Gate Station (on the Lynton to Barnstaple line), was to run from a point just below the Main Drift at Cornham Ford, which had been cleared out and was currently being extended towards the Roman Lode, where it was expected to open up the vast iron ore reserves believed to lie under the old surface workings. Once across the Barle, the railway was to run between the old miners cottages and the river, and continuing beside it, the first section would have ended near Driver Cottages—on the Challacombe-Simonsbath road.

The plans of the next section are missing, but the line would probably have run beside the lane leading to Driver Farm, where it would have curved westward across the moorland between Pinkery Pond and the farm, crossing the higher reaches of the Barle by way of a short viaduct, to join the next stage, which began beside the hedge south of Longstone Barrow. From this point it was proposed to follow the contours of the hillside, circling around the head of Longstone Water, before turning westwards again. This section ended on the hillside above the ruins of Radworthy Farm.

The plans for the remainder of this proposed railway route have not been found, but once across the head of Swincombe Valley the ground is comparatively level, and little difficulty would have been encountered in taking it to its proposed destination at Blackmoor Gate, to link with the

---

*Fortescue papers D.R.O. Exeter. Plan dated 14.9.1909.

now defunct Lynton-Barnstaple railway, for carriage of the iron ore to Fremington Quay for shipment to South Wales.

Early in 1911, Henry Roberts was granted a years extension to his mining agreement. In the summer of the same year, Edward Willey, a civil and mining engineer, spent a month on Exmoor examining the mining property and the transport problem. His report of 28th August 1911, shows that much of the route for the railway to Blackmoor Gate (which was to be of two feet gauge) had already been pegged out. The steepest part of this line was a manageable one in 50 from Cornham Ford to Swincombe. The most expensive obstacle to overcome was in getting the line across the upper end of the Swincombe Valley. Willey estimated that this alone would cost £2,000. Although this railway was a sound engineering project, its total estimated cost of £23,000 was way beyond the means of the syndicate. An alternative suggestion to use an aerial ropeway over the same route, was found to be no less expensive.

Other routes suggested at or about this time included a railway to Glenthorne on the coast near County Gate. Frederic Knight's earlier projected railway to Porlock Weir was also looked at, but here again the cost was prohibitive. Probably the most ambitious scheme was a proposed aerial ropeway from Cornham Ford to Porlock Weir. The feasibility of this proposal was thoroughly gone into, and on the completion of the survey, a detailed report was issued on 19th August 1910. This ropeway, 16,268 yards long, was to consist of three sections, with a total of 130 trestles and 435 carriers, each holding eight hundredweight. The ropeway was capable of carrying 40 tons per hour, at a speed of 130 yards a minute. Furthermore, only a modest 30-40 horse power engine would have been required to work it. Permission to carry this ropeway over Porlock Common and down to Porlock Weir had been granted by the Blathwayt family in 1909, so there can be little doubt that the syndicates intentions were sincere, but the estimated cost of the ropeway at £17,000, plus £4,000 required to improve the handling facilities at the harbour, were beyond the syndicates means and the whole project had to be called off.

In the final analysis, none of the projected rail or ropeways were affordable, and throughout the period this company was at work on Exmoor (23rd October 1909-12th January 1912), the 500 tons or so of iron ore raised, was taken by traction engine to South Molton and loaded on rail, at a cost of £140, which meant that nearly half the value of the ore sold was swallowed up in transport charges.

In January 1911, work was suspended on the extension of the Main Drift at Cornham Ford, with only 18 yards added to the 413 yard tunnel cut by Dowlais. This was a major setback to Henry Roberts, who believed that had it been continued 130 yards or so more to the Roman Lode, it would have opened up a block of ore beneath the so called 'Roman' surface workings, some 500 yards long by one and three quarter yards wide and 120 feet deep, with an estimated yield above the adit level of at least 124,000 tons of fine quality iron ore.

It is interesting to note that Edward Willey believed that 60-70,000 tons of ore had already been taken out of the old workings by the 'Romans'. This tremendous achievement, regardless of who the ancient miners were, was all the more remarkable because it happened long before John Knight had carried out his road improvements, and we are left to wonder just how many pack horse trains, and how many years passed, before this huge quantity of ore was removed from this remote hill on Exmoor, and as to where did it all go?

Alex Tucker and Edward Willey were not the only mining engineers called in to examine and advise on the development of the Exmoor mining property, nor were either of these two men responsible for closing down the Main Cornham Drift. This was done on the advice of William Dixon, who had come down from Whitehaven at Henry Roberts request in 1908. He returned again in 1910, to inspect the mines and report to the syndicate. Dixon was not at all happy with the slow progress being made in driving the Main Drift forward, and he now believed it was more important to prove the Roman Lode by sinking a shaft directly on it from the surface, before resuming work in the tunnel. In the latter half of 1910, work began on sinking this shaft on the hillside 100 yards east of the Burcombe Valley Shaft sunk by Dowlais in the mid 1850's. After sinking the new shaft to a depth of 70 feet the miners broke through into what was at first believed to be the collapsed remains of the Roman Drift (also cut by Dowlais), but subsequent mining operations proved that this drift was still some way below them, and that they were in fact in the mining deads left behind by the 'Romans'.* From the bottom of the shaft, Roberts drove a level eastwards on the lode, and on August 28th 1911, the miners cut into a solid body of ore, and some was certainly raised. Roberts considered this proof enough, but Willey advised sinking a second shaft 200 yards to the east, in order to prove the lode conclusively. This shaft, roughly in the centre of the old surface workings, was begun late in 1911, and was sunk very close to where Robert Smith had sunk an exploratory shaft for Frederic Knight some 60 years earlier. By January 5th 1912, 30 tons of good quality iron ore had been raised from the new shaft, where the lode was five feet wide, and it was anticipated that 15 tons of ore a week would be brought out for the next four weeks, after which, production would be stepped up to 40 tons a week.

We will call a temporary halt here to the progress reports on the Roman Mine, and take a look at the developments that had been taking place at the other Exmoor mines during the same period, because early in January 1912, the mining syndicate broke up, and though for a short while E.P. Davis and Henry Roberts carried on alone, the remainder of Exmoor's mining history belong to the new Exmoor Mining Syndicate, Ltd. that was formed soon after.

When Dowlais abandoned Llewellyn's Level in 1857, it was 212 yards

---

*These old workings varied in depth from 30-80 feet.

long and not one lode of value had been cut. On William Dixon's recommendation, Henry Roberts was driving it forward, with the express intention of proving the assumed westward extension of Rogers Lode. It is difficult to understand why Dixon was so insistent that this level should be continued, when Comers Level—driven earlier by Dowlais for the same purpose—had failed to find it, even though it had been carried some way beyond its expected position. One cannot help feeling that the money spent on extending Llewellyn's Level, would have been put to better use elsewhere. Work here had been progressing favourably, and by July 20th 1910, the level was 264 yards long. A year later it had been driven to 310 yards, to where the flow of water had increased considerably, leading Roberts to suspect that they were very near the lode, but shortly after, with no lode in sight, the miners were pulled out and the drift abandoned. A crosscut tunnel had also been driven from the level by Roberts, but although it had proved a little more successful, when a lode one foot wide was cut, there was insufficient ore in the vein to work, and this too had been given up.

When William Dixon first examined the Exmoor mining property in 1908, Rogers Shaft on the Deer Park was full of water. According to Roberts—in a later report—it was not pumped out until June 1910, when Dixon returned to examine it thoroughly. The lode at the bottom of the 90 foot shaft was ten feet six inches wide, and had been in solid ore from the surface down. Levels had been driven from the bottom, 162 feet east and 152 feet west, and at nine feet from the shaft in the west level, a crosscut had been driven 132 feet south to the Double Lodes, which were two feet four inches and one foot six inches thick, but the iron ore in these lodes, although of good quality, was more costly to work because of a high quartz content.

By the end of 1911, coal to the value of £146 had been consumed by the boiler working the steam operated pump in an attempt to keep the workings dry, but for all this expense, very little ore was taken up Rogers Shaft, as the pump was broken down more often than not. This was certainly the case when Edward Willey was doing his month long tour of inspection in the summer of 1911, for he too reported the shaft full of water, and work there at a standstill.

Most of the ore taken from the Deer Park—or Bluegate Mine—at this time, came from a shaft being sunk beside the Simonsbath road to the west of Rogers Shaft—on the same lode. At the same time, an adit level, known as the Upper Drybridge Level, was being driven southwards from the head of the valley west of the Simonsbath-Bluegate road, from a point about 200 yards south-west of the Hon. John Fortescue's memorial cairn, with the object of intercepting the shaft at a depth of 50 feet, and by following the lode eastwards, not only take out the iron ore encountered, but eventually connect with Rogers Shaft some distance away, thus reducing considerably the cost of pumping there.

At some time during the life of this syndicate, Henry Roberts contracted to drive an adit level for a distance of 130 feet, at a cost of £104. 12. 0, and though it is not stated where this level was to be driven, it is believed to be the adit level that passes under the Simonsbath road at Drybridge, because this adit is exactly the right length. This level, driven eastwards on what was believed to be an extension of the Roman Lode, certainly contained some good iron ore, but by the time the miners had completed their contract the vein had narrowed to a few inches, and no further development took place there.

The adit level (east of the shaft) at the Picked Stones Mine, first opened up by Anthony Hill and the Plymouth Iron Company in 1857, had been cleared out very early on by Henry Roberts, and by the time William Dixon completed his second tour of inspection of the Exmoor mines (20th July 1910), it had been considerably extended.

A serious problem had been encountered in the driving of this level, when, after following the lode eastwards for a distance of 67 yards, it was cut off by a slide or fault. The Plymouth Iron Company had driven through this fault but on failing to find the lode on the other side, had abandoned it. Dixon, in his earlier investigation of the Exmoor mines, believed that the lode had been heaved southwards, and Henry Roberts had followed a leader of ore in that direction for a distance of 39 yards, to where it turned south-eastwards on what was believed to be its proper course, but after carrying the level forwards for a further 41 yards the lode split into two small branches, neither of which contained workable quantities of ore, and all work there ceased.

It was now thought that the adit had not been on the main lode at all and a further attempt to find it was made by driving a crosscut tunnel northwards, but after 30 yards had been completed, without any sign of either the lode or the big deposit of ore that lay close to the surface nearby, this tunnel too was abandoned. A shaft sunk to a depth of 39 feet close to the fault in the primary adit (but not sunk directly on this level), proved to be of greater benefit when a lode ten feet six inches wide was discovered, and some ore was certainly raised from a level driven westward from the bottom of this shaft.

This then was the state of mining on Exmoor when Sir George Hingley and Joseph Ellis withdrew from the syndicate after £4,050 had been expended in a little over two years with a corresponding income of only £337. It is not unlikely that both men considered enough money had been spent on the search and were not prepared to speculate further on the offchance that one day the venture might prove a success.

Edward Prosser Davis and Henry Roberts, however, were still very optimistic, and more than ready to carry on, and for a few months continued to do so alone, but the burden was too great and Lord Fortescue was approached and invited to join the two men in forming a new syndicate. He accepted the proposal, and an agreement to this effect was drawn up on June 18th 1912, although the new company, known as the Exmoor Mining Syndicate, Ltd., was not formerly registered until the 16th December 1912.

The proposed working capital of the new company was £10,000, divided into one pound shares, and the original; in fact, the only subscribers, were

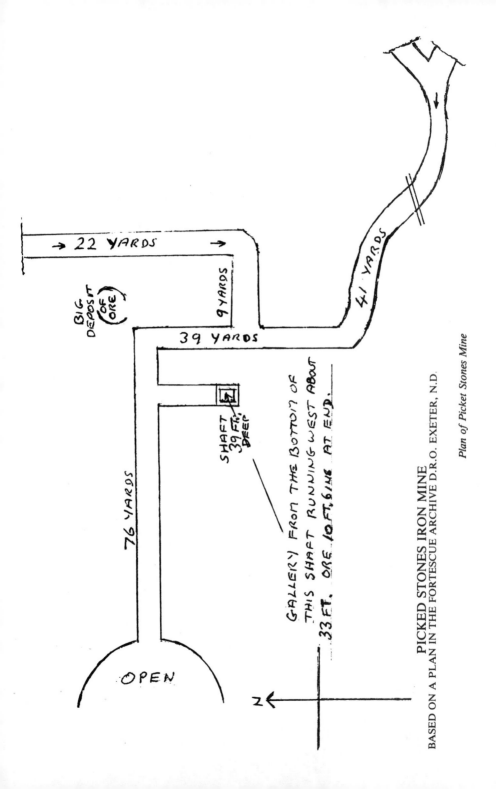

→ 22 YARDS →

BIG DEPOSIT (OF ORE)

9 YARDS

41 YARDS

39 YARDS

SHAFT 39 FT. DEEP

76 YARDS

OPEN

N ←

GALLERY FROM THE BOTTOM OF THIS SHAFT RUNNING WEST ABOUT 33 FT. ORE 10 FT. 6 INS AT END.

PICKED STONES IRON MINE
BASED ON A PLAN IN THE FORTESCUE ARCHIVE D.R.O. EXETER, N.D.

Plan of Picket Stones Mine

Henry Roberts in retirement (former manager of the Exmoor Mining Syndicate)

Trevor Waltho inside the Picket Stones Adit Level.

Lord Fortescue, with an initial holding of 1,000 shares, and E.P. Davis with 2,000. In a rather unusual arrangement, 4,550 fully paid up shares were allotted for a consideration other than cash, and though it is not stated what this consideration was, it was probably a form of compensation to the remaining members of the former syndicate for work done, and for the plant and mining machinery on site. In the case of Lord Fortescue and G.C. Smyth Richards; for their part in getting the new company off the ground and certain other concessions.

Be that as it may, E.P. Davis's shareholding was doubled to 4,000 and Lord Fortescue's increased to 1,900. Henry Roberts was allotted 1,250, and John Lester, a mineral and metal broker from Wolverhampton—who was secretary to both the former and new syndicate—was given 250 and G.C. Smyth Richards 150. The number of shares issued, 7,550, must have looked reasonably impressive on paper, but in effect it left the E.M.S. with only £3,000 in working capital, which was a totally inadequate sum when we consider the work that needed to be done in order to produce iron ore on the scale required to make the mines self financing. Under the new agreement the syndicate had the right to search for minerals on the Roman Lode, Rogers and Double Lodes, Picked Stones and the area west of White Water (south of the track to Winstitchen), for five years, at an annual dead rent of £250; with an option on all lodes on the Exmoor Estate.

A worse time for the new company to begin mining on Exmoor is hard to imagine. The early part of 1912 had been particularly wet, and by the end of July, Henry Roberts was complaining that he was having to use eight tons of coal a week at the Bluegate Mine to keep the workings dry, as against 35 hundredweight in normal conditions. To add to his problems, the steam operated Pulsometer pump was no more reliable now than it had been in earlier years, and being broken down so often, was the main reason why very little ore had been raised from Rogers Shaft. In December of 1912, the weather was so atrocious that water was pouring into the shaft from the surrounding moorlands, and trenches had to be cut around it to divert this water away.

According to the Rev. Ramsay—the Vicar of Exmoor—1912 was the wettest year since he had begun keeping records, but even worse was to follow, because the first four months of 1913 were wetter still, with virtually no let up, when, for much of the time, it was raining five days out of six, and Henry Roberts must have been exceedingly thankful when towards the end of April he was able to report that in the last few days there has been some improvement in the weather, with only 12 hours rain in 24.

The Bluegate Mine was not the only mine on Exmoor to suffer as a result of this continuous downpour, and as we shall see shortly, Picked Stones in particular was hard hit, with mining operations and other work there severely curtailed.

For the miners working on Exmoor at this time, conditions were appalling; soaking wet from morning till night, both above and below ground, it was nigh on impossible to have a dry change of clothing ready before the next shift began. Accommodation for some of these men had been provided in the form of large wooden or corrugated iron huts equipped for the purpose, placed on site at each of the three main mines. Apparently the old miners cottages at Cornham Ford were by this time beyond repair, and of all the cottages built on Exmoor these must surely have had the shortest useful life. Completed in 1857, they were deserted by the Dowlais miners only a year later when the company ceased operations. In every Kelly's Directory for Somerset from that date until 1889, Cornham Ford is described as a hamlet, but a deserted hamlet it must have been, because in the Census Returns of 1861, 71 and 81, they are not even listed, and in all that time I have found only one reference to a tenant there, when for 12 months from Michaelmass 1871, a John Nott rented one of the Cornham Ford cottages, for which he paid £2. 3. 0.

Not all of the 14 or so miners employed by the E.M.S. lived on site, three of them at least walked each day from Challacombe to the mines, and though it hardly seems credible, Tom Little, who went to live at Driver Cottages in 1910, when he was only eight years old, can remember clearly these men passing the cottage door each day before he set off for school, their clothes coloured red from working underground in the mine. It is even more remarkable that he can still recall their names: Charlie Coward, George Hawkes and Fred Adams. Two other local men working in the mines at the time were Harry Hunt and Herb Antell. The latter, who came from Lynton, did the blasting. Henry Roberts, the manager or overseeer at the mines, lived in Simonsbath, first in one of the West Cottages and later at South View.

Although the first agreement made between Lord Fortescue, Henry Roberts and E.P. Davis, in regards to forming a new syndicate to work the Exmoor mines, does not date earlier than June 1912, it is probable that Lord Fortescue was already giving the two men all the help he could to keep the mining going, and it is now time to pick up the threads and continue the history of mining on Exmoor from the breaking up of the former syndicate in January 1912, to the time all mining on Exmoor ceased. The easiest and perhaps the only sure way of covering the ground properly, is to take each of the three remaining mines, Roman, Bluegate and Picked Stones separately, and follow their progress individually to the time they were closed down.

Roman Mine

When the Roman Mine was last looked at on June 5th 1912, 30 tons of iron ore had just been raised from the number two shaft that was being sunk on the Roman Lode, at a point roughly in the middle of the old surface workings. Shortly after, a tramway was laid from the shaft to a loading bay 160 yards away beside the rough track leading down to Cornham Ford. About 800 yards of this track to the Simonsbath-South

Molton road was also made up, to allow the traction engine* to collect the iron ore direct from the mine—to save double handling. Morale at the mine at this time was high, and great were the expectations, but early in September, after sinking the shaft to a depth of 34 feet, it was found to have been sunk through a pillar of ore left by the 'Romans' to keep their mine from collapsing in on them. The last six feet of the shaft was not in the pillar at all, but had been cut through the mining deads left behind by the miners of old, and Roberts estimated that in order to get down into the solid ore ground he would have to sink the shaft 26 feet deeper through the mining waste. This was decided against, and the sinking of the shaft ceased forthwith. The pillar of ore was then worked out, and after yielding a total of 100 tons of fine quality ore, the shaft was abandoned for good.

In the meantime, the Burcombe Valley Shaft (sunk by Dowlais) had been partially cleared out, and an open cutting and a short tunnel driven to meet it from lower down the valley. After connecting with the shaft, a new level was begun towards the Roman Lode, and 100 yards or so of the tramway that had been taken out of the abandoned Main Drift at Cornham Ford, was laid in the new workings and on the tip outside (12.9.1912). Work on driving this level continued steadily, and on the 5th April 1913, the Roman Lode was cut. A month later the miners were well into a solid body of ore. Shortly afterwards they broke through into the old 'Roman Workings', which at this point must have been the best part of 100 feet deep. The course of the lode was followed for a total distance of 165 feet, the whole of which had been removed, although iron particles still adhered to the walls of the lode. The first 60 feet of this work was believed by Roberts to have been done by the 'Romans', and 36 feet beyond, by Dowlais, although he could find no reference of this work having been done by them.

After clearing through the old workings, and proving that the lode continued beyond, all work ceased on 27th August 1913, with Roberts stating that 'from his experience in driving levels he would have no hesitation in advising the directors of the syndicate to continue the Main Drift at Cornham Ford through the Roman Lode to the bottom of the Valley Shaft, when finance permitted', but as it turned out, this was not to be.

On November 15th 1913, three men under a foreman named Loosemore** were back in the Roman Mine; not in the lower Roman Level, but in the level that had earlier been cut from Number One Shaft, and after carrying it forward a few more feet, the miners came to a wall or pillar of ore going up as far as the eye could see. This pillar or ore (as it was found to be) was five feet wide by 12 feet six inches long, and was estimated to contain 2-300 tons of fine quality ore, but promising as it appeared to be, very little of this ore was removed, as it could not be brought out at a profit, and on 29th November 1913, the men were pulled out and the Roman Mine closed down.

*Driven by Bert Sparkes of Filleigh.
**Probably the same man who was superintendent of a mine at Charles, and another at Spreacombe in the First World War.

Bluegate Mine

Early in 1912, miners in the Upper Drybridge Level, begun by Henry Roberts in the spring of 1911, cut the Rogers Lode at a point some 330 yards west of Rogers Shaft, and levels were begun east and west on the course of the lode. Westwards the lode was poor, and after driving 30 feet, with no sign of improvement, work there was stopped. Eastwards, the first 40 feet was also poor, but the next 40 feet yielded 65 tons of good quality iron ore, and with this improvement a tramway was laid in the level and on the bank outside.

By the middle of November 1912, the miners had driven the level eastwards for a total distance of 120 feet on the lode, which varied in width from six feet down to three feet, most of it ore worth saving, but only a month later the men were pulled out, with Roberts stating that anything more done there will be from a shaft sunk on the best part of the lode.

The original intention when the Upper Drybridge Level was commenced, was to drive it on the course of Rogers Lode, first to the shaft beside the Simonsbath road, and then on to Rogers Shaft, but from Henry Roberts mining reports this level does not appear to have even reached the first shaft, where it was expected to intercept at a depth of 50 feet, because less than a month before the level was abandoned, the miners were only an estimated 30 feet below the rising hillside, and thus still some distance from the shaft.

As we have already seen, very little ore was raised by the first Exmoor mining syndicate from Rogers Shaft, and it was not until May 1912 that permanent timber and the headgear were fixed to the top of the shaft, and compressors installed to ventilate the mine and provide compressed air to the drilling rig. At the same time, a tramway was constructed to connect the shaft to a loading stage beside the Simonsbath road, some 250 yards away, and all was seemingly ready to recommence mining on what was hoped would prove to be a large and profitable scale.

There were certainly some grounds for optimism at this time, and a great deal of thought was again given to the problem of transporting the ore away from the mine, only this time, an entirely new route was proposed; in fact, the shortest possible to a railway. It would have involved the construction of an aerial ropeway from the Bluegate Mine to the abandoned Florence Mine, just three miles away in the parish of North Molton, from where the ore would have been transported to South Molton by reconstructing—and using—the Florence Mine's disused tramway. Once again there were problems, either in obtaining permission, or more likely, in raising the money to finance the project, even though it was the least expensive of all the ropeway and railway proposals put forward, with an estimated cost of £5,000 for the ropeway, plus £4,000 for rebuilding the tramway, and so, like all the earlier schemes, and later proposals, nothing ever came of it.

Apart from solving the transport problem, all was now ready to begin raising ore from Rogers Shaft, but as usual, when all else was ready, the

Pulsometer pump broke down once again. Engineers from the manufacturers were sent for, who, after examining the pump, intimated that there was nothing wrong with it and the fault lay in the pipework. New pipes were ordered, but it was the end of November before they arrived, were fitted, and pumping begun. This—as we have already stated—was at the time when Exmoor was experiencing the wettest weather since records had been kept; nevertheless, by the first week in December, the mine was half drained, but it was not until January 21st 1913 (after yet another pump failure) that the mine was dewatered. On February 10th the pump failed again and the water in the workings rose rapidly. After it was repaired, Roberts reported that it took 96 hours of constant pumping to drain the mine once more. Shortly after this, an additional pump (a Tangye) was fitted in the shaft to help with the pumping operation and as an additional precaution against further breakdowns, and at long last, after nearly 12 months of frustrating breakdowns and demoralising weather, the miners settled to their task.

By June 1913, 82 tons of ore had been raised, and ten tons a day were leaving the mine by traction engine, bound for the railway station at South Molton, that is, when the roads were not too waterlogged and soft to travel over.

By the 1st of July, the miners had cleared the shaft down to the sump at the bottom of Schneider and Hannay's workings, and a new type of power drill to speed up sinking the shaft deeper, was ordered from Sheffield. It was around this time that six of the eight miners working at Bluegate downed tools, when their demands (unspecified) were not met, but the rest of the men employed by the E.M.S. refused to support them, and the troublemakers were dismissed. Wages at this time were 24/- for a 41 hour week, which was a shilling more than the miners in the Somerset Coalfield received, and 3/- more than their Cornish counterparts, but they worked three hours a week less.

With the arrival of the new power drill, work was concentrated on sinking Rogers Shaft deeper as quickly as possible, and it was during this period that production at the mine reached its peak of about 50 tons a week, but as the shaft was sunk deeper it made more water, and the cost of pumping increased accordingly, and on reaching a depth of 150 feet sinking was suspended.

From the surface of the mine to the bottom of the shaft the miners had been in solid ore all the way, and with levels driven east and west at 90 feet the existence of a large body of ore was proved beyond any reasonable doubt, but having reached this stage, the Directors of the syndicate appeared to be unable to make up their minds on the next step. The obvious answer—and one that Henry Roberts had repeatedly advocated— was to drive a drainage level from lower down the Drybridge Combe to come into the shaft at its maximum depth of 150 feet below the surface, thus obviating completely the need and expense of pumping for all the mining area above this level. In the meantime, Roberts suggested two alternatives to keep the mine working, either he should put all his available men to work driving levels east and west of the bottom of the shaft for a distance of 150 yards in both directions on the course of the lode, to prove once and for all that the expense of the proposed drainage tunnel was warranted, and bring out a considerable quantity of ore in the process; or, to confine pumping to the 90 foot level and concentrate on extending the levels there, and at the same time reduce by half the cost of pumping.

Nothing more had been done at the 150 foot level when two independent mining consultants, Messrs. Sylvester and Charlton, were called in by the syndicate to examine the lodes and advise on how best to overcome the problems of the mine. Samples of ore taken from the lode in Rogers Shaft yielded a respectable iron content of 56.73%, but the present situation, whereby all the profits from the mine were being swallowed up by pumping and haulage costs, could not be tolerated for much longer, and the E.M.S. wished to know what alternatives, if any, they had to keep the mine going.

Sylvester's advice was to bring out all of the mining plant from Rogers Shaft and stop working there, but Charlton took a little longer in exploring all the alternatives before coming to his conclusions. His detailed examination of the mine and proposals for its future, were set out in his report of 27th October 1913, which gives the depth of Rogers Shaft as 148 feet ten inches, with levels driven east and west at 90 feet. The east level was about the same length (165 feet)* as it was when Dixon examined the mine in 1910, but the west level had been extended by 113 feet, and was now 265 feet long. Charlton's comments on the mine reveal that the ladderway in the footwall of the shaft was not in accordance with mining regulations, and there were no platforms (one recommended). Pumping arrangements to deal with 2,000 G.P.H. rising to 5,000 G.P.H. in the wet season were also far from satisfactory. The Pulsometer pump brought the water from the shaft sump to the 90 foot level, and two pumps—a Tangye and an Evans—took the water from there to the surface, an expensive way to bring such a small quantity of water out of the mine, but in the light of what we know of the Pulsometer pump and its unreliability, the other two pumps were an essential part of the mine machinery; because they did at least ensure that the mine was kept drained to a working level.

It was Charlton's opinion that the levels so far driven proved the existence of 27,000 tons of iron ore, and he proposed that an adit level should be driven from a point 542 yards away in the Drybridge Combe, to come into Rogers Lode at a depth of 250 feet, with the shaft deepened accordingly to meet it, thus opening up a potential 657,000 tons of iron ore from the three Deer Park Lodes, and removing all the water above this level in the process. Henry Roberts' proposed shorter drainage adit of 440 yards, to meet the shaft at a depth of 150 feet was also considered, but Charlton was more concerned with the long term future of the mine. He

*At the eastern end of this level, problems were encountered with the falling away of ground from above, which proved difficult to stop.

also believed that the adit level, dressing floors to concentrate the ore, an aerial ropeway to the Florence Mine, and other essential work at the mine could be done for £10,500. If the work was carried out according to his recommendations, it was expected that 5-600 tons of ore a week would be raised, or a minimum of 25,000 tons a year, which, with a profit of 5/- per ton, would yield £6,250 per annum. The time estimated to carry out the necessary work was two years; and there lay the problem.

The trouble was, the E.M.S. had been undercapitalised from the start, and had relied almost entirely on quickly raising sufficient quantities of ore to finance further development. This had not happened, and the company were now in a *Catch 22* situation, where they could neither afford to drive the drainage adit so essential tó opening up the mine—and thus cut out the enormous cost of pumping—or afford to continue mining from Rogers Shaft for that very reason, and by the 3rd November 1913, all of the mining plant had been brought out of the mine and stored ready for use, as and where needed, and the levels and shaft all timbered to stand for a long time, in the hope that at some time in the not too distant future the money would be found to develop the mine properly.

This was the end of serious mining at Bluegate, but during clearing up operations a little more work was done in the Upper Drybridge Level, and 34 tons of ore brought out. Out of a total workforce of 14 miners working on Exmoor on November 3rd, seven were given a fortnight's notice due to the closure of both the Roman and the Bluegate mines, the remaining seven were either already at Picked Stones, or moved there shortly after.

Picked Stones Mine

Of the three mines working on Exmoor in the early 20th century, Picked Stones was the most productive, but the problem of transporting the ore away from this isolated mine, served only by the rough and very inadequate track from Picked Stones Farm to Winstitchen, caused even more difficulties than usual, with a decided reluctance on the part of owners of suitable transport to call there to collect it. A little of this ore had been taken to South Molton Station, and some by the more expensive route to Barnstaple Quay for shipment to Wales, but the stock of ore at the mine continued to build up faster than it could be got away, and in May 1912 it was proposed that a tramway should be constructed to carry the ore from the mine to a more accessible loading stage a mile away beside Gypsy Lane.

At a meeting held at the mine on 5th June, the estimated cost of this tramway was given as £200. Lord Fortescue gave permission to cut down fir trees at Cornham Brake, planted many years earlier by Frederic Knight, to provide 2,000 sleepers for the tramway and some 12-15,000 feet of two inch thick timber for use in the mine. Work in the mine at this time appears to have been mainly confined to driving a level westwards from Anthony Hills shaft, at a depth of 26 feet below the surface, and from levels driven from the shaft sunk by Henry Roberts prior to 20th July

1910, and it was from these workings that the present company expected to raise some 60-80 tons of ore a week, which was perhaps a little optimistic, because in fact the weekly output rarely exceeded 50 tons. Nevertheless, by September 1912, 300 tons of ore, over and above that taken away by traction engine, lay in stock at the mine.

By this time, ladders, pumps and winding gear had been fixed at the shaft, but the exceptionally wet weather that had been largely responsible for the problems at the Bluegate mine also caused a temporary suspension of all underground working at Picked Stones as the hand pumps installed there were incapable of dealing with such a large volume of water. A new shaft was begun 50 yards west of Henry Roberts earlier shaft, but this was not yet on the lode, and for the time being all available manpower was put to work on the construction of the tramway, the foundations of which were completed by January 21st, 1913, when the bulk of the men were back at work in the mine, although much of the tramway was still to be laid.

In February, a syphon was fitted in the mine to drain the shafts and workings, and proved to be a great success. Other work completed soon after was an incline to connect the mine to the tramway, and a winch fitted at its head for winding up the ore.

By March, ore was coming out of the mine at a steady 30 tons a week, and early in May, Edward Mare, who had previously been employed by the syndicate hauling coal from South Molton and Yarde Down to Rogers Shaft at the Bluegate Mine, was engaged with his horse and cart at 6s. 8d. a day to haul ore from the Picked Stones Mine to the depot at Gypsy Lane. After the completion of the tramway in July, he was employed in hauling the ore wagons over the line to the same depot. To speed up operations a horse whim was erected at the mine and it was then possible to move 60 tons of ore a day from the pithead to Gypsy Lane. A rough estimate of working costs at this time was 4-5s. a ton for mining the ore, plus a total of 15s. a ton haulage costs from mine to the Welsh ports. With the ore making 25s. a ton, a modest profit of 5s. per ton was left after all expenses had been met, which was hardly likely to make a fortune for the syndicate on the small tonnage they were producing, and certainly left very little margin for any further development of the mines.

In the six month period April to September 1913 when all three mines, Roman, Bluegate and Picked Stones were at work, 718 tons of ore were sold, with 180 tons more in stock, 898 tons in all, which was 406 tons short of Henry Roberts estimate and he was called on by the Directors of the E.M.S. to explain the deficiency. Roberts replied that when the ore was brought out of the Bluegate Mine, where he spent most of his time, it was saturated with water and after drying out it weighed about 60-70 tons less. The foreman at Picked Stones, a man called Nott, was about 100 tons out in his calculations, the remaining shortfall could not be accounted for, but Roberts accepted that it must have been the result of his own miscalculations!

ROMAN MINE

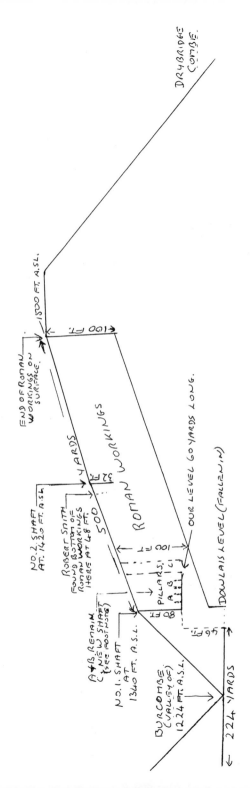

HEIGHT ABOVE SEA LEVEL 1122 FEET. THE LEVEL AT WHICH THE MAIN DRIFT WILL CUT THE ROMAN LODE VERTICAL SECTION OF ROMAN MINE: BASED ON HENRY ROBERTS PLAN OF THE MINE DEC. 10.1913. FORTESCUE ARCHIVE D.R.O. EXETER

FOOTNOTE: THE REFERENCES TO THE PILLARS OF ORE A&B AND THE DOTTED LINES OF THE NEW SHAFT C (PROPOSED) WERE NOT IN HENRY ROBERTS HAND, SO WERE PRESUMABLY PART OF LATER PROPOSALS TO WORK THE MINE: DATE & COMPANY UNKNOWN.

Plan of Roman Mine

Plan of Bluegate Mine

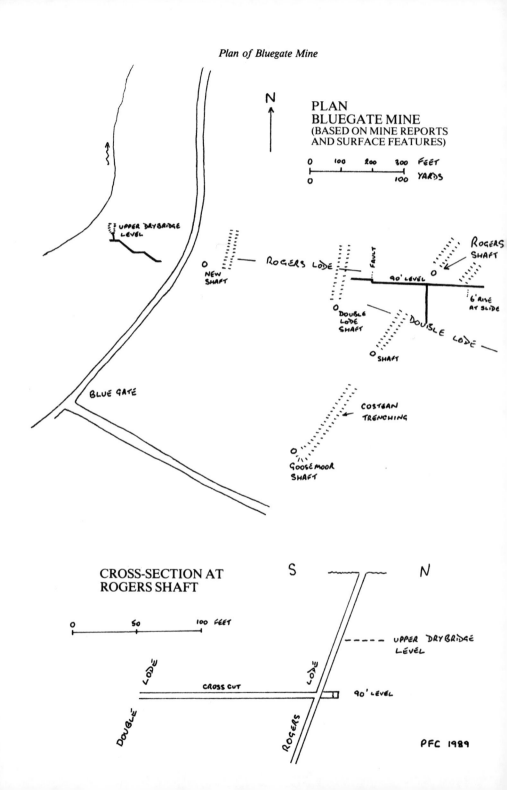

PLAN
BLUEGATE MINE
(BASED ON MINE REPORTS
AND SURFACE FEATURES)

After the closure of the Roman and Bluegate mines in November 1913, the men not under notice, namely Loosemore and his team of four miners, moved to Picked Stones, replacing the three men working there, who, having become dissatisfied with their conditions of employment, were also paid off. Picked Stones was now the only mine on Exmoor still working, and all efforts were concentrated on increasing its output. For some time past, most of the ore raised from the mine had come from the level driven west of Anthony Hills shaft, and more latterly from a new shaft which had been sunk in the latter half of 1912, some 50 yards west of Henry Roberts earlier shaft. By January 1914 much of the available ore at this level had been worked out and the flow of underground water was altered, and the syphon resited, so that the workings could be sunk 40 feet deeper in order to open up new ore ground.

The full extent of mining work done by the E.M.S. and its predecessors at Picked Stones, is not certainly known. This is partly due to the absence of records of the Plymouth Iron Co., but more to the wording of Henry Roberts reports, which, although no doubt perfectly clear to the Directors of the syndicate, who were familiar with the layout of the mine, do not always make sense to an ignorant layman with no access to the relevant underground workings, or final abandonment plans (not located). Nevertheless, we do know that in March 1914 some work was being carried on in the area of the shaft sunk earlier, near to where the lode was cut off by a fault in the primary adit, because Roberts reported that the miners were too close to this old shaft and old levels for safety, and they were pulled out to begin again 20 feet deeper, which meant cutting through the shaft and making it safe.

By April 1914, the mine workings were below the depth at which the syphon could work effectively and the Pulsometer pump was brought out of storage at Bluegate and fixed in the mine, and once installed kept the workings dry at a minimal cost of five hundredweight of coal a day. A month later the mine had reached the required depth of 65 feet, and at this level the lode was found to be 12 feet wide, and full of good clean ore.

In the past few months the iron ore had been coming out of the mine at a faster rate than it could be disposed of, and by the middle of May there were 600 tons in stock. Moving this ore from pithead to Gypsy Lane was easy enough, but finding transport to take it from there to the nearest port or railway station was much harder to come by. A letter from J.N. Lester, the company secretary, to Lord Fortescue, dated 18th May, reveals that because of the transport difficulties the syndicate was now suffering from a severe cashflow crisis, with only enough money in the kitty to pay the men's wages to the end of the month. Approaches were quickly made to practically every firm for miles around who had suitable transport for moving the ore, and by the end of June two firms were hauling the ore away on a regular basis.

The Devon Traction Co., contracted to haul it to Dulverton Station and load it on rail 'en route for Wales' for £15 for every 50 tons that passed through Taunton, and by the 4th July they had taken away 22 lorry loads (135 tons). At the same time a Mr. Pope had taken ten lorry loads (50 tons) in the opposite direction to South Molton Station, where this ore too was loaded into trucks headed for the same destination (Ebbw Vale, cost of rail transport 6/- per ton). Berry's of Barnstaple also contracted to haul ore for the E.M.S., but on finding it could not be done for the money, refused to honour their agreement, a decision that, but for Lord Fortescue's intervention, could have cost them dear. Squires of Barnstaple had also been approached, but the price they quoted was prohibitive and they were not employed.

The damage done to the roads of North Devon and West Somerset, particularly those leading from the Exmoor mines to South Molton and Dulverton, by the heavily laden traction engines and lorries, caused the Highway Board of both Councils a great deal of concern, and to meet the cost of reinstatement the E.M.S. agreed to pay the South Molton Council 4d. a ton for every ton of ore passing over their roads. How many payments were made is not known, but a cheque for £10. 9. 0 was forwarded to the Council in June 1914, which, at the agreed sum of 4d a ton, means that at least 627 tons of ore were transported to South Molton Station. A similar agreement was worked out with the Dulverton Board, but no details of the cost to the E.M.S. have been found.

It would appear that by the middle of July, the two regular haulage firms decided to call it a day, there being little if any profit in it for them. This setback to the syndicate left some 500 tons of iron ore still in stock, which could not be converted into cash to keep the mine going. This sealed its fate, and on 17th July 1914, all work at the Picked Stones Mine ceased; not because the miners had run out of ore, or—as it is claimed in the *Reclamation of Exmoor Forest*—because all the profits were swallowed up in haulage costs, but simply because Henry Roberts just could not get the transport in the first place, and after the outbreak of World War One in August, what little chance there had been of hiring lorries evaporated completely, when all available transport was commandeered for more essential duties elsewhere.

In the last six months of its working life (9.1.1914 to 17.7.1914) 687 tons of ore had been raised from the Picked Stones Mine. There was certainly no intention on the part of the Exmoor Mining Syndicate to permanently withdraw from the mining scene at this time, and though all the miners had been dismissed, Henry Roberts was retained to keep the mines and mining plant in good order, while negotiations were being carried on, in the hope of forming a new company with sufficient working capital to exploit to the full the potential of the Exmoor mines.

With this intention firmly in mind, several large iron masters were approached. By November 1914, negotiations were well under way with a large iron and steel company, Stewarts and Lloyds, who, it was hoped, would be persuaded to invest £50,000 in the proposed new company; an essential part of the development plans being the aerial ropeway to

Porlock Weir, but after investigating the prospects they declined to proceed with the deal, and negotiations were broken off.

Throughout 1915 and most of 1916, efforts were still being made to form a new company to work the mines, but although there were several inquiries, and plenty of correspondence passing to and fro, nothing came of it, and towards the end of 1916 it was decided to try and negotiate a sale of the mining property for the sum of £15,000.

From a number of inquiries, only one came close to fruition, and this, from a firm with the unlikely name of Mudros Syndicate Ltd. The promoter of this company, Henry St. John Wileman of London, showed a very keen interest in the mining property, which he proposed to take for a term of 42 years, at an annual dead rent of £1,000, after a first year payment of £500. This was agreed on certain conditions. These were:

1. To continue the Main Drift at Cornham Ford to cut the Roman Lode, and then drive beyond it to prove the Rogers Lode at a depth of 450 feet below the surface.
2. To drive an adit from Drybridge Combe, to meet Rogers Shaft at a depth of 150 feet.

Wileman argued that the second stipulation was unnecessary as he intended to work both lodes from the Main Drift. Agreement appears to have been reached on this point, but not on the £2,000 deposit Lord Fortescue insisted on before allowing mining to begin; money that Wileman was either unwilling, or unable to pay. On making further inquiries into Wileman's background, he was found to be a man of very dubious character, with a bad record, a financial agent and a bankrupt, with many judgements against him, and without further ado it was decided to reject his offer.

It was now March 1917, and the mines had been closed for two and a half years, but still the Exmoor Mining Syndicate soldiered on in the hope that a company could be found—or formed—to re-open the Exmoor mines, and it is possible that this would have been achieved, if an experiment conducted by the Ministry of Munitions had proved successful.

In July 1917, the Minister of Munitions inspected the iron ore lying at Picked Stones. Henry Roberts was instructed to put 25 tons of this ore on rail at Dulverton at £3 a ton.* The ore was wanted for making hydrogen gas for the Air Service, and if the result of the experiment was favourable the Ministry would require a regular supply. It was not to be, and what might have been a very profitable venture came to naught.

Later in the year, after examining the Exmoor Mining property, a mining engineer, Forster Brown, estimated that the cost of work needed to re-open the mines and bring them into production as £2,500-£3,000, but it is extremely doubtful if it could have been done for this kind of money, which made no allowance whatever for the drainage adit at Bluegate, or for a railroad or ropeway to a station or the coast.

---

*Thirty shillings of which was paid to Roberts for haulage.

Very early in 1918, a Mr. Llewellyn Davies from Glamorgan was granted a three month licence to investigate the Exmoor minerals. His report of 18th April, shows that he envisaged a much more ambitious undertaking. On his calculations be believed that 7,575,200 tons of iron ore were available for mining; assuming that the three major lodes, Roman, Rogers and Double extended 4,000 yards. His plans for working the mines were: To continue the Main Drift at Cornham Ford. Drive a drainage adit to Rogers Shaft, and to construct an aerial ropeway to Porlock Weir—working from a central station. He also proposed that the River Barle should be dammed to provide power via a turbine driven generator (three phase), and that a stand-by steam engine should also be provided.

Llewellyn Davies believed the mines would stand a capitalisation of £250,000, and with an expenditure of £150,000 made, produce 1,000 tons of ore daily when fully developed, and pay a dividend of ten percent, with capital redeemed in 15 years.

Shortly after Davies completed his exploration of the mineral resources of Exmoor, the Exmoor Mining Syndicate went into voluntary liquidation, the company being wound up on the 13th May 1918. At this time the number of fully paid up shares totalled 9,410, the only shareholders to have increased their original holdings being Lord Fortescue, who now held 2,520, and E.P. Davis, with 5,210. On July 24th, all the mining plant and machinery, accommodation huts, tramways, etc., and about 330 tons of iron ore, were put up for sale by auction and realised a total of £844. 9. 8, which, after outstanding accounts were settled, left £338. 6. 0 for distribution among the shareholders on the basis of the number of shares held. Lord Fortescue received £90. 10. 0, Edward Prosser Davis £188, Henry Roberts £44. 18. 0, J.N. Lester £9 and G.C. Smyth Richards £5. 18. 0. With this division of all that was left of the company assets, the Exmoor Mining Syndicate ceased to exist.

In the *Reclamation of Exmoor Forest* Llewellyn Davies is credited with only a three month licence to investigate the Exmoor minerals, but there is reason to believe that he held an option on the Exmoor mines for much longer than this, because on 30th August 1918, G.C. Smyth Richards met Davies and arranged for him to have an option for the Exmoor mines on the following terms; £100 for the first year, £150 second year, £175 third year and £200 fourth year. On the 15th October—the same year—Davies signed a licence for the Exmoor mines and paid over, £100 for the next years option. A subsequent perusal of the Exmoor Estate accounts show that under the heading of 'Mines', the years 1918, 19, 20 and 21 give a corresponding income of £125, £165, £175 and £200, figures that are accurate enough to suggest that Llewellyn Davies did in fact keep his mining options open, but whether any mining actually took place during this four year period is not known. We do know, however, that when G.C. Smyth Richards met Davies on 15th April 1919, he was having trouble in getting the mines financed—the Banks having had bad reports. At this time he was taking a Professor Jones to inspect the mines, and he was advised by Smyth Richards to see Loosemore, the old man who worked these mines with Roberts.

It is extremely unlikely that even if Llewellyn Davies grandiose plans for the development of mining on Exmoor had been carried out, that they would have resulted in either a short or long term profit. His assumption that the lodes were continuous over a distance of two and a half miles was unfounded; the ore along the line of the Exmoor lodes being confined to a few large and small deposits. It is possible, however, that a smaller company could have made a go of it, providing they could afford the initial development costs, including either the aerial ropeway or a railway to the coast, because all the evidence pointed to there being substantial proven deposits of ore at two of the three major mining areas, Bluegate and Picked Stones.

At Bluegate, Rogers Shaft had been sunk through solid ore to a depth of 150 feet, and with levels driven east and west at 90 feet, the existence of a large body of ore had been proved, but because of the cost of pumping there, and the lack of sufficient funds to drive the drainage adit, it had been abandoned with practically the whole of this body of ore intact.

The potential of the Picked Stones mine was also considerable; two massive lodes of exceptionally good clean ore had been encountered there, and this, too, was virtually untapped.

Although the Roman Lode cannot be said to have been proved at depth, because the Main Drift had been abandoned before reaching it, Henry Roberts was convinced that the ore was there in quantity, and a short extension to the Drift would have quickly proved if this was so. Similarly, work in Llewellyn's Level had also ceased before reaching the assumed position of the westward extension of Rogers Lode, and by continuing this level for about 25 feet more, the lode—or its non existence—would have been proved beyond doubt, but it was not to be, and apart from a little exploration work at Bluegate in 1934, all mining on Exmoor had ended.

In is impossible to walk the length and breadth of Exmoor today, without becoming increasingly aware of the tremendous amount of time and effort that had been put into locating and opening up the mineral bearing lodes that traverse the Moor. In the early 1850's, Frederic Knight and his able lieutenant, Robert Smith, had discovered no less than 26 such lodes, all of which had been exposed by sinking pits or cutting trenches upon them where they outcropped near the surface. Such pits and trenches are as common as the small quarries that once yielded stone for the many miles of walled banks that provide fences for the field boundaries and larger enclosures of Exmoor, but in spite of this, and the mining activities of three iron mining companies in the latter half of the 1850's, and later mining by Henry Roberts and the Exmoor Mining Syndicate, mine buildings and associated relics are very scarce on the ground: Not for us the huge engine houses that are so much a part of the Cornish landscape; hauntingly beautiful as they are in their own way, and we are spared the huge unnatural spoilheaps that so often accompany them. A few of the underground levels on Exmoor can still be entered, but the shafts have, for the most part, been either capped or filled in.

Although Picked Stones was the last mine to be abandoned on Exmoor it is now very difficult to visualise it as it was when it was working. This is due not only to the reclamation work that has been carried out over a large area surrounding the mine, which has destroyed all trace of the incline and tramway to Gypsy Lane, but also because the 76 yards long primary adit begun by Anthony Hill in 1857, and extended by Henry Roberts in the early part of this century, has collapsed into the workings below, leaving behind an open work double its earlier length.

Much easier to reconstruct, is the layout of the Bluegate Mine, where the shafts and adit, although now filled or blocked can be easily identified; the bed of the tramway leading from the Simonsbath road to Rogers Shaft leaving no doubt as to its position. The buildings used by Roberts in the early part of this century—being of a portable nature—were included in the sale of mining plant and effects in July 1918, but remnants or traces of the buildings erected earlier by Schneider and Hannay can still be found; overgrown cinders giving away the location of the Engine House and Boiler; a mixture of iron slag and cinders—that of the Blacksmiths Shop; both buildings being alongside the mining trench that runs from Rogers Shaft towards the road from Bluegate into Wintershead and Horsen farms. A little to the west of the Blacksmith's Shop, in a sunken hollow, the remains of a circular stone building nine feet in diameter can also be found. This is almost certainly all that is left of the Powder House or Magazine of the same date.

It is, perhaps, the mining area around Cornham Ford, and Burcombe in particular, that evokes the deepest thoughts of the discerning explorer into Exmoor's mining history, for nowhere else on Exmoor is the presence of the 'Ancients' felt more strongly than when one pauses for a while within the confines of the so called 'Roman Workings', to contemplate the mining there of long ago. For a brief moment the imagination runs riot and the mists of time roll back, to clear with a sudden realisation of just how magnificent were the achievements of the old time miners, who, despite the isolation and lack of any permanent accommodation on the Moor (there was none), and the obvious technical limitations of the age, raised and transported away more iron ore from these workings than all the later mining men and companies put together—in the centuries that followed.

No relics of this by-gone age of mining on Exmoor have been discovered, or if they have, are unrecorded, but in the stream bed of the Burcombe Water, a few bits and pieces from more recent mining can still be seen; a twisted tramrail here, a broken ore wagon there, an axle and wheel from the same, protruding from the debris beside the stream. We come to the filled in wheelpit at the junction of the Water with the Barle, now incorporated into the footbridge across the river. An adit or two within the vicinity of Cornham Ford are still open, or partly so and the large spoil heap from the Main Drift bears witness to the time and efforts that were wasted in the abortive attempts to win the iron ore from these reluctant hills. Across the river, the ever dwindling ruins of the miners cottages bear testimony to one mans hopes and dreams, but neither Frederic Knight—or Lord Fortescue's efforts at a later date—have destroyed the beauty of this particularly lovely spot. The hustle and bustle of mining passed, the miners moved away, and the ugly scars they left behind upon the hills and in the valleys were given over to the hand of nature, which in her own forgiving way has slowly but surely softened the effect of this rough intrusion into her privacy, and all but healed the ugly man made wounds.

The chances of mining ever again being restarted on Exmoor can be said to have passed with the creation of the National Park, and though the powers that be have been unable to prevent the so called improvement of thousands of acres within its boundaries, the granting of a licence to mine within these same boundaries is an entirely different matter, and one that would surely arouse the wrathful indignation of all who hold dear the preservation of our fast declining moorlands: A strong deterrent indeed, to even the most stout hearted mining company.

CHAPTER 12

EXMOOR IN WARTIME AND CHANGES THEREAFTER

OUR twelfth and final chapter begins around 1939, when the dark clouds that had for some time been looming ominously on the horizon became a reality, and for the second time in just 25 years the Country was plunged into war.

Once again the Nation was forced to rely on its own resources in order to survive. Home grown food production was stepped up, aided by ploughing grants and subsidies on corn growing and fat stock, which were introduced by the Government in July 1939. The benefits of this, however, were mainly confined to the lowland areas, and it was not until 1941 that a subsidy was given to hill farmers to encourage them to increase their sheep flocks. This was followed two years later by a similar subsidy on beef cattle.

A look at Lord Fortescue's Exmoor Estate in 1938, reveals that at this time it consisted of 29 farms—including smallholdings. Out of a total of 14,368 acres, 6,368 were classified as cultivated land, mainly improved grassland. The remaining 8,000 acres consisting of rough moorland grazing. The estate farm (including Cornham Farm, which came in hand in 1936) was 9,000 acres, divided into six herdings, plus another at Badgworthy, which had been leased back in 1926. The total number of breeding ewes and replacements were about 4,600, plus 157 head of cattle, increased in the summer months by the influx of about 100 in calf Shorthorn heifers from Castle Hill and the purchase of some 50-70 Irish Shorthorns at Bristol. In addition, a number of cattle were taken in for the summer grazing from the surrounding districts of North Devon and West Somerset.

The steady improvement of the estate farm—which recommenced with the introduction of subsidies on lime and slag in 1937—continued, and by 1944 some 800 acres of old pasture at Cornham, Toms Hill, Winstitchen, Duredon and Hoar Oak had been ploughed up and reseeded. Because the new grass matured nearly a month earlier it was now possible to make hay in June, when the weather was usually more settled. It was during this period that for the first time since the Knights began the reclamation of the old Forest, the estate farm reached a state of near self-sufficiency. This was just as well, because Castle Hill, which had been relied on in the past to provide winter keep for the ewe hoggs, had, for the most part been ploughed up and tilled to corn. A certain amount of oats were also grown on Exmoor, but in most years failed to ripen and had to be cut green.

Comparisons of stocks numbers recorded in 1939 and 1945, show that although the numbers of sheep kept on the Exmoor Estate herdings had risen only slightly, the cattle herd had been greatly increased, and had risen from 157 in 1938 and 39, to 418 in 1945, and remained at about 400 head for the next few years before in was again increased. A breakdown of the herd, taken in July 1945, reveals that the pure bred Galloways were now 136 strong and consisted of 80 cows and 20 heifers, the rest were steers and calves. Other breeding stock consisted of 10 GallowayXDevon cows and 10 heifers, 12 GallowayXHereford heifers, 110 Shorthorn heifers (from Castle Hill) and 42 DevonXShorthorn cows and 120 heifers. The remainder of the estate farm herd consisted mainly of one and a half to two year old steers and some calves, which brought the total herd of cattle kept that year to 552. Furthermore, because much of the lower lying land around Exmoor had been ploughed up and tilled to corn, some 500-600 head of cattle had been sent to the Moor for summer pasturing annually over the past few years. In 1944 the number was 550.

Such had been the improvements to much of the grassland on the estate farm that it was now possible to fatten the Galloway Devon crossbred steers at two and a half years, which at this time were selling for an average of £32. 10. 0 apiece, as against the pure bred Galloways, which made no more at three to three and a half years.

Elsewhere on Exmoor similar improvements were made, particularly at Honeymead. A considerable acreage of land was also broken up in the Sandyway area in the south-east corner of Exmoor, some of it for the first time. Land tilled to corn had the usual mixed results; dependance on the weather for harvesting being just as much of a problem as it had always been.

Exmoor, as was usual, took a little time to adjust to the realities of war, but with the issue of gasmasks to the 20 children attending Simonsbath School, on May 27th 1940, and the arrival of 30 evacuee children, 23 boys and seven girls from Goodall Road School, Leyton, on 17th June 1940, accompanied by their teacher Mr. Frank Betts, there were no longer any doubts. A week later, an evacuee school was set up in the Meeting House, and there it remained until the two schools merged in April 1942. One cannot help but wonder what the reactions of the evacuee children were, when they found themselves set down in the middle of nowhere on Exmoor, after being uprooted from their homes in the densely populated suburbs of London.

The young evacuees from Leyton were not the only such arrivals on Exmoor at this time. A private girls school was set up in Simonsbath Lodge (Boevey's old house). This school remained in occupation for about three to four years, before departing from the Moor. They were replaced by a private boys school, whose residence there was of even shorter duration.

In the preparation for D-Day, a large moorland area around Larkbarrow, Toms Hill and Brendon Common was requisitioned by the Military as a training ground and artillery range. Big field guns, stationed on North Molton Ridge and elsewhere, guided by spotter planes, fired shell after shell in the direction of the old farmsteads and shepherds cottages, shattering the moorland silence and severely damaging their targets. There was to be no rebuilding programme in this area after the war and the ravages of storm and time have completed their destruction.[1]

Sheep continued to graze on their accustomed herdings during lulls in military training and gun practice, but Jim Little and his son Cecil, second the third generation shepherds of the Little family of Toms Hill, had been transferred to Warren Cottage in 1943, and into the farmhouse itself when it came in hand in 1946. Warren Cottage, which adjoined the farmhouse, was converted out of the farm dairy around the turn of the century by the 4th Earl Fortescue, but after Jim Little moved into the farm it was let only briefly. It is still there, but needs a considerable amount of money spent to refurbish it.*

When the Military were using the training area, the sheep flock was driven back to Warren, but records reveal that they did not all escape unscathed and there were some sheep losses.

Wartime casualties were, unfortunately, not confined to the animal population. A number of RAF aircraft crashed on Exmoor during operational duties, and there was inevitably some loss of life. The first plane known to have crashed on the Moor came down behind Lower Sherdon Farm late in 1939. This aircraft (type unknown) remained undiscovered for some time. It was eventually found by Jack Little, the former shepherd of Mines herding, who since his retirement in September 1939 had been living at Lower Sherdon with his wife and son Stan (a bachelor), who was then farming there. When Jack discovered the plane the four crew members were still inside, all dead. A tragic loss of young lives, but an all too frequent occurrence at that time.

Lower Sherdon was also the scene of a later disaster, when, shortly after the was ended, a jet flew into the implement shed and demolished it. Stan Little, who was working there had a miraculous escape, but Eli Buckingham who was with him was not so fortunate. He was hit on the head by a piece of the plane, and spent some time in Hospital and convalescing, but never fully recovered.

One of the West Gate cottages on the Challacombe road was badly damaged when a Wellington bomber crashed into it in 1940. One man was killed, the other members of the crew—who had baled out—were unhurt. One turned up at Aclands with no idea of his whereabouts, and was much relieved to find the occupants spoke English. Another Wellington made a forced landing in soft ground behind Warren Farm. No one was hurt, and little damage was done to the plane. It could not, however, take off again, and was dismantled and carried away. A Flying Fortress crashed on Long Holcombe, but it is not known if there was any loss of life.

The Germans dropped a couple of land mines near Hoar Oak but little damage was done; one failing to go off. This was taken away by horse and cart.

---

*Now being carried out (1988).

The Army, too, suffered a severe blow, when Colonel R.H. MacLaren, MC, OBE (Military), the Commanding Officer of the experimental branch of the Royal Engineers, stationed at Lynton, was demonstrating a new explosive device to Government officials and fellow officers. Something went wrong, and without thought for his own life he threw himself onto the weapon. He was killed instantly, but no one else was hurt. A memorial stone was erected on the spot.* The inscription reads:

IN
MEMORY OF
COLONEL R.H. MACLAREN, O.B.E.
M.C. COMMANDER C.W. TROOPS
ROYAL ENGINEERS, WHO WAS
KILLED ON DUTY ON THIS SPOT
MAY 20th 1941.
THIS STONE WAS ERECTED
BY HIS BROTHER OFFICERS

The damage done to Larkbarrow Farm and Toms Hill by shells fired from the big field guns stationed on North Molton Ridge has already been recorded, but there were other casualties. One of these was Larkbarrow Cottage, which was built about the same time as the farm it served. Few people have heard of this old cottage, or know just where it stood. Even less can recall the sad story that will forever be associated with it. All that is now left of what was once a happy home, can be found about 400 yards from Larkbarrow Farm, beside the track to Toms Hill, where a few small piles of rubble and a little section of wall here and there can still be seen by those who care to look.

It was in this cottage that Will Little—the son of William 1st of Toms Hill—lived with his wife, son and daughter, assisting his father with the Larkbarrow herding, and it was close to the cottage that Will's life was tragically ended on July 13th 1923. Will had gone to Warren Farm for the day, to help with the hay harvesting there. A storm came on, haymaking was abandoned, and be began to make his way homeward. When he was nearly there, he collected up his two cows and drove them on before him. Will was within sight of his home and coming over a low bank when lightning struck and he fell to the ground, killed instantly.

Although this happened over 60 years ago, Tom Little can still vividly recall the sad funeral procession leaving the cottage. Six bearers on horseback led the way, followed by George Webber with Lord Fortescue's market cart bearing the coffin. Next came Harry Prout and Tom Little with pony traps carrying the family mourners, with Harry Bond bringing up the rear with the floral tributes. The procession did not keep to the road out of Larkbarrow, but went up over the Forest to Warren, and on to Simonsbath for the burial service and interment. By the time they reached

---

*On Brendon Common.

Warren, Tom—who had been leading his pony through the long sedge grass—was soaking wet, and wet he remained throughout the service.

Badgworthy Cottage was also destroyed by the big guns. Many shepherds had come and gone from this lonely place in the course of the 80 years or so of its existence. Tom Little stayed there for a short time when he was a young man, to help the shepherd (Jim Barwick) dig his peat. Tom was most unhappy when he was within the confines of the cottage at night. In fact, he refused to stay. There was a strange but distinct atmosphere about the place that upset him. Many people have experienced this feeling at some time in other places, and found it impossible to give a logical explanation to its cause. In the case of Badgworthy, is it not just possible— if all, or even some of the stories we have read about the Doones are true— that the spirits of this infamous family continue to haunt this spot. For let us not forget, the shepherds cottage is said to have been built with stones taken from the old 'Doone Cotts'. Stranger happenings than this have been recorded!

The last shepherd to live at Badgworthy was Jack Jones, who in the 1930's was taken ill with acute appendicitis and had to be carried over the common to Brendon Two Gates—a distance of nearly two miles—to reach the ambulance, which could get no nearer to his home. It was the same Jack Jones who later moved to Coventry to live with his daughter, where the only work he could obtain was as a grave digger.

Time passed; the war ended. The evacuees returned home, and the army gave up their training grounds. Exmoor settled down once more to its accustomed routines, and it was not until recent years that the army returned to the Moor to clear the area around Larkbarrow and Toms Hill of unexploded shells and other wartime objects. They did a thorough job as far as they went, with their marking tapes trailing across the Moor as they cleared acre after acre. They did not, however, find all of the relics of the wartime years, and beside one of the old drainage ditches on Trout Hill (cut by the Knights many years before) I came across a number of spent ·303 cartridges, 133 in all, some of which were embedded in the peat to a depth of seven and a half inches below the surface. The date stamped on the cartridge cases was 1943, and if they could reach this depth in only 40 years, how much more of Exmoor's past lies hidden from our eyes?

The end of the last war was not the signal for a post war depression in the agricultural economy, such as had happened shortly after the cessation of hostilities in the First World War. Guaranteed prices for farm products were introduced in 1947, and the subsidies of earlier years were continued. Grants were made available for the improvement of hill farms. These grants were taken full advantage of, and a considerable modernisation programme of the farms, buildings and cottages on Exmoor was carried out.

The severe winter of 1946/47, which resulted in heavy sheep losses on and around the Moor, was followed a few years later by an even greater catastrophe; the Lynmouth Flood Disaster, which caused the destruction of the greater part of the lovely village of Lynmouth, with the sad loss of 34 lives; with further loss of life and extensive damage to property, roads and bridges on and around Exmoor.

In 1953, John Purchase, the Exmoor Estate farm bailiff—since George Molland's death in 1936—retired. He was replaced by John Hayes, who had previously been farming at Morebath and had been practically ruined when foot and mouth disease struck his farm and the livestock had to be destroyed. About the same time, Mr. F.G. Smyth Richards, the Agent to the Fortescue's Castle Hill and Exmoor Estates, also retired. He was replaced by Mr. J.M.B. Mackie.

In the ten year period (1944-54) a further 700 acres of land had been reseeded, and the estate farm, including Warren and Badgworthy, was now a little over 10,500 acres in extent, with another 5,000 acres let; for the most part in seven farms; Pinkery, Driver, Duredon, Simonsbath Barton, Emmetts Grange, Wintershead and Horsen.

In the 1950's, with the aid of the hill farm improvement grants, some of the old shepherds dwellings way out on the Moor were replaced by new bungalows nearer to the main roads and to Simonsbath. Two were erected beside Winstitchen Lane; one for the shepherd of the newly formed Ashcombe herding, created in 1958 to replace the Hoar Oak herding, which was given up about this time. The other bungalow, completed a few years earlier in 1951, was built to replace Wheal Eliza Cottage, which, since 1903, had been the home of the shepherd of Mines herding. The last shepherd to live in the old cottage was William Little's grandson (also William) who took over the herding when his father—Jack—retired in 1939. Jack Little, who spent all his working life on the Exmoor Estate, the last 14 years at Mines, was unquestionably the finest shepherd of his generation, and possibly of all time, although he only just had the edge on his brothers Jim and William (killed by lightening), who were also extremely competent men. Family rivalry was keen, but it was Jack Little who was called upon time and again to move around the Moor and improve herdings that had been let back.

William Little moved into his new bungalow in 1952, and continued on as shepherd of the Mines herding for a further 21 years, before semi-retiring to one of the West Cottages at Simonsbath. Even there he did not entirely foresake his flock, but retained a half herding at Simonsbath Barton practically to the time of his death in October 1982, at the age of 77. With his passing, 110 years of continuous shepherding on Exmoor by William Little 1st and his descendants—came to an end. William Little was also the last shepherd on the Moor who was a direct descendant of the Scottish shepherds brought down by Frederic Knight when he began his vast sheep ranching enterprise around 1871. The only member of the Little family now left on Exmoor Proper is Jack's daughter (William's sister) Mrs. Harry Prout—née Maggie Little—of Rose Cottage, Simonsbath.

After William Little's departure from Wheal Eliza the cottage was abandoned, and it was not long before one more ruin was added to the

Exmoor list. Two hundred yards from the cottage, tucked away behind Flexbarrow, lies the garden created by Jack Little with the help of two of his sons, and here, amongst the wilderness to which it has returned, Lilac flourishes* and a couple of Gooseberry bushes and a small patch of Rhubarb struggle for existence. The original garden of Wheal Eliza, nearer to the cottage, was not a great success, as it was often waterlogged and very prone to frost.

A replacement bungalow was also built at Blackpits, for the shepherd of the Blackpits cum Badgworthy herding, but the former corrugated iron structure, built there in 1920, was retained for use as a store and for orphan lambs, etc.

Titchcombe was also replaced by a new bungalow, which was built close to the main Challacombe road, about half way between Bale Water and Cornham Farm. The old Titchcombe bungalow—some distance away between Driver Farm and Duredon—was never an attractive building, with its corrugated iron exterior, and after it was given up it soon became a sorry sight, with its windows all blown out and the porch and outhouses falling down. I am happy to record that on my last visit there it had been given a new lease of life by 20 youngsters on a Youth Training Scheme. The exterior has been clad with tanolised timber and new windows fitted. It has also been refurbished inside and is now quite presentable.

A little to the north of this bungalow, on the west bank of Bale Water, lies the turf covered remains of what appears to have been a rectangular building, but who built it and for what purpose is not known. A similar building (if such it was) can be found on Brendon Common, 175 yards north of the ruins of the cottage above Hoccombe Water, and close to the wall fence separating the common from the Badgworthy enclosures. The internal measurements of this building are approximately 25 feet by 11 feet, but here again we know nothing of its origins or history.

The shepherd of the Limecombe herding, who was based at the lonely Limecombe Cottage, also changed his place of abode around this time. Not into a new bungalow, but into No. 1 West Cottages. These cottages, six in number, are divided into two blocks of three. The older and smaller cottages, built by the Knight family, were sold by the Fortescue Estate to a local builder in the early 1970's. He attractively restored them from a near derelict state, and then sold them off individually.

The three larger cottages, retained by the estate, are of a little more interest to connoisseur's of Exmoor's history, because No's 2 and 3 are conversions from the building built by Frederic Knight to house the steam ploughing engine he purchased in the mid 1870's. The ploughing tackle was stored in a large shed between the engine house and the older cottages, and a Blacksmith's Shop was erected on the opposite side of the road. This building, an essential part of the set up, enabled repairs and maintenance to be carried out on the spot. The conversion of the engine house to two

---

*Planted by Jack's daughter, Maggie.

cottages (no. 1 was already there) was carried out in the late 1890's by Viscount Ebrington, shortly after he took possession of the Exmoor Estate.

At certain times, when the front wall of the cottage is damp and the light is right, it is still possible to see the outline of the old archway through which the steam engine entered. Incidentally, the engine and ploughing tackle were still there when Lord Fortescue and Viscount Ebrington took possession, but shortly afterwards the steam engine was removed to his Lordship's Brick and Tile works at Filleigh, where the wheels were removed and the engine used as a stationary unit. The ploughing tackle was sold off.*

It is reassuring to find that when the shepherd of the Limecombe herding moved to West Cottages, the last of the Limecombe cottages did not suffer the same fate as Wheal Eliza Cottage. It has been let on and off for a number of years, and is at present used by one or two schools for field studies and adventure holidays.

Of all the herdings on the Exmoor Estate, Hoar Oak alone retained its former shepherd's cottage, but even there the end was near. The rearrangement of the shepherd's accommodation was no doubt much more acceptable from the point of view of the shepherds and their wives and families, because it brought them into closer contact with the rest of the community around Simonsbath, and enabled them to partake more easily in everything that was going on; social functions, etc. There were certain disadvantages in the new arrangements, however, in that the new bungalows and other shepherds accommodation were now placed on the very edge of the herdings in their charge, and not, as formerly, in the centre of operations, where a watchful eye could be kept on their flocks, and a helping hand was never far away when needed. A great advantage when heavy snow arrives on Exmoor with little or no warning.

In 1954, Exmoor Proper and large areas of land around it, were designated a National Park, although there was not—as is commonly believed—any change of land owndership. Three years later, the National Park Committee entered the first of its many battles to maintain the 'Status Quo' when it became involved in the controversy concerning the future of the Chains and Hoar Oak herding, which the Fortescue Estate had agreed to lease to the Forestry Commission. This herding, which was on the most exposed, wettest, and least productive part of the Exmoor Estate had never been a great success, but whether the planting of this large area with conifers would have been any improvement is debatable. At 1,500 feet and more above sea level, and exposed to the worst gales, it is extremely doubtful if the plantation would have reached maturity. Such was the opposition to the proposals by the National Park Authority and the newly formed Exmoor Society, that the Forestry Commission withdrew from the scene, and for the second time in less than 50 years, the Chains

---

*From a conversation with Jack Buckingham of Rose Cottage.

were saved from destruction. Conservationists won the day, but a thought should be spared for Lord Fortescue, whose proposal to lease the Chains for afforestation was not taken solely with the view to increasing the income of his estate, but because of his concern over the future safety of Lynmouth and other moorland villages, following the devastation and loss of life caused by the terrible flood disaster of August 1952; a disaster that largely emanated from the Chains.

According to Mr. Hugh Thomas, the present Agent of the Fortescue Estates, Lord Fortescue's honourable intentions have been much misunderstood, and most people have forgotten that the proposal to plant trees on the Chains watershed was to avoid a repetition of the Lynmouth Flood Disaster, because afforestation of areas like the Chains has the effect of slowing down the rate at which water drains away, thus providing a built in safety factor, and one that would certainly have been of considerable value in lessening the severity of flooding in the future: A well known technique that has been used with great success elsewhere in this country and overseas.

The deaths of the 5th Earl Fortescue and Lady Fortescue within a few days of one another in June 1958, left the family without a direct heir,* and with crippling death duties to pay. This necessitated the sale of not only a large number of properties around their home at Castle Hill, but the whole of the Challacombe Estate and a considerable part of Exmoor. It is sad to find that the sale of the Brendon properties in 1916, and parts of Exmoor in 1921 and 1927 by the 4th Earl, had failed to secure the long term future of the Fortescue Estates, even though the 5th Earl had been able to retain his Exmoor interests without further sacrifice of farms or land.

The sale of the Challacombe Estate of some 5,080 acres, together with 4,640 acres of the Exmoor Estate, which included Hoar Oak and about 200 acres in Devon, took place on Friday 18th September 1959, in the Bridge Buildings, Barnstaple, when the whole was put up for auction in one lot. In the tense atmosphere of an overcrowded room, a consortium of tenants were outbid by a Crewkerne investment company, who secured the properties on offer with a bid of £163,100; £100 more than the tenants could raise.

Within a day or so it had changed hands again, when a Mr. R. Spiere purchased the whole for an undisclosed sum (believed to have been considerably more than the Crewkerne company paid for it). Mr. Spiere commented that his purchase was not a speculation, and that he would sell off all he could to the tenants, 'they have nothing to worry about'. In the case of the Challacombe tenants he was as good as his word, and a little later they were able to puchase their farms and other properties, but the offer was not extended to the Exmoor tenantry of what was now known as the Emmetts Grange Estate, and in less than a fortnight this estate was sold

---

*Their only son Peter (Lord Ebrington) was reported 'Missing Presumed Dead' during the Second World War: The 5th Earl was succeeded by his brother, the Hon. Denzil Fortescue, who died in 1977. He was succeeded by his eldest son, Richard, the 7th Earl.

intact to a Mr. Darby Haddon of Bourton-on-the-Water in the Cotswolds Gloucestershire.

The Emmetts Grange Estate comprised of the Grange and 419 acres, Wintershead and 736 acres, Horsen and 690 acres, Pinkery and 331 acres, and Driver and 448 acres. Also included was Hoar Oak and the Chains herding, 1,210 acres in all; and allotments on Hangley Cleave (218 acres), Long Holcombe, (255 acres), and Sherdon Allotment and fields, together totalling 324 acres. The Exmoor Forest Hotel and eight miles of fishing completed the property sold at this time. The annual rents received by the Fortescue's from this part of their estate prior to the sale was given as £2,087, 10. 0.

Details in the sale brochure of the Emmetts Grange Estate reveal that all the farms sold had been modernised and equipped with bathrooms and septic tank drainage. All had their own electric lighting plants, mainly Lister Start-O-Matics, although Pinkery was generating its supply with the aid of a windmill. Driver Cottages and Hoar oak were less fortunate. They had neither electricity or bathrooms, and were still using the old bucket closets. The water supply to Driver Cottages was limited to a shared tap on the wall outside, but Hoar Oak did have water laid on to a sink in the scullery.

It is generally believed that the Scotch Blackface sheep remained on the Hoar Oak and Chains herding until it was sold with the Emmetts Grange Estate, but in fact they were gone prior to the 5th Earl Fortescue's death a year earlier, when Abe Antell, the last shepherd to live in the Hoar Oak Cottage, was transferred to Blackpits to replace a younger shepherd who had moved to Simonsbath, to take charge of the newly created Ashcombe herding.

After Mr. Darby Haddon became the owner of the Emmetts Grange Estate, his tenants were given to understand that they could remain in their farms, but it was not long before it became clear that Mr. Haddon was intent on taking possession of the whole of his estate. There was little the tenants could do to resist this move. At that time there was virtually no security for the tenant farmers, no matter how good a farmers they were, and these men were among the best on Exmoor, and slowly but surely, one farmer after another was forced to give up and move on. Over 20 years later there are still bitter feelings about the way this affair was handled, and I know of one family in particular who shed many tears when they in turn had to leave their farm and the Exmoor they so dearly loved.

Mr. Haddon took up residence at Emmetts Grange, and as his farms came in hand he turned them into herdings, stocking them with a mixture of Cheviot, Scotch Blackface and Exmoor Horn sheep, and Galloway Cattle. One or two local men were employed as stockmen, others were brought down from Scotland as Frederic Knight and Lord Fortescue had done before him. A number of hedges, vital as protection for livestock on the high moorlands, were bulldozed down, and some modernisation was carried out at the Grange, and new cottages built close by. Two of the older cottages that formerly served Wintershead and Horsen Farms were deemed to be beyond repair and were put to the torch and burned down. In the 1970's the present owner, Mr. Geoff Ward, a Barnstaple business man with many interests, built two new cottages on this site as replacements, but it was not until the summer of 1988 that they were first occupied.

Mr. Reg Westcott of West Ley Farm, Exford, was born in one of the old cottages, which his parents occupied for a time while working for his grandfather, who was then farming at Picked Stones. During the long winter months, Reg's father trapped rabbits, which, before myxomatosis reached the Moor in 1952-53, thrived in large numbers. Pests they may have been, but welcome ones, for in many cases they paid—or largely paid—the rents of the farms, and records kept by Mr. F.J. Westcott show that on Wintershead Farm alone, where he was trapping in 1932/33/34, no less than 3,932 rabbits were killed over the three year period.

The purchase of the Emmetts Grange Estate by Mr. Haddon, and the subsequent taking in hand of the farms, which resulted in the ejectment of long established tenant farmers, destroyed almost totally the traditional farming and social fabric of Exmoor that was begun in Frederic Knight's time and built up over many generations. This was completed when the last two tenanted farms on the Exmoor Estate, Simonsbath Barton and Duredon, came in hand in 1969 and 70, and neither were let again. Duredon Farmhouse and about nine acres of land were sold off; the rest of the land on this farm was split between the Titchcombe and Limecombe herdings.

On the estate farm, time and other factors had also taken a heavy toll of the old and familiar shepherding and estate worker families, and, sad to say, Exmoor became a land of strangers.

Old customs were again in danger of dying out. Where once the occupants of every cottage and farmhouse on the Exmoor Estate had their own turf (peat) pit and cut 8,000 and 20,000 turves respectively each year for consumption in their hearths, only two men, Sante Lafuente, the stockman at Cornham Farm (now semi-retired (1988) and living at Jubilee Villas Simonsbath), and Jack Buckingham, were left to keep the home fires burning.

Sadly, Jack is no longer with us. His death on 13th January 1988, came suddenly and totally unexpectedly after a short illness: For close on 50 years Jack Buckingham had been a loyal and conscientious worker on the Exmoor Estate farm. He drove the first permanently based tractor on the estate—a Standard Fordson—and survived an horrendous accident on the same machine in 1947, when he lost control of his charge and it rolled over and over down the steep cleave—close to where Cornham Bungalow now stands. Later, as additional tractors were brought into use, Jack began to spend more of his working days on repairing the old wall and bank fences erected by the Knights many years earlier. He became a skilled craftsman in this field, taking a great pride in his work, and in the process gained an unrivalled knowledge of his 'patch'. For many years too, Jack helped out at lambing and shearing times, and in later years, when the weather was too severe to work out on the Moor, he assisted Den Westlake in the saw mill at Simonsbath. On fine summer evenings and at weekends he was often to be found on Buscombe (east of the road, about midway between Blackpits Bungalow and Brendon Two Gates) cutting Turf for Rose Cottage, where, for many years until his death, he lived with his friends the Prout family. He also cut turf for a few of his neighbours in the village, and for Dick French of Brendon Barton; the latters turf pit being on Brendon Common, where Dick is one of the few commoners who have continued to exercise this right. In the last four to five years some of the younger generation Exmoor Estate workers have shown an interest in burning peat as an alternative fuel and there has been some revival of this ancient practice.

Peat comes in two forms: Spine turf, where the deposits are shallow, is cut on the slant. Pit turf, where the peat beds are much deeper, is cut straight down. The deeper the beds, the blacker the peat, but harder to harvest as it is inclined to break up when being dried. The lumps that have broken off are known locally as 'Biddocks'. These are bagged up separately, and are highly prized as they give out exceptional heat, equally as good as the best coal when used in the old time Bodley Stoves, now for the most part replaced by Rayburns. A man on day work cutting peat was expected to turn out 1,000 turves a day, a figure that was usually doubled when on piece work. An exceptional 7,000 turves were reputed to have been cut in two days by the late Tom Elworthy,* at Kittuck (behind Larkbarrow Farm), and this was after walking from Duredon Farm, a distance of some five miles away, returning home at night, and repeating the journey the following day. A feat, which, if it could be verified, would surely qualify him for an entry in the *Guinness Book of Records*. Tom Elworthy, who was familiar with all the peat beds on Exmoor, believed that the deepest beds were situated on Warren Allotment, where it was possible to dig five spits deep (about eight feet) with little trouble.

Another entitlement or concession held by the shepherds and Exmoor Estate workers, was that of keeping a cow. The shepherds—as we have already noted—were provided with two; the estate workers—one. This custom began to die out about the time of the Second World War, not because Lord Fortescue ceased to supply the cows on request, but, because of a tendency towards smaller families, less milk was required, and where a cow was kept, it usually supplied milk to one or more neighbours. In the past, cows belonging to the estate workers—who for the most part lived along the Challacombe road at West Cottages and at West Gate—were driven along the road to the far side of Limecombe and up on to Big Duredon field to graze, each cow on returning in the evening turning into its own shippon to be milked, and in the winter bedded down. The

---

*Son of Tom Elworthy who lived at Wheal Eliza Cottage for 40 years.

shepherds out on the lonely Moor were the last to give up their cows, and this was not until after they moved into their new bungalows and alternative accommodation in the 1950's. The nearness to civilisation, plus a six day a week delivery of milk from Minehead to their doorstep, meant they were no longer dependent on their own resources, and the keeping of a cow or two was not worth the bother it entailed. Only the shepherd at Blackpits, and the stockman at Cornham, carry on the custom today (1986).

It was during the war years—or thereabouts—that the old style gypsy caravans, once a familiar sight, stopped travelling the Moor. There were at least two stop-over sites on Exmoor Proper. One was on the three cornered piece of open land at Withypool Cross. The other, at Bale Water, just above the road and close to the stream. Neither were used for more than a day or two at a time, but Tom Little remembers the gypsies cutting the withies (willow) at Bale Water and turning them into clothes pegs. Another site, just outside the boundary fence, was at Brendon Two Gates, and the accompanying drawing, copied from an old postcard, was taken along this stretch of road. On one occasion prior to 1916 the gypsies overstayed their welcome here, and Lord Fortescue was forced to take steps for their removal.

In 1967, Mr. Darby Haddon sold the Emmetts Grange Estate (with the exception of the Exmoor Forest Hotel and fishing, which he gave to his daughter) to Mr. J. Bradley, who farmed it in much the same way as his predecessor. Two years later it was again on the market, and it was at this time that the National Park Department of the Somerset County Council were able to purchase all that part of the estate north of the Challacombe road; namely Pinkery and Driver Farms, and Hoar Oak and the Chains; 1,991 acres in all, at a cost of £53,000. Driver and Pinkery farms were once again let, but not Pinkery farmhouse and two acres adjoining, which were reserved as an outdoor activity and field studies centre for the use of older school children in the summer months. At the time of the purchase the farmhouse was in an almost derelict state, but young volunteers under the guidance of Mr. Arthur Phillips—the resident warden—soon made it habitable and brought it into use. Mrs. Matthew Waley Cohen of Exford, in the unavoidable absence of her husband,* performed the opening ceremony. It was a unique occasion, when, instead of cutting a ribbon, she cut a Caerphilly cheese, which proved to be a sensible idea and must more palatable.

It is sad to relate that Hoar Oak Cottage did not receive the same treatment. Deserted before the first sale in 1959, when Abe Antell moved to Blackpits, it was now in a sorry state, but not beyond repair. Semi-derelict it may have been, but even worse was to follow when its interior was gutted out, the windows walled up, and the natural slate roof torn off and replaced by one of ghastly galvanised iron. Rightly or wrongly, I

---

*Brother of Sir Bernard of Honeymead.

Gypsy caravans on Brendon Common (from an old photograph)

Avery Cattle weighbridge at Simonsbath c1898

believe the intention was that part of the old cottage would be retained as a hay store, etc., by who ever took the tenancy of the former herding, the other part, for use by anyone requiring shelter, day or night, like many of the old 'Bothies' in Scotland. It is still possible to shelter there, if you do not mind wading ankle deep through animal manure and the occasional dead sheep, for the doors are all gone and sheep and ponies wander in and out at will, and more repairs will be necessary soon as the roof is again beginning to blow off.

A year after the purchase of the northern part of the Emmetts Grange Estate, the National Park Authority decided to sell off Driver Cottages, which were also in need of extensive renovation. The two cottages were afterwards knocked into one, and now go under the name of 'Moorland Way'.

The sale of the Emmetts Grange Estate by Mr. J. Bradley in 1969, increased the number of landowners on Exmoor still further. Mr. Geoff Ward purchased Wintershead and Horsen Farms, and Mr. A. Brown —Emmetts Grange. These properties are still in the same ownership, but the former two farms have, I believe, been on the market for some time, and a few years back one the 'Beatles' was showing a keen interest in the Grange.

Part of the Honeymead Estate was also sold off in 1967, following Sir Bernard Waley Cohen's* decision to reduce his farming activities. Picked Stones Farm on Exmoor and Thorne Farm in Exford Parish, together with nearly 400 acres of land were sold to Mr. Graham Leeves of Exford. Red Deer Farm and some 460 acres were sold to Mr. Tom Gage of Gallon House. A further 60 acres of land opposite the old inn were purchased by Mrs. Gundrey of Exford.

Over the years a small hamlet has sprung up at Honeymead. Sir Bernard Waley Cohen's residence, Honeymead House, was destroyed by fire in April 1954. It was rebuilt, and a managers house and workmens cottages have also been erected.

At Simonsbath, the Lodge, former summer residence of the Fortescue family, had been little used by them in recent years. For a short while after the private boys school departed it was let as the Diana Lodge Hotel, but was unoccupied when Major John Coleman Cooke, an army colleague of my father, saw it, fell in love with it, and shortly afterwards acquired a lease for it and moved in. Major Cooke, a Fellow of the Zoological Society and lover of Exmoor, became a successful author, but he is perhaps better remembered for his work for conservation, and it was due almost entirely to his efforts that the Exmoor Society was formed as an Amenity group to fight for the preservation of the natural character of the moorlands, which, because of ever increasing reclamation, was in grave danger of being completely destroyed. Not all of their battles have ended in success, but a growing awareness of the need to conserve our national and natural

---

*Succeeded his father in 1952.

heritage for future generations to enjoy is at last beginning to have its effect, and working side by side with the National Park Authority some progress is being made in achieving these aims.

It was shortly after Major Cooke moved into the Lodge that I first made my acquaintance with the old house, when I cycled from Umberleigh to collect wages due for tidying up the Majors smallholding at Langridge Ford, prior to its sale. Major Cooke and his wife remained at the Lodge for close on 20 years, and three of their four children were born there. In 1968 the Cookes moved to Braunton, where the Major continued his work for conservation, even though his health was deteriorating. He died in London on 16th February 1978, aged 64. His ashes were brought back and interred at Simonsbath.

Following Major Cooke's departure to Braunton, Simonsbath Lodge was put on the market. It was purchased by Mr. J. Morley, who ran it as an hotel for five years before selling out to Mr. M. Woods. He continued the business for a further five years before he sold out to Mr. and Mrs. Brown. They restored the old house to a high standard, and at the same time built up a fine reputation for their cuisine, but after five years, they too have moved on.

When the Fortescue Estate sold Simonsbath Lodge to Mr. J. Morley, the sale did not include the old mansion building to the rear. This was retained as accommodation for an estate worker and his family, as it had been since 1961. Prior to that date the House and Mansion were occupied and run as one unit, apart from the west wing between Boevey's old house and the woolstore, which, for a few years from 1957-1965, was also occupied by an estate worker.

Of the many changes on Exmoor in recent years, the closure of Simonsbath School in 1970 is perhaps the saddest, though not entirely unexpected; this school being but one of countless village schools throughout the country that have suffered a similar fate in recent years. A number of reasons can be found for the closure of these fine schools, but basically it was due to the movement of a large part of the rural population to the towns and cities, following the rapid expansion of farm mechanisation after the last war, which inevitably led to a reduction in the level of manpower needed on the land. This, coupled with the trend towards smaller families, and the change of education policy in the 1950's, whereby village schools taught their pupils only to the age of 11 before they were moved to the nearest senior school to complete their education, also had its effect in reducing the number of pupils in the village schools at one time, and undoubtedly hastened the day of closure.

Having received my earliest education in schools of this kind I mourn their loss. Thay had a place and a great contribution to make to the close knit rural and social life of our villages, and their loss has in many cases destroyed the very soul of the rural community: Unfortunately, schools without pupils cannot and do not survive, and records show that when Simonsbath School closed on 17th July 1970, only three pupils were transferred to other schools; two to Exford Primary and one to Dulverton Middle School. Although Simonsbath School had provided education to most of the children living within a three mile radius of the village since 1857, many children living in the outlying farms and cottages on Exmoor attended the village school nearest to their homes; Twitchen in particular, where virtually all of the pupils from the Sandyway area were educated.

Of the moorland parishes surrounding Exmoor Proper, the schools of Barbrook, Brendon, Oare, Hawkridge, Withypool, Molland, Twitchen, Heasley Mill and Challacombe have all closed. We shall not see their likes again! Some of these schools have been sold off and converted into private houses. Others, like Simonsbath and Withypool, are now used as activity centres.

In June 1970, John Hayes, the Exmoor Estate bailiff since 1953, died in harness, and since that time farming on the Exmoor Estate has been managed from Filleigh by the Farms' Manager. Subsequent bailiffs on Exmoor have been regraded as Sub or Under Managers. John Hayes was followed by a quick succession of Under Managers, none of whom lasted more than two years until the arrival of Mr. Peter Brook in 1977. He has since moved (Michaelmas Day 1986) to Luckworthy, Molland, to begin farming on his own account.

In the year prior to John Hayes death, Simonsbath Barton came in hand, and the Fortescue Estate decided that future Under Managers would have the benefit of the farmhouse at Barton as their residence. In consequence, the brick house, built for—and first occupied by—George Molland early this century, and later by his successors, was no longer required, and this house, known as Hillcrest, situated beside the Lynton road out of Simonsbath was therefore sold off with its out-buildings and a little over three acres of land as a residential holding.

In 1980, Mr. H.R. Thomas, FRICS, the Agent to the Fortescue Estates since 1974,* approached the National Park planning department on his employer's behalf, with a proposal to rebuild Larkbarrow Farm and to add a small silage barn and lean-to lambing shed. The improvement of this part of the Exmoor Estate had been long delayed by the unexploded shells and wartime debris left behind when the army forces withdrew from their training area, but with the recent clearance of this land it was now possible to break up the old pastures and renew the grassland there. Once this work was completed, the Larkbarrow herding, which, since 1943, had been run from Warren, would have been re-established and Warren would then have become a separate herding: This had been deemed necessary for two reasons:

1. To make better use of the Larkbarrow land and thus improve its profitability.
2. Because Mr. Ernie Duke, who had been shepherding the combined herdings with his son Brian, had just retired.

*He succeeded Mr. I.M. Lang, who took over from Mr. J.M.B. Mackie, Chistmas, 1960.

Father and son had lived together at Warren in a convenient arrangement, but this was unlikely to happen again, and with no other house available in the area difficulty was expected in finding a replacement shepherd.

Neither the Exmoor Park Authority or the Exmoor Society were happy with the proposals, and the planning application was withdrawn pending negotiations with the National Park Authority, who accepted that something would have to be done to remedy the situation. Representatives of the Department of the Environment and the National Park, proceeded to work out a compromise with Lady Margaret Fortescue and the Fortescue Estate, and after long negotiations a solution acceptable to all parties was worked out. The D. of E. and the National Park Department of the Somerset County Council agreed to purchase Larkbarrow and 880 acres of land lying around it, in order to conserve it and to allow access to the general public over this somewhat remote and very beautiful moorland area, whilst allowing the Fortescue Estate to lease it back, but this was not on the moderate terms that some local news reports indicated, because the rental paid was nearly four times that of comparable adjoining land. Justified perhaps as a return on capital investment, but not in terms of agricultural production capability.

The sale of this land released much needed capital for re-investment on the improvement of other farms on the Exmoor Estate, whilst retaining Larkbarrow as a sheep and cattle herding. From the financial point of view this was undoubtedly a reasonable solution to the problem, but it did not resolve the question of accommodation for a new shepherd. This was partly got over when Brian Duke moved to Jubilee Villas with his father and mother, and Pat Watts, the son of Eric Watts, the last tenant of Duredon, moved into Warren. It was not an entirely satisfactory arrangement because it meant that Brian Duke was now some distance from his herding. Not the easiest of ground to cover when the moorland roads are blocked with snow.

Thus things stood until 1982, when it was found necessary to sell off a further portion of the Exmoor Estate to finance the payment of a family trust settlement. This time it was the turn of Warren Farm and 2,260 acres to come under the hammer (10th August 1982). This part of the estate consisted of Warren Farm and 518 acres of in-bye land, of which about half had been improved. The remainder of the land—apart from Toms Hill where there had been some reclamation many years earlier—was rough moorlands, comprised of East and West Pinford, Trout Hill and Hayes Allotment.

Once again the National Park Authority stepped in, and with the aid of money from the National Heritage Fund—set up by Parliament in 1980— they were able to raise the purchase price of £447,000, which would have been much higher had it not been for the Capital Gains tax concessions introduced for the benefit of Heritage land purchases *(viz.* Tax allowed for at time of purchase rather than paid by the Fortescue Estate at a later date, thus keeping the money required for the purchase to a minimum). With

Warren sold, it was no longer possible to continue with a herding on the Larkbarrow land and this was given up. This ground is, I believe, now shared between four licencees.

Eight months after the National Park Authority purchased the Warren Estate, tenders were invited for the purchase of Warren Farm and the 518 acres of in-bye land. This was secured by Mr. P. Hawkins, who had purchased Red Deer Farm and 200 acres on the same day that Warren was first sold. Mr. Hawkins was also able to lease the remainder of the Warren Estate, subject to certain covenants.

The Exmoor Estate was now reduced to about 6,500 acres, plus Badgworthy, which they still rent. All of this land, apart from Emmetts Allotment (Burcombe) is in hand. This allotment has been let continuously for many years, first with Emmetts Grange, and more latterly by Victor Tucker of Rocks Farm, Exford, until his death in 1985. Emmetts Allotment has now been taken in hand by the estate, but Victor Tucker's son, John, will (by arrangement), continue to use this land for summer grazing.

The number of sheepherdings since Warren and Larkbarrow were given up has remained steady at five, but with the improvement of so much of the pasture around Simonsbath, and with the taking in hand of Duredon and Simonsbath Barton, it has been possible to increase the number of breeding ewes and replacements per herding from 550 to 800 plus. These herdings, each with one shepherd, are Titchcombe, Limecombe, Blackpits, Ashcombe and Mines. Extra help is provided at lambing time. All sheep are sheared by the estate shepherds.

The Cheviot flocks, a familiar sight on Exmoor since 1871 (with all replacement ewes bred on the Moor), are all but gone, and have for the most part been replaced by Scotch BlackfaceXCheviot ewes, which in their turn have also been put to Blackface rams. A Blueface Leicester ram has also been used with some success. Although the ewe lambs produced by this breed of ram are not retained for breeding on the estate herdings there is a good demand for them in the local markets, where they are sold as Two Tooths. Texel rams are also used, but none of the progeny of these rams are retained or sold for breeding, but are used solely because they produce the type of lamb carcase required by the housewives of today.

Although no one with any feeling for Exmoor's past can fail to mourn the passing of the Cheviots, which for well over 100 years were the mainstay of the Exmoor Estate farming economy, their ultimate downfall has been brought about by the great improvement in pasture quality, which has caused them to become too fat, and thus require considerable shepherding because of the tendency to get on their backs, incurring heavy losses. The Scotch Blackface sheep do not have this fault and thus require less shepherding, a great advantage with increased flock numbers and limited manpower to look after them. Nevertheless, it remains to be seen whether or not the crossbred ewes have retained the hardiness of their forebears and the ability to survive the harsher winter conditions that are from time to time encountered on the Moor.

Despite the sale of nearly two thirds of the original Exmoor Estate, the Fortescue farming enterprise has reached a degree of self sufficiency undreamed of at the turn of the century and it is no longer necessary to send stock off the Moor to winter. Approximately 380 cows, descendants of the Galloways introduced in 1935, are calved down annually,* and, after having the run of the herdings in the summer, are winter quartered at Cornham and the Barton. A vast quantity of silage is made each year to sustain both cattle and sheep through the winter, but tillage is limited to rape crops grown to fatten the lambs.

Throughout the 90 years the Exmoor Estate has been in the possession of the Fortescue family, there has been a steady and continuous improvement of their property. Financial problems, death duties and family trust settlements have all helped to reduce the size of the estate, but never in all this time has the efficiency of management been in question, and I believe the Fortescues have been well blessed with their choice of Agents, Farm Managers and Bailiffs, and well served by them and the shepherds and estate workers in their employ. The present workforce consists of a resident under-manager, who resides at the Barton.[2] Five shepherds, two cattlemen, a carpenter, a mason—who is a jack of all trades, four tractor drivers and two or three part time workers. Accommodation is provided rent free and craftsmens rates are paid. Perks include wood and peat for fuel, but the custom of supplying potatoes to all workers is now dying out and they are no longer provided to new staff taken on. A non-contributory pension scheme was introduced some years ago, which is of great benefit to long service employees, who on retirement have either been allowed to stay on in their cottages, or, where these cottages are required for service workers, found alternative accommodation in the village.

We have dealt at some length with the break up of the Exmoor Estate, and it would not be right or proper to conclude this book without a brief account of the progress made by a few of the long established Exmoor families during the time that they were living on the Moor.

One or two of these we have already covered, but of the numerous working men employed by John Knight in the early stages of his reclamation, only three other families, the Frys, Kingdoms and Steers, remained on Exmoor Proper to the present century, and nearly all of the descendants of later arrivals are also gone from the Moor.

The first recorded Fry on Exmoor (apart from Ursula Fry of Pinkery) was John Fry, who is listed on John Knight's labour accounts for 1836 as a bullock herd. He was probably working on Exmoor before this date, and was certainly there for a long time after. By 1866, John and his son William were farming 217 acres around Simonsbath and on Ashcombe. John retired prior to 1871, but continued to live in Simonsbath until his death at the grand age of 93 in 1884. At some time about 1880, William

---

*About two thirds are calved in the spring, the remainder in the autumn.

Fry gave up the cottage and land he was renting at Simonsbath in favour of Picked Stones Farm and 140 acres, increased a few years later to 163 acres, and there, he, and later his son Charles, farmed until 1902, when this branch of the Fry family appears to have left the Moor. William's brother James, with a partner William Smith, took over Simonsbath Inn, a grocers shop and 32 acres of land in 1864, when Robert Holcombe—the former tenant—moved to Sandyway to take the Sportsman's Inn. When William Fry took the tenancy of Picked Stones, James and his partner took over 140 acres of the land his brother had previously rented, and at some time between 1886 and 1898, James became the sole tenant. Simonsbath Inn, delicenced by Frederic Knight in 1862, was run as a refreshment house and hotel, and during the time that James Fry was the tenant—and for that period only—it was known as the William Rufus Hotel, a name that was changed to the Exmoor Forest Hotel in 1902 when Mr. R. Moyle took over.

The Walter Fry who purchased Kinsford in 1864, was certainly a close relative to James and William Fry, probably another brother, and after he died in 1885, William moved in, but in 1896, James, who had been left a third share of Kinsford, purchased the other shares and became the sole owner. He did not keep it for long, and by 1902 Kinsford was in the possession of a Mr. R. Marsh. Shortly after, all the remaining members of the Fry family slipped quietly off the Moor.

William Kingdom and his descendants also prospered on Exmoor, William, who was employed as a blacksmith by John Knight in 1836, and afterwards by Frederic, had three sons, William, Alfred (also known as Arthur) and Alex. William junior continued the family blacksmith tradition after his father's death, and by 1866 he was renting a cottage and the blacksmith's shop in Simonsbath and a little land close by. He later became the Postmaster-cum-Postman of the village, and was also the Registrar of Births, Deaths and Marriages* and the relieving school attendance officer. William had one son, Ernest, who, for a few years after his father's death in 1915, continued at the Post Office, but about the year 1922 gave this up to concentrate on his farming interests, remaining on Exmoor until 1936.

For a few years, Arthur Kingdom farmed 540 acres at Warren Farm, but in 1898 he gave notice to quit, and appears to have left the Moor soon after. Alex, the other brother, took the tenancy of Driver Farm and 317 acres about the year 1875. He, and later his son John, continued to farm there until 1920, when John sold up and moved up country. Alex had another son, William, who took Cornham Farm in 1899 and remained there for 21 years, retiring to North Molton in the same year that his brother gave up Driver, and when Ernest departed from Simonsbath some 16 years later, the name of Kingdom died out on Exmoor.

Joseph Steer, ploughman to both John and Frederic Knight, was also on

*Appointed January 1886.

Exmoor in 1836. He lived first at Limecombe and later at Bale Water, before taking the tenancy of a cottage in Simonsbath and 22 acres of land. This was accomplished before 1861, and when he died in 1880, his second son, William—who had been living at home—carried on the tenancy. William was also a ploughman on the Exmoor Estate, and was in fact the driver and operator of Frederic Knight's steam engine and ploughing tackle, purchased in 1876. William died in 1893, a year after the death of his elder brother John, who for over 30 years had been farming the White Rocks smallholding of 27 acres. John was succeeded by a younger brother, Richard, who had also been employed by Frederic Knight, first as a labourer and more latterly as the shepherd of the Deer Park herding. Richard died in 1906, and it was his son William who was destined to be the last of the Steer family on Exmoor. Shortly before his father's death, William had taken the tenancy of half of the Exmoor Forest Hotel. He continued in the hotel business until 1916, when he moved to South View and became the tenant of the cottage and 65 acres, moving on to take the larger farm of Cornham in 1920 when William Kingdom retired. William Steer remained at Cornham until 1936, when he left the Moor to live at Exford, where he died in 1954.

A James Watts was also working for John Knight in 1836, employed as a quarryman, but he was long gone when a family of the same name, still resident on Exmoor, came to live on the Moor from the adjoining parish of North Molton in the early part of this century.

Of the many families who arrived on Exmoor in the latter half of the last century, only a handfull remained beyond the turn of the century. Some, like the Scottish shepherds and William Carter and Robert Cann we have already dealt with, but others who spent many years there and took part in the making of the Exmoor we know today, are, or soon will be forgotten.

One such family were the Blackmores, who, for some years around 1851, lived in one of the old Warren Cottages. Whether the Frederick Blackmore who was renting a cottage in Simonsbath and 19 acres of land in 1866 was a descendant of this family is not clear, but it was almost certainly this man who was looking after the Duredon herding prior to Robert Tait Little's arrival in 1871. The last of the family to work on the estate was John Blackmore, who was living at No. 6 West Cottages when World War II broke out, but died shortly after.

A family by the name of Coward were living in one of the Honeymead Cottages by 1846, where Robert, the head of the household, was employed by Henry Matthews as a farm labourer. Robert was still on the Moor in 1871, and by 1877, a son, Charles, was living in one of the two Driver Cottages. His descendants were still there up until 1937, when Arthur, the last of the Coward family on Exmoor, moved away. His brother, Ned, who followed Thomas Little as the shepherd of the Limecombe herding, left the Moor some 15 years earlier in 1922. Strange to say, the Cowards were one of the few long established families on Exmoor who did not better themselves, despite the fact that they were hard workers, and the nearest they came to farming on their own account was when Arthur rented a couple of cows and a small corner of Titchcombe—on which to keep them—from Lord Fortescue for £4 a year.

Evan Jones, a Welsh miner and his family probably came over from his native country in the late 1850's, to work for one of the mining companies. They were certainly on Exmoor in 1861, when his three children were baptised, and remained on the Moor long after mining had ceased. Evan's son, John (Jack) and his wife became caretakers at Simonsbath House for Sir Frederic Knight in his latter years, and afterwards took the Cloven Rocks smallholding; progressing to the larger farm of Winstitchen a little later on.

Jack Jones had three sons, Richard, Sidney and Jack. All three worked for a time on the estate. Jack junior we have already come across as the last shepherd to live at Badgworthy. Sid also worked in a shepherding capacity, as and where needed on the estate herdings. He later moved to Riscombe, Exford, where he oft recalled the old days, when the annual autumn draft of moorland sheep were driven on foot to Bridgwater Fair to be sold. Great care had to be taken when the drovers and their charges reached the monument in Bridgwater, for should the sheep fail to go straight on past it, and turned around it instead, they became tightly packed and were very hard to part.*

Dick Jones, the other brother, followed his father at Cloven Rocks when the latter moved to Winstitchen. Later, Dick was able to take the tenancy of Red Deer Farm. He remained there until 1937, when he sold up. For a couple of years after, he was still about the Moor, but then moved away into the Barnstaple area; returning in 1947 to live once more at Cloven Rocks. Dick died in 1971 at Little Crocombe, Winstitchen Lane; the home of his daughter Dorothy, who was the wife of the last William Little on Exmoor. Dorothy still lives in Simonsbath,* one of the very few people on Exmoor today who can trace their roots on the Moor back as far as 1861.

Thomas Elworthy, the first of three men of that name on Exmoor, came to Simonsbath in the early to mid 1850's, and is said to have been employed on the building and equipping of some of Frederic Knight's farms. By 1861 he was firmly established in a cottage in the village and was listed on the Census of that year as a farmer. His son, Thomas Bale Elworthy, we have already met with as the long time occupant of Wheal Eliza Cottage and father of a large family, and there are few of the old families on or within the close proximity of Exmoor that do not have some Elworthy blood in their veins. Three of his sons, Thomas, John and William, all became successful farmers on the Exmoor Estate. Young Thomas, famed for his considerable ability in the peat diggings, was farming 70 acres on his own account by 1898. In 1904 he took the other half of the Exmoor Forest Hotel and a further 19 acres. He had the sad

*Conversation with Reg Westcott of West Ley Farm, Exford.
**Moved to North Molton in 1987.

misfortune to lose his wife in 1909, and shortly after handed the tenancy of the hotel and some of his rented land to his brother John. Thomas then moved into one of the West Gate cottages, vacated by Donald MacDougal in 1910 when he moved to Wheal Eliza to take the Mines herding. Tom married again in 1912, and a year later was renting Warren Farm, moving on to Honeymead in 1925, when Robert Cann came out, and there he remained until his retirement in 1939.

In 1918, John Elworthy's wife Mary asked Lord Fortescue for the sole tenancy of the Exmoor Forest Hotel; her husband to guarantee the rent. This was agreed, and while John continued to farm, Mary ran the hotel, which prospered in her capable hands. Mary purchased two cars for use as taxis, her brother, William Watts (former carpenter and coachman to Lord Poltimore of North Molton), drove one; her cousin, Seymour Watts—the other. Both men were kept on in the winter months, helping John with the stock on the farm and on maintenance work in the hotel. A full licence was restored to the hotel in 1933, just three years before Mary retired from the business. She and her husband moved back into Lower House, or Pound Cottage as it is now known, where they had lived prior to taking the Hotel. They remained there until about 1945, but after Carl Rich the village blacksmith died, they moved into his cottage at Jubilee Villas, where Mary died in November 1947 and John in October 1953. John was the last of the male Elworthys to live on Exmoor Proper, as William, his other brother, who was farming Winstitchen in 1911, and later at Duredon, predeceased him in 1945. William's daughter Gwendoline, who married Eric Watts in 1933, took on the farm, and when they retired in 1970, Duredon—the last of the Exmoor Estate tenanted farms—was taken in hand.

Shortly after Mary Elworthy's retirement she purchased Kinsford, but never lived there. In the same year (1938), in a corner of the property close to the main road, the wooden bungalow known as Dunmoor* was erected, and it was there that Mary's brother William lived in his retirement. In the hard winter of 1962-63 he nearly froze to death, and it was said afterwards that even his dinner had to be consumed in two goes, as it was freezing to the plate as he was eating it. He survived the ordeal, and lived on until October 1983, when he died at the ripe old age of 93.

For the whole of the time that Mary Elworthy owned Kinsford, and for many years after, it was let to Samuel Denby and his wife, who ran it as a farm and guest house, and also served delicious cream teas. After Samuel's death in 1968, Mrs. Denby retired to North Molton, and William Watts four children, who had inherited Kinsford from their Aunt, sold it for £7,000 to a Mr. Hart, who had recently purchased Buttery Farm in North Molton parish. He used to arrive on Exmoor by helicopter.** He spent a

*Named after a Mr. Dunning of Barnstaple who built it, and Moore's of South Molton who supplied the materials.
**He was not the first to arrive on Exmoor by air. In the mid 1930's, the Hon. Denzil Fortescue regularly visited his brother, the 5th Earl and his family during their summer vacation at Simonsbath. He landed a light plane in the big field west of Cornham Farm, where a hanger was built to house his aircraft.

small fortune at Kinsford, adding an annexe and refurbishing the old house, and even more at Buttery, but his business empire collapsed, and he left the district owing local tradesmen a considerable sum of money.

Another name that crops up from time to time in the records of Exmoor, is that of Hooper. The earliest of which we have mentioned was the John Hooper who was living with his family in Boevey's old house at Simonsbath, which they also ran as an inn from 1801 until it was purchased by John Knight in 1818. Whether the William Hooper who married Mary Coward in Simonsbath Church in 1858 was related, is not known. A year later, when their first child was born, their place of abode was given as Slate Quarry, the old cottage beside White Water, close to Cow Castle. In 1884, a John Hooper was renting Red Deer Farm and 286 acres, but he was not listed on the Exmoor rent roll of 1898. Another John Hooper (probably his son) drove a team of horses, first for Frederic Knight, and later for Lord Fortescue. He began farming in a small way, renting a little land known as Duredon Bottom and Cornham Brake, before taking the tenancy of Driver Farm in 1920, where he remained until he retired and left the Moor to live at Bridgetown in 1934.

Most of the families we have been looking at arrived on Exmoor with little more than confidence in their own abilities and the hope of a better future for themselves and their children. That they succeeded beyond their wildest expectation is a tribute not only to their own endeavours but to the help and encouragement given them, firstly by Frederic Knight, and later by the Fortescue family. As a matter of interest, these self made men and women, many of them born on Exmoor, remained on the Moor for a longer period of time than their counterparts—the farmers who came from away to take Frederic Knight's farms.

Of the latter group, only three names that appeared on Exmoor before 1871, Red, Richards and Hayes, are to be found on Lord Fortescue's rent roll of 1898. William Red became the tenant of Simonsbath Barton in 1867, and farmed there until his death in 1911. His only son died of congestion of the lungs in 1900, when he was only 34 years old, but a daughter married William Gammin in 1912, and they continued at the Barton until their retirement in 1935, when they left the Moor to live at Exford.

George Richards was farming 300 acres at Wintershead before 1861, increased in stages to 570 acres at the time of his death in 1878. His widow and sons, George and Albert, carried on the farm until 1881, when Albert left to take the tenancy of the adjoining farm of Horsen and 736 acres, and there he and his wife remained until 1899 when they moved to Wellington (Somerset) to take possession of a smallholding of about 40 acres they had purchased.

George and his mother remained at Wintershead until 1885, but gave up the farm in that year in favour of Newlands Farm, Exford. George married another of William Red's daughters* and around 1901/02 moved

*George Molland the Exmoor Estate bailiff married a third.

to Flitton Barton in North Molton parish, where they farmed until George died in 1911. He left behind a widow and 13 children, and as was the custom in those days when the breadwinner of such a large family died, some of the children were farmed out among relatives. Such was the case with Bob Richards, who was only nine years old when his father died. He went to live with his Uncle and Aunt at Simonsbath Barton, and remained there working for his Uncle until the latters retirement in 1935. For the next two years he continued at the Barton working for George Thorne, the new tenant, but in 1937 Bob moved to Twitchen to begin farming on his own account, and a year or two later married a fine young woman from Heasley Mill. In 1947, they moved back on to Exmoor as tenants of Horsen Farm, the self same farm his Uncle Albert had been farming in the latter part of the last century. It was at Horsen that their children, two girls and a boy, grew up in a happy and peaceful environment, more than content with their lot, and had it not been for Mr. Darby Haddon's decision to take all his farms in hand, it is not unlikely they would still be there today. It was not to be, however, and around 1962/63 their landlord took possession and the Richards family moved to Surridge Farm, Skilgate, and it is there that Mr. and Mrs. Richards and son George live today. Around about 1967, the opportunity came to renew old links with Exmoor, and for a few years they rented Honeymead Allotment (this was shortly after Sir Bernard Waley Cohen had sold off this part of his Honeymead Estate) but the venture was not a great success, as some of the sheep placed there disappeared without trace, and the remains of others found there revealed the unmistakable signs of having been butchered on the spot. Mr. Bob Richards, a leading breeder and exhibitor of the Exmoor Horn breed of sheep for many years, and winner of countless prizes, is now 86,* and one of his earliest recollection of life at Flitton Barton, where he was born in 1902, was taking butter produced on the farm to his grandfather, William Red, at Simonsbath Barton, who in turn took it on to Eastcott Farm, Porlock, from where it is believed to have been retailed in the Porlock area.

The Hayes family has also been long associated with Exmoor, although their actual time of residence there was limited to a few years around 1886, when a John Hayes was renting Warren Farm,** and for 17 years prior to 1970, when a later John Hayes was the Exmoor Estate bailiff. The first Hayes—Exmoor connection was when old farmer Hayes of Exford took the tenancy of the newly created farm of Larkbarrow in 1846. He never lived there, and two years later gave it up. A later member of the family, William Hayes, was renting Sparcombe Allotment on Elsworthy before 1864, and this was still held by the family as late as the mid 1920's. This allotment of 400 acres is one of the few places on Exmoor that has unofficially taken the name of the tenant, and is always referred to locally as Hayes Allotment. Comerslade near Kinsford is another: This is known

*1988.
***Rented by the Hayes family since 1871, occupied by a stockman.

locally as Strangers Allotment, after a long term tenant, and the same applies to an allotment on Great Woolcombe, which is known as Spooners Allotment; named after an early tenant of Wintershead Farm.

A self conducted survey, cross checking the families living on Exmoor in the last century against those living there in 1986, revealed that at the latter date only two male descendants of the first group were still living on Exmoor, and one of these was from a late arrival.

The first of these men, Jack Buckingham of Rose Cottage, has since died (13th January 1988). He was the last surviving member (on Exmoor) of the large family of Buckingham that descended from the John Buckingham who was farming at Kingsland Pits in 1851. The family moved to Woolcombe before 1888, and they also farmed at Lower Sherdon where Jack was born. In this century members of the same family were farming at Horsen, 1899-1919; Picked Stones, 1903-1916/17; and Pinkery, 1920-1951: Jack was the fifth generation of his family to live on Exmoor, and with his passing the Moor has lost one of its finest sons. He will be sadly missed by all who were privileged to know him.

The other family we are concerned with, is that of William Thorne, but not the man who for over 50 years farmed at Ferny Ball, for his children were all daughters. The other William Thorne, a descendant of the large North Molton family of Thornes—who, in the 1722 Forest Book of Exmoor, had no less than nine representatives sending sheep to the Moor for the summer grazing—took the tenancy of Emmetts Grange and 658 acres, which included Hangley Cleave Allotment, plus an additional allotment on Burcombe (Emmetts). William had previously been farming at Cheriton in the parish of Brendon. He is believed to have moved to the Grange, either at Michaelmas 1888—shortly after Mrs. Tucker (the outgoing tenant's) retirement sale—or Lady Day 1889. William died in 1901 at the early age of 41, leaving a widow and three sons; John, the eldest, was 16; William Christopher five; and George—who was born in the same year that his father died.

Despite the loss of her husband, Mrs. Eva Thorne did not give up the farm. A year or two later she married for the second time, and with her new husband—Daniel French from Brendon—continued at the Grange. By 1912 her eldest son John was renting Hangley Cleave Allotment on his own account, and there he began a remarkable career in farming that was probably unmatched by any other farmer in Devon or Somerset in his time. At his peak, John Thorne was said to have been farming nine farms plus numerous other parcels of land, some of which he owned, some rented; the whole of which were combined into a huge sheep ranching enterprise. Two of his farms were on Exmoor; Driver, which he rented, and Barkham, which he purchased about 1925. It was this man, known as 'Old' John Thorne—to distinguish him from his son, 'Young' John—who became a great champion of the working classes, and many a successful farmer in the area today owes his position in life to the help he or his family received from 'Old' John.

Home to John Thorne in the latter years of his life was at Bentwitchen, not far from Heasley Mill, a farm, which after being rented by the Thorne family for many generations, he was able to purchase when Lord Poltimore sold off part of his North Molton Estate and emigrated to South Africa. Driver Farm and Hangley Cleave were given up when Mr. Darby Haddon took possession of the estate he had purchased in 1959. 'Old' John Thorne died in 1964, and soon after, 'Young' John moved to Bentwitchen from Higher Sherdon, where he had been living and farming for many years, and this farm was also given up. Barkham was sold in 1968, but 'Young' John Thorne did retain one property on Exmoor; Ferny Ball, which he had purchased in the late 1950's. This offlying farm has, since the death of 'Young' John Thorne in 1981, been in the possession of his son Jeremy, but the stock there is tended daily by the celebrated Exmoor authoress Miss Hope Bourne, who lives in a caravan close to the old farmhouse, which was gutted by fire in 1954 or 1955 when the property was owned by a Mr. Craven Wilkinson. The house was reroofed but not refurbished, and is now used as a store.

George Thorne, 'Old' John's youngest brother, took the tenancy of Simonsbath Barton in 1935, after farming for a few years at Western Ball, Twitchen. He married one of George Molland's two daughters, the other married his brother, Christopher. George and his wife had no family, and after farming at the Barton until 1969, retired to Exford, where George died ten years later.

Chris Thorne spent all of his life at Emmetts Grange, taking over after his mother's death in December 1915, and farming it until his own demise in 1952. He left a widow and three sons, George, Chris and Joe. George remained at the Grange with his mother. He married Kathleen Denby of Kinsford in 1956, and when Mr. Darby Haddon took possession, all three moved to Sandyway Farm, which they purchased from Major King Fretts who was retiring. George Thorne and his wife are still living there, and this branch of the family is the only one left who are still resident on Exmoor, although young Chris Thorne, who farms at Eastern Ball, Twitchen, does own a small piece of Exmoor, having purchased Greenbarrow from Leslie Carter in 1971.

Of the farms in the Sandyway area, Ferny Ball, Higher and Lower Sherdon, and Woolcombe are all now farmed by non resident farmers. Lower Sherdon was purchased by Jim Hayes of Sheepwash, Molland, in the early 1970's. He sold off the house, buildings, and a little land, and a kennels has now been established there. The rest of the land is stocked in the traditional way.

Most of the old families are gone from the Moor, many of the old cottages and farms also, but a certain amount of building development has been carried out in more recent years. A bungalow was built at Sandyway Farm in the 1950's by Major King Fretts for a workman, and another at the end of Litton Lane in the 1970's. The old Sportsman's Inn has been

---

*For Mr. Porter of Litton Farm.

completely refurbished, and a new bungalow erected opposite. Two Council Houses were built in Simonsbath in 1960-61 but as there was no local demand for them they were let to families from Exford. New bungalows for the Exmoor Estate shepherds we have already mentioned, and last, but not least, a new private house has been recently built on the site of the Gospel Hall in School Lane, where all that can be found of the old place are two stone pillars, which reveal the where-abouts of the entrance from the lane outside.

For many years the sheep and beef farmers of Exmoor have successfully held their own against all competition in the open markets, but the harsh milk quotas recently imposed on the dairy farmers of this country by the powers that be in the European Community Headquarters in Brussels, in their efforts to reduce the huge butter mountain, has had a knock on effect and is causing problems. This has come about because many dairy farmers— seeking an alternative source of revenue—have turned to beef and sheep as a way out of their troubles. This in turn has resulted in a greatly increased amount of beef, lamb and wool coming on to a market that was already close to saturation point, and for which there has been no increased demand. It is a crazy situation, and one that needs to be quickly resolved before untold damage is done to the economy of the hill farming regions, where farmers have no alternative but to carry on with their traditional way of farming.

Because of the pressures hill farmers are facing, with ever increasing costs, while incomes remain all but static, some farmers in the Exmoor region have sought to increase their incomes by ploughing up hitherto untouched rough moorland grazing pastures, so that more sheep and cattle can be kept. This is not the answer to the problem, but merely adds to it. Nor can the long term future of these farms be secured by the so called management agreements worked out by the Exmoor National Park Authority, in their efforts to conserve the natural beauty of the moorland region, whereby, farmers are paid sums varying from £10-£40 an acre each year to leave the land as it is and not plough it up. The ploughing grants of yesteryear for the improvement of rough moorland pasture were withdrawn in 1984, and it does perhaps seem a little odd that moorland landowners, who did not take advantage of these subsidies when they were available, should suddenly show such an interest in turning to the plough now. Such is the perversity of human nature. One cannot entirely blame the farmers for taking advantage of the management agreements in their efforts to increase their incomes in very difficult times, and it is of course a very hard decision to make as to whether or not an application to plough is genuine, but unless great care is taken, the trickle of applicants could become a flood, and an intolerable strain would then be put on the Government department responsible for finding the bulk of the money for this scheme, which would quickly lead to its collapse. I cannot foresee any long term advantage to the Exmoor hill farmers from the management agreements, and believe it to be only a temporary solution to their problems, but Exmoor has survived troubled times in the past, and one way or another it will survive in the future.

NOTES

CHAPTER 1

Page 22 1. The Roman patrol boats are believed to have been based at Sea Mills (now Avonmouth) but were apparently kept at sea in the Bristol Channel, except when bad weather ruled out the threat of invasion.

CHAPTER 2

Page 33 1. There is nothing in the Forest Records so far discovered to indicate when the first Telling Houses came into being, nor have either of those known been dated.

CHAPTER 5

Page 61 1. An advertisement placed in the *North Devon Journal* in 1828, re. steers and heifers taken in to keep on the South Forest, reveals that the prices charged from 1st May-1st November, were 35/- for three year olds (and over), and 25/- for two year olds. A similar advertisement in 1831 shows that the prices charged for each group had been reduced by 10/-.

Page 90 2. It is now known that there were two earlier bailiffs employed on the Exmoor Estate, both men being recorded in the Exford Parish Registers in 1830: James Berwick, who resided at Cornham; and William Hunter at Honeymead: Their occupations were given as 'Agents to John Knight, Esq.', as were Edward Henderson and James Aynsley in later Church records.

Page 73 3. John Haynes was the landlord of the Inn at Countisbury, a mason by trade.

Page 77 4. Unlike John Knights other early cottages, which are all believed to have been slated with locally quarried slate, Oar Oak was almost certainly thatched. In the labour accounts of July 1835, Ambrose Ridd's bill for laying on 17 square of thatch at 2s. 6d. a square, came to £2. 2. 6. Ordinary rick thatching at that time was 5d. a square.

Page 84 5. Greenbarrow was recorded in the Exford Parish registers as Green Down, an Extra Parochial place on Exmoor Forest near Crooked Post—when George Passmore died there in April 1838, aged 28. His daughter, Elizabeth, was listed on the Census of Exmoor 1841, aged four, living at Greenbarrow with John Carter and his family.

CHAPTER 6

Page 86 1. According to William Hannam, the first tenant of Cornham Farm, the first days sale of livestock was held in atrocious weather with very few buyers attending. On the second day the weather was even worse; no one turned up and the sale was cancelled. This would account for the further livestock auction later in the year, but as there was no machinery or husbandry implements on offer at this time, this would tend to confirm my belief that the machinery, etc., that was for sale in 1851, following John Knight's death, was in fact that listed in the Cornham sale of March 1845.

Page 89 2. An advertisement in the *North Devon Journal* (5th November 1846), re. the sale at Honeymead of all of Mr. Matthews 90 North Devon dairy cows (giving up the dairy), also included 50 hundredweight of cheese in suitable lots.
   Three years earlier, in September 1843, John Knight's annual livestock sale advertisement in the *North Devon Journal* reveals that he too had gone in for cheese making, with 60 hundredweight of prime cheese on offer, 'made on Exmoor and equal in richness and flavour to the produce of the best dairies in England'.

Page 91 3. John Knight's sale of live and dead stock at Cornham 12th and 13th March 1845, (prior to William Hannam taking the farm), included threshing and winnowing machines and a circular saw mill, but nothing to say how they were powered. Subsequent investigation in the field has revealed that a leat to provide water power can be traced from the easternmost building of Cornham Farm, all the way back across Titchcombe, Driver, Goat Hill and Pinkery, to join the River Barle just below the dam of Pinkery Pond. This water carriageway is mentioned in John Knight's labour accounts of 1835, and what is most interesting is that is was cut in such a way that his later farms, Pinkery and Driver, and probably also a proposed farm at Titchcombe, would all have been able to make full use of this water power.

Page 107   4.   *A Chronicle of Castle Hill 1456-1918,* compiled by the 4th
Earl Fortescue, reveals that the 3rd Earl purchased the
Reversion of the Exmoor and Brendon Estates more to
please his sons than himself, for he was nearly 70, but
notwithstanding his misgivings he refused to bargain about
the terms and gave Sir Frederic Knight the excessive price he
asked. This involved raising a large sum by mortgage, besides
which, the 3rd Earl had a dozen children requiring
allowances, and his brother and the Dowager Lady Fortescue
were also entitled to a large income from the Estate; all at a
time when because of the agricultural depression, rents
throughout the land were being reduced. By 1895, Lord
Fortescue was in grave financial difficulties, and in the next
ten years, partly as a matter of policy, but more essentially to
pay off mortgage charges, some 8,000 acres of his Lordships
offlying properties in this Country and in Ireland were sold
off, realising a total of nearly £171,000.

CHAPTER 7

Page 112   1.   There is a complete absence of advertised sales of Cattle and
Sheep in the *North Devon Journal* in regards to the Exmoor
Estate, for the period 1846-1865 inclusive, and it is now
believed that Frederic Knight kept no cattle of his own during
this time, and few if any sheep, as it was not until 1866 that his
first annual sale took place, when 362 sheep were up for
auction at Simonsbath, on Monday 27th August. Frederic's
second annual sale took place the following year, when 857
Exmoor Horn sheep were on offer, but it was not until 1868
that the draft sale of 1,025 sheep included any Cheviots,
when 348 ewe and wether lambs of that breed were auctioned
off.

Page 112   2.   The *North Devon Journal,* 10th June 1852, records the safe
arrival of the 'Glendower' at Ilfracombe with a cargo of
1,100 sheep from the Isle of Skye on board. All but four
'which died on the voyage' were landed safely, and
temporarily placed in a field belonging to a Mr. Nugent,
before proceeding on to their destination, Wintershead Farm
on Exmoor, the home of Gerard Spooner, a Scot who had
recently taken the tenancy of the farm. Spooner had hired the
'Glendower' to bring down the sheep, which were to form
part of his stock. The woolly immigrants were accompanied
by five shepherds and their families who were expected to
settle on the Moor and look after their charges.

Page 122   3. A little more information concerning the place of origin of other Northern and Scottish shepherds is now to hand. William and Adam Dunn came from Elsdon, Northumberland: Robert Tait Little from Torthorwold, Dumfries: William Little from West Linton, Peebleshire: Thomas Graham from Ashkirk—(also in the border country): John Gourdie was the son of a farmer of Markinch, Fife; and Donald MacDougal from Loch Lomondside.

CHAPTER 8

Page 136   1. The Census of North Molton for 1861, records two children named Burgess living with Mr. and Mrs. John Hayes of Brinsworthy Farm. Jane who was 17, and Charles who was 12: Neither names tally with those given by the Reverend Thornton, but whether he deliberately called them Tom and Emma in order to try and shield them from the limelight, and offer them some degree of anonymity is not known. What is certain, is that Jane and Charles were the children of William Burgess who married Jane Shapland at Exford in 1838. Altogether there were five children of this marriage, all recorded in the Exford Parish Registers. The eldest was Mary, baptised in 1840, followed by Jane in 1843, John 1846, Charles 1849 and Anna Maria in 1852. So much for Anna Maria being an only child!

Page 143   2. Closer investigation of this rather unusual adit at a more recent date has raised serious doubts that it was driven to find iron ore. There are, however, distinct similarities between the lay out of the adit and the pit at its higher end, with the set up of the drainage tunnel and sump at Pinkery Pond. There is some reason therefore to believe that John Knight intended to construct a dam across the Tangs Bottom Water to create another pond or reservoir. The water from this pond would have been released into the stream below, as and when required, to augment the water supply to the leat that comes off it further down the valley. This leat crossed the Simonsbath-Challacombe highway just to the east of Bale Water, and continued beside the road to the mill at Simonsbath, picking up the Limecombe Water on the way. The back up reserve of water from the pond would have ensured that an adequate supply of water was available at all times to keep the water powered machinery at the mill working.

CHAPTER 9

Page 154 1. An even earlier advertisement re. the sale of Barkham, Sandyway and Coles Cross farms has since been discovered in the sale columns of the *North Devon Journal* of 14th June 1849. At that time, the estate also included the Sportsman's Inn and five acres, and a cottage and two acres adjoining; five lots in all. Sandyway farmhouse is described as being newly erected, so it is to be presumed that the other premises on offer are more likely to date from the early 1840's, rather than the latter half of the decade.

Page 159 2. According to local knowledge passed down through the family to Mrs. Anne Buckingham of North Molton— daughter of Mr. and Mrs. Henry (Harry) Watts, who lived and farmed at Kinsford for about six years prior to 1922— Kinsford once changed hands for a barrel of beer. On another occasion it was sold for £100.

Page 162 3. Former tenants of the Acland Arms at Moles Chamber had also looked after the stock taken in to keep on the Acland Allotment.

CHAPTER 10

Page 177 1. The green prickly leaves of the gorse bush are a rich source of protein, and it was once common practice where gorse grew in profusion for farmers to cut the prickly greenery during the winter months, and after running it through a specially designed machine—fitted with sharp knives and granite rollers—it was ready for feeding to the farm horses and other stock, providing them with a valuable addition to the normal diet of hay or chaffed oats. As there are very few acres on Exmoor Proper where gorse forms a natural part of the vegetation, it is now believed that G.C. Smyth Richards had it planted in Limecombe to help feed the 14 or more carthorses kept on the estate farm.

Page 172 2. The normal procedure when cutting peat is to take off the first couple of inches and place it to one side, and after all the peat has been removed from the pit the toppings are laid face up in the bottom of the pit to grow on again naturally.

Page 181 3. When the plugs were removed from the pipes at Pinkery Pond in 1913, they were found to be rotten. New plugs were made by Charlie Elworthy, the Exmoor Estate carpenter, who carved his initials on them (C.D.E.) prior to replacement.

CHAPTER 12

Page 224   1. Badgworthy Cottage, Toms Hill Farmhouse and buildings, together with Larkbarrow Cottage, were severely damaged by mortar and shellfire, and because of their dangerous condition explosive charges were later set off around these buildings, reducing them to piles of rubble. In the case of Larkbarrow Big House and farm buildings, wartime damage was less severe, and it was not until the war in Europe was over that American troops stationed on Gallon House Allotment (behind the old inn), with nothing better to do, fired salvo after salvo in the direction of the farm. According to Jack Buckingham, very little additional damage was done as the Americans were lousy gunners. By the time the troops departed, however, many of the slates were gone off the roofs of the house and buildings, and the remainder were later removed by estate workers.

Page 240   2. Since Michaelmas 1986, the Exmoor Estate farm has been run from Filleigh by the Farms Manager, Mr. Ron Smith. At the present time the Under Manager's house at Simonsbath Barton is let.

Cornham miners cottages, c1857

A typical Knight farmhouse, Horsen.

Gross income of the Forest taken from the Forest Books of Exmoor
1718-1764 inclusive

1718 £550;	1719 £581;	1720 £616;	1721 £625;
1722 £644;	1723 £622;	1724 £620;	1725 £613;
1726 missing;	1727 missing;	1728 £513;	1729 £476;
1730 missing;	1731 490	1732 £490;	1733 £492;
1734 £525;	1735 missing;	1736 £495;	1737 missing;
1738 £553;	1739 £507;	1740 missing;	1741 £357;
1742 £309;	1743 £274;[1]	1744 £292;	1745 £401;*
1746 £409;	1747 £446;	1748 £547;[2]	1749 £771;[2]
1750 £529;*	1751 £592;	1752 £554;	1753 £518;[2]
1754 £470;	1755 £378;*	1756 £448;	1757 £406;
1758 £369;	1759 £416;	1760 £426;*	1761 £417;
1762 £535;	1763 £435;	1764 £438;	1765 £412;*
1766 £370;*	1767 £468;*	1768 £466;*	

[1]Lowest income recorded in the Forest Books.
[2]Included Pony clearance sales.
*Taken from other accounts in the Acland records, not the Forest Books.

Numbers of sheep before and after shearing (in parentheses), and where placed on Exmoor, as taken from the Forest Book of 1722. Also the parishes from whence the sheep flocks came: The place names on Exmoor are given firstly in the abbreviated form in which they are recorded, followed by the full modern equivalent—where known. The parishes that have been parenthesised are those which did not send their sheep to the place shown until after they had been sheared.

Abbetts hill	Abbetts Hill?	145 (140) South Molton:
Ald bur	Aldermans Barrow:	nil (68) (Exford):
Ashc	Ashcombe:	1658 (1498) Bishops Tawton, Chittlehampton, East Buckland, Landkey, South Molton, Swimbridge, Tawstock, Warkleigh:
Binchin	Benjamy:	nil (60) (Lynton):
Bilhill	Bill Hill:	nil (10) (Challacombe):
Bl Burr	Black Barrow:	nil (130) (Porlock):
Bl hill	Black Hill:	45 (10) (High Bray):
Bl pitts	Black Pits:	269 (97) Tawstock, Yarnscombe:
Br mead	Broad Mead:	nil (40) (Challacombe):
Burcom	Burcombe:	865 (740) Goodleigh, North Molton, Swimbridge:
Burscom	Buscombe:	728 (638) Arlington, Chittlehampton, Pilton, Swimbridge, Tawstock:
Chains	Chains:	162 (112) Loxhore:
Clannicom	Clannacombe:	nil (360) (Oare):
Colepitts	Coal Pits:	358 (354) Bishops Nympton, North Molton, Twitchen:
Cole +	Coles Cross:	251 (248) Chittlehampton, South Molton:
Combeslade	Comerslade:	207 (180) North Molton:
Corn	Cornham:	1090 (1132) Bishops Tawton, North Molton, South Molton, Swimbridge, Tawstock:
Dreford	Driver:	530 (386) Loxhore, Shirwell, Tawstock:
Dryhill	Dry Hill:	292 (326) Marwood, Swimbridge:

Dryslade	Dryslade:	191 (180) North Molton:
Duran	Duredon:	1639 (1300) Bishops Tawton, Chittlehampton, Landkey, South Molton, Stoke Rivers, Swimbridge, Tawstock, West Buckland:
Ecmead	Acmead:	nil (230) (Porlock):
Edgerl Stone	Edgerley Stone:	nil (40) (Challacombe):
Emetts	Emmetts:	642 (862) Bishops Tawton, Chittlehampton, East Buckland, North Molton:
Ex b	Exe Barrow:	116 (70) East Down:
Excleave	Exe Cleave:	nil (562) (Exford):
Ex h	Exe Head:	234 (166) Goodleigh, Tawstock, West Buckland:
Exridge	Exe Ridge:	nil (170) (Challacombe), (Exford):
Ffernb	Ferny Ball:	548 (496) Bishops Nympton, Chittlehampton, Filleigh, North Molton, Warkleigh, Yarnscombe:
5 bur	Five Barrows:	38 (60) Goodleigh, (North Molton):
Goat Hill	Goat Hill:	648 (600) Arlington, Loxhore, Shirwell, Stock Rivers, Swimbridge, Tawstock:
Gormead	Gormead:	nil (82) (Porlock):
Halscom	Halscombe:	490 (382) Bishops Tawton, Chittlehampton, East Buckland, Goodleigh, Landkey, Swimbridge:
Hang cleave	Hangley Cleave:	nil (70) (North Molton):
Herliv	Hereliving:	nil (95) (Exford):
H. Oake	Hoar Oak:	361 (450) (Brendon) Goodleigh, Landkey, (Tawstock):
H. Tarr	Hoar Tor:	164 (150) Landkey:
Hocom	Horcombe?:	497 (170) North Molton:
Honym	Honeymead:	548 (716) Bishops Tawton, Chittlehampton, (Exford) Filleigh, Landkey, Swimbridge, Warkleigh, West Buckland:

Horsen	Horsen:	856 (710) East Buckland, Filleigh, North Molton, (Withypool):
Keemead	Keemead:	nil (135) (Porlock):
Kinsford	Kinsford:	179 (251) North Molton:
Kitoake	Kittuck:	nil (329) (Porlock):
Lannic(om)	Lanacombe:	541 (412) Landkey: Swimbridge: West Buckland:
Little h	Little Hill:	379 (270) Swimbridge:
Lyddon	Litton:	805 (965) Molland, Twitchen:
L combe	Long Combe:	nil (130) (Exford):
L occam	Long Holcombe:	141 (536) Bishops Nympton, (North Molton):
Longway h	Longway Hill?:	nil (200) (Lynton):
Occam	Holcombe?:	27 (20) Shirwell:
Pinkry	Pinkery:	537 (415) Fremington, Loxhore, Shirwell, Westleigh:
Pinford	Pinford:	793 (660) Arlington, Charles, West Buckland:
Ramscom	Ramscombe:	264 (285) (Exford), North Molton:
Recom	Reycombe:	180 (400) (Exford), Landkey, North Molton:
Redway	Redway:	nil (50) (North Molton):
Rexib	Ricksy Ball:	276 (250) Heanton, High Bray:
Rostic	Roostitchen:	246 (240) (Challacombe) High Bray:
Ruccom	Ruckham Combe:	883 (750) Ashford, Challacombe, Loxhore, (Lynton) Shirwell, Westleigh:
Saddle Stone	Saddle Stone:	nil (100) (Lynton):
Settibur	Setta Barrow:	20 (50) (High Bray):
Settic	Settacombe:	nil (40) (High Bray):
Sherd	Sherdon:	2354 (1268) Atherington, Bishops Tawton, Chittlehampton, East Buckland, North Molton, Swimbridge:
Shortridge	Short Ridge:	nil (92) (North Molton):

Smallacom	Smallacombe:	209 (200) Chittlehampton:
Spracom	Sparcombe:	22 (938) Landkey (Exford):
Squallacom	Squallacombe:	264 (230) High Bray, Stoke Rivers:
Stoford	Stowford Bottom:	nil (110) (Oare):
Swaphill	Swap Hill:	28 (165) (Exford), (Porlock), Stoke Rivers:
Tangs	Tangs Bottom:	381 (174) Arlington, Charles, East Down, Shirwell:
3 combs	Three Combes Hill:	424 (327) Bishops Tawton, Charles, High Bray, Filleigh, South Molton, Swimbridge, Tawstock, West Buckland:
Titsc(com)	Titchcombe:	604 (488) Bishops Tawton, Chittlehampton, High Bray, Tawstock:
Tomshill	Toms Hill:	371 (620) Arlington, Landkey, (Porlock):
Trouth(ill)	Trout Hill:	498 (400) Landkey, Swimbridge:
2 burr	Two Barrows:	nil (110) (North Molton):
Venns	Venns:	nil (100) (North Molton):
Vex b	Flexbarrow:	153 (120) Swimbridge:
Ventc(om)	Vintcombe:	594 (610) Charles, Heanton, (High Bray), Landkey, (Oare), Shirwell, Stoke Rivers, Swimbridge:
Warren	Warren:	591 (506) Ashford, Braunton, Chittlehampton, Heanton, High Bray, Swimbridge, West Buckland:
Waterslade	Waterslade:	147 (150) Molland:
White c	White Combe?:	nil (50) (North Molton):
White Ladder	White Ladder:	nil (50) (North Molton):
Withycom	Withycombe:	155 (148) North Molton, Swimbridge:
Wemst	Winstitchen:	873 (825) Charles, Chittlehampton, Molland, South Molton, Swimbridge, Warkleigh, (Withypool):

Wind H	Wintershead:	830 (877) High Bray, North Molton, South Molton, Yarnscombe:
Wood b	Wood Barrow:	nil (20) (Challacombe):
Woolcom	Woolcombe:	988 (1039) Braunton, North Molton, Shirwell, Swimbridge, Twitchen:
Worcom	Warcombe:	215 (150) East Down, Loxhore:
Yeocom	Yeocombe?:	98 (88) North Molton:
Yellake	Hearlake:	488 (337) Bishops Tawton, Chittlehampton, Heanton, Swimbridge, Tawstock.

Notes

1. In the Forest Books of Exmoor 1718-1744, a number of other places where sheep were depastured are recorded. Some of these places were in almost continuous use during the period concerned, others were used on rare occasions only. I have therefore divided the list into two groups in the same order as given above.

   Group 1. Beccom (Beckham): Butt Corn (Buttery Corner): Crooked Post: Hecom (Heccombe?): Lark bur (Lark Barrow): Ravens Nest: Shirc ridge, Shorcridge and Shircome ridge are all believed to be alternative spellings for Shirkham Ridge; (now Fyldon Ridge): Shortcombe Ridge or Shortridge believed to be alternative names for an area of moorland thought to lie between Coles Cross and Buttery Corner.

   Group 2. Berkham (Barcombe or Burcombe): Dar Corner (Darlick Corner): Horsehead (Horsehead Stone): King pitts (Kingsland Pits): Medicom (Madacombe): Moles Chamber: Swarcom (Swarcombe): Wareball: White b (White Barrow?): Whitemead Head?: Weanaway H^d (Winaway):

2. A notable omission from the Forest Books is the large area of moorland in the north-eastern part of Exmoor known as Elsworthy. It is not unlikely that this was one of the places that was reserved for 'colts or bullocks' taken in to keep, or the residential herd of Exmoor ponies belonging to the Warden. Madacombe and Wareball, close by, may also have been used for this purpose because they were only very occasionally stocked with sheep.

3. A large part of the south-eastern corner of Exmoor appears to have been grazed almost entirely by the sheep and other stock belonging to the Free Suitors of Withypool and Hawkridge, who, because of their rights of free pasture on the Forest, do not appear in the Forest Books. It is difficult to determine the exact boundaries of the land in their use but we do know that it was only on very rare occasions that there were any sheep from other parishes recorded within the following boundaries: Green Barrow Cattle Grid to Sandyway Cross, and from there to Barkham and down the stream below to Sherdon Water, continuing along the same to a point just short of the River Barle where it meets the Forest boundary and follows it right handed up over the hill and back to the Green Barrow Cattle Grid on the Withypool road.

THE EXMOOR ESTATE SHEPHERDS 1861-1986

IN compiling a list of shepherds on the Exmoor Estate herdings it has become clear that the mass exodus of sheep and shepherds from Scotland to Exmoor was by no means completed by the time that John Gourdie is said to have brought down the last large consignment of Cheviots in 1871.* Neither Cornham or Pinkery were in hand at this time, and it was not until 1873 that these farms became herdings, and though we do not know if James Crawstown—who is believed to have been the first shepherd of the Cornham Herding—brought a flock of sheep with him to Exmoor, we do know for certain that William Little, the first shepherd of the Pinkery Herding, did not arrive on Exmoor with his flock of Cheviots until 1874.

The names of the Exmoor shepherds prior to 1910 have been obtained from many sources, principally Robert Tait Little's records; Church and school records, Fortescue Estate records, and Census Returns, but the latter give little indication as to the date the shepherds arrived, which could have been some years before they show up on a Census.

The list of shepherds from 1910 to the present day is that given me by Jack Buckingham of Rose Cottage, with additional information supplied by Tom Little and Mrs. Harry Prout (née Maggie Little). Dates are approximate, but believed to be accurate within a few months.

Abbreviations used are as follows: Scot or Scottish Descent, S or SD: Robert Tait Little, RTL: Church, Ch: School, Sch: Fortescue, F: Census, C: Not known, NK: *Reclamation of Exmoor Forest,* REF.

One shepherd on Exmoor that we have been unable to place was called McCreadie. His name has been passed down, but neither the herding he was associated with or any dates are known.

WINSTITCHEN HERDINGS CREATED BY 1861

Shepherd	S or SD	Date first Recorded	Source	Left	Source
John Scott	SD	1861	C	NK	
Thomas Scott	SD	1871	C	gone by 1876	Sch
William Davidson	S	1876	Sch	gone by 1903	F

Note: In 1903 Winstitchen and 225 acres let. Herding retained and run from Wheal Eliza Cottage. Afterwards referred to as Mines Herding.

William Bain	S	June 1903	Sch	Lady Day 1910	Sch
Donald MacDougal	S	1910		1920	

Hugh Buckingham and Jack Jones (temporary shepherds) 1920-early 1921.

William Dagg	S	13.6.1921	Sch	9.10.1923	Sch
Jack Jones?		1923		Sept. 1925	

*See *Reclamation of Exmoor Forest,* Orwin and Sellick, pages 120 and 297.

The Exmoor Estate Shepherds 1861-1986—*continued*

Shepherd	S or SD	Date first Recorded	Source	Left	Source
Jack Little	SD	9.1925		Retired 9.1939	
William Little (Jack's son)	SD	9.1939		1971	

Note: William Little moved into a new bungalow in Winstitchen Lane (Little Crocombe) in 1952. Mines Herding afterwards run from there.

Bill Rawle		1971		1974	
Reg Pincombe		1974		1974	
Bill Land		1974		1977	
Miss Kay Charman		1977		1979	
John Bristow		1979		1982	
Brian Duke		1982		Still there	

SIMONSBATH HERDING CREATED BY 1871

James Easeman?	S	1871	C	NK	
John Gourdie	S	1871?	REF	1885	RTL
Robert Little	SD	1885	RTL	1888	RTL
Richard Steer		1888/9	RTL	1894	RTL
Donald MacDougal	S	1894	RTL	1910	F

Notes: The Simonsbath Herding became known as the Deer Park Herding about 1887. From 1898 until it was given up in 1910 it was known as South Forest Herding.

When the herding was given up in 1910 part of the land was let, the remainder was amalgamated with Mines Herding when Donald MacDougal, the last shepherd of the South Forest Herding, moved to Wheal Eliza to take charge of the Mines Herding.

LARKBARROW HERDING CREATED ABOUT 1864
DOUBLE HERDING

Shepherds	S or SD	Date first Recorded	Source	Left	Source
William Dunn		1870 (probably from 1867)	Ch	NK (still there 1877)	Ch
Adam Dunn		1871 (probably from 1867)	C	Died 13.11.1875 (at Larkbarrow)	Ch
Thomas Graham	S	1878 (probably from 1875)	Ch	NK Still there 1881	C
Peter Murray ⎱	S	1880 (probably from 1878)	Ch	30.9.1892	RTL
Bob Murray ⎰	S	1881?		1892?	

Shepherds	S or SD	Date first Recorded	Source	Left	Source
John Blackmore		2.10.1892 (temporary)	RTL	17.12.1892	RTL
John Hewitt	S	13.12.1892	RTL	1896	RTL
Thomas Davidson	SD	1893	RTL	1898	RTL
Andrew Black	S	1896	RTL	26.5.1897	RTL
Thomas Hewitt	S	26.5.1897	RTL	1898	RTL
William Little	S	1898	RTL	Retired 9.1925	
William Little (son)	SD	1898	RTL	13.7.192 Killed by lightning	
William Little* (son of above)	SD	1923 (with his grandfather)		9.1925	
Hugh Buckingham	SD	1925		1928	
William J. Little	SD	1925 (Jack Little's son)		1928	
James Little	SD	1928 (old William Little's son)		retired 1950	
Cecil Little	SD	1928 (Jim Little's son)			
Will Land		1950		1953	
Cecil Little Sante Lafuente		1953		1955	
Cecil Little Jim Chapman		1955		1958	
Cecil Little				left 1959	
Ernie Duke		1958		Retired 1980	
Brian Duke (son)		1959		1981	
Pat Watts		1980		1982	
Sarah Watts (daughter)		1981		1982	

Note: Larkbarrow double herding run from Toms Hill and Larkbarrow until 1925. From 1925-1943 it was run from Toms Hill, afterwards from Warren. Warren sold in 1982, herdings given up.

BADGWORTHY HERDING CREATED MID 1860's

Shepherd	S or SD	Date first Recorded	Source	Left	Source
David Bryden	S	1871 (probably before)	C	NK	
William Howeston	S	1881	C	NK	
William Hepburn	S	1881 (assistant shepherd)	C	NK	

*For a short while prior to his father's death (in 1923) they had worked together with his grandfather.

Shepherd	S or SD	Date first Recorded	Source	Left	Source
Adam Reid	S	1885	RTL	20.5.1887	RTL
George Anderson	S	26.5.1887	RTL	20.5.1888	RTL
Thomas Graham	S	24.5.1888	RTL	1893	RTL
Thomas Armstrong	S	1893	RTL	NK still there 1901	
William Blythe	S	1906 (probably before)	Sch	15.11.1907	Sch
Jack Little	SD	1908		9.1916	

Note: Badgworthy Herding given up September 1916 when the Brendon Estate was sold to Sir Edward Mortimer Mountain. In September 1925, Badgworthy was leased back. Restocked in 1926.

James or Charles Barwick	1926	1923
Jack Jones	1932	See under Blackpits

BLACKPITS HERDING CREATED 1916

Note: From 1916-1920 Blackpits Herding was run from Simonsbath by Jack Little. In 1920 he moved into a newly erected bungalow at Blackpits.

Shepherd	S or SD	Date first Recorded	Source	Left	Source
Jack Little	SD	9.1916		9.1925	
William Little	SD	9.1925		About 1936	

Note: Blackpits Herding given up about 1936; land split between Badgworthy, Limecombe, and possibly Hoar Oak herdings: Great and Little Buscombe and Lanacombe added to Badgworthy: Prayways, Great and Little Ashcombe added to Limecombe. In 1940, Jack Jones, the Badgworthy shepherd, was moved to Blackpits, and since that time Badgworthy Herding has been run from there. Prayways restored to the Blackpits-Badgworthy Herding in the 1970's.

Jack Jones	1940	1946
Frank Curtis	1946	1953
Jim Chapman	1953	1955
Tom Perry	1955	1956
Brian Smith	1956	1957
Denzil Curtis	1957	1958
Abel Antell	1958	1963
Edwin Antell (son)	1963	1967
Jim Chapman	1967	1971

Shepherd	S or SD	Date first Recorded	Source	Left	Source
Eric Maggs		1971		1973	
Mervyn Jones		1973		1974	
Ralph Gubb		1974		1975	
Mervyn Jones		1975		1976	
Dave Williams		1976		still there	

CORNHAM HERDING CREATED 1873

Shepherd	S or SD	Date first Recorded	Source	Left	Source
James Crawstown?	S	1873	Ch	NK	
William Carey		1881	C	NK still there 1885	
Robert Cann		1892	RTL	1897	RTL
James Cann		1898	RTL	1899	F:RTL

Note: Cornham Farm let Lady Day 1899, Herding given up.

TITCHCOMBE HERDING CREATED ABOUT 1910

Note: Titchcombe Bungalow built about 1910, was not always occupied by the shepherd of the Titchcombe Herding. Abode of shepherds given between dates.

Shepherd	S or SD	Date	Abode	Left
James Little	SD	1910	Titchcombe	1928
Hugh Buckingham		1928	Titchcombe	1934
Sid Jones		1934	Limecombe	1936
Bob Little		1934	Simonsbath	1936
John Purchase		1936	Cornham	1937
Sid Jones		1937	Cornham	1939
Fred Land		1939	Cornham	1947
Charlie Lovegrove		1947	Cornham	1950
Sante Lafuente		1950	Titchcombe	1953
Jack Jones*		1953	Titchcombe	1954
Bill Land		1954	Titchcombe and Cornham Bungalow	1973 (from 1958/9)
Bob Pattenden		1973	Cornham Bungalow	1977

*Not the Jack Jones of Badgworthy and Blackpits.

Shepherd	S or SD	Date first Recorded	Source	Left	Source
John Bristow		1977	Cornham Bungalow	1979	
Mervyn Benallack		1979	Cornham Bungalow	1982	
Ken Prouse		1982	Cornham Bungalow	still there	

CHAINS OR HOAR OAK HERDING, CREATED BY 1870

Shepherd	S or SD	Date first Recorded	Source	Left	Source
William Davidson	S	1870	Ch	1876	Sch
John Renwick*	S	1881 (probably from 1876)	C	1886	RTL
James Johnstone	S	22.11.1886	RTL	19.3.1904 Died at Hoar Oak	Ch
Archie Jackson	S	1904		1913	
Will Hobbs		1913		1932	
William Little	SD	1932 (Jack's son)		1938	
Abel Antell		1938		1958	

Note: Hoar Oak Herding given up in 1958. Best of the Hoar Oak sheep transferred to Ashcombe.

ASHCOMBE HERDING CREATED 1958

Shepherd	S or SD	Date first Recorded	Source	Left	Source
Denzil Curtis		1958		1969	
Will Hobbs		1969 (not the Hoar Oak Shepherd)		1976	
Jeff Moule		1976		still there	

---

*Taken away to Exeter Asylum 1886.

DUREDON HERDING CREATED 1868

Shepherd	S or SD	Date first Recorded	Source	Left	Source
Frederick Blackmore		1871 (probably from 1868)	C	NK	
James Crocombe		1871 (probably from 1868)	C	NK	
Robert Tait Little	S	1871		17.9.1907 Died in a London Hospital	
Robert Little (son)	SD	1881 (assistant shepherd)	C	1885	RTL
Thomas Little	SD	1892	RTL (son of)	1919	

Note: Duredon Farm and 198 acres let in 1901. Herding retained.
Robert Tait Little and his wife and son Thomas moved to Limecombe.
Herding still on the books as Duredon but referred to as Limecombe
Herding.

Ned Coward		1919		1922
Sid Jones		1922		1937
Fred Land		1937		1939
Cecil Barrow		1939		1946
Bill Westcott		1947		1961

Note: Since 1956 Limecombe Herding run from West Cottages,
Simonsbath.

Russell Hicks		1961		1968
Henry Prout		1968		1969
Jeff Moule		1969		1976
Edgar Hillier		1976		1977
Mervyn Benallack		1977		1979
Miss Kay Charman		1979		still there

PINKERY HERDING CREATED 1873

Shepherd	S or SD	Date first Recorded	Source	Left	Source
William Little	S	1874	Mrs. H. Prout	1898	RTL
John Hewitt	S	1898	RTL	NK	
Jack Little	SD	1903 (possibly earlier)	Mrs. H. Prout	1908	
William Hunt		1908		Lady Day 1912	

Note: Pinkery Farm let 1912. Herding given up.

WINTERSHEAD HERDING CREATED 1885

Shepherd	*S or SD*	*Date first Recorded*	*Source*	*Left*	*Source*
John Gourdie	S	1885	RTL	1898	F

Note: Wintershead Farm let to John Gourdie Lady Day 1898; Herding given up; sheep transferred to Honeymead.

HONEYMEAD HERDING CREATED 1897/98

Shepherd	*S or SD*	*Date first Recorded*	*Source*	*Left*	*Source*
Robert Cann		1897	RTL	1898	RTL
James Cann		1899 (brother of above)	RTL	1900	RTL
Jack Little	SD	1901 (For a few months prior to Lady Day)			

Note: Robert Cann took part of his former herding as a farm in 1898, and after taking more land the herding was given up in 1901.

Acland Archine (D.R.O. Exeter)
Acland, Sir A.H.D., *Memoirs and Letters of Sir T.D. Acland* 1902
Acland, Sir T.D., *The Farming of Somersetshire* 1851
Allen, N.V., *The Waters of Exmoor* 1978

Billingsley, John, *General View of the Agriculture of Somerset* 1795
Blathwayt Archive, (S.R.O. Taunton)
Bourne, Hope L., *A Little History of Exmoor* 1968
Burton, S.H., *Exmoor* 1952

Census Returns for Exmoor and Bordering Parishes 1841-1881
Chanter, J.F., *The Swainmote Court of Exmoor* 1907
Collinson, J., *History and Antiquities of the County of Somerset* 1791
Cotton, R.W., *Barnstaple and the Northern part of Devonshire
    during the Civil War* 1889

Dowlais Iron Company Papers (Glamorgan R.O.)

Eardley-Wilmot, H., *Ancient Exmoor* 1983
Exmoor Review 1959-1986

Fortescue Archive (D.R.O. Exeter)
Fox, Lady Aileen and Dr. W.L.D. Ravenhill, *Early Roman Outposts
    on the North Devon Coast: Old Barrow and Martinhoe* 1966

Grinsell, L.V., *The Archaeology of Exmoor* 1970

Hurley, J.E., *Murder and Mystery on Exmoor* 1971

Jones, C. Brynner, and Others, *Livestock on the Farm,*
    Vol. IV, Sheep Breeds 1912

Kelly's Directories of Devon and Somerset
Knight Archive, (Kidderminster Reference Library)

MacDermot, E.T., *The History of the Forest of Exmoor* 1911
Madge, R., *Railways Around Exmoor* 1971
Mining Journals 1846-55 and 1875

North Devon Journal 1824-1986

Orwin, S.C., *The Reclamation of Exmoor Forest* 1929
Orwin, S.C.and R.J. Sellick, Updated version of above 1970

Page, J.L.W., *An Exploration of Exmoor and the Hill Country
    of West Somerset* 1890

Parish Registers of Exmoor and Bordering Parishes

Rawle, E.J., *Annals of the Ancient Forest of Exmoor*   1893
Roberts, Henry, Mining Reports 1912-1914. (Fortescue Archive
    D.R.O. Exeter)

Sidney, S., *Exmoor Reclamations:* Journal of Royal Agricultural Society
    of England   1878
Slader, J.M., *Days of Renown*   1965
Smith, Robert, Articles in the Journals of the Royal Agricultural
    Society of England, and the Bath and West of England
    Society. (also extracted in the *North Devon Journal)* Viz.
    The Cultivation of the Moorlands (R.A.S.)   1856
    Irrigation (B.&W. of E.)   1856
    The Exmoor Cottages (B.&W. of E.)   1858
    Agriculture (N.D.J.)   1859
    Established Breeds (N.D.J.)   1860
    Grasslands (N.D.J.)   1862
Smyth Richards, G.C., Diaries (Fortescue Archive D.R.O.)   1897-1920
Snell, F.J., *A Book of Exmoor*   1903
Snell, F.J., *The Blackmore Country*   1906
Somerset Ale House Records of the Hundreds of Carhampton and
    Williton. (S.R.O. Taunton)
Somerset Archaeological and Natural History Society, (Proceedings of)
Stenton, Sir Frank and Others, *Saxon England* 3rd Edition   1971

Thornton, Rev. W.H., *Reminiscences and Reflections of an Old
    West Country Clergyman.* Vols. I and II   1897
Transactions of the Devonshire Association

Victoria History of Somerset   1906

Whybrow, Charles, *Antiquarry's Exmoor*   1970

Other Sources of information, as stated in the Text.

INDEX